MARY HALL

# Coaching, Athletics, and Psychology

ROBERT N. SINGER
*Florida State University*

# Coaching, Athletics, and Psychology

McGraw-Hill Book Company
New York   St. Louis   San Francisco   Düsseldorf   Johannesburg
Kuala Lumpur   London   Mexico   Montreal   New Delhi
Panama   Rio de Janeiro   Singapore   Sydney   Toronto

# Coaching, Athletics, and Psychology

*Library of Congress Catalog Card Number 76-149719*

07-057465-0

345678 KPKP 79876543

# Contents

*Preface*                                                                ix

**ONE**  Introduction

*Determiners of Success in Coaching*                                       1
*What Is Psychology?*                                                       5
*Application of Psychology to Society*                                      9
*Application of Psychology to Coaching*                                    10
*Skills and Abilities*                                                     12
*All-round Athletes*                                                       18

**TWO**  Growth and Development Factors

*General Considerations*                                                   24
*Elementary School Athletes*                                               28
*Junior High School Athletes*                                              32
*High School Athletes*                                                     40
*College Athletes*                                                         49
*Postcollege Athletes*                                                     50
*Optimal Age for Achievement in Athletics*                                 50
*The Aging Process*                                                        56
*Summary*                                                                  60

**THREE**  Personality Factors and the Athlete

*Ways of Studying Personality*                                             65
*Personalities of Athletes and Nonathletes*                                70
*Personality Changes Due to Athletic Experience*                           73
*Personality Comparisons of Various Sport Groups*                          74
*Recreational and Activity Interests and Personality*                      78
*Physical Fitness and Personality*                                         79
*Personality of the Superior Athlete*                                      79
*Personality Data and the Coach*                                           84
*Personalities of Coach and Team*                                          85
*Personality and Type of School*                                           85
*Tactical Advantages*                                                      86
*Psychological Injuries*                                                   87
*Summary*                                                                  89

**FOUR**  Personal Factors and the Athlete

*Body Build*                                                               94
*Physical and Motor Measures*                                             110
*Sensory Factors*                                                         111
*The Perceptual Mechanism*                                                118

*Intellectual Attributes*                                      121
*Emotions*                                                     125
*Staleness*                                                    129
*Expression*                                                   129
*Form*                                                         130
*Summary*                                                      131

FIVE    Social Factors and the Athlete

*Group Interactions*                                           135
*Competition and Cooperation*                                  138
*Competitive Ability*                                          141
*Relationships between Individual and Team Performance*        145
*Morale and Spirit*                                            145
*Attitudes and Values*                                         147
*Sportsmanship*                                                154
*Leadership*                                                   155
*Family*                                                       159
*Social Mobility and Status*                                   162
*Handling Individual Athletes*                                 165
*Special Considerations*                                       177
*Social Facilitation (Effect of Spectators)*                   181
*Summary*                                                      184

SIX    Practice Factors and the Athlete

*Practice Sessions*                                            192
*Practicing for Perfection*                                    197
*Warmup*                                                       202
*Improvement as a Result of Practice*                          207
*Fatigue*                                                      212
*Summary*                                                      215

SEVEN    Learning Factors and the Athlete

*Learning*                                                     219
*Motivation*                                                   221
*Reinforcement*                                                231
*Transfer of Learning*                                         240
*Retention*                                                    248
*Summary*                                                      253

EIGHT    Training Factors and the Athlete

*Knowledge of Results (Feedback)*                              259
*Drill*                                                        262
*Whole Method versus Part Method*                              268
*Mental Practice*                                              270

*Verbalization*                                                           272
*Process Versus Product*                                                  272
*Application of Principles*                                               273
*Habit Interference*                                                      274
*Guidance, Demonstration, and Instruction*                               275
*Psychological Tolerance*                                                 278
*Cues and Aids*                                                           281
*Summary*                                                                 293

NINE    Research and Sports

*Baseball*                                                                304
*Basketball*                                                              309
*Football*                                                               319
*Golf*                                                                    325
*Gymnastics*                                                              326
*Judo*                                                                    327
*Karate*                                                                  327
*Swimming*                                                                327
*Tennis*                                                                  332
*Track and Field*                                                         333
*Volleyball*                                                              335
*Wrestling*                                                               336

TEN    The Coach

*Impression on Athletes (Frame of Reference)*                            351
*Predicting Success in Athletics with the Aid of Psychological
    Research*                                                            353
*Treatment of Individual Players*                                        356
*Treatment of Winning and Losing Teams*                                  357
*Mental Attitude and Preparation for the Contest*                        358
*The Coach as an Individual*                                             361
*The Successful Coach*                                                    363
*Summary*                                                                365

*Name Index*                                                             367
*Subject Index*                                                          371

# Preface

The intricacies of modern-day athletics far surpass the imagination of any forecaster years ago. Educational offerings in general have become quite sophisticated, and athletics, as a part of the educational structure, is an example of how complex skilled behavior can be taught through systematic programs of training.

The superior athlete and the outstanding team do not appear out of nowhere. Many grueling hours of practice, with meaningful interactions between coach and athlete, serve as a basis for athletic achievement. The coach, however, as educator-trainer, has the prime responsibility for molding skilled athletes and better human beings; and in order that he may serve this function, he must have training in the many diverse areas that contribute to success in coaching.

The coach of today is becoming increasingly more aware of the scientific information related to the athlete's potential proficiency in a sport. Research in nutrition, physiology, body mechanics, sociology, anthropology, and psychology can provide guidelines for the coach. The concern of this book is the last-mentioned of these fields, psychology.

Unfortunately, when the average person thinks about psychology and athletics, his thoughts go to psyching someone out, maintaining morale, game strategy, and other mentalistic concepts. Actually, however, when the total scope of psychology is considered, a completely different picture emerges. An attempt will be made to familiarize the reader of this book, whether coach or athlete, with scientific psychology as it relates to sport.

The basic assumption of the author is that the coach of today does not want to live in a fantasy land, far removed from the intellectual pursuits that are related to his occupation. He is seeking the actual knowledge that can be blended with common sense to produce desired outcomes. Moreover, he is academically and intellectually capable of reviewing, interpreting, and applying research and sophisticated literature to actual situations.

To make this task a little easier for the coach, this book interprets the research. The topics covered in this book have been neither over-simplified nor presented superficially; for the observation of the author is that there has been too much watering down of these subjects for too many years. Typical books for the coach have been extremely general and non-scientific, and have taken a commonsense approach. The time has come to utilize the tremendous amount of research being done in psychology, in order to help the coach to be more effective in his work.

The plan of the book is to begin with a general introduction to the psychological domain and to demonstrate the relationship of psychological subdisciplines to coaching and athletics. Following the introductory material, developmental factors and the athlete are considered. Characteristics of different age groups are explained, and hints are given to those coaching at the various levels.

Next, personality factors are examined in relation to success and choice of activities. Data from Olympic athletes and college champions are reviewed. Information is given next about the effects of the athlete's physical, intellectual, and emotional qualities on his success in sports. The relationships between social factors and the athlete are discussed next, including the effects of competition and cooperation, values, spectators, and group interaction on performance.

The next three chapters are concerned with learning, and an application from learning and training research is made to athletic situations. The nature of practice and the variables influencing more effective practice results are discussed. Individual differences are explained, and the effects of warmup and fatigue on learning and performance are suggested. Motivation, transfer, and retention—all standard topics in the psychology of learning—are discussed, with their special implications for the coach. Training factors, such as drill, knowledge of results, verbalization, guidance, instruction, cues and aids, and technological equipment, are examined and analyzed according to learning principles.

Many research sources are then reviewed for each sport. Training factors and personality studies are categorized by sport. Finally, some general personal comments are made about the nature of the coach and his relationship with his athletes.

It is hoped that the information provided in this book will be evaluated as stimulating, as based on scientific study, and—most important—as meaningful to the coach.

*Robert N. Singer*

# CHAPTER ONE

# Introduction

Techniques in coaching have become increasingly more scientific during this century. The intricacies and complexities in the coaching situation reach far beyond the grasp of the average person. The spectator watches the contest: he sees the basketball go through the hoop, the fullback score the touchdown, or the golf ball go into the hole. But does he realize the strategies involved in various maneuvers? Is he aware of the nature and the number of practice sessions that preceded the contest? What does he know of the athlete, this wonderful complex machine that can perform highly skilled movement patterns? Can he visualize the type of person who becomes a coach and the necessary preparation associated with successful coaching?

Toward the end of the nineteenth century and in the beginning of the twentieth, college and high school athletic competition encompassed a variety of sports. But not until relatively recent years has the coach had available much scientific data of practical application to his work. Not only are these data now available, but the coach is taking advantage of them. He reads medical, physiological, and psychological journals; communicates with researchers; and applies what he learns to given situations. Research is one of the keys to progress and is being utilized to a greater extent than ever before in all aspects of coaching.

Recruiting is as important as ever. Competition is keen at the college and professional levels for the services of outstanding athletes. Nevertheless, the personal qualities, experiences, and knowledge the coach brings with him enable him to increase the probability of success. Let us now examine the factors underlying coaching success.

## DETERMINERS OF SUCCESS IN COACHING

It is difficult to understand what it takes to be a champion athlete, and the same problem exists in attempting to determine how a person becomes a successful coach. The ideal contribution and interaction of many variables probably exists in both cases. However, it should be emphasized here that successful coaching is not dependent on successful participation in athletics. Although there are a number of outstanding athletes who are winning coaches, there are certainly many who have not excelled in sports.

The coach assumes multiple roles. As Tutko & Ogilvie (1967, p. 355) so aptly put it, "Although the coach prefers to see himself as an encyclopedia of knowledge and master of strategy, he is called upon to perform the roles of salesman, public relations man, counselor and psychologist." In other words, the coach, besides his preparation in athletics and mastering of pertinent information, is (1) a public relations man for the team to the public, (2) a counselor, to assist the individual athlete with his personal problems, (3) an organizer, and (4) a motivator, who must inspire each athlete to his best performance.

## Personal Qualities

The coach must be motivated and inspired to achieve. Superb athletic performance occurs under conditions of optimal motivation; a coach with an intense need to achieve will demonstrate energy and vigor in fulfilling his responsibilities. If there is such a thing as "mechanical sense," or the ability to be a "natural hitter," we might think of the outstanding coach as having "coaching sense." Such senses are not easily defined, and yet, one must have a feel for what he is doing, an aptitude for the work he is undertaking. Psychologists like Spearman talk in terms of a general intelligence factor, Cattell proposes two factors, and other psychologists have identified numerous types of intelligence. Perhaps there are an academic intelligence, a social intelligence, and a motor intelligence. Perhaps coaching success partially depends on the interaction of a number of these kinds of intelligence.

Leadership qualities are a prerequisite for achievement in coaching. A leader is one who is respected for what he says and does, and who is admired by his team. The coach gains respect by giving respect, and by possessing knowledge and skills associated with the sport. There are many "successful" coaches who are domineering, forceful leaders, gaining power more through fear and even hate than through respect. These military-type men are primarily from the old school of thought, and many younger coaches are achieving their goals through more humanistic approaches.

If we can assume that many of the attributes associated with the recognized good teacher also are associated with the good coach, let us examine Knapp's findings (1962) on the characteristics of superior teachers. Knapp's article, one of many in *The American College*, contains a summary of the research literature on the ideal factors ascribed to college teachers. Evidently, social and personal qualities are deemed very important by students. Some of the qualities that students desire the teacher to have are a pleasing personality, the ability to show warmth and compassion, a sense of humor, enthusiasm, sympathy, and a sense of fair play. Intellectual distinction and mastery of the subject were often not mentioned or were considered less important.

## Human Relations

Understanding and respecting individual differences, being perceptive, being sensitive to the problems of others, relating to the group, and the like, all contribute to the results the coach is seeking. Athletes, although distinguished from the normal population by attainment of skill in a given endeavor, have problems similar to those of other people. Athletes are people, too. Their unique personalities, problems, goals, and abilities must be considered. For the coach to impose his will continually on all athletes in his charge, to expect the same behavior from them all, may be detrimental to the desired performance. In spite of the convenience of and the necessity for treating athletes at times as a group, sensitivity to and respect for individual differences should always prevail.

The ability to be an inspiration to others certainly is an important attribute of the coach. Inspiration implies a knowledge of motivational techniques to be applied to individuals with various personality profiles. It also implies setting an example, and being looked up to, by the athletes. Tutko & Ogilvie (1967) state that countless coaches indicated that motivation was 50 to 90 percent of the coach's responsibility.

Ability to communicate is an important aspect of human relations. The coach must be able to communicate with his team, with their parents, with the public, and with the teachers and administrators of the school. Articulation makes the difference between understanding and misunderstanding, and therefore communication should occur often and should be of a high quality. The coach should express intentions, objectives, and explanations to every concerned party, as he must gain the support of the students, the alumni, and the public.

## Personal Experience

The old adage that there is no substitute for experience certainly has merit in coaching. We all learn and profit from experience, whether in athletics, coaching, or any other endeavor. One "matures on the job"; he learns from his mistakes as well as from his successes. Academic and vocational preparation and words of advice can go just so far in preparing the coach for his tasks. Just as each athlete performs skills in an individualistic manner, every coach develops his own coaching techniques in accordance with successful results. The same methodologies do not necessarily work satisfactorily for all people.

For the coach, personal experience may be gained from previous coaching ventures and from actual participation in the sport. As mentioned before, achievement in the particular sport is not a requirement, but it certainly is of value in a few ways. Athletes will probably quickly learn to respect a former athlete, and gaining immediate respect from the team is a decided advantage. Second, the coach who has himself played a particular game may feel greater empathy, may be able to sense the feelings of the athletes in particular situations, since he has experienced similar situations himself.

However, there is no experience like actual coaching experience. Many athletes have found it easier to perform than to coach, for coaching demands time, talent, and countless other ingredients that go unrecognized by the typical spectator and often by the athlete himself.

### Formal Education: A Continuing Process

In order to be well prepared, the coach of today draws upon the contents of a variety of books and research articles as well as upon his formal academic education. Courses in anatomy, physiology, kinesiology, psychology, sociology, and anthropology offer much content matter of relevance to the coaching situation. The actions of the coach should be based upon scientific evidence and tempered with common sense and experience. The different types of determiners of coaching success discussed so far are listed below for concise reference.

### Foundation Blocks of Successful Coaching

#### Experience

Previous coaching
Athletic participation
Other

#### Personal qualities

Common sense
Intelligence
Dedication
Leadership
Decision making
Character
Other

*Human relations*

Sensitivity to others
Respect for others
Ability to communicate
Ability to be an inspiration to others
Ability to organize
Ability to motivate others
Other

*Education*

College preparation
Courses in physiology, psychology, sociology, kinesiology, coaching, administration, etc.
Knowledge gained from books, articles, and research

The pure and behavioral sciences continually provide information of importance to the coach. Therefore, his education should not stop on graduation day, but should continue in the years to come; that education does continue for many is evidenced by a sustained interest in newly published books and journal articles. Training methods and coaching techniques are moderated and changed with the advent of new scientific knowledge.

For many years the coach has relied primarily on medical and physiological information as the basis of his actions. This leaning toward the physiological area is only natural, as nutrition, strength and endurance development, health, and the training and care of the athlete are of great concern to the coach. In addition, mechanical principles associated with movements of the body and of projectiles are useful in analyzing and correcting the athlete's movement patterns. For some reason, however, the typical coach has only superficially examined the psychological and sociological disciplines, and they have made little impact on him. Considering the potential contributions these disciplines can make to the coach's productivity, it remains a mystery why they have been neglected thus far.

## WHAT IS PSYCHOLOGY?

The word "psychology" dates back to ancient Greece; it is formed from the Greek words *psyche*, "mind" or "soul," and *logos*, "study," and originally meant the study of the mind or soul. For many years, psychology, as a part of philosophy, was concerned with exactly that study.

Many disciplines became separated from philosophy during the sixteenth, seventeenth, and eighteenth centuries, notably such natural sciences as physics, chemistry, and mathematics. Toward the end of the nineteenth century, psychology began to dissociate itself from philosophy, to be remodeled and recognized as a distinct science. People concerned with psychology were no longer interested in metaphysics (the nature of the soul, for instance); they were interested in psychology as a science, and they began to study events that were observable and measurable, rather than the difficult, if not impossible, problems of the mind and soul.

The main aim of a science is to express the regularity of relationships that exist in nature. This aim is more easily achieved in some disciplines than in others. Through scientific statements resulting from extensive research and observation, it is hoped that the truth will be discovered. Although there are certainly many ways of finding the truth, disciplines classified as sciences are supposed to follow certain procedures that enable them to make statements based on more than mere hearsay or general observation. Because of this rationale, the contents of this book are based primarily on scientific research. Presumably, there is a certain amount of confidence in the actions of an individual when they are dependent on scientific statements.

The important thing to remember is what constitutes a science, and there is fairly good agreement that the *method,* not the *material,* determines whether or not we are dealing with a science. In science, the attempt is made (1) to discover, (2) to describe, and (3) to explain. Experimentally derived facts became the basic data of the sciences, as facts determine laws. In psychology, the subject matter is behavior. The methodology employed in and applied to the study of behavior is scientific, for the "truths" of behavior are arrived at by rigorously controlled experimentation. In fact, psychology is often referred to as the "science of behavior."

Because human behavior is so complex, so difficult to study scientifically, and so unpredictable, there are many skeptics and critics of psychology as a science. At least, however, it does attempt to study behavior in a scientific manner. The purely observational stage has passed, and we can understand more about human behavior every day because of the extensive experimentation going on in this area. Psychologists ask why humans behave as they do; they attempt to explain and predict behavior. Psychology, then, offers one approach to the understanding of man.

The study of behavior is dependent upon the biological as well as the social sciences, and there is a certain degree of overlap between the disciplines in subject matter. Although people look to psychology for the explanation of secrets, and talk in terms of hypnotism, ESP (extrasensory perception), and the like, the average psychologist studies practical events. In fact, the content of this book and its applications to coaching and athletics comes primarily from psychological research.

Experimental psychology probably received the greatest impetus from the efforts of Wilhelm Wundt, founder of the first recognized laboratory of experimental psychology in the year 1879 in Leipzig, Germany. German researchers during this period at the end of the nineteenth century exerted a great influence on American psychologists.

Wolman (1960) states that in the early 1900s psychologists were most concerned with mental tests, experimenting with animals, and psychiatry. These areas, of course, are still of interest to psychologists, as are many more. Figure 1-1 contains some of the more important discoveries and events leading up to and associated with psychology as a science at the end of the nineteenth century.

Through tests of mental ability, prediction of future achievement and behaviors is attempted. The work of Binet in France and the revision of his intelligence tests at Stanford University in the early 1900s have had a tremendous continuing effect on education and research. We are still not sure what intelligence is, or how it can best be measured to exclude socio-economic and cultural differences and yet include all those attributes that might fall under the heading of intelligence. Nevertheless, the state of present knowledge about intelligence has allowed psychologists to make important contributions to education and to society in general.

Animal experimentation may provide insight into human behavior. It is much easier to control and experiment with lower forms of life than with humans, and inferences may be made from one organism to another. Although it is true that there is danger in applying laws of behavior from a rat to man, certain aspects of behavior can never be studied in the human to the extent they can in animal subjects. Pavlov's work with dogs earlier in the twentieth century permitted us to develop a better understanding of the reflex and other neural processes.

Animal experimentation continues. Its value lies in the continuing information provided on behavioral variables which leads to further experimentation, sometimes to experimentation with humans. When human experimentation is not possible, concepts and broad generalizations can certainly be advanced to explain and describe human behavior.

Psychiatry, the study of the subconscious processes, continues to be a challenge to certain psychologists in clinical and diagnostic work who are interested in studying behavior for which we are probably not aware of the causes. Repressed feelings and hidden situations, which may have occurred many years in the past, are brought out into the open in psychiatric treatment. Freud, with his attempt to discover what is going on below the conscious mind, developed techniques to be followed in this area. Various therapeutic methods are employed by psychologists who favor different schools of thought, but each method is an attempt to reveal subconscious matter, explain behavior, and help patients to a better adjustment.

At present, there is still interest in psychiatry, animal experimenta-

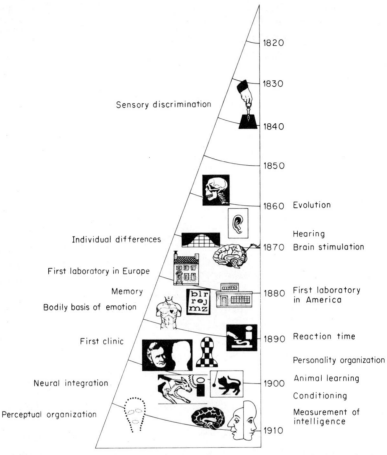

FIGURE 1-1 *Some of the most important events in the early history of scientific psychology. Before psychology was established as an independent science, some of the events of behavior were studied by scientists in related fields.* (Source: *Karl U. Smith & William M. Smith.* The behavior of man: an introduction to psychology. *New York: Henry Holt, 1958. P. 23.)*

tion, and intelligence tests. Nevertheless, changing degrees of emphasis in certain areas and the development of other areas have been observed through the years. Perhaps the strongest influence on psychology was the origin of behaviorism in 1913. Behaviorism is a concept of how psychology should be approached. In response to behaviorism, psychologists came to be primarily concerned with overt behavior or "outer experiences," rather than with the mind, consciousness, or "inner experiences."

Behavior was studied with an attempt at precision methodology. Human behavior was investigated in a variety of ways—in the laboratory as well as in the "field" situation. In the laboratory it was possible to control many confounding extraneous variables, to isolate the variable of interest. However, with the gain in precision came a loss in realism. The artificiality of the laboratory situation came under attack.

Field research, represented by experimentation in classrooms and the like, although more realistic, was less controlled than laboratory research and permitted only general conclusions. Obviously, both types of research are needed. They need not be antagonistic; rather, they can be complementary, can contribute knowledge to specific areas. In this book, an attempt has been made to synthesize the findings of research in both laboratory and field (gymnasium, athletic fields, swimming pools) and to interpret data for the benefit of the coach and the athlete.

After behaviorism, other schools of thought came into existence. Gestaltists, neo-behaviorists, cognitive psychologists, field theorists, and many others influenced the direction psychology was to take. At present, psychology encompasses a wide assortment of fields. Let us turn to the specialists in psychology and see how their work is applied to society. We will also examine implications to athletics from the research completed in these areas.

## APPLICATION OF PSYCHOLOGY TO SOCIETY

Psychology today has an enormous impact in industry, in the military, in classrooms, in the area of mental health, in various professions, and in the gymnasium. Although all psychologists receive similar training at the basic level, most also do some special preparation for a specific area of interest.

In *industry*, the need is for knowledge about efficiency and optimal conditions for work output. When should "breaks" be given? How long should they be? How can workers be motivated? Should they work in groups or alone, if the choice exists? Tests to predict aptitude or performance are also in demand. These are but a few of the questions and problems which are raised by industry which industrial psychologists are attempting to resolve.

Similarly, *military* problems are concerned with output effectiveness and efficiency and with aptitude testing. During World War II, the Korean War, and the war in Vietnam, psychologists played an important role in assisting military personnel to improve training methods and techniques. Many training and predictor devices were developed by these psychologists. The results of studies in vigilance or attentiveness, training methods, simulation, and aptitude testing were applied to military situations.

Educational psychologists promote more effective teaching and learning conditions in the *classroom*. Research from the laboratory and the classroom help to formulate principles of learning for children and adults. Teaching aids and cues are developed, programmed teaching methods and other improvisation become useful and practical, and knowledge of group dynamics and individual differences is improved.

In *mental illness*, therapeutic methods are advanced and personality factors studied. The entire range of neuroses and psychoses is examined, and ways of overcoming such personal problems are developed. Clinical psychologists make a major contribution to society in helping their patients overcome personal problems and become better adjusted so that they can live more effectively within themselves and within society.

In the *professions*, such as law, medicine, and dentistry, psychology is applied to communication and interaction with clients, suspects, and patients. An understanding of human behavior is essential in dealing with people. Professional people will attest that the accumulation of knowledge and facts related to medicine or law per se is not enough; the psychology of "handling" or "dealing with" people helps to further the attainment of goals.

Finally, those who work in *athletics* can benefit from knowledge gained from the various areas of psychology. The coach and the athlete want answers to such questions as: How can highly skilled performance be developed? What factors should be emphasized to enhance the learning situation? What growth and developmental factors need to be considered? What is the role of personality profiles or specific traits in contributing to outstanding achievement? These are the main categories, although this book will also deal with many others.

## APPLICATION OF PSYCHOLOGY TO COACHING

The obvious intention of this book is to apply psychological research to athletic situations. The reader is now aware of the many ways in which athletics can benefit from such research. Many branches of psychology contribute pertinent knowledge, and none of these branches can be neglected. Psychologists who concentrate on specific endeavors are classified accordingly. Some of these specialties are developmental, social, clinical, physiological, and learning.

The *developmental psychologist* is interested in the origins of behavior, in hereditary factors and environmental interactions, especially in relation to the behavior of infants, children, adolescents, and young adults. Developmental psychology provides us with normative data on the expected physical, social, emotional, and maturational characteristics of groups by age or maturational levels. Any coach dealing with a group of athletes, whether on a Little League team, elementary school team, junior high school team, high school team, or college team, should be aware of the characteristics associated with his team's age group.

The *social psychologist* supplies information on the social dimensions of human behavior: how attitudes and values are formed, the nature of group dynamics, and the effect of cultural influences. We live in a group-oriented culture. Competition and cooperation with others affect the manner in which objectives are reached. Certainly the athletic situation, in which people of assorted backgrounds and occupations are involved in some way, is one of the most unusual social phenomena of our times. Teachers, administrators, players, coaches, students, parents, and the public at large are brought together by their interest in athletic contests.

The *clinical psychologist* is involved in understanding personality, intelligence, personality disorders, and individual differences in behavior. He is also referred to as a "differential psychologist," "personality psychologist," or "psychology of adjustment psychologist." The coach must organize a group of athletes who come to him with various behavioral differences. Problems occur if all athletes are treated similarly in all situations, if no respect and understanding is given to the nature of individual differences. Emotional, physical, learning, temperamental, and cognitive differences are apparent from person to person.

The *physiological psychologist* attempts to bridge the gap between physiology and psychology. He explains learning from both viewpoints and is concerned with the underlying chemical and neural activity of behavior. Neurological information dealing with the learning process helps to broaden one's understanding of skilled performance.

The *learning psychologist*, primarily associated with experimental psychology, investigates the learning process and the factors pertinent to learning. Usually noted for laboratory work involving human and infrahuman organisms, these investigators also undertake research in practical situations. Learning psychologists attempt to provide a basis for learning principles in such areas as motivation, retention, acquisition, reinforcement, and transfer. A definite need arises for coaches to learn, understand, and apply the research and concepts, for these factors and many others operate in skilled performance.

All these psychologists have something to offer the coach. Their research provides a basis for understanding and predicting human behavior at various age levels. Principles of learning are offered, the growth and nature of abilities are explained, and the nature of individual differences is elaborated upon. Suggestions are made about how environments can be reshaped for more effective behavioral results. Similarly, direction is provided for possible approaches to teaching. The worth of tests in predicting achievement in academics or athletics is evaluated.

We are now ready to examine the vast stores of psychological material applicable to coaching and athletics. Perhaps, since motor skills and abilities are of such importance to coaches and athletes, they should be discussed first. After all, the ultimate aim is to mold a highly skilled athlete. How are the terms "skills" and "abilities" related, and how do they differ? More importantly, how are they developed?

## SKILLS AND ABILITIES

The terms "skill" and "ability" are frequently employed in industry, the military, education, and athletics. The coach is concerned with developing the abilities that are related to skill. There are numerous abilities and even more skills, and the relation of the two terms to one another is somewhat confusing.

An understanding of the concept "skill" may be approached in two ways: (1) "skill" may be a noun referring to an act, a task, or a particular pattern of responses and (2) "skilled" or "skillful" may be an adjective describing the status of the performer of the task. A skill can be almost anything—typing, the jump shot, piano playing, or the sidestroke. A specific act, whether executed at home, in the classroom, in the street, or in the gymnasium, may be called a "skill." Such a skill may also be associated with verbal materials, athletic activities, social transactions, and mechanical techniques. For this reason, skills have been classified according to their nature.

The skills in which the coach and the athlete are interested are termed "motor." As defined elsewhere (Singer, 1968), a *motor skill* concerns "muscular movement or motion of the body required for the successful execution of a desired act." No skill is purely motor, perceptual, conceptual, or verbal; rather the degree of emphasis in any skill allows us to refer to it in a certain way. Certainly the interaction of many processes is involved in athletic or motor skills, although overt movements are most obvious.

A person's level of achievement in a particular task is his *skill level*; it is described in relation to the accomplishment of others and in terms of specific objectives. Skill is determined by the effectiveness of results within a framework of minimum energy expenditure. In skilled performance, there is a certainty and consistency in the responses. The qualities of the skilled performer have been elaborated upon by many other writers and investigators in connection with the efficiency of laborers, bombardiers, pilots, dancers, and athletes. Many criteria of successful performance are common to different tasks.

For example, Annett and Kay, writing in the *Occupational Psychology Journal* (1956), list the following qualifications of the skilled worker. He anticipates more quickly and therefore has more time to react. He responds to fewer environmental cues by isolating and disregarding the irrelevant ones. He displays less variability and more consistency in performance. Finally, he receives a maximum amount of information from a minimum number of cues. Do these statements not also describe the skilled athlete?

In the following delightful folk tale by Harry Johnson, associations can be made between the story and performance in athletic events.

---

## SKILL = SPEED × ACCURACY × FORM × ADAPTABILITY[1]

Harry W. Johnson

This is an age of change. In industry, especially, every day brings new developments. And each new product, each new process, each new package is likely to bring with it the necessity for new skills. Manifestly, it behooves the leaders in industry to search for (a) means of selecting people capable of learning new skills readily, and (b) means of teaching new skills efficiently.

Even the briefest contemplation of the teaching of skills brings to mind another need—(c) means of determining the amount of a new skill acquired.

But what do we mean by "skills"? As Maier pointed out a psychologist entering a shop would be likely to find that the "unskilled workers" there possessed a higher degree of what he considered skill than the "skilled workers." But the skill of the latter, he would find, was backed up by understanding and knowledge, and so our definition of skill must be carefully framed: *Skill is the ability to execute a pattern of behavioral elements in proper relation to a certain environment.* The environment may include a wrench or a tennis racket. It will most certainly include the floor or ground. In sports it often includes a ball. And the elements may be simultaneous or in a sequence. The definition, it is to be hoped, is sufficiently broad to include all "skills" as the term is ordinarily used, only excluding those abilities commonly subsumed under the headings of understanding and knowledge.

[1] Reprinted from *Perceptual and Motor Skills*, 1961, **13**, 163–170.

But this definition has no particular value until we consider the dimensions of the skill. When these dimensions have been clarified, we can see how to measure a skill or develop a skill. We can even make a beginning in evaluating aptitude for a skill. And the dimensions are probably most readily made apparent by the following foolish little fable.

### The woodchoppers' ball

Once upon a time there lived in the Great North Woods two lumbermen. One was a Swede and one was a Finn, and both of them were experts with the axe. All the Swedes in the Great North Woods thought that the Swede was the greatest axeman in the world. All of the Finns in the Great North Woods thought that the Finn was the greatest axeman in the world. Nobody else in the Great North Woods, if there *was* anyone else in the Great North Woods, really mattered.

Naturally, this division of opinion led to arguments. Frequently, especially on weekends, these arguments led to fights. Since none of these seemed to settle the point, someone, more intelligent than the rest, suggested that a contest be staged. It was further suggested that the contest be followed by a party with a dance and that the entire affair be called the Woodchoppers' Ball.

Elaborate plans for the Woodchoppers' Ball were made. A huge hall with a stage was engaged. A Judge was chosen who happened to be half Swede and half Finn and was trusted by everyone. A band was hired to play for the dance. And loads and loads and loads of wood were brought for the use of the contestants.

Meanwhile, all over the Great North Woods, wagers were made on the outcome of the contest. People who had money bet money. People who had principles, or who simply didn't have money, put up all sorts of personal possessions or agreed to do things that were dangerous or ridiculous or difficult or tedious if their protagonist lost. As the time of the Woodchoppers' Ball approached, feeling was running very high.

When the great day came, the Judge got up on the platform and called the meeting to order. "Ladies and Gentlemen," he shouted in a very loud voice. "This here is a contest to decide which of these two men is the better man with an axe. This is not a contest of luck, and it is not a contest of popularity. It is a contest of skill. We are here tonight to decide which of these two men is the most skillful axeman in the world."

"That being the case," he went on, maintaining his remarkable volume, "my assistants and I have spared no effort to keep things fair. These chopping blocks you see before you are standard in size and shape and absolutely identical. On either side of the stage, and carefully guarded, you will see two tremendous piles of wood which have been perfectly matched, stick by individual stick. And the lights for the positions of the two contestants are as nearly identical as we can make them. We will now flip a coin to see who gets the east end of the stage and who gets the west end, and then the contest can get under way."

The coin was flipped, positions were taken, and the contestants were ready to begin. Each contestant was given ten cords of wood, specifications which the men must meet in chopping the wood were carefully explained, and the Judge raised the starting gun. The crowd went quiet, waiting for the signal to begin.

When the Judge fired the starting gun, the Swede and the Finn began to chop and the audience began to yell. The more the men chopped, the more the people shouted, especially since it became increasingly evident that the finish would be very close. In fact, as nearly as anyone in the audience could tell, the two men struck their last blows at exactly the same time, and the crowd hushed tensely, waiting for the Judge's decision. There was considerable delay while the Judge consulted with the people who had planned the party, but finally he bravely stepped forward to the edge of the platform, and announced, "Ladies and Gentlemen : I hereby declare the contest you have just witnessed to have ended in a draw !"

The first reaction to this was a moan of disappointment, but, as the full import of the decision sank in, this swiftly gave way to manifestations of indignation. The murmur of the crowd grew louder, and several angry remarks were shouted. The Judge raised his hands for silence. "We knew you'd feel this way," he said loudly, "so me and the committee has decided to do something about it." His judgemanship, leadership, and diplomacy were much better than his grammar. After all, English was a third language. "We have plenty of wood, and skill ain't all speed. We're going to test the *accuracy* of these two men and decide who the skillful one is that way."

So, the axemen competed in splitting matches and they competed in splitting straws. They competed in hitting pencil marks and they competed in hitting bird shot. In short, they competed in about every test of accuracy the Judge could devise. But anything the Swede could do the Finn could do likewise, and anything the Finn could do, the Swede could do as well. In accuracy, it gradually became clear, the Swede and the Finn were as evenly matched as they were in speed.

Finally, an old man with a long white beard whispered something lengthy in the Judge's ear, and the Judge made the following announcement: "Ladies and Gentlemen," he said, although by this time nobody was either, "since this ain't gettin' nowhere, I'd like to ask your opinion of a suggestion that's just been made. These men are obviously equal in speed and they're just as equal in accuracy. But there's still a side to chopping wood that we haven't tested. The more skill an axeman has, the less effort he'll use to get the job done. These two men are of an age and of a size. We propose that they be given all the wood they want and both chop until one of them drops. If that's agreeable to the contestants and agreeable to the audience we'll test their skill by that." The two heroes glanced at each other grimly and nodded their heads. The crowd shouted its approval.

But they didn't know what they had let themselves in for. At the end of an hour, the men were still chopping, and keeping up the required cords per hour. At the end of two hours, they were chopping yet, and many of the spectators had found entertainment of their own. To make a long story short, some time later, ninety-nine per cent of the crowd was mightily surprised by a loud thud and a louder silence which signified that both contestants had dropped to the floor.

This third tie, showing the Swede and the Finn to be equal in "form" as well as in speed and accuracy, was almost too much. The contest had just about lost an audience. But the old man with the beard stepped up to the Judge once more. This time he didn't consult so long, but he gestured quite a bit. When the Judge stepped forward this time he had a proposal that, as it turned out, let the gamblers settle their bets and the dancing begin. "We've compared these men in speed, we've compared them in accuracy, and we've compared them in what you might call smoothness. But in all this, they've worked on standard chopping blocks and they've used their own axes. Now, let's see how adaptable they are. They will now be asked to chop wood of various kinds on blocks of various heights. They'll chop under various conditions and they'll chop with various axes."

At this suggestion, the Finn grew pale and gripped his axe. However, he gamely entered this strange new kind of battle. But the truth was quickly out. The Swede could chop any wood under any conditions that the Judge saw fit to impose. Moreover, he chopped on any block and he chopped with any axe. Without his own axe and block, the Finlander was an ordinary man. In terms of adaptability, the Swede was easily superior, and nobody argued, although half of them were sad, when the Judge declared the Swede the Most Skillful Woodchopper in the World.

And so the story is ended. But one word remains to be said. The writer hastens to take this opportunity to assure the fair-minded reader that the outcome of this contest is unrelated to the writer's nationality.

So, skill has four dimensions: speed, accuracy, form, and adaptability. Do these dimensions apply to other skills than chopping wood?

———————

Johnson goes on to show the applications of these factors to a variety of skills. Each needs to be considered in dealing with any athletic skill.

The nature of a skill is closely related to the nature of an ability. An *ability* is a developed capacity, or what a person brings to a new task. Since there are a variety of learning situations, the specific abilities that interact for success in each situation should be understood and developed to maximum potential.

There is no one motor ability; instead, there are a number of motor abilities, as there are many cognitive abilities and other abilities. An ability, as Fleishman (1967) writes, is a general trait, depending on heredity, environmental factors, and learning. It is related to success in a number of tasks. On the other hand, skill is the level of proficiency in a particular task. It is a specific sequence of responses. One of the basic assumptions, according to Fleishman, is that skills representing a number of activities can be described in terms of basic abilities. Therefore, if it were known that a person possessed a particular high ability, it might be predicted that he could learn a specific skill easily. Obviously people differ in many ways, and ability is one of them. As Gagné and Fleishman (1959) point out, two people may practice equally long and with equal earnestness but attain different levels of proficiency. Differences in abilities brought to the task may help to explain this result.

An ability is rather permanent and enduring once maturity is reached. Genetics sets limits on potential, but abilities are developed in youth. With adulthood, the relative permanence of abilities over the span of many years show little if any decrease in performance. However, under favorable conditions, specific skills are improved upon with practice, regardless of age.

Verbal ability underlies the potential for success in a number of academic courses. Ability in manual dexterity is associated with proficiency in a wide range of industrial and mechanical tasks. Motor abilities, such as balance, eye-hand coordination, and speed, are associated with achievement in a number of sports.

The kinesthetic sense, or awareness of one's body parts in relation to the whole body, is important in a variety of motor skills. The "sense of feel" has been measured in a host of tasks, none of which seem to correlate too highly with each other. That is, doing well on one task which supposedly measures kinesthesis does not necessarily indicate good performance on a second kinesthetic task. The point is that an ability can be measured in a variety of tasks, and that in many cases, although a certain common ability is presumed to underlie achievement in these tasks, success may be specific to the particular task.

How ability to perform a particular athletic skill may be developed is open to speculation. If a person learns about logic and reasoning in a course, can his knowledge be transferred to other situations? If an athlete practices kinesthetic acuity or balancing ability in the laboratory, will his performance be improved in the gymnasium or the swimming pool? These questions serve to remind the reader that we are still talking in general terms when we refer to "abilities." Abilities may be defined, but accurate measurement and prediction of them is still far in the future.

## ALL-ROUND ATHLETES

The word "athlete" is defined, for the purposes of this book, as any person competing on an organized sports team under the guidance of a coach. For many years the youngster who excels in numerous sports has been spoken of as the "all-round athlete" or the "natural athlete." Such an athlete acquires new skills with ease and efficiency. He is poised, smoothly coordinated, and agile. He is the center of great acclaim by ardent admirers, sought after by ambitious coaches, and envied by rival coaches. That there are such athletic individuals is taken for granted, especially since we can all think of at least one person who would exemplify the preceding description. But is it possible that the all-round athlete is a myth, or at least a rarity, a freak of nature?

Reexamination of the concept of natural athletes, gifted performers in many sports, is necessary because of the increasing number of investigations which shed light on the problem. It has frequently been thought that an outstanding performer in one sport would have little difficulty in acquiring skill in other activities, that he would at least do better than the so-called "nonathlete" or the person who has participated in athletics without great success. It has been supposed that the athlete's natural and innate skill would sharpen his insight and hasten his progress in the acquisition of new motor skills.

The soundness of this line of reasoning is questionable. Many coaches have welcomed to their squads athletes who have excelled in other sports. They have expected proficiency to be generalized, to be applied to any sport in which the athlete is interested. Unfortunately, high expectations can lead to disappointments and frustrations. For every coach satisfied with the performance of an athlete in his new endeavor, there are many other coaches who are disappointed.

Laboratory and field research refute the notion of a general motor ability. These studies have tended to justify Franklin Henry's theory of motor specificity, which first appeared in a 1960 edition of the *Research Quarterly*. The theory is that all learning is specific and is stored, conceptually speaking, on a memory drum. When a response is called for, it is made as effectively as it has been stored on the drum. A person will tend to perform a new skill with a certain degree of proficiency only to the extent that he has previously experienced similar elements underlying the skill.

We can expect tennis to have a certain amount of transfer to the learning of badminton or squash. If an athlete performs well in more than one sport, it is because he is familiar with the movements necessary for success, because previous experiences have permitted him to develop general motor abilities common to and underlying a few sports. Hereditary factors are also important in determining potential success in various sports. Finally, in the area of personality, the athlete is likely to be highly motivated, and motivation to perform well in one sport might easily transfer over to other sports.

The author has recently completed two studies which would seem to support Henry's theory. In one study (Singer, 1966), the subject stood behind a 9-foot restraining line and repeatedly threw a softball with his preferred arm at a 4- by 4-foot target for 30 seconds. The process involved throwing with one hand and catching with either one or both hands. The subject then threw the ball at the target with his nonpreferred arm. The same subject then kicked a soccer ball continuously at a 4- by 4-foot target for 30 seconds, first with his preferred leg, then with his nonpreferred leg. The throwing and kicking skills involved individual limb speed and accuracy, as well as the ability of the person to coordinate upper extremities and then lower extremities.

The results indicated low positive relationships between the performance of the limbs. In other words, there was a slight tendency for persons who received the higher scores when throwing with their preferred arms to do the same with their nonpreferred arms. The same type of correlation existed between the preferred legs and the nonpreferred legs, the preferred arms and the preferred legs, and the nonpreferred arms and the nonpreferred legs. A further analysis revealed a tendency for success in these movements to be fairly specific rather than general. Evidence from this investigation suggests the questioning of a general motor ability and lends further support to Henry's theory of motor specificity.

In another study (Singer, 1965), athletes and nonathletes were compared in ability to perform on a stabilometer with and without spectators. The stabilometer is an apparatus which measures one's ability to balance on a board, and for this particular test, fluctuations of the board were recorded on moving graph paper inserted in the kymograph. Ten 30-second trials were administered to each subject. It was hypothesized that the athletes, who were outstanding at Ohio State University in such sports as basketball, tennis, wrestling, golf, track, and baseball, would learn how to balance more quickly and better than the nonathletes. Every sport requires a certain amount of balance, and although the balance required for the stabilometer is not the same as that needed for the specific sport, it was nevertheless believed that some positive transfer would be noted. Another hypothesis was that the athletes would perform more efficiently in front of a group of spectators because they were accustomed to performing motor skills in front of numbers of people. In the experimental situation, none of the subjects knew that people were going to watch them perform on the stabilometer. Two secretaries, two faculty members, and two students made up the audience, which watched the athletes and nonathletes without speaking during three 30-second trial periods.

Contrary to expectations, the nonathletes performed at a higher rate throughout practice. They also balanced more efficiently in front of the spectators than did the athletes.

A concept of general motor ability is of course incompatible with the results of such studies as this. The all-round athlete who exhibits general motor ability should perhaps be thought of as the exceptional case rather than the expected. More and more studies are indicating motor specificity rather than a general all-round ability to perform well in a variety of skills.

Even the ability to perform a motor skill in front of people appears to be specific to the motor skill which has been constantly practiced before spectators. The transfer of situation to situation and skill to skill cannot be taken for granted. Also, successful practice is no indication of success in the game situation, as every coach and performer will attest.

There will always be people whom we can term "all-round athletes." They have a wide range of athletic skills, movements, and coordinated patterns that transfer easily to newly introduced skills. They are highly motivated motor performers. They have been born with a certain degree of motor coordination and athletic aptitude, just as people are born with varying intelligence levels, creative abilities, and hair colors. Heredity, experience, and personality interact to influence the person and his actual and potential athletic status.

However, coaches should not expect too much of an athlete who has achieved success in another sport. The athlete also may expect too much of himself. Great success in one sport does not necessarily mean similar satisfaction in other sports. Only an extraordinary human being, possessing remarkable talents and skills, is able to be an outstanding performer in more than one sport.

Coaches would do well to take a realistic approach to the situation in which an athlete who is good in one sport attempts to succeed in an activity for which he has less talent. Achievement may or may not be demonstrated. But there is one consolation for the athlete: his highly developed skill in one sport which has brought him personal satisfaction and the admiration of others, has contributed as much to his growth and to his life in general as has probably any other experience. Disappointments in other sports have to be accepted along with the success in one, for participation in athletics is a preparation for life, and both athletics and life have their share of ups and downs.

## REFERENCES

Annett, John, & Kay, Harry. Skilled performance. *Occupational Psychology,* 1956, **30**, 112–117.

Fleishman, Edwin A. Development of a behavior taxonomy for describing human tasks: a correlational-experimental approach. *Journal of Applied Psychology,* 1967, **51**, 1–10.

Gagné, Robert M., & Fleishman, Edwin A. *Psychology and human performance.* New York: Holt, 1959.

Henry, Franklin M. Increased response latency for complicated movements and a "memory drum" theory of neuromotor reaction. *Research Quarterly,* 1960, **31**, 448–458.

Knapp, Robert H. Changing functions of the college professor. In N. Sanford (Ed.), *The American college.* New York: Wiley, 1962.

Singer, Robert N. Effect of spectators on athletes and non-athletes performing a gross motor task. *Research Quarterly,* 1965, **36**, 473–482.

Singer, Robert N. Interlimb skill ability in motor skill performance. *Research Quarterly,* 1966, **37**, 406–410.

Singer, Robert N. *Motor learning and human performance.* New York: Macmillan, 1968.

Tutko, Thomas A., & Ogilvie, Bruce C. The role of the coach in motivation of athletes. In R. Slovenko & J. A. Knight (Eds.), *Motivations in play, games and sports.* Springfield, Ill.: Charles C Thomas, 1967.

Wolman, Benjamin B. *Contemporary theories and systems in psychology.* New York: Harper & Row, 1960.

# CHAPTER TWO

# Growth and Development Factors and the Athlete

No matter what the coach would like, guiding an athletic team goes far beyond disciplining athletes and teaching skills. Among the many personal matters that the coach must be aware of are growth and developmental factors: factors that dictate how skills must be taught and how the athlete must be treated, and that also indicate behavioral expectancies. In coaching youths, adolescents, and young adults, the anatomical, physiological, emotional, cultural, psychological, and sociological factors that are pertinent to chronological age or maturational age must be taken into consideration.

Children develop as they grow older and confront emotional problems. They need to develop control and yet to retain enough aggressiveness to succeed in competitive sports. With development and maturation, their motor movements come under control, and it becomes possible for them to execute complex behavior and motor skills. Language mastery makes communication easier; the translation of oral commands into appropriate movement patterns is a natural result of growing and learning. Thought, understanding, reasoning, concept formation, and the learning of strategies and tactics also improve in normal developmental patterns.

Children develop in other ways. Socially, they learn to compete, to cooperate, and to maintain the balance necessary in sport. Personality, although originally shaped from genetic factors, is modified by experience. The child acquires identity, a self-image, and behavioral tendencies. His attitudes, interests, and values are formed and modified, and are reflected in athletic situations. He adjusts to life's problems and handles his conflicts and frustrations in acceptable or socially unacceptable ways. His family, peer group, and culture influence his patterns of development.

The coach receives the product of all these variables. Even if all the athletes of a team are the same age, each has different problems. Fortunately, there are a number of general expectations with regard to age and the factors mentioned previously. An understanding of patterns of growth and development, of individual similarities and differences, is necessary if the coach is to handle a group of athletes effectively. The problem is most severe with young children, who require much attention and understanding. There are vast differences in body structures and maturational levels between young children. Their many incomplete phases of development necessitate special sensitivity on the part of the coach. As the child develops into adolescence and early adulthood, the coach becomes more free to concentrate on skills, tactics, and the high-level promotion of his team in the sport represented.

In many relationships between coach and athlete there is a gap of a generation or two. The adult coach typically knows his sport and the skills involved quite well. But does he understand his athletes? Can he relate to children? To adolescents? To young adults? Communication is extremely important, and it comes through understanding, knowledge, and a will to succeed. We will discuss some of the typical characteristics of athletes who form teams equivalent to age groups found in upper elementary school, junior high school, high school, and college. But first, an elaboration of some of the general growth and developmental considerations is in order.

## GENERAL CONSIDERATIONS

At a tryout the average coach is not interested in the kinds of experiences and developments that the athlete has had before he tried out for the team. What the aspirant can produce at the tryout will usually determine whether he will be selected or rejected.

Preschool children rarely perform in structured competition, and coaches do not usually have direct formal contact with them. Coaches' experience with very young children is usually restricted to playing with and observing their own or neighbors' children. Only when the child is about 7 or 8 years of age, at the earliest, does he begin to take part in organized athletic competition. Nevertheless, preschool years are significant and meaningful. Motor, intellectual, physical, and personality development provides the foundation for the learning of complex motor acts at a later stage in life.

Since there are many books on child development for the coach who is interested, it is unnecessary to discuss all such material here. Only the aspects of early childhood that are relevant to later athletic performance need to be included.

Patterns of motor development in the preschool child have been fairly well established. Their sequence is fairly similar from child to child, although their rate of development is different in each child. Youngsters of similar ages differ widely in maturational status, a fact that parents and coaches should always consider.

### Distinction by Age and Maturational Readiness

A fair amount of research has established norm expectancies for boys and girls of various chronological ages in such characteristics as IQ, developmental tasks, and physical characteristics. These data are meaningful, to a point. They are readily available and are helpful for purposes of comparison. Unfortunately, however, interpreters of these data sometimes forget that individual children differ in maturational progress even though they age chronologically in similar fashion.

One of the greatest complaints of those who are against organized competitive athletics in elementary school and junior high school is that although boys of similar age are competing with one another, wide dissimilarities in maturational growth create a dangerous situation in sports like football and wrestling. Competition in other sports is also criticized, on the grounds that students with a great assortment of physical shapes and forms may be in the same contest. In such unequal contests, danger to the less mature children is always present.

Some young athletes whose physical size is large for their age give the impression of early maturity even though they are actually immature. If these athletes are trained hard, they may appear lazy but in truth may be unable to perform the refined movement patterns that would coincide with their mature-looking body characteristics. Such athletes incur the wrath of uninformed and insensitive coaches, and emotional problems and physiological dangers may result. The junior high school athlete who is making the transition to adolescence is most affected by these circumstances.

Any coach who deals with athletes, especially those below college age, should be aware of differences in maturational rate within specific age groups. Biographical data in the form of height and weight growth charts provide insight into each athlete's progress in development. Other measures, such as wrist-bone X rays, also help to indicate the stage of development. The young athlete should not be trained beyond his physical, physiological, and emotional limitations.

## Are Athletes Born or Made?

Is genetics or experience more important? Coaches have not been the only ones to debate this issue. For many years, educators and psychologists have argued on this point, with the primary focal point being intelligence. Modern-day researchers and writers, interested in the topic, have generally agreed that both factors interact to determine traits and abilities.

Genetics provides the means, the instruments which make movements possible. Environmental influences, the quality and quantity of training experiences, shape the degree of skill achieved by the individual. Research on body build and athletic achievement, further discussed in Chapter 4, indicates that a hereditary stereotype for a particular sport or event is advantageous. However, developed desire and motivation can have a strong effect and can even enable those who are less well endowed to succeed in athletics. Hard training can overcome many personal limitations. Although a certain body type or build may lead to achievement in specific activities, it is by no means necessary. Nevertheless, the presence of certain bodily, emotional, and intellectual characteristics will probably contribute to the probability of success in particular endeavors. These and other attributes are both genetically and environmentally determined.

Anne Anastasi, who has written considerably on the subject of individual differences, believes that asking how much effect environment or genetics has on any human characteristic is almost meaningless. She suggests (Anastasi, 1966, p. 83): "The question should be reformulated in terms, not of how much, but of how. What we need to know is the *modus operandi* —the way in which specific hereditary and environmentary factors operate in producing specific differences in behavior."

The exceptional athlete is, then, both born and made; he displays abilities and skills reflected by the interaction of hereditary and environmental variables. If the coach knows something about the athlete's family characteristics and his experiences in sports, he should be able to predict the athlete's future status with some accuracy.

### Optimal Learning Periods

Two different types of research have strongly indicated that life's early and timely experiences are meaningful. Freud's clinical observations at the beginning of this century have been, to some degree, verified in subsequent case studies. The degree of satisfactory adjustment to various stages of development from approximately age 2 to age 6 will ultimately determine behavior later in life. Freud contended that there are certain periods in a child's life when he is particularly sensitive to certain experiences. The adult personality may be modified by later personal experiences but is largely shaped during these critical years.

The second area of research has to do with the effects of early enriched or deprived experiences on subsequent behavior. The main subjects on which data have been collected are rats, dogs, apes, chickens, and ducks. Animals raised in culturally deprived environments exhibit lower forms of intellectual behavior in adult years than do animals raised in culturally rich environments. Young rats deprived of food demonstrate hoarding behavior at maturity. Animals raised in competitive situations are aggressive at maturity.

A phenomenon termed "imprinting" is associated with this line of research. Somewhere between 24 and 36 hours after hatching, mallard ducks will follow the first moving object they see and will thereafter look on it as their mother. Imprinting must occur during a critical period in the organism's life span, if it is to occur at all.

We might speculate that there are periods in the life of every human during which specific experiences can have the most meaning for later life. If this were true, sports skills could be introduced and taught effectively in modified form much earlier than is usually the case. Many champion athletes report that they had some experience in the sport of their choice quite early in life.

This is not to say the earlier the better. Timeliness is more important than earliness. "Timeliness" refers to the stage in development when physiological, psychological, emotional, and other capacities are primed to be most responsive to the introduction of particular experiences. The optimal learning period for a skill is not dependent on age but rather on the relative rate of maturation. Critical periods are therefore different for each learning situation and for each person with regard to age. Critical periods do seem to come earlier than was previously supposed, however.

Findings from McGraw's famous twin study (1935) suggest that motor skills involving balance and the overcoming of fear might be taught when the youngster is in the first or second year of life. Unfortunately, there are no guides to the critical points at which one learns specific sports most effectively. It does appear, however, that good experiences in sports early in childhood are beneficial in the years that follow.

## *Considerations about Early Movements*

In the discussion of the all-round athlete in Chapter 1, two points were made that need elaboration here. One had to do with general movement experiences, the other with training in specific skills during formative childhood years—both factors that contribute to successful athletic endeavors.

A childhood filled with rich and varied movement experiences serves as a foundation for learning of the more complex athletic skills later in life. Many sports contain skills and subskills that call for basic movement patterns like swinging, striking, running, jumping, and throwing. Since the sequence and timing of these acts are unique from sports skill to skill, there is a general impression that sports skills are diverse and unrelated. Very often, however, acts can be broken down into simple patterns of movement, the kinds experienced to some degree in childhood. If a child has not been encouraged or allowed to participate in varied movements and explorations, the foundations of movement patterns will be weak, and such a lack is difficult to compensate for later. Poor throwing patterns are hard to unlearn, and yet passing a football, throwing a baseball, flinging a basketball pass, hitting an overhead volleyball serve, and serving a tennis ball all require elements of coordinated throwing behavior.

It is foolish to attempt to teach complex skills to infants. As Scott (1968, p. 123) warns, "Most children are not able to perform activities requiring good coordination of the whole body much before the ages of 7 or 8, and introducing them too early to such activities only results in unskilled performance or failure." This does not mean, however, that sports skills cannot be simplified and modified appropriately for the age of the child.

Another consideration is that proficiency in specific skills and sports increases the probability of success in learning new, related ones. The skills involved in swimming and gymnastics are quite far apart; those involved in badminton, squash, tennis, and paddle ball are more related. Therefore, the background of the athlete may yield a clue to his probabilities of success in specific sports.

Coaches should develop case histories of potential athletes. Previous experiences, honors, and interests of each athlete provide insight into possible achievement, and family interests and accomplishments are useful supplementary information. A number of people become outstanding athletes in spite of minimal athletic participation and status in childhood, but childhood activities should not be neglected as clues to possible future proficiency in sports.

## ELEMENTARY SCHOOL ATHLETES

From the material presented thus far, it should be evident that wide experience in play activities early in life is desirable. No one has qualms about play as activity that contributes meaningfully to the child's development. The urge to play is natural in children, and the benefits are obvious. Controversy arises, however, when youngsters below the age of approximately 13 are allowed, encouraged, or pressured to join athletic teams organized in the school or in the community.

Although spontaneous activity for children under minimal adult supervision is advocated by almost everyone, some people are concerned about the control, intensive specialized training, and emotional climate surrounding organized athletic competition. The issue probably began with the formation of Little League baseball in 1939 under the direction of Carl Stotz in Williamsport, Pennsylvania. Everything, starting with facility and equipment dimensions, was scaled down to meet the ability and size limitations of youngsters between the ages of 8 and 12. There are other sports, including football, in which the community may offer organized athletic activity for children of elementary school age, but Little League baseball is a good example of the issue.

The scope and magnitude of the Little League are indicated by the following data, recently reported in a popular journal: (1) the average Little League schedule contains about 20 games; (2) there are district, state, regional, and world series playoffs; (3) better and poorer players are distinguished by acceptance to major and minor Little League teams within a town; and (4) more than 1 million boys are involved in 5,400 Little Leagues throughout the world (Schoenstein, 1969).

Many elementary schools offer athletic programs for those gifted or interested in them. These programs sometimes assume the same characteristics as their high school and college counterparts. At other times they are administered in quite a limited fashion and with minimal organization and show. Essentially, the controversy is about whether athletic teams and leagues sponsored by the school or the community are beneficial or harmful to the participants. The controversy has gone on a long time, with ethical, philosophical, psychological, physiological, and sociological parameters. The obvious need is for research to provide data that might help to resolve some aspects of the issue.

A report published through the combined efforts of the American Academy of Pediatrics, the American Medical Association, the American Association for Health, Physical Education, and Recreation, and the Society of State Directors of Health, Physical Education, and Recreation contains suggestions and guidelines with regard to children under age 13 who participate in competitive athletics (*Desirable Athletic Competition,* 1968). The report warns against commercialization and overemphasis on athletics at this age level. A narrow sports experience for the student should be avoided, and all students should have access to a physical education program of high quality. Rule modifications and careful grouping of children according to their physical characteristics are recommended.

Controversy about athletic programs for youngsters still rages, however, and though guidelines for action have been suggested, many people would like the issues to be resolved with the aid of research support. Rarick (1968), in a recent speech at the National Conference on the Medical Aspects of Sports, stated that about one-third of the elementary schools in this country sponsor interscholastic athletic competition. One of the major concerns about such programs is their effect on normal growth and development. Injury to the epiphysis, because this part of the bone is vulnerable during the growing years, is a special problem with regard to competition. Rarick indicated that the incidence of this type of injury is rare. When it does occur, it can be treated in most cases so that permanent damage will not result.

Rarick went on to say that in a roentgenographic study, Little League players aged 9 to 12 were reported to have various kinds of conditions, such as epiphysitis and osteochondrosis in their throwing arms. It was recommended that pitchers below the age of 14 pitch only a few innings of each game and that the curve ball not be allowed. Rarick also commented that research evidence did not support the idea that competitive sports and intensive training adversely affect the physical growth of children. In fact, physical activity probably has a positive effect on the growth of bone and muscle tissue. According to Rarick, whether young athletes can handle the psychological stress of competition has not yet been resolved, although there are indications that the tension of competition disturbs their sleeping habits. However, he suggested that the tension is probably not excessive, nor of any greater magnitude than that following competition in the classroom.

Another matter of public concern is the nature of the leaders of the young athletes. Criticism is often leveled at the lack of preparation these leaders, whether teachers and coaches in school or members of the community, have for directing the fate of their charges. The teaching of athletic skills is one thing, but an understanding of or sensitivity to growth and development patterns is something else. Normative information as well as knowledge of expected individual differences in anatomical, physiological, emotional, motor skill, social, psychological, intellectual, and anthropological characteristics are necessary in order to guide any group of youngsters competently.

Another area in which formal knowledge would be advantageous is the development of appropriate cooperative and competitive attitudes. For the most part, the college athlete displays appropriate competitive behavior. When a problem does exist, it is usually less serious than with younger athletes. Coaches of young athletes should be aware that, although cooperative attitudes are a function of increasing age, training can lead to better cooperation, and that the best results are obtained with young children (Heise, 1942).

The tendency to compete or cooperate is learned, but children find it easier to compete than to cooperate. A child at the age of 2 or 3 strives for an object. Other children go unnoticed; they are not as yet a source of possible competition to him. At about 3 or 4, he begins to recognize other children as competitors. A desire to excel is shown from 4 to 6, and at 6 or 7, the child becomes aware of the obstacles to his goal. In many activities, competition becomes basic and cooperation becomes incidental. Healthy and appropriate competitive and cooperative behaviors have to be taught if they are to be shown in proper perspective, and future attitudes can be determined by early experiences. In any sports event, the athlete has to cooperate with his teammates and has to compete aggressively but within the rules against his opponents. The successful athlete is one who has learned to do both.

Very few studies have been completed on athletic groups of elementary school age. In the middle 1950s, a series of studies were done on Little League baseball players, and the results of the reports are helpful in forming a better understanding of some of the relationships among sports participation, age, and other variables. In response to the argument that competitive athletic situations overstimulate the young athlete to the extent that he is not capable of handling them emotionally, Skubic (1955) undertook the project described below. In reviewing the literature, the investigator had found numerous discrepancies concerning the value of competitive athletics for boys. Some wrote that personal security and emotional stability would result from participation, whereas others stated that the result of intense competition is physical, psychological, and emotional harm. Skubic tested the emotional responses of Little League and non-League players. The League players were tested before and after competition, and the non-League players were tested before and after softball competition in physical education classes. Emotional responses were measured by a galvanic skin response (GSR) test. The youngsters were found to be equally stimulated by competition in class and Little League games. These data do not, of course, provide any information on the long-range effects of competitive athletics.

In a follow-up study (1956), Skubic attempted to obtain further information on Little League players. The conclusion was that

> . . . boys chosen on teams show greater achievement in school subjects, possess greater motor ability and are better adjusted socially and emotionally than boys who are not members of teams. . . . Boys participating in the program and their parents approved the program wholeheartedly. Their main criticism was that many boys who were members of teams did not get a chance to play in the games [p. 97].

Skubic further concludes that "it appears that the boys who display the best baseball techniques, play the most intelligent game, have emotional stability, and get along best in a group are the ones who are chosen to play competitive baseball" (p. 107).

In another investigation, Seymour (1956) studied Little League players and non-League players. The boys evaluated themselves and were evaluated by teachers and by other children before and after a season of play. The boys in the two groups were between ages 10 and 12, and were equated by age and by grade in school. Seymour, after analyzing the data, wrote that (1) it is difficult to ascribe any change, favorable or unfavorable, to a season of Little League baseball; (2) the problems and needs of Little League players and non-League players are fairly similar; and (3) the Little League players scored higher on personality traits and social acceptance than did the non-League players both before and after the season of competition.

From a physiological and an anatomical point of view, it appears that outstanding young athletes are more mature than their nonathletic counterparts. Skeletal maturity is evidently related to the athletic performance of athletes in later childhood. Physiological maturity, as determined by the Crampton Pubic Hair Index, is also associated with athletic accomplishments. For example, Hale (1956) examined 112 participants in the 1955 Little League World Series. Their average chronological age was 12.53 years. It was determined that approximately 50 percent of the boys were postpubescent, as mature as the average 14- or 15-year-old. Interestingly enough, the majority of the postpubescents batted in from third to sixth position in the batting order.

Further support for the importance of growth and maturity variables underlying motor aptitude in preadolescents in 10- to 12-year-olds has been offered by Ismail and Cowell (1961). Other factors identified as being relevant were speed, kinesthetic memory of the arms, body balance on objects, and body balance on the floor.

Thus it can be seen that the coach of an athletic team composed of children of upper elementary school age typically deals with those who are more advanced than the average, socially, physiologically, anatomically, emotionally, and psychologically. Advanced athletic skills seem to be associated with advanced maturity. The extent to which maturity encourages athletic participation and leads to proficiency and the extent to which athletic experience encourages early maturity are difficult to ascertain. From a psychological point of view, the long-range effects of high-level athletic competition are of great interest and concern. At the present time, unfortunately, we can only speculate on these outcomes.

## JUNIOR HIGH SCHOOL ATHLETES

Junior high school competition, although not quite as controversial as elementary school athletics, has had its share of debate. The transition from late childhood to adolescence is a marked one. Junior high schools contain students with wide dissimilarities in body size and proportion as well as in athletic ability. Strong distinctions are apparent between late and early maturers. Because of these differences among boys and girls of similar chronological age, misunderstandings are widespread about how they should be treated, individually and collectively, with regard to athletic competition.

A number of students at this point in life appear to have adult bodies, and others possess the physical characteristics of elementary school children. These varying degrees of development have led to two important questions: (1) To what extent can competition be allowed or encouraged among students of varying physical and ability characteristics? (2) To what extent can and should junior high school athletes be trained for competition? The coach is of course concerned with all dimensions of the athlete. The student's physiological limitations, needs, interests, social interactions and values, emotional stability, and motor development are all involved in setting the pattern for an effective training regimen.

Much has been written about expected development and individual deviations during the period of change from late childhood to adolescence, typically encompassing the ages from 12 to 15, the junior high school years. Strength, height, weight, and various motor performance data have been published and republished elsewhere. In early adolescence (ages 13 to 15) there is usually a rapid growth in height, weight, and strength, as well as a steady gain in eye-hand coordination.

Attitudes, expectations, and values for this age group have also been reported on. For example, these children admire achievement in physical skills and try to be good at a number of sports and games. Their popularity is significantly related to their strength and motor skills. They question and defy adult authority—a possible source of conflict between the unsuspecting coach and his team members.

Among the various safeguards that can help to make athletic programs at the junior high school level acceptable to more people are (1) mandatory medical examinations; (2) acceptable equipment and facilities; (3) grouping of athletes according to such variables as size, maturation level, and skill; and (4) qualified and competent coaching and officiating. As with younger children, contact sports must be especially well supervised. Similarly, winning and losing should be placed in proper perspective because of the possible psychological effects of undue emphasis on either. Emotion-packed contests and too much pressure may be psychologically damaging to emotionally immature youth, it has been reasoned. As there are few if any objective data to support or refute such accusations, common sense must prevail.

Although junior high school interscholastic athletics has become increasingly widespread in the United States, powerful arguments may be found on either side. As educators, medical men, psychologists, and sociologists are divided on the issue, it is obvious that there is no clear-cut evidence either for or against.

Some reasons why junior high school interscholastic competition may not be a good idea are:

1  The boys have not yet matured anatomically. Bone growth has not yet terminated and will probably not do so until the late teens. Contact sports create a situation in which injury may occur to the bone and especially to the end (epiphysis) of the bone, resulting in the possibility of deformity or decreased growth.

2  Physiologically, boys in early adolescence vary extensively. There is a great extreme in sizes and shapes, creating a situation in athletics in which boys sometimes compete against others twice as large. Also, a large body frame is deceiving at this age. These boys are not ready for extensive endurance activities, for although their bodies may appear mature, their circulatory and respiratory systems are less well developed.

3  In a youngster who is not completely healthy, the heart may be damaged.

4  The expense is prohibitive.

5  There is a lack of trained personnel who will have only the best interests of the boys at heart.

6  Junior high school athletics should not be a training ground for high school varsities.

7  Junior high school boys should not be subjected to the competitive way of life. They are too young and will have plenty of time to experience competition in later life.

Some reasons why interscholastic athletics should be included in the curriculum are:

1  If planned and guided leadership were not offered in the school program, the boys would probably participate in sports through outside agencies or on their own.

2  Sports, especially competitive team sports, are basic to the American way of life. Probably more junior high school boys participate in basketball, football, and baseball or softball than in any other physical activities.

3  Increasing scientific research has shown that the normal, healthy heart of a youngster cannot be injured through vigorous activity or strain.

Supposedly, the body itself knows when to retire before the heart is taxed too much.

4   It has been demonstrated that junior high school athletes are more mature physically than boys who do not participate in varsity athletics. Therefore, they should be able to handle themselves adequately in physical competition.

5   Sociological studies have shown that athletic boys are usually better accepted by their peers than nonathletic ones, that they are respected and liked by others, and that they tend to be leaders in a group.

6   Physical education, as a part of the total education process, is supposed to meet the needs and interests of all the students. This means activities not only for the "average" student, poor athlete, and non-athlete, but also for the superior athlete.

7   American democracy stresses competition in life. If junior high school boys experience competition in athletics, they will be better prepared for later life. (This position has been neither supported nor refuted by the research literature.)

8   High school and college varsity teams need boys who have been previously well coached in fundamentals. Junior high school coaches have the opportunity to develop and prepare these boys for high school and college competition.

Whatever the arguments for and against various organized athletic activities, boys will probably participate in athletic activities no matter what adults plan for them. It is therefore the schools' responsibility to provide good leadership, excellent guidance, and the best facilities possible to ensure that athletics may be of value to the participants.

As to the athletic proficiency of junior high school students, Espenschade (1940) has written that motor performance is related to age, weight, and height during elementary and junior high school years but shows a small correlation with body build. More recent and complete cross-sectional and longitudinal data are reported by Clarke (1967). Measures of maturity, physique, body size, strength, endurance, motor ability, academic aptitude and achievement, interests, and personal-social relations were recorded over a 10-year period. Athletes in football, basketball, track and field, and wrestling were studied. Among the conclusions were the following:

Boys who make and are successful on interscholastic athletic teams in both elementary and junior high schools are definitely superior to their peers in maturity, body size, muscular strength, endurance, and power [p. 49].

Although successful young athletes generally have common characteristics, the pattern of these characteristics varies from athlete to athlete; where a successful athlete is lacking in such a trait, he compensated by strength in another [p. 53].

Outstanding elementary school athletes may not be outstanding in junior high school athletics, and outstanding junior high school athletes may not have been outstanding in elementary school athletics [pp. 54–55].

On the last point, of the 20 outstanding athletes studied, only 5 demonstrated superior skills in both elementary and junior high school. Furthermore, 9, or 45 percent, were outstanding only in elementary school while 6, or 30 percent, were outstanding only in junior high school. Figure 2-1 shows the average profiles of the three groups of athletes: (1) superior at both 12 and 15 years of age; (2) superior only at 12 years; and (3) superior only at 15 years.

Personality data have been collected by Schendel (1965) on ninth-grade athletes and nonathletes. Using the California Psychological Inventory, substitutes, regular players, and outstanding players were compared; their respective profiles are shown in Figure 2-2. Profiles of the nonathletic group and the total athletic group appear in Figure 2-3. None of the 18 personality traits listed in Table 2-1 distinguished the three groups of athletes. However, when athletes and nonathletes were compared, these conclusions were drawn (Schendel, 1965, p. 66):

> Ninth grade athletes generally possess desirable personal-social psychological characteristics to a greater extent than nonparticipants in athletics from the same grade. Ninth grade athletes, compared to ninth grade non-participants in

---

TABLE 2-1    Personality scales used for Figures 2-2 and 2-3

| | | |
|---|---|---|
| 1. Dominance (Do) | 7. Responsibility (Re) | 13. Achievement via conformance (Ac) |
| 2. Capacity for status (Cs) | 8. Socialization (So) | 14. Achievement via independence (Ai) |
| 3. Sociability (Sy) | 9. Self-control (Sc) | 15. Intellectual efficiency (Ie) |
| 4. Social presence (Sp) | 10. Good impression (Gi) | 16. Psychological mindedness (Py) |
| 5. Self-acceptance (Sa) | 11. Tolerance (To) | 17. Flexibility (Fx) |
| 6. Well-being (Wb) | 12. Communality (Cm) | 18. Femininity (Fe) |

---

*Source:* Jack Schendel. Psychological differences between athletes and nonparticipants in athletics at three educational levels. *Research Quarterly*, 1965, **36**, 52–67. P. 65.

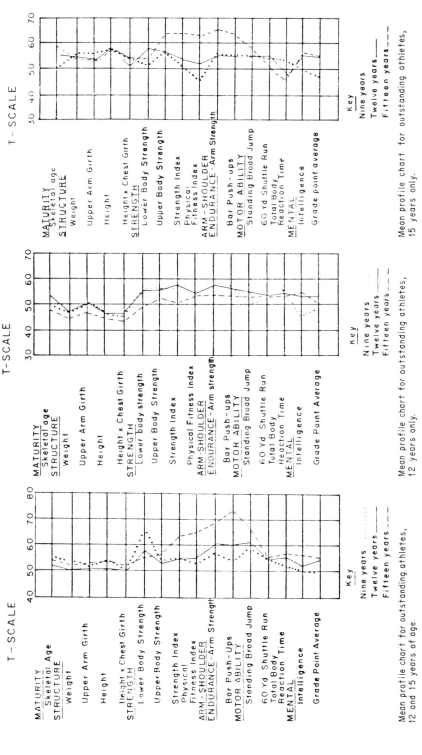

T-SCALE

MATURITY
  Skeletal Age
STRUCTURE
  Weight

Upper Arm Girth

Height

Height x Chest Girth
STRENGTH
  Lower Body Strength

Upper Body Strength

Strength Index
Physical
Fitness Index
ARM-SHOULDER
ENDURANCE-Arm Strength

Bar Push-Ups
MOTOR ABILITY
  Standing Broad Jump

60 Yd Shuttle Run
Total Body
Reaction Time
MENTAL
  Intelligence

Grade Point Average

Key
Nine years ........
Twelve years ———
Fifteen years — — —

Mean profile chart for outstanding athletes,
12 and 15 years of age.

---

MATURITY
  Skeletal age
STRUCTURE
  Weight

Upper Arm Girth

Height

Height x Chest Girth
STRENGTH
  Lower body strength

Upper Body Strength

Strength Index
Physical Fitness Index
ARM-SHOULDER
ENDURANCE-Arm strength

Bar Push-ups
MOTOR ABILITY
  Standing Broad Jump

60 Yd Shuttle Run
Total Body
Reaction Time
MENTAL
  Intelligence

Grade Point Average

Key
Nine years ———
Twelve years ———
Fifteen years — — —

Mean profile chart for outstanding athletes,
12 years only.

---

MATURITY
  Skeletal age
STRUCTURE
  Weight

Upper Arm Girth

Height

Height x Chest Girth
STRENGTH
  Lower Body Strength

Upper Body Strength

Strength Index
Physical
Fitness Index
ARM-SHOULDER
ENDURANCE-Arm Strength

Bar Push-ups
MOTOR ABILITY
  Standing Broad Jump

60 Yd Shuttle Run
Total Body
Reaction Time
MENTAL
  Intelligence

Grade point average

Key
Nine years ———
Twelve years ———
Fifteen years — — —

Mean profile chart for outstanding athletes,
15 years only.

FIGURE 2-1   *A comparison of three groups of athletes in various characteristics at three different age periods.* (Source: *H. Harrison Clarke. Characteristics of the young athlete: a longitudinal look.* Proceedings of the 8th National Conference on the Medical Aspects of Sports, 1967, **8**, 49–57. Pp. 55–56.)

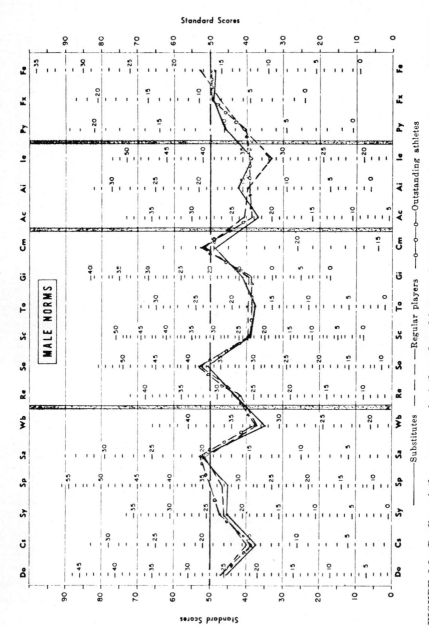

FIGURE 2-2 *Profiles of three groups of ninth-grade subjects: substitutes, regular players, and outstanding athletes. (Source: Jack Schendel. Psychological differences between athletes and nonparticipants in athletics at three educational levels. Research Quarterly, 1965, 36, 52-67. P. 57.)*

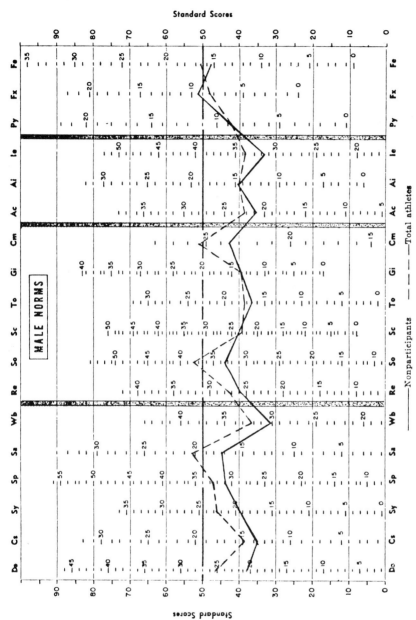

FIGURE 2-3 *Profiles of two groups of ninth-grade subjects: nonparticipants and all the athletes.* (*Source: Jack Schendel. Psychological differences between athletes and nonparticipants in athletics at three educational levels.* Research Quarterly, *1965,* **36,** *52–67. P. 56.*)

———— Nonparticipants    — — — Total athletes

athletics: (*a*) possess more of the qualities of leadership and social initiative, (*b*) possess more of the qualities which lead to status, (*c*) are more sociable, (*d*) possess a greater sense of personal worth, (*e*) have less self-doubt and make fewer complaints, (*f*) have more social maturity, (*g*) are more conventional in their responses to social situations, and (*h*) possess greater intellectual efficiency.

In another study of personality, Ogilvie (1968) administered varied tests to competitive male and female swimmers, members of the internationally famous Santa Clara Swim Club, as they progressed from 10 to 14 years of age. Ogilvie reports that as 10-year-olds, the boys were typified by such traits as coolness, reservation, and introversion. After training in the club until age 14, they became more warm-hearted, outgoing, extroverted, emotionally stable, self-assertive, independent, and aggressive. The girls demonstrated similar changes in personality development. Ogilvie concluded that high level competition makes a positive contribution to personality development.

There have been very few studies dealing with the psychology of learning and training factors on junior high school athletes, or for that matter, nonathletes. Most of the research, as shown below and in Chapter 9, which deals with research and sport, has been on high school and even more on college subjects. One investigation in which the performance outcomes of modified basketball practice techniques were compared with traditional techniques has been made by Takacs (1965). Three groups of eighth-graders were tested: group I shot free throws at a regulation basket; group II shot at a smaller basket; and group III did not shoot at all. Group II did significantly better than group III in later performance with a regulation basket, and did the same as group I. Evidently, for this group, small-basket shooting neither facilitated nor hindered the learning process.

Since organized athletic competition in junior high schools is increasing, more physiological and psychological research is needed and will certainly be done. Many of the kinds of studies on older subjects dealing with the acquisition of motor skill can be and perhaps should be repeated with younger students. Learning does not necessarily occur in all age groups in a consistent pattern. Exceptions and modifications should be noted and further explored.

## HIGH SCHOOL ATHLETES

Although patterns of growth irregularity are still evident in high school students, many outstanding athletes at ages 17 and 18 have completed their growth spurts and are nearing maturity. The growth spurt for boys usually occurs between 10 and 15 years of age, and then many of the growth and developmental problems that athletes have in elementary school and junior high school become less pressing. Emotional and social matters become more urgent, for the adolescent is attaining physical maturity but not necessarily social maturity. Because social and emotional problems can interfere to some extent with acquisition of skill and proficiency in athletics, the coach needs to recognize them and to help the students to resolve them as effectively as possible.

During adolescence, the individual's motor performance reflects the combination of increased eye-hand and overall body coordination and strength. Body control and the completion of complex spatially and temporally timed tasks are demonstrated. Much rapid growth in strength is shown in boys between 15 and 16 years of age, and in general throughout adolescence. With the development of abilities and the acquisition of skills through practice and experience, potential athletic accomplishments come closer to being realized. Tanner (1961) writes that throughout adolescence physical qualities, such as power and endurance, as well as athletic skills, increasingly improve with great rapidity. General maturity and athletic maturity bring about high, stable levels of performance. Many athletes do not achieve this maturity until the college years.

Performance curves on various physical tasks for boys and girls are illustrated in Figures 2-4 and 2-5. Trends from age 12 to age 18 are about the same for the boys on almost all tasks; that is, a general increase is apparent. Girls, however, are more inconsistent in performance on the tests.

For the adolescent, there is an important relationship between his physical development and his psychological attitudes toward himself. Psychological factors can influence physical appearance, and physical development affects personal attitudes. Popularity has been shown to be more related to strength and athletic skills than to academic achievements. Therefore, the high school athlete often enjoys high status among his peer group. Although many reasons may be offered for participation in athletics, social approval and prestige are certainly important. Other influencing factors are the desires to excel, to master, to express oneself, and to experience adventure and excitement.

The popularity of high school athletes has been well documented by Coleman (1961). He studied all students in 10 selected midwestern high schools. Of all possible variables, the "elite" students (those who were mentioned most often by their peers) selected going out for the football team as being most associated with their popularity. All the boys were asked what they most wanted to be: a famous athlete, a missionary, or an atomic scientist. The athlete was most frequently checked by all the boys (37 percent) and this response was even greater among the elite students.

As for status, Coleman's study indicated that athletic achievements rated

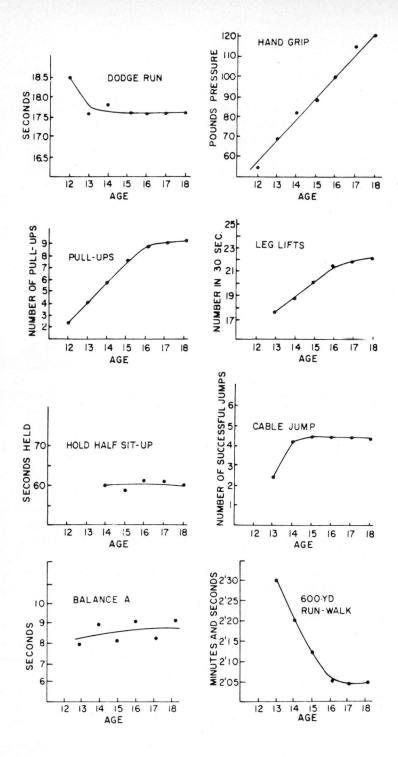

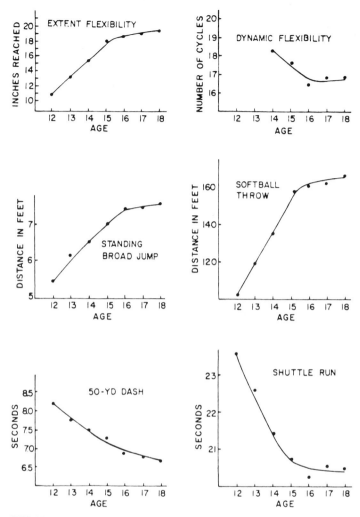

FIGURE 2-4 *Developmental curves for boys on various physical tests.* (Source: *Edwin A. Fleishman.* The structure and measurement of physical fitness. *Englewood Cliffs, N.J.: Prentice-Hall, 1964. Pp. 122–123. Copyright 1964 and reprinted by permission of Prentice-Hall, Inc.)*

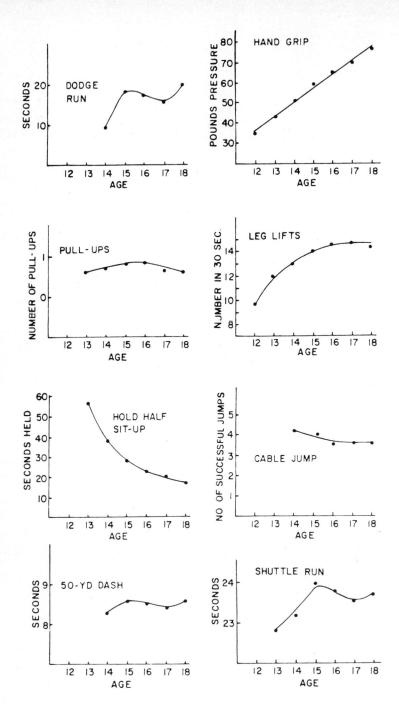

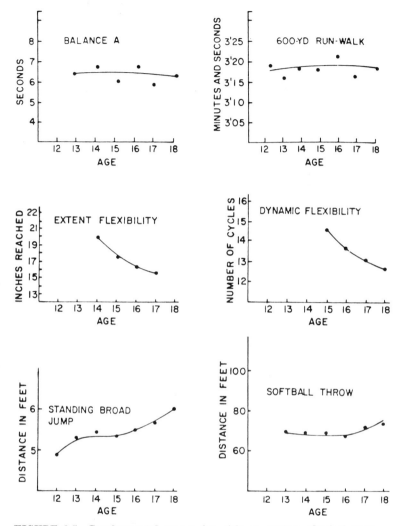

FIGURE 2-5  *Developmental curves for girls on various physical tests.*
(Source: *Edwin A. Fleishman.* The structure and measurement of physical
fitness. *Englewood Cliffs, N.J.: Prentice-Hall, 1964. Pp. 124–125. Copyright
1964 and reprinted by permission of Prentice-Hall, Inc.)*

higher as a symbol of success than did scholastic achievements. To be an athlete-scholar was found to be most desirable for status, but few boys could fit into the category of athlete-scholar.

Most coaches prefer athletes who are dedicated to "the cause"—serious-minded, competitive boys with a strong desire to sacrifice and to accomplish. Unfortunately, coaches overlook the complexity of the human organism, and a boy's reasons for participating may not be congruent with the coach's ideals. Activities are inspired by many interacting variables, some of which may not be realized by the athlete himself. Sports must be placed in proper perspective with all the other obligations and interests of the adolescent. Growing up is difficult, and participation in athletics is but one experience among many that take part in this process.

Jersild (1967) indicates that, toward the middle and end of adolescence, numerous children begin to show less interest in being continuously physically active. Many activities are curtailed; specialization occurs in some. "Even the boy who still feels his oats and knocks himself out on the college football field (while the girls, seated, look on) is likely to be much more sedentary between games and practice periods than he was in high school or in the elementary grades" (p. 98). Jersild warns that "during adolescence many persons reach not only their peak performance in several motor activities but also the peak of their desire to be active" (p. 97). Therefore, it is entirely possible that the high school coach works with the athlete in his state of maximum enthusiasm.

High school athletes have served as subjects in a number of interesting psychological studies, in such categories as (1) prediction of athletic ability; (2) the relationships of personality and participation in sports; (3) learning and training techniques; (4) instructional methods; and (5) the relationships of character, leadership, and sports. Let us briefly review some selected investigations and the conclusions reached.

In the area of predicting athletic ability in a given sport, Knox's work (1937) is well known. The four skills tests developed for the Knox Basketball Test were the dribble shoot, the speed dribble, the penny cup, and the speed pass; one test score was derived from the four tests. The tests were administered at the beginning of a basketball season to 260 boys in eight high schools. At the end of the season it was found that the test was able to predict how 61 of the 68 squad members tested would do. Of 36 first-team members, it had been predicted from scores on the test that 29 would achieve that status. Knox also found his basketball skills test to be an excellent predictor of which high school teams would make a tournament. Other investigators, however, though conceding that the Knox test has merit as a squad predictor in distinguishing between varsity and nonvarsity performers, have concluded that it is not subtle enough to differentiate among levels of ability within a squad.

Tests for archery and bowling, because they are essentially the same as contest conditions, are good predictors. In team and dual sports the situations become more intricate as athletes interact with team members and against their opponents. Successful prediction of performance is much more likely with an isolated skill, such as batting, than with overall baseball-playing ability. Bates (1948) registered the batting averages of high school baseball players over a two-year period. He then administered a pendulum target test to the players, in which the maintenance of eye contact with the object was extremely important. The high correlation of .81 between scores on the pendulum test and the batting averages indicated the strong predictive value of this test. Films also showed that batters who usually followed the ball longest on the pendulum test got the best results in hitting the ball.

Many personality traits are also being investigated as they affect, or are affected by, athletic competition. For example, Newman (1967) tested high school varsity wrestlers for anxiety with the IPAT 8 Parallel-Form Anxiety Battery 40 minutes before all home matches and also on a nonwrestling day. After the matches, wrestling performance was evaluated by three judges. No relationship was determined between anxiety and performance evaluations. Rinne (1968) found evidence to support the hypothesis that high school football players tend to be no more aggressive, as measured by the Edwards Personal Preference Schedule, than their peers who do not play football. Newman (1968) noted that certain personality traits distinguished slower and faster swimmers on a high school squad. Also, certain traits were more associated with specific events.

Research in learning, training, and instruction is only one field of study. Appropriate practice techniques, instructional media, and training schedules, as related to the maturity level of the athletes, are reflected in acceptable or excellent performance. So many variables need to be considered that selecting a few isolated studies could be misleading. Nevertheless, in order to give the reader a "feeling" for this area, some research efforts will be briefly summarized.

Deliberate and controlled rehearsal of motor skills benefits performance greatly. Clark (1960) studied varsity, junior varsity, and novice high school subjects. The effects of physical practice were compared to the effects of mental practice on the acquisition of skill in shooting a one-hand foul shot. After 14 days of practice, testing indicated that the physical-practice varsity group improved 16 percent while the mental-practice varsity group improved 15 percent. The junior varsity groups improved 24 percent and 23 percent, respectively. The novice groups showed a gain of 44 percent through physical practice and 26 percent through mental practice. Apparently, for these athletically inclined students, mental practice was about as effective as physical practice in performance outcomes.

Howell (1967) attempted to determine the effect of 2½-pound ankle weights on the jumping performance of 18 high school basketball players. The control group consisted of 18 other players, who did not wear weights during the four weeks of the experiment. On a final test of jumping ability (in which none of the groups wore weights), no difference was observed between the groups.

The effectiveness of films, slides, videotapes, and other media as instructional aids has been investigated. An interesting approach discussed, though not reported in research form, by Dupont (1966) is the use of programmed instruction to teach football play formations and other matter before the start of practice. Dupont uses this method instead of the traditional distribution of playbooks. He states that the material is learned better when presented in a programmed manner. Extensive work is being done on programmed instruction in all academic areas and is based on sound learning theory. Approaches in this line usually yield productive results.

Although formalized written reports present much information on an athlete's behavior and performance, much information on the psychological aspects of sport cannot be handled in such a manner. Common sense and even anecdotes provide valuable insight and direction. The sociological and psychological values of sport can be investigated in countless ways. Perhaps nothing will really say more than an account in the *New York Times* (January 31, 1965) of the impact of a lost basketball game. This was no ordinary defeat. The high school team involved was New York City's Power Memorial Academy, the star of the team was Lew Alcindor, and the loss occurred after 71 consecutive victories over a period of years.

After the game, which took place in Maryland, the head coach Jack Donohue, the assistant coach Jack Kuhnert, and the team could not get to sleep until the early morning hours. They talked about everything—the past, the loss, and the future. In the sensitive words of the head coach, "It was good, the talk. . . . The boys were very close. They needed to be close. They needed the companionship. It was something they didn't need so much when they were winning."

A perceptive coach like Donohue demonstrates not only some value in the experience of losing but an important aspect of sport as well. The coach's psychological approach to athletics and winning and losing has a great influence on the impressionable minds of adolescents. The "psychology" that Donohue used after the game is not easy to teach; it has to be felt, and it has to be sincere. A final remark in the article which reflected the optimism of the team was the coach's statement that the boys were thinking about a new winning streak.


## COLLEGE ATHLETES

During the college years, which usually coincide with termination of adolescence and entrance into early adulthood, athletes demonstrate the kinds of talents that can be present only as a result of many years of dedicated practice, a mature body structure, enthusiasm and interest, and expert coaching.

With maturity, or stability in growth and other developmental features, the individual is less bothered by his sources of concern, anxiety, and tension, and can concentrate on the tasks at hand. The college athlete still has his share of personal and social problems, however. The role and methods of guidance of the college coach are different from the approach of the coach who works with younger athletes. The athlete in late adolescence and young adulthood has the ability to endure physically and to tolerate psychologically the punishment of intensive and extensive practice sessions and grueling contests. He can concentrate on the tasks to be learned and can practice for hours, whereas young athletes have a shorter attention span and get bored easily. They also tire more quickly because of the changing chemical and physiological structures of their bodies. Whereas young athletes tend to be quite dependent on the coach, the older athlete is more questioning. He likes to have explanations, where possible, for the things he and the team are told to do.

Strategies and techniques for future contests can be resolved to some extent by group effort. If the coach is of a democratic nature, coach and team members can participate in the ultimate decisions affecting the group. Autocratic decisions are necessary and effective in certain times and places, but it stands to reason that mature athletes can help in solving the problems of the team. College athletes also probably have a greater interest in participating in this manner than they had in their earlier years. (The nature of leadership and group dynamics are discussed in Chapter 5.)

By now, the reader has obtained a fairly good idea of the directions psychological research on athletes has taken. The remainder of the book will continue along the same lines and will take up many other topics related to athletes in general, regardless of age, sex, or sport affiliation. The exception is Chapter 9, where research pertinent to each sport is briefly summarized.

## POSTCOLLEGE ATHLETES

Professional sports, the Olympics, and organized teams and tournaments everywhere are available for athletes after they graduate from college. The same opportunities are, of course, open to athletes of postcollege age who did not go to college, as well as to younger athletes. Many athletes achieve their highest expectations and performance levels in their twenties, and are at their best in their thirties or even later.

The role of coaches with professional athletes is interesting. Since these athletes are so highly proficient, there is little left to teach them with regard to skills. It is true that slight changes in the execution of certain acts can make a difference in performance, but primarily, the coach is a morale builder who attempts to keep the team functioning as a cohesive and purposeful unit. Tactics and strategies have to be developed for each event, and the coach plays a major role in directing patterns of attack. Because the athletes are mature, the coach's role in dictating training regimens and evening hour schedules is a sticky issue. Still, the assumption must be that the outstanding athlete is that way because he is highly motivated and possesses the ideal components necessary for superior performance. He should be "up" or "loose" when he has to be, and pep talks can play a less dramatic role than with the younger athlete.

## OPTIMAL AGE FOR ACHIEVEMENT IN ATHLETICS

Performance levels and learning abilities do not necessarily diminish with age, but some physical, motor, and sensory abilities do seem to decrease gradually. For example, reaction-time peaks are usually reached in the early twenties, and performance gradually lessens with succeeding years. Nevertheless, through hard training, man demonstrates superior skills at earlier and later ages than ever before. From a psychological point of view, performance decrements can be explained in terms of loss of interest and motivation, changing attitudes and values, and new interests and responsibilities. Well-learned acts are not easily forgotten, but discontinued training results in a lowering of strength, endurance, flexibility, speed, timing, and other variables related to effective performance of skills. A person's physical characteristics and pertinent motor abilities must be developed to and sustained at a maximum point in order for his true learning levels to be demonstrated.

At what point in life can the most productive performances be expected? It has been suggested earlier that this is an individual matter, that various factors can influence achievement at a given age. Nevertheless, it is possible to ascertain roughly when the average athlete reaches optimal performance levels. World record holders, Olympics athletes, tournament winners, and professional athletes are the sources for the data.

Some researchers have extensively studied the Olympics athlete. Jokl (1964) reported his analysis of data collected from the 1952 Olympic Games in Helsinki. Male Olympics champions in all the events ranged in age from 13 to 66, a phenomenal spread which demonstrates the possibilities of athletic success at almost any point after early adolescence. Jokl in fact points out that middle-aged men can perform well. The data were analyzed according to sport and event, and the swimmers were found to be represented by the lowest mean age, 21.5 years. Boxers, cyclists, runners, hurdlers, and jumpers were, on the average, under 25. Weight lifters, decathlon participants, freestyle wrestlers, and runners in events over 5,000 meters were usually between 25 and 30.

Woman athletes, Jokl discovered, generally achieve full maturity in competition at a younger age than men. Their earlier physiological and emotional maturity may be a partial explanation, and lack of sustained motivation to train and compete after the adolescent years is probably another reason why female participants are younger. Marriage and child rearing probably also have some bearing. Social and cultural disapproval of women's competing in sports is difficult to overcome, though it is gradually diminishing throughout the world; it has no doubt been one factor in curtailing the athletic aspirations of young women.

Hirata (1966) has also observed Olympic athletes, and his data from the 1964 Olympics in Tokyo are of great interest. His data on the physiques and ages of the male and female athletes in the many events are shown in Table 4-3. He indicated that male champions ranged in age from 15 to 54, with a mean age of 26.3 years. As might be expected, the male athletes were mainly in their twenties and thirties. Female athletes ranged from 13 to 35 years of age, with a mean age of 22.8, and most of them were 17 to 25 years old.

Perhaps the most extensive effort to determine the ages of maximum proficiency in various endeavors has been undertaken by Lehman. He did an early study on sports (Lehman, 1938), and a later publication (Lehman, 1953) contained facts pertinent to achievement in every type of activity, e.g., painting, exploration, scientific discovery, movie making, and sports.

In the first report (Lehman, 1938), a tabulation was made of the ages of athletes who appeared in *Who's Who* types of books from 1916 to 1938. As they were primarily professionals, the sample was somewhat biased; also, when the study was made, social and cultural conditions in America were

TABLE 2-2    Age and proficiency at sports

| Type of activity | No. of cases | Mean age | Standard deviation | Years of maximum proficiency |
|---|---|---|---|---|
| Professional baseball (not including pitching)......................... | 3,126 | 29.07 | 4.04 | 28 |
| Professional baseball (pitching)........ | 1,666 | 29.50 | 4.39 | 27 |
| Major league batting championships.... | 96 | 29.16 | 3.46 | 26–29 |
| Major league pitching championships... | 88 | 28.18 | 3.72 | 26–31 |
| Major league stolen-base championships | 63 | 27.96 | 3.46 | 25–29 |
| Professional boxers.................. | 448 | 26.98 | 3.98 | 25–26 |
| Tennis champions (French, English, and American)...................... | 317 | 27.63 | 5.25 | 25–27 |
| Professional ice hockey players........ | 823 | 27.56 | 4.00 | 24–25 |
| Professional football players.......... | 485 | 25.72 | 2.33 | 24 |
| Corn-husking champions............. | 87 | 30.39 | 6.20 | 26–30 |
| Automobile racers................... | 54 | 28.81 | 4.50 | 27–30 |
| Bowling champions (individual performance)........... | 58 | 32.78 | 7.56 | 30–34 |
| Bowling champions (team performance) | 238 | 33.38 | 7.83 | 27–37 |
| Rifle and pistol shooters.............. | 630 | 32.05 | 8.13 | 27 |
| Duck pin bowlers (men).............. | 91 | 32.19 | 4.36 | 30–34 |
| Duck pin bowlers (women)........... | 90 | 28.13 | 3.47 | 25–29 |
| Billiards (world record breakers)....... | 42 | 35.67 | 5.83 | 30–34 |
| Billiards (world championship winners) | 136 | 34.35 | 8.75 | 25–29 |
| Golf (professional championships— English and American)............. | 48 | 32.33 | 6.49 | 30–34 |
| Golf (open championships— English and American)............. | 88 | 31.01 | 6.37 | 25–34 |
| Golf (amateur championships— English and American)............. | 74 | 29.88 | 7.66 | 25–29 |

*Source:* Harvey C. Lehman. The most proficient years at sports and games. *Research Quarterly*, 1938, **9**, 3–19. P. 17.

considerably different than they are at the present time. Nonetheless, the data are interesting to examine. Table 2-2 contains Lehman's information on the ages of maximum proficiency in sports, and Table 2-3 presents more specific data classified by age intervals. As expected, participants in aggressive activities like football and ice hockey do not last as long as those in less violent sports. The peak performance years in most sports appear to be the

late twenties. Lehman was quite optimistic about the direction his work
might take. He wrote:

> Indeed, it should be possible to construct, for each specific type of measurable
> behavior, of a given standard of excellence, something analogous to the mor-
> tality tables that have long been utilized by life insurance companies. Like the
> mortality tables, the probability tables that are here suggested would apply
> only to groups of individuals of a given chronological age. Such tables obviously
> would not apply to every individual within a given age group [p. 19].

We have yet to see such tabular material. Though the degree to which age
handicaps or facilitates performance is difficult to predict with certainty,
normative data do suggest general expectations with respect to athletic accomplishments and age.

In the later investigation (Lehman, 1953), data on sports skills were
compared with data on other talents. The athletic events studied are presented in Table 2-4. When athletic proficiency (in all the events listed in
Table 2-4) is compared with scientific output, the figures reproduced in
Figure 2-6 are obtained. Peak performance years are fairly similar for both
groups. They become identical when scientific accomplishments are compared with sports that involve movement precision, fine motor coordination,
and no physical contact, such as rifle and pistol shooting, billiards, golf, and
bowling (see Figure 2-7).

Optimal ages of performance of football players are compared with
optimal ages of performance of composers of lyrics and ballads in Figure

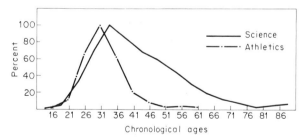

FIGURE 2-6  *Ages of best output in science and most
proficiency in athletic skills involving fine motor coordination. (*Source: *Harvey C. Lehman.* Age and achievement.
*Princeton, N.J.: Princeton University Press, 1953. Figure
130, p. 257. Copyright 1953 by the American Philosophical
Society and reprinted by permission.)*

TABLE 2-3  Number of outstanding performances per five-year interval

| Type of activity | \multicolumn{11}{c}{Age interval} |
| --- | --- | --- | --- | --- | --- | --- | --- | --- | --- | --- | --- |
| | 15–19 | 20–24 | 25–29 | 30–34 | 35–39 | 40–44 | 45–49 | 50–54 | 55–59 | 60–64 | 65–69 |
| Professional baseball (not including pitching) | 12 | 476 | 1,443 | 944 | 226 | 25 | | | | | |
| Professional baseball (pitching) | 8 | 216 | 763 | 501 | 137 | 37 | | | | | |
| Major league batting championships | | 9 | 51 | 31 | 5 | | | | | | |
| Major league pitching championships | 1 | 17 | 41 | 26 | 3 | | | | | | |
| Major league stolen-base championships | | 13 | 33 | 16 | 1 | | | | | | |
| Professional boxers | 6 | 142 | 208 | 75 | 14 | 3 | | | | | |
| Tennis champions (French, English, and American) | 12 | 84 | 133 | 54 | 28 | 6 | | | | | |
| Professional ice hockey players | 6 | 235 | 375 | 167 | 37 | 3 | | | | | |
| Professional football players | | 214 | 242 | 29 | | | | | | | |
| Corn-husking champions | 2 | 16 | 27 | 23 | 13 | 4 | 1 | 1 | | | |
| Automobile racers | 1 | 4 | 26 | 15 | 7 | | 1 | | | | |
| Bowling champions (individual performance) | 2 | 5 | 13 | 18 | 12 | 6 | | 1 | | 1 | |
| Bowling champions (team performance) | 5 | 24 | 60 | 54 | 50 | 25 | 10 | 7 | 1 | 1 | |
| Rifle and pistol shooters | 33 | 95 | 153 | 137 | 97 | 82 | 20 | 5 | 7 | 1 | |
| Duck pin bowlers (men) | | 4 | 25 | 37 | 22 | 3 | | | | | |
| Duck pin bowlers (women) | 1 | 17 | 43 | 29 | | | | | | | |
| Billiards (world records) | | | 5 | 15 | 12 | 5 | 5 | | | | |
| Billiards (world championships) | 1 | 19 | 32 | 25 | 24 | 16 | 12 | 5 | 1 | | |
| Professional golf (English and American) | | 7 | 8 | 20 | 9 | 3 | | | 1 | | |
| Open golf (English and American) | 1 | 16 | 24 | 23 | 15 | 8 | 1 | | | | |
| Amateur golf (English and American) | 1 | 21 | 24 | 14 | 4 | 7 | 2 | | 1 | | |

Source: Harvey C. Lehman. The most proficient years at sports and games. Research Quarterly, 1938, **9**, 3–19. P. 18.

54

**TABLE 2-4**  Ages at which individuals have exhibited peak proficiency at athletic skills

| Type of skill | No. of cases | Median age | Mean age | Ages of maximum proficiency |
|---|---|---|---|---|
| United States outdoor tennis champions | 89 | 26.35 | 27.12 | 22–26 |
| Runs batted in: annual champions of the two major baseball leagues | 49 | 27.10 | 27.97 | 25–29 |
| United States indoor tennis champions | 64 | 28.00 | 27.45 | 25–29 |
| World champion heavy-weight pugilists | 77 | 29.19 | 29.51 | 26–30 |
| Base stealers: annual champions of the two major baseball leagues | 31 | 29.21 | 28.85 | 26–30 |
| Indianapolis-Speedway racers and national auto-racing champions | 82 | 29.56 | 30.18 | 27–30 |
| Best hitters: annual champions of the two major baseball leagues | 53 | 29.70 | 29.56 | 27–31 |
| Best pitchers: annual champions of the two major baseball leagues | 51 | 30.10 | 30.03 | 28–32 |
| Open golf champions of England and of the United States | 127 | 30.72 | 31.29 | 28–32 |
| National individual rifle-shooting champions | 84 | 31.33 | 31.45 | 32–34 |
| State corn-husking champions of the United States | 103 | 31.50 | 30.66 | 28–31 |
| World, national, and state pistol-shooting champions | 47 | 31.90 | 30.63 | 31–34 |
| National amateur bowling champions | 58 | 32.33 | 32.78 | 30–34 |
| National amateur duck-pin bowling champions | 91 | 32.35 | 32.19 | 30–34 |
| Professional golf champions of England and of the United States | 53 | 32.44 | 32.14 | 29–33 |
| World record-breakers at billiards | 42 | 35.00 | 35.67 | 30–34 |
| World champion billiardists | 74 | 35.75 | 34.38 | 31–35 |

*Source:* Harvey C. Lehman. *Age and achievement.* Table 45. P. 256. Princeton, N.J.: Princeton University Press, 1953. (Copyright 1953 by the American Philosophical Society and reprinted by permission.)

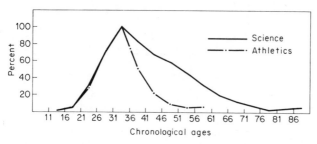

FIGURE 2-7    *Ages of best output in science and most proficiency in specific athletic skills. (Source: Harvey C. Lehman. Age and achievement. Princeton, N.J.: Princeton University Press, 1953. Figure 131, p. 258. Copyright 1953 by the American Philosophical Society and reprinted by permission.)*

2-8. In the same figure, the ages when chemists made important contributions are compared with the ages of world championship billiard shooters. An examination of athletic performances and intellectual achievements reveals very similar optimal performance curves. The best performances in self-pacing, fine motor activities, and creative thinking occur at similar age points. Lehman concludes:

> This marked agreement in such widely different fields as regards the age level at which peak attainment is most likely to be achieved, seems to be too consistent to be the result of mere coincidence. Could it result largely from some fundamental characteristic of the human organism—something in the nature of a fixed order of human development? Or is it more the result of motivational factors? . . . These data seem to conceal something that needs to be explained and which, when better understood, can hardly fail to be significant.[1]

The aging process reveals interesting performance data on many measures. Let us further examine patterns of stability and change in these performances across the adult years.

## THE AGING PROCESS

Industrial research indicates that worker output is effectively sustained until the age of 60 or 65 in tasks that are self-initiating and self-pacing. In sports events that require similar qualities—golf, archery, and bowling, for example—athletic output is demonstrated at reasonably skilled levels for many, many years. The aging process is more detrimental to abilities

[1] Harvey C. Lehman. Age and achievement. Princeton, N.J.: Princeton University Press, 1953. P. 265. Copyright 1953 by the American Philosophical Society.

associated with externally paced events. When the older individual has to perceive quickly and respond accordingly, or when he performs tasks requiring large amounts of strength, endurance, speed, flexibility, and the like, he is at a slight disadvantage.

But learning can take place throughout life. Besides the physical and psychological limitations associated with older age, unlearning fixed patterns of responses in order to learn new things also causes the older person some difficulty. Nevertheless, the learning process can operate at a reasonable rate at all ages, assuming the person is healthy and motivated. Thus athletes who select sports more easily performed at older ages can participate with a high degree of skill for many years of their lives.

Older people perform best in skills that emphasize accuracy rather than

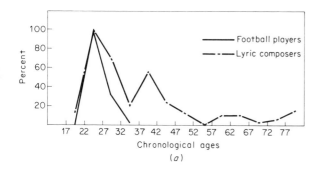

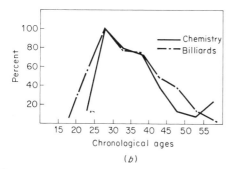

FIGURE 2-8  (a) *Optimal ages of performance in football and composing.* (b) *Ages of best output in chemistry and most proficiency in billiards.* (Source: *Harvey C. Lehman.* Age and achievement. *Princeton, N.J.: Princeton University Press, 1953. Figures 134 and 135, p. 261. Copyright 1953 by the American Philosophical Society and reprinted by permission.)*

speed. They need more time to finish a task, and they complete fewer tasks in a given time period than younger people. They process information more slowly, and as Welford (1958) states, their slower motor performances are due not so much to losses in speed of movement as to the time taken by the central nervous system in initiating, shaping, and monitoring movement. Apparently there is a decreased efficiency of the central nervous system with age, and declines in performance are associated with a slowing down of the ability to receive and transmit information. Another symptom of the aging process is development of a tendency to pay attention to irrelevant information. Even warning signals are not of much help. All these factors support the advocation of self-pacing sports events for older people.

Further physiological evidence on the aging process is provided by Birren (1964). He writes that sensory and perceptual changes occur in older persons, that the fibers responsible for mediating sensory impressions decrease in number with age. Although Birren feels that the sensory systems are hampered in this way when a person reaches approximately 70 years of age, disease and other factors can become more of a handicap than intrinsic age-related changes. Stimuli that are not strong enough or that are unexpected, unfamiliar, or complex cause an especially noticeable slowness of behavior in the aged. Perhaps there is an age change in the speed of neural activity, as evidenced by a slowing down in reaction time. The data illustrated in Figure 2-9 show how response speed decreases as a function of age for both sexes approximately after the age of 20. Both sexes improve dramatically in reaction time performance from age 8 to age 20.

In tests of times taken by people of various ages to complete series of tracing tasks, all subjects become faster with each practice trial. Older subjects have been found by Welford (1951) to perform substantially slower than younger ones in the first series of trials. However, "Proportional drop in time [to execute the tasks (see Figure 2-10)] did not vary greatly or very consistently with age" (p. 64). In fact, it can be seen in Figure 2-11 that, as the experiment proceeded, the speed tended to increase with age.

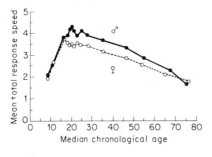

FIGURE 2-9  *Mean total response speed as a function of median chronological age for the two sexes. Each point is based on the data for 20 subjects, averaged over the entire practice period. (*Source: *Clyde E. Noble, Blaine L. Baker, & Thomas A. Jones. Age and sex parameters in psychomotor learning.* Perceptual and Motor Skills, *1964,* **19**, *935–945. P. 941.)*

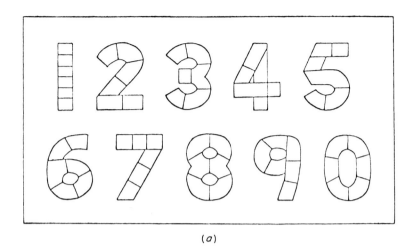

(*a*)

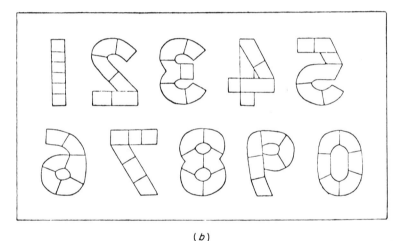

(*b*)

FIGURE 2-10   *Tracing tasks completed by subjects in different age groups. The times taken to complete the tasks were recorded and are shown in Figure 2-11. (*Source: *A. T. Welford.* Skill and age. *Published for the Nuffield Foundation by the Oxford University Press, London, 1951. P. 62.)*

Even by the end of the experiment, though, the fastest older subjects were slower than the slowest younger subjects.

When performance accuracy is analyzed according to age group, however, a different picture emerges. It can be seen in Figure 2-12 that essentially there is much similarity among ages in various throwing tasks. The only substantial rise in inaccuracy with age was on one kind of throwing task (the top performance curve in Figure 2-12). Accuracy in general is apparently much less affected by age than is response speed.

SUMMARY

The chronological age, and more important, the maturational readiness of the athlete dictate special considerations on the part of the coach. Sex differences, prior personal experiences, genetic factors, and the like are other

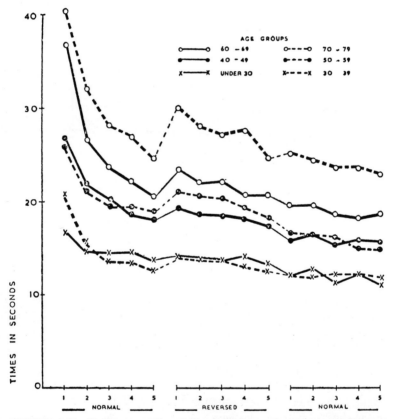

FIGURE 2-11    *Performance times to trace 10 figures for subjects in different age groups. (Source: A. T. Welford. Skill and age. Published for the Nuffield Foundation by the Oxford University Press, London, 1951. P. 64.)*

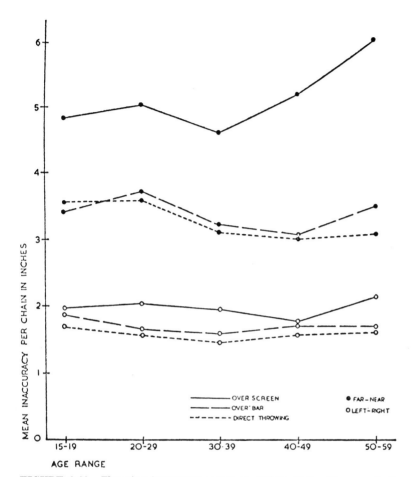

FIGURE 2-12   *Throwing inaccuracy scores on various tasks.* (Source: *A. T. Welford.* Skill and age. *Published for the Nuffield Foundation by the Oxford University Press, London, 1951. P. 50.)*

considerations for the coach in determining behavioral expectations and appropriate training techniques. The manner in which skills are taught should be determined by the maturational and experiential level of the learner.

*Distinction by age and maturational readiness*   Coaches who deal with younger athletes should be aware of maturational differences within age groups and should take them into consideration in the treatment, training, and competitive handling of these athletes.

*Are athletes born or made?*   The outstanding athlete is one who has been born with athletic ability and has developed it to the extent that genetics and experience interact in a meaningful way to produce his athletic status.

*Optimal learning periods*   There appears to be an optimal learning period, although it is difficult to isolate, for any behavior or skill. Although meaningful early experiences should be encouraged, timeliness, with regard to maturational readiness of the organism, is a more important consideration.

*Considerations about early movements*   A childhood filled with enriched and varied movement experiences serves as a foundation for learning the more complex athletic skills later in life.

*Elementary school athletes*   There is much controversy today about the benefits and harms that can result from athletic competition by children of elementary school age on school and community teams. Although much research is still needed, present reports tend to demonstrate that many fears are exaggerated. Generally speaking, the elementary school athlete is more advanced maturationally, socially, physiologically, anatomically, emotionally, and psychologically than nonathletic counterparts of the same age.

*Junior high school athletes*   Similar controversy, sparse research, and research findings are associated with junior high school athletes. With the change from late childhood to early adolescence come personal and social problems not encountered before. Coaches should be especially aware of great differences in the maturational levels of these children, and should also be sensitive to their needs, attitudes, and trainability.

*High school athletes*   Athletes of high school age are generally easier to train than younger athletes. They can concentrate and practice for longer periods of time, and in many cases they possess the physical characteristics and motor skill necessary for high levels of athletic proficiency. High school athletes, like younger ones, are extremely impressionable. The coach's psychological approach to athletics and to winning and losing has a great impact on them.

*College athletes*   The average college athlete is comparatively free of his previous sources of concern, anxiety, and tension, and can concentrate on the tasks at hand. The nature of effective leadership is probably different for college athletes than for younger ones, as older athletes are able to and want to participate in decisions affecting the team.

*Postcollege athletes*   The coach's role with professional athletes is primarily to maintain or elevate team morale and to prescribe or suggest tactics and strategies.

*Optimal age for achievement in athletics*   The ages of Olympic medalists and record holders in general vary widely. However, in most events, champion athletes are in their middle to late twenties.

*The aging process*   A number of bodily changes occur with age, but older people are usually able to compete favorably in events that require accuracy. They are hampered in activities involving speed of reaction, quickness of perception, speed of movement, strength, and endurance.

REFERENCES

Anastasi, Anne. *Differential psychology*. New York: Macmillan, 1966.

Bates, Frank H. Relationship of hand and eye coordination to accuracy in baseball batting. Unpublished master's thesis, University of Iowa, 1948.

Birren, James E. *The psychology of aging*. Englewood Cliffs, N.J.: Prentice-Hall, 1964.

Carder, Brent. The relationship between manifest anxiety and performance in college football. Unpublished master's thesis, University of California, 1965.

Clark, L. Verdelle. Effect of mental practice on the development of a certain motor skill. *Research Quarterly,* 1960, **31**, 560–569.

Clarke, H. Harrison. Characteristics of the young athlete: a longitudinal look. *Proceedings of the 8th National Conference on the Medical Aspects of Sports,* 1967, **8**, 49–57.

Coleman, James S. *The adolescent society*. New York: Free Press, 1961.

*Desirable athletic competition for children of elementary school age.* Washington, D.C.: published by the American Association for Health, Physical Education, and Recreation through NEA, 1968.

Dupont, Jim. Programmed learning in the athletic program. *Athletic Journal,* 1966, **46**, 62, 91.

Espenchade, Anna. Motor performance in adolescence. *Monographs of the Society for Research in Child Development,* 1940, **5** (No. 1).

Hale, Creighton J. Physiological maturity of Little League baseball players. *Research Quarterly,* 1956, **27**, 276–284.

Heise, Bryan. *Effects of instruction in cooperation on the attitudes and conduct of children.* Ann Arbor: University of Michigan Press, 1942.

Hirata, Kin-Itsu. Physique and age of Tokyo Olympic champions. *Journal of Sports Medicine and Physical Fitness,* 1966, **6**, 207–222.

Howell, William T. The influence of ankle weights on jumping height of high school basketball players. Unpublished master's thesis, Drake University, 1967.

Ismail, A. H., & Cowell, C. C. Factor analysis of motor aptitude of preadolescent boys. *Research Quarterly,* 1961, **32**, 507–513.

Jersild, Arthur T. *The psychology of adolescence*. New York: Macmillan, 1967.

Jokl, Ernst. *Medical sociology and cultural anthropology of sport and physical education.* Springfield, Ill.: Charles C Thomas, 1964.

Knox, Robert D. An experiment to determine the relationship between performance in skill tests and success in playing basketball. Unpublished master's thesis, University of Oregon, 1937.

Lampman, James J. Anxiety and its effects on the performance of competitive swimmers. Unpublished master's thesis, University of Florida, 1967.

Lehman, Harvey C. The most proficient years at sports and games. *Research Quarterly,* 1938, **9**, 3–19.

Lehman, Harvey C. *Age and achievement.* Princeton, N.J.: Princeton University Press, 1953.

McGraw, Myrtle B. *Growth: A study of Johnny and Jimmy.* New York: Appleton-Century, 1935.

Newman, Earl N. Personality traits of faster and slower competitive swimmers. *Research Quarterly,* 1968, **39**, 1049–1053.

Newman, Richard E. A comparison of the anxiety measures and match performance evaluations of high school wrestlers. Unpublished master's thesis, South Dakota State University, 1967.

Ogilvie, Bruce C. Psychological consistencies within the personality of high-level competitors. *Journal of the American Medical Association,* 1968, **205**, 156–162.

Rarick, G. Lawrence. Competitive sports for young boys: controversial issues. Speech presented at the 10th National Conference on the Medical Aspects of Sports, Miami Beach, Fla., 1968.

Rinne, James L. A descriptive study of the aggressive attitudes of high school football players as compared to the aggressive attitudes of non-participating students. Unpublished master's thesis, Sacramento State College, 1968.

Schendel, Jack. Psychological differences between athletes and nonparticipants in athletics at three educational levels. *Research Quarterly,* 1965, **36**, 52–67.

Schoenstein, Ralph. Little League baseball. *Pageant,* July, 1969, **25**, 47–50.

Scott, J. P. *Early experience and the organization of behavior.* Belmont, Calif.: Brooks/Cole, 1968.

Seymour, Emery W. Comparative study of certain behavior characteristics of participant and non-participant boys in Little League baseball. *Research Quarterly,* 1956, **27**, 338–346.

Skubic, Elvera. Emotional responses of boys to Little League and Middle League competitive baseball. *Research Quarterly,* 1955, **26**, 342–352.

Skubic, Elvera. Studies of Little League and Middle League baseball. *Research Quarterly,* 1956, **27**, 97–110.

Takacs, Robert. A comparison of the effect of two methods of practice on basketball free throw shooting. Unpublished master's thesis, Arkansas State College, 1968.

Tanner, James M. *Education and physical growth.* London: University of London Press, 1961.

Welford, A. T. *Skill and age.* London: Oxford University Press, 1951.

Welford, A. T. *Ageing and human skill.* Published for the Nuffield Foundation by the Oxford University Press, London, 1958.

# CHAPTER THREE

# Personality Factors and the Athlete

$O$f the various aspects of psychology that are related to sport, personality comes to mind more frequently than most others. In many respects, personality represents a mystical conglomeration of qualities. Yet the attitudes of the athlete toward self-development, self-realization, competition—attitudes which shape his unique behavior—may very well make the difference in skill attainment and athletic status. How and to what extent an athlete's personality determines success is difficult to ascertain, but certainly such knowledge would provide valuable insights into the effectiveness of the coach, the athlete, and the team.

The coach is in many ways an amateur psychologist: He tries to understand the emotional problems of his athletes. He attempts to use motivational techniques that are appropriate for athletes of given temperaments. He places team members in situations where their skills and personalities will give them the best possible chance of succeeding. If the coach is sensitive to athletes' behavioral tendencies, he may be able to predict their behavior in certain situations, and to position and deploy them to best advantage. He may also be able to correct or eliminate undesirable behavior, or may be able to remove the athlete from the situation that produces such behavior. Understanding people and their personalities can pay dividends.

One basic observation, which is verified by research, is that there is a remarkable difference in personality traits from athlete to athlete. The lack of consistency in patterns has made it difficult to generalize about the behavioral expectancies of all athletes. The same is true of superior athletes. Certain traits are frequently encountered in superior athletes, but unique differences make it necessary to deal with all athletes on an individual basis. Research findings on personality differences and similarities of athletes and nonathletes, athletes in different sports, and superior and average athletes are presented and discussed in this chapter. But first let us look more closely at the term "personality," to see what it means and in what context it is usually employed.

## WAYS OF STUDYING PERSONALITY

As is the case with so many terms, "personality" defies a single definition. To some people, it is synonymous with the word "type"; to others, it means "temperament"; still others conceive of it as encompassing far more. Geneticists believe that personality is primarily influenced by heredity, but learning theorists view it as mostly affected by environmental experiences. Historically and traditionally, understanding of personality has come from three sources.

One source of understanding of personality is provided by many playwrights and authors, who are notorious for their ability to characterize people. Literary and philosophical works provide much insight into the nature of the human being. Authors' sensitivity to people enriches our knowledge and understanding of human behavior. This source, however, is obviously limited by its very nature; it is far from scientific, and much of the information it provides cannot be used in practical ways—for example, in understanding the relationship between athletic achievement and personality dynamics.

Another approach to the analysis of personality is primarily a result of the work of Freud and others during this century. In developing the technique of psychoanalysis, psychiatrists and clinical psychologists advanced concepts and terminology related to the adjustment process. A person's activities were explained in terms of previous experiences, many of which occurred in early childhood. Psychiatrists and clinical psychologists are usually interested in investigating so-called "abnormal behavior," and can sometimes help the athlete who has severe emotional problems. Most coaches and athletes, however, have found little practical value in studying clinical psychology, as they are not qualified to analyze and help others who demonstrate abnormal behavioral patterns.

Thus, these two avenues to the understanding of human behavior do not lead to practical results. Researchers and laymen alike have therefore looked for more scientific and meaningful methods, and instruments have been developed for this purpose. They are usually in the form of questionnaires and other types of self-reporting inventories, the data from which enable description of a person's personality profile or certain aspects of it. In turn, these profiles constitute the basis for comparing the personalities of athletes and nonathletes, champion and nonchampion athletes, and athletes in different sports. Certainly, there are other ways to obtain information on a person's personality, but the ease with which these tests can be administered and interpreted by people who do not have professional psychological training explains their great popularity. Almost all personality studies of athletes use such forms, and a wide assortment of personality tests is available.

There are certain drawbacks to personality tests, however. Their validity (the degree to which they measure what they purport to measure) and reliability (performer consistency in response) are surely open to question.

Any good test contains high statistical confirmation of validity and reliability, but unfortunately, inventory measures are notoriously insensitive indicators of personality. Still, they are better than nothing, and their limitations warn us to expect inconsistency in conclusions from study to study.

## *Definitions of Personality*

Because personality is a broad area, any definition of it must be general. This necessity becomes apparent when one considers such descriptive sayings as "He has a great personality" and "He has no personality." Even more specific descriptions of people are too general to be truly accurate. "He is athletic," "He is an introvert," and "He is happy-go-lucky," although they may be perceptive statements, are still not sensitive descriptions of personalities.

It is interesting to note in passing that many years ago "personality" referred to what a person appeared to be: it was an actor's mask, a facade. Today, "personality" refers to what a person actually is. In accord with this current view, Allport's definition of personality (1961) ranks as one of the most often quoted and accepted: "Personality is the dynamic organization within the individual of those psychophysical systems that determine his characteristic behavior and thought" (p. 28).

To know someone's personality is to understand him. Although the goal of understanding someone is desirable, the task of developing such understanding is filled with difficulties. "Personality" encompasses a conglomeration of personal characteristics, reflects the way the person behaves, and predisposes him to act in a certain way when faced with a given situation. The study of personality requires scientific preparation and such personal qualities as perceptiveness, sensitivity, and concern for others. Presumably, the effective coach possesses such attributes, and they help him to predict the actions of his athletes. The athlete, like everyone else, develops tendencies to behave in certain ways in particular situations. To know an athlete, then, is to come to expect that he will probably produce a certain set of responses in a given situation. Cattell (1965), the noted personality psychologist, writes that a man's personality indicates what he will do when he is in a given mood and is placed in a given situation.

## *Research on Sports and Personality*

Instead of merely discussing personality in a theoretical manner, we shall attempt to identify the *traits* that personality comprises. Determination of a person's traits, behaviors, or aptitudes and examination of the way these characteristics work in his adjustment to a situation is a scientific approach to the study of human behavior. A "trait" is a relatively permanent and broad behavioral reaction tendency which represents behavior and generalized feelings or responses. For example, aggressiveness may be considered a trait, and other examples are emotional stability, a tendency toward group affiliation, and introspection. There are numerous qualities that might be called "traits," and psychologists have attempted to identify the few that are reasonably independent of each other. Since there is no agreement about their particular descriptions, the various tests of personality often attempt to measure different traits. Or, if you like, some conceivably similar traits are referred to in different terms.

Nevertheless, even an unsophisticated knowledge of human behavior would allow us to believe that most traits are interrelated and difficult to isolate. When we refer to someone as a particular "type," what we probably have in mind is a pattern of trait measures. "Type" refers to the person's distinguishing characteristics—for example, "athletic type," "scholarly type." Each person is unique, and attempting to classify a person according to type is dangerous. From a scientific point of view, the process is also meaningless.

The assumption in scientific measurement is that traits can indeed be measured. At best, depending on the nature of the instrument used, the honesty of the respondents, and the competencies of the test administrator, individual traits can be isolated and analyzed according to norms or compared between groups. Certain behavioral scientists are currently attempting to discriminate between champion and average athletes in personality traits as well as in personality profiles, or patterns of trait scores. Personality comparisons are also being made from athletic group (team) to athletic group, as well as from athletes to nonathletes.

One final note should be stressed to broaden our understanding of personality dynamics. Both genetics and learning affect personality. Heredity frames and shapes the potential for development, but personality is also strongly affected by environmental variables. Inherited tendencies influence us to behave in certain ways. The structures, abilities, and aptitudes a person is born with are a part of his personality and influence his development, and many other aspects of personality are formed early in life. In adulthood, personality is the end product of a number of years of social learning and social experiences. One's personality is modified by his culture, his family, his peer group, and a host of interacting experiences.

Is body build related to personality? Although extravagant claims were made for a while, the answer to this question seems to be, "Yes, but only to a limited extent." A muscular person, inclined toward athletic endeavors, may gain social prominence for his achievements and may be influenced to learn other athletic skills. At one time it was thought that the heavy-set, obese person was jovial and good-natured; that the slender, linear type was introverted, scholarly, and sensitive; and that the muscular, athletic person was most perfectly adjusted. Because of the complexity of human behavior and individual experiences, however, attempts at determining relationships between body build and personality are rarely made any more. Although Cortes & Gatti, in a recent article (1970), are quite optimistic about determining the relationship between physique and many aspects of personality, generally such efforts are not very fruitful and, furthermore, could be inaccurate.

## The Coach's Influence on the Athlete's Personality

By the time a coach encounters an athlete for the first time, the athlete's personality is fairly well established. Still, the coach's potential influence on the child should not be taken lightly. Meaningful relationships and experiences have a telling effect on personality. Participation in sports is one of the most important experiences in the life of the typical athlete. Since the coach inevitably has a strong effect on the athlete's role in sports, and since the time he spends with the athlete is considerable, he can have an enormous impact on the child's personality.

The effect of the coach, like that of any other teacher, may be negative or positive. But unlike most relationships between teacher and student, the relationship between the coach and the athlete is extensive and intensive. A large amount of time and energy are spent in participation in a sport. Little wonder, then, that of all the student's teachers, the coach may make the most profound impact on his behavioral tendencies. The closer the relationship between any two people, the better the chance that one will meaningfully affect the other.

A maladjusted coach may serve as a poor model and have bad effects on the team members. Emotional instability and irrationality on the part of the coach pose a threat to the personality development of the athletes. Emphasis on winning at any cost, with disregard and lack of respect for the feelings of individual team members, might lead impressionable students to have similar attitudes. Competition should be encouraged, but there are healthy as well as inappropriate ways of attempting to beat an opponent. Young people tend to emulate those whom they admire and respect. The coach's personality and behavior may influence the student's actions, and a child can gain much from associating with a coach who has desirable personality characteristics.

Furthermore, an understanding and respected coach may assist the athlete in periods of inner conflict. The athlete's conflicts between desired and attained goals, conflicts about competitive feelings, and conflicts between personal and team interests can sometimes be resolved in a satisfactory manner with the help of the coach. When the athlete exhibits inappropriate withdrawal, regression, or aggression, the perceptive coach can sometimes provide help. The coach thus becomes a sort of guidance counselor. In his own behavior and in the services he renders, the coach's influence on the athlete's personality can be of major consequence.

## PERSONALITIES OF ATHLETES AND NONATHLETES

What differences in personality can we expect between athletes and nonathletes? Before attempting to answer this question, an explanation of the terms "athlete" and "nonathlete" is in order. From study to study, both terms have been used to represent dissimilar samples. An "athlete" may be any member of a school team, or the term may be restricted to letter winners. Other criteria have also been suggested for designating the athlete. A "nonathlete" might be a person who had never participated in interscholastic or intercollegiate sports, or a person who had never played on an organized team. These sample definitions of the two terms serve at least to make the reader aware of the nature of the subject groups. Since there is no agreement on what truly constitutes either an athlete or a nonathlete, researchers have much leeway in selecting subjects and forming groups. This is an important point to remember in examining research evidence concerned with differences between athletes and nonathletes, for it might help to explain inconsistent findings in different reports.

In any case, many researchers have attempted to find out whether there are personality dissimilarities between so-called "athletes" and "nonathletes." Various groups of athletes have also been compared with each other and with nonathletes. Perusal of the research indicates that personality inventories have typically been administered to college subjects or, in fewer cases, to high school subjects. When the tests have shown differences in personality, the issue that is still unresolved is: Are the differences caused by athletic participation, or do individuals with certain personality profiles tend to participate in various forms of athletics? Or are the two factors interrelated? How to determine the answers to these questions is a perplexing problem, but one which needs to be faced.

In estimating possible personality changes due to athletic exposure, longitudinal studies are more useful than the typical cross-sectional study. Strategy for such research has been discussed elsewhere (Singer, 1967). Unfortunately, longitudinal studies are time-consuming and elaborate, whereas cross-sectional studies are easy to construct, and the results are obtained quickly. The cross-sectional study does not inform us how or whether individual persons change over a period of time, as the analysis is from group to group only. Some typical investigations in this area are described below.

Booth (1958) used the Minnesota Multiphasic Personality Inventory (MMPI), a highly clinical personality instrument, to compare 141 college athletes with 145 nonathletic college students. The investigator found that the nonathletes scored higher on the anxiety variable than did a corresponding group of athletes. Further analysis was done with athletes in individual and team sports, and the team athletes made notably lower scores on the depression variable.

In an earlier study, Sperling (1942) tested 171 varsity athletes, 138 intramural athletes, and 126 nonathletes on the Human Behavior Inventory, the Bell Adjustment Inventory, and the Clark-Thurstone Scale. The varsity and intramural groups demonstrated higher scores on ascendance, extroversion, personal adjustment, and motivation for power than the nonathletic group. The nonathletes scored high on aesthetic and theoretical values. No differences in personality were noted between the varsity and intramural players, and with all the athletes, longer experience in athletics seemed to be related to more favorable adjustment scores, extroversion, and ascendancy.

Many other studies could be described, but a summary will suffice: most researchers have found some personality differences (as indicated by the different personality-measuring devices employed) between designated groups of athletes and nonathletes. There is no agreement on specific differences, although some trends are apparent. Cooper's (1969) and Ogilvie's (1967) analyses of the literature will serve to illustrate the major implications. Cooper finds that, after the athlete and the nonathlete are contrasted, the following profile of the athlete emerges:

> The picture painted of athletes describes them as follows: (*a*) more outgoing and socially confident; (*b*) more outgoing and socially aggressive, dominant, and leading; (*c*) higher social adjustment as rated by both teachers and peers and also higher in prestige and social status and self-confidence; (*d*) stronger competitors; (*e*) less compulsive; (*f*) less impulsive; (*g*) greater tolerance for physical pain; (*h*) lower feminine interests and higher masculine ones.
>
> While there are occasional exceptions to this picture, . . . there is no striking contradiction and by and large the picture is quite consistent. Much of the research in the area as a whole seems an attempt to justify participation in athletics and physical education as both important and helpful aspects of growth and maturity in a physical and psychological sense. While many of the conclusions seem positive, crucial issues about the psychological nature of physical athletic activity are still unanswered. The general personality picture for

athletes should not be taken to mean that the primary issues have been resolved [p. 19].

Ogilvie has studied in great detail the personalities of athletes of all ages and assorted skill levels. As a result of his work, he feels justified in writing of the typical athlete in descriptive terms. Many of the traits he mentions confirm Cooper's conclusions from a survey of the literature. In turn, Ogilvie (1967) lists still other aspects of the athlete's personality structure. He states:

> The male competitor is basically an emotionally healthy person who tends toward extroversion. He is tough-minded, self-assertive, self-confident, with a high capacity to endure the stress of high level competition. He is a person who sets high goals for himself and for others. He has great psychological endurance and tends to be a "dominant, take charge" type of person, yet does not seek leadership. Moreover, he is slightly freer to express his natural aggressiveness tendencies with a high need to affiliate with others. He is basically an orderly, organized sort of person with a lower than average tendency to act impulsively. He will seek to lead a more structured life and to live in a socially highly desirable manner [p. 48].

Some people believe that the athlete is characterized by a high need to achieve, but there are data to the contrary; that is, athletes' need to achieve is no higher than that of corresponding groups of nonathletes. In one study, for example, junior high school participants in interscholastic athletics were compared with intramural participants and nonparticipants. No difference was found in the achievement needs of the three groups (Meyers and Ohnmacht, 1963). The findings of a recent master's thesis (Gorsuch, 1968) indicate a similar need for achievement by nonathletes, team-sport athletes, and individual-sport athletes. Need for achievement was measured by McClelland's Thematic Apperception Test.

Nevertheless, there is little reason not to believe that superior athletes possess a reasonably high need to achieve within their respective athletic endeavors. Although the need to achieve is not necessarily a generalized trait, the usual instruments do measure it as a general aspect of personality. Since it is highly probable that nonathletes have high needs to achieve in such areas as scholarship, social prominence, and performance in the arts, a generalized needs instrument would yield balanced data from athletes and nonathletes.

Discovering that selected groups of people have unique personality traits helps us to understand the individual members of the groups. Recent developments have included attempts to discriminate among the personality profiles as well as among the traits of athletic and nonathletic groups. With appropriate statistical analysis, trait scores are combined, and their degree of interaction provides a profile score. Profile scores for individual persons and for groups of people are thus formed. The study of personality through the formulation of profiles is more dynamic and perhaps also more realistic than the study of separate traits. Some such research endeavors are reported later in this chapter.

## PERSONALITY CHANGES DUE TO ATHLETIC EXPERIENCE

Because personality is determined by genetic factors but modified by environmental experiences, a strong possibility exists that personality influences activity preferences as well as being modified by activity experiences. The personality mold is formed early in life but can be changed by later experiences.

Is the athlete born with physical and psychological characteristics that give him a greater probability of success than the average person? A moderate correlation of about .50 is usually found when succeeding generations of a family are compared on such physical qualities as height, weight, and body build. To the extent that physical characteristics are associated with athletic achievement, therefore, the indication is that heredity does play a role in the athlete's success.

Further, research by Gedda and others (1964) demonstrated that the Olympic athlete and his family practice similar activities, indicating that specific physical and psychological qualities could be attributed to heredity. Evidently, a certain ideal combination of personality traits is associated with outstanding athletic accomplishments, and because this combination seems to occur within the athlete's family, genetics is thought to play a role in determining success. It is also possible, indeed probable, that participation in certain activities is strongly encouraged within the family.

On a more empirical basis, opinions are often expressed on the personality changes that occur due to participation in sports. It is thought, or hoped, that desirable changes will occur as a result of the experience. From his observations on competitive girl swimmers throughout preadolescence and adolescence, Ogilvie (1968) states that (1) with success in competition, the girls become more outgoing and less reserved; (2) competition increases their emotional stability and tough-mindedness; and (3) with age, tension and anxiety are reduced, more self-control and self-discipline are demonstrated, and there is a shift from apprehension and worry to self-confidence.

One of the few reported longitudinal research projects, by Werner and Gottheil (1966), was concerned with the personality development of cadets in relation to participation in college athletics. The Cattell Sixteen Personality Factor Questionnaire was administered to 340 athletic cadets and 116 nonathletes shortly after they entered the United States Military Academy and before they were graduated. When the groups were compared upon entrance, the athletes were found to be more sociable, dominant, enthusiastic, adventurous, tough, group-dependent, sophisticated, and conservative than the nonathletes. Despite four years of regular athletic participation, the nonathletic group did not change measurably in personality structure. More specifically:

> If participation in athletics in college has an effect on personality structure, the effect would be expected to be greater on individuals with little previous athletic participation than on accomplished athletes. However, despite four years of regular athletic participation, the designated non-participant group was *not* found to change in personality structure as measured by the 16 P-F Test: (*a*) to a greater extent than the athletes; (*b*) in a different pattern than did the athletes; (*c*) nor so as to become more like the athletes [p. 126].

Thus, data from the study do not support the view that participation in athletics influences personality. It may be that college-age men are fairly resistant to changes in personality traits, and it is also conceivable that the Cattell test was not sensitive enough to identify changes if they did indeed occur. Also, the cadet sample was quite unusual and does not allow inferences to typical college students.

Other evidence points to the undesirable association of athletics and values. In one study (Kistler, 1957), it was found that poorer sportsmanship attitudes were displayed by college students who had varsity experience than by nonathletes. In another study (Richardson, 1962), varsity letter winners showed less favorable sportsmanship qualities than did nonletter winners. Subsidized athletes (perhaps the better athletes) scored poorer than nonsubsidized athletes. (These two studies are discussed in more detail on page 149). It is difficult to state definitely whether these characteristics were the result of athletic experience, or whether the athletes were successful because they had these characteristics. However, there does seem to be some conflict between the ideals of our society and the perhaps realistic (or perhaps materialistic) attitudes which athletes have toward competition.

## PERSONALITY COMPARISONS OF VARIOUS SPORT GROUPS

If athletes can be shown to be dissimilar to nonathletes in particular traits, we might guess that athletes in different sports are different from each other in certain identifiable ways. Presumably, the very nature of individual differences in skills, abilities, interests, and temperaments at least partially reflects differences in activity pursuits and ultimate achievements. It is conjectured that particular personality characteristics motivate and sustain interest in learning and succeeding in selected sport skills, and that such learning and success cause further distinctions among the athletes associated with various sports.

Belief in such propositions is fairly universal, but confirmation by research results is lacking. Some investigations show personality differences between groups; others do not. The major complaints about the inconsistency of all studies of personality and sport certainly hold true here: questionable samples of athletic subjects of varying levels of proficiency, variations in the statistical treatments of the data, dissimilar personality-measuring devices, and in general, a haphazard approach in methodology. All these problems make it impossible to determine whether research findings are "true."

Essentially, personality research on sport groups has taken one of two directions: (1) the personalities of athletes associated with specific sports are compared; or (2) athletes from various sports making up the area of team sports are compared with individual-sport or dual-sport athletes, or both.

## Differences in Personality between Sport Groups

A number of investigations yield data supporting the hypothesis that weight lifters differ from other athletic groups in various personality traits. Generally, weight lifters have feelings of masculine inadequacy and inferiority, withdrawal, and the like. It has been concluded (e.g., by Thune, 1949, and Harlow, 1951) that weight lifting appeals to a group of people who differ in needs, interests, and personality from other people.

Slusher (1964) tested various high school athletic groups—wrestlers, swimmers, baseball players, basketball players, and football players—with the MMPI, and found a number of significant differences among the groups. The least neurotic group was the swimmers, while football players and wrestlers were similar in displaying strongly neurotic profiles. Basketball players were very concerned with themselves, were easily depressed, and showed the greatest deviation from the other groups.

Contrarily, Lakie (1962) observed no differences among 230 athletes from different colleges, in the following sports: wrestling, track, tennis, golf, football, and basketball. He used five scales of the Omnibus Personality Inventory, and also analyzed the athletes according to the type of school they attended, e.g., state college, university, or private school. He found that they differed on certain measures according to the nature of their college affiliation. Specific types of schools apparently attract athletes of similar characteristics who are dissimilar to athletes who go to other types of schools.

### Differences in Personality between Team-sport Athletes and Individual- or Dual-sport Athletes

Peterson, Weber, & Trousdale (1967) investigated possible personality differences between women in team sports and women in individual sports. The Cattell Sixteen Personality Factor Questionnaire was administered to 156 women AAU athletes and to the 1964 United States Olympics team. Numerous trait dissimilarities were observed between team- and individual-sport athletes. The individual-sport athletes were higher in dominance, adventurousness, sensitivity, introversion, radicalism, and self-sufficiency, and were lower in sophistication than the team-sport athletes.

Using the Edwards Personal Preference Schedule (EPPS) with Ohio State male athletes, Singer (1969) was able to distinguish team-sport athletes (baseball players) from individual-sport athletes (tennis players) in certain traits. Table 3-1 contains the comparisons made between these groups, and the comparisons with normative data. The tennis group scored significantly higher than both the baseball and the norm groups on the achievement variable. The norm group was significantly higher than the baseball group in autonomy. The tennis and norm groups scored higher than the baseball group on the intraception variable, and the tennis group demonstrated a higher dominance factor than the baseball group. The baseball team scored significantly higher on the abasement factor than the other two groups. On aggression, the norm group achieved a lower score than the tennis group.

Schreckengaust's results (1968) with college women paint a somewhat different picture. The EPPS was administered to 33 female individual-sport athletes and 38 female team-sport athletes. The only trait distinguishing the groups was heterosexuality, in which the individual-sport group scored higher.

Walter Kroll is a leader in the application of multiple discriminant analysis. Kroll and Crenshaw (1968) reported a comparison of four groups of highly skilled athletes. Using the Cattell Sixteen Personality Factor Questionnaire, they collected data from football players, wrestlers, gymnasts, and karate athletes. Significant differences in personality profiles were noted when the football players and wrestlers were compared with gymnasts and karate athletes, and gymnasts and karate athletes also differed from each other.

The information presented in this study supports the idea that football players and wrestlers may have similar personality characteristics. Surely aggressiveness is common to both sports, and perhaps participation in one

TABLE 3-1    Means, standard deviations, and univariate $F$ tests of the EPPS variables*

| Variable | Means | | | Standard deviation | | | Univariate $F$ |
|---|---|---|---|---|---|---|---|
| | Base-ball | Tennis | Norm | Base-ball | Tennis | Norm | |
| Achievement..... | 16.07 | 18.90 | 15.66 | 3.79 | 3.30 | 4.13 | 3.29† |
| Deference....... | 11.78 | 9.10 | 11.21 | 4.01 | 4.01 | 3.59 | 2.40 |
| Order.......... | 10.34 | 7.90 | 10.23 | 4.81 | 4.37 | 4.31 | 1.44 |
| Exhibition....... | 14.17 | 16.00 | 14.40 | 3.69 | 3.95 | 3.53 | 1.14 |
| Autonomy....... | 12.80 | 15.00 | 14.34 | 4.36 | 3.90 | 4.45 | 3.45† |
| Affiliation....... | 14.54 | 14.00 | 15.00 | 4.47 | 5.20 | 4.32 | .55 |
| Intraception..... | 14.34 | 16.90 | 16.12 | 4.24 | 5.30 | 5.23 | 3.40† |
| Succorance...... | 10.64 | 11.00 | 10.74 | 3.94 | 4.78 | 4.70 | .03 |
| Dominance...... | 15.25 | 18.50 | 17.44 | 4.75 | 3.26 | 4.88 | 5.85† |
| Abasement...... | 15.31 | 12.10 | 12.24 | 5.10 | 4.72 | 4.93 | 10.54† |
| Nurturance...... | 14.02 | 12.40 | 14.04 | 5.45 | 4.52 | 4.80 | .56 |
| Change......... | 14.47 | 14.30 | 15.51 | 4.49 | 4.92 | 4.74 | 1.55 |
| Endurance....... | 14.12 | 12.50 | 12.66 | 4.92 | 4.61 | 5.30 | 2.11 |
| Heterosexuality.. | 17.98 | 14.70 | 17.65 | 5.21 | 5.50 | 5.48 | 1.56 |
| Aggression....... | 13.98 | 16.20 | 12.79 | 4.93 | 4.90 | 4.59 | 4.37† |
| Consistency score........ | 12.67 | 12.30 | 11.53 | 1.30 | 1.10 | 1.88 | |
| $N$ ............ | 59 | 10 | 760 | | | | |

* The EPPS is claimed to measure 15 relatively independent normal personality variables: (1) achievement (doing one's best), (2) deference (following others and conforming), (3) order (being neat and orderly), (4) exhibition (liking to be the center of attention), (5) autonomy (independence), (6) affiliation (being part of a group, having friends), (7) intraception (analyzing others), (8) succorance (seeking help and affection from others), (9) dominance (being a leader), (10) abasement (willingness to accept blame, having inferiority feelings), (11) nurturance (assisting others, being sympathetic), (12) change (willingness to try new things), (13) endurance (completing tasks), (14) heterosexuality (being attracted to the opposite sex), (15) aggression (attacking, criticizing, blaming).
† Significance at .05 level or better.
*Source:* Robert N. Singer. Personality differences between and within baseball and tennis players. *Research Quarterly*, 1969, **40**, 582–588. P. 585.

sport strengthens the desirable personality characteristics for the other sport, though interestingly enough, one is a team sport, the other an individual sport. Why karate athletes and wrestlers did not have similar personality profiles is difficult to explain.

So far the most research has been done on male athletes. With the recently changing attitudes toward women's competitive athletics and with the numerous tournaments that have been sponsored by women's organizations, research on the personalities of women athletes is increasing at a rapid rate.

## RECREATIONAL AND ACTIVITY INTERESTS AND PERSONALITY

Thus far we have looked only at organized athletic groups. But what of people who select particular activities in an elective physical education program? Are dissimilarities in personality reflected in activity or recreational preferences? There does seem to be some relationship between personality and activity interest. A number of investigators have noted trait distinctions between various physical activity groups. It should be pointed out, though, that in some studies the students were in their specific activity classes not necessarily by choice but because other classes which they might have preferred were already full. For instance, Flanagan (1951) studied 221 male college students in six physical education classes: fencing, basketball, boxing, swimming, volleyball, and badminton. A personality inventory constructed from several instruments was used to measure such traits as masculinity-femininity, ascendance-submission, extroversion-introversion, and emotional stability-emotional instability.

Among the results were the following: (1) fencers were found to be more ascendant than basketball players, volleyball players, and boxers, and more feminine than basketball players; (2) badminton players were the most extroverted; (3) basketball players were the most masculine, and swimmers and boxers scored higher in masculinity than did badminton and volleyball players; and (4) volleyball players were more submissive, more introverted, and less emotionally stable than members of the other groups. According to Flanagan, then, personality evidently does play a role in activity selection.

In another representative study, this time with college women, Riddle (1968) administered a physical activity preference form, and also recorded the students' own estimates of their skill level and socioeconomic status. A number of personality need variables were found to differentiate significantly between activity selection. Once again, the conclusion was that personality variables do influence choice of activities.

Ibrahim (1969) investigated the relationship between personality and recreational participation during leisure. Male and female college students were analyzed on the California Psychological Inventory (CPI) according to degree of participation in recreational activity, as well as according to type of activity favored, e.g., physical, social, communicative, aesthetic, or learning. The "recreationally outstanding" or above-average person (i.e., the recreationally inclined person, who participates to a great extent in these activities) was stereotyped as ". . . more confident, versatile, outgoing, enthusiastic, outspoken, and energetic than the recreationally average or below average" (p. 81). A number of traits distinguished the groups according to type of recreational pursuits, but Ibrahim feels that the evidence is not strong enough to make any sweeping statements.

## PHYSICAL FITNESS AND PERSONALITY

Research on physical fitness and personality falls into two basic areas: (1) personality comparisons of groups that score high and low on physical fitness test scores, and (2) study of changes in personality that occur along with improvement in physical fitness. Since the need to develop the body is interrelated with the need to participate in certain kinds of sports and recreational activities, personality can be expected to be related to physical fitness to some degree.

In a study of college women, Harris (1963) appraised the fitter women as being more stable and less anxious than less fit women. Tillman (1965) administered three personality tests to two groups of public school boys— an extremely physically fit group and a less fit group. The fitter group was more dominant, extroverted, and socially oriented than the less fit group. As a second part of the study, the less fit group was divided into two subgroups. The experimental subgroup then experienced a 9-month strenuous physical fitness program, while the control subgroup did not. Although the experimental subjects improved much more in physical fitness than their counterparts, they differed from the control group on only one personality trait (ascendance-submission). Evidently personality changes does not develop as quickly as changes in physical development.

It is interesting to observe that the fitter group demonstrated many of the personality traits associated with the typical athlete. In many respects, this should not be too unexpected. Physical development underlies potential for success in athletic endeavors. Many athletes score quite high on fitness tests, and whether they are grouped as athletes or as persons high in physical fitness, they have similar personality traits, in general. This statement is true to the extent that athletes and nonathletes or fitter and less fit persons might be distinguished on personality measures. Naturally, people differ considerably among themselves in personality.

## PERSONALITY OF THE SUPERIOR ATHLETE

If superior athletes could be identified and agreed upon, a logical analysis would be to determine whether they possess a unique personality profile.

That is to say, do champion athletes differ in personality from average athletes? Earlier in this chapter an attempt was made to determine the psychological characteristics of the athlete, or to differentiate him from the non-athlete. It stands to reason that the superior athlete would have many if not all the traits associated with the average athlete, but perhaps in slightly different combination and interaction. It is possible that the greater or lesser presence of certain personality traits might distinguish the superior athlete. By the same token, it is highly probable that his skills and abilities would also tend to differentiate him.

Some researchers have compared outstanding and average athletes from specific sports, and others have attempted to characterize the superior athlete in general, regardless of sport affiliation. The reader is once again reminded of the difficulty of gaining agreement about the criteria for designating a champion. Olympic athletes, professional athletes, and "starting" players are all called "champion" in the research; and even establishing criteria for the average athlete is not easy. Therefore, the research is presented with reservations and must be understood so.

Kroll (1967) examined the personality profiles of wrestlers across different levels of demonstrated achievement in wrestling: (1) a superior group composed of 28 United States Olympic wrestlers; (2) an excellent group composed of 33 collegiate wrestlers who were rated by their coaches as being excellent; and (3) an average or below average group of wrestlers. Discriminant function analysis failed to establish any differences in personality profile among these three groups.

Other researchers also have observed little difference in personality when comparing groups at various skill levels within a sport. For example, Ruhling (1966) administered an introversion-extroversion scale to intramural and varsity players in wrestling, tennis, and basketball. Within each group, no differences were noted. Gold's findings (1955) indicate that professional and varsity tennis players score similarly on the Guilford-Martin Personality Inventory, as do professional and varsity golf players. Carlson & Kroll (1967) stated that no personality profile components or patterns distinguished three classifications of karate participants.

In a study reported earlier in this chapter, Singer (1969) compared higher-ranked with lower-ranked baseball and tennis players at Ohio State University. Near the end of each sport schedule, a roster of subjects who had completed the EPPS personality test was given to the coaches, who were asked to rank the players according to skilled performance. For statistical analysis, the 10 highest-ranked varsity and the 10 highest-ranked freshman baseball players were placed in one group and were compared with a group composed of the 10 lowest-ranked varsity and the 10 lowest-ranked freshman baseball players. The top five tennis players were compared with the five lowest-ranked players. A multivariate technique, multiple discriminant analysis, was used to determine profile differences from sport to sport, and skill level achieved within each sport. Also, each of the 15 traits of which the EPPS is composed was analyzed separately within and between groups, and was compared with norms, using separate univariate $F$ tests. The resulting data are shown in Tables 3-2 and 3-3.

It was determined that the lowest-ranked baseball group scored lower than the norm group in dominance. In abasement, both baseball groups scored higher than the norm group; in endurance, the lowest-ranked baseball group was found to be significantly higher than the norm group. The highest-ranked tennis players scored higher than the norm group in achievement. On the order variable, the lowest-ranked tennis group was significantly lower than both the norm group and the highest-ranked tennis group. When the highest- and lowest-ranked tennis players were compared,

TABLE 3-2   Means, standard deviations, and univariate $F$ tests for the highest and lowest rated baseball groups and the normative group

| Variable | Means | | | Standard deviation | | | Univariate $F$ |
|---|---|---|---|---|---|---|---|
| | High | Low | Norm | High | Low | Norm | |
| Achievement..... | 16.15 | 16.35 | 15.66 | 3.94 | 3.17 | 4.13 | .40 |
| Deference....... | 12.05 | 11.40 | 11.21 | 4.99 | 3.51 | 3.59 | .54 |
| Order.......... | 9.90 | 11.75 | 10.23 | 5.24 | 4.28 | 4.31 | 1.26 |
| Exhibition....... | 15.90 | 13.25 | 14.40 | 3.27 | 3.24 | 3.53 | 2.88 |
| Autonomy....... | 14.25 | 12.10 | 14.34 | 4.64 | 4.01 | 4.45 | 2.47 |
| Affiliation....... | 13.90 | 13.50 | 15.00 | 4.31 | 4.98 | 4.32 | 1.74 |
| Intraception..... | 14.15 | 15.95 | 16.12 | 4.27 | 4.09 | 5.23 | 1.41 |
| Succorance...... | 10.90 | 9.35 | 10.74 | 4.17 | 3.20 | 4.70 | .88 |
| Dominance...... | 15.40 | 15.00 | 17.44 | 5.27 | 4.85 | 4.88 | 4.01* |
| Abasement...... | 14.85 | 16.35 | 12.24 | 5.06 | 4.50 | 4.93 | 9.29* |
| Nurturance...... | 13.05 | 13.30 | 14.04 | 4.65 | 6.15 | 4.80 | .62 |
| Change......... | 14.05 | 13.85 | 15.51 | 4.98 | 3.76 | 4.74 | 2.08 |
| Endurance....... | 13.60 | 16.20 | 12.66 | 4.86 | 3.95 | 5.30 | 4.66* |
| Heterosexuality.. | 17.05 | 17.40 | 17.65 | 4.76 | 6.10 | 5.48 | .13 |
| Aggression....... | 14.75 | 14.00 | 12.79 | 3.13 | 5.39 | 4.59 | 2.40 |
| Consistency score........ | 12.33 | 12.98 | 11.53 | 1.14 | 1.21 | 1.88 | |
| $N$............ | 20 | 20 | 760 | | | | |

* Significance at .05 level or better.

*Source:* Robert N. Singer. Personality differences between and within baseball and tennis players. *Research Quarterly*, 1969, **40**, 582–588. P. 586.

TABLE 3-3   Means, standard deviations, and univariate $F$ tests for highest and lowest rated tennis players and normative group

| Variable | Means | | | Standard deviation | | | Univariate $F$ |
|---|---|---|---|---|---|---|---|
| | High | Low | Norm | High | Low | Norm | |
| Achievement..... | 20.60 | 17.20 | 15.66 | 1.02 | 3.87 | 4.13 | 3.90* |
| Deference....... | 10.40 | 7.80 | 11.21 | 3.98 | 3.60 | 3.59 | 2.35 |
| Order.......... | 10.60 | 5.20 | 10.23 | 4.72 | 1.17 | 4.31 | 3.41* |
| Exhibition....... | 16.40 | 15.60 | 14.40 | 4.50 | 3.26 | 3.53 | 1.07 |
| Autonomy....... | 14.20 | 15.80 | 14.34 | 3.71 | 3.92 | 4.45 | .27 |
| Affiliation....... | 13.20 | 14.80 | 15.00 | 6.77 | 2.64 | 4.32 | .43 |
| Intraception..... | 16.40 | 17.40 | 16.12 | 3.38 | 6.65 | 5.23 | .15 |
| Succorance...... | 9.00 | 13.00 | 10.74 | 4.86 | 3.74 | 4.70 | .92 |
| Dominance...... | 19.80 | 17.20 | 17.44 | 1.72 | 3.87 | 4.88 | .59 |
| Abasement...... | 12.20 | 12.00 | 12.24 | 4.22 | 5.18 | 4.93 | .01 |
| Nurturance...... | 12.60 | 12.20 | 14.04 | 5.95 | 2.32 | 4.80 | .58 |
| Change......... | 11.40 | 17.40 | 15.51 | 3.56 | 4.22 | 4.74 | 2.28 |
| Endurance....... | 12.40 | 12.60 | 12.66 | 4.63 | 4.59 | 5.30 | .01 |
| Heterosexuality.. | 14.40 | 15.00 | 17.65 | 3.88 | 6.72 | 5.48 | 1.44 |
| Aggression....... | 15.80 | 16.60 | 12.79 | 3.97 | 5.64 | 4.59 | 2.75 |
| Consistency score........ | 12.75 | 12.51 | 11.53 | .95 | 1.26 | 1.88 | |
| $N$............ | 5 | 5 | 760 | | | | |

\* Significance at .05 level or better.
*Source:* Robert N. Singer. Personality differences between and within baseball and tennis players. *Research Quarterly*, 1969, **40**, 582–588. P. 586.

there was a significant difference in only one of the 15 variables; between the highest- and lowest-ranked baseball players, no differences were noted. With multiple discriminant analysis, no significant differences in personality profiles were observed between the highest- and lowest-ranking baseball players. Because of the small number of subjects, the data from the tennis players could not be analyzed in a similar way.

On the other hand, other research has found distinctions in personality between champion athletes and average athletes. For instance, Ogilvie & Tutko (1967), after collecting information on countless athletes, feel they can characterize the outstanding athlete and distinguish him from lesser athletes. They describe him as one who has a high need to achieve, can resist the stress of competition, has great psychological endurance, and is self-confident and self-assertive.

Olson (1966) attempted to discern personality differences among categories of outstanding male tennis players. He described champions as more inner-directed, more pragmatic, and more extroverted than "near-great" tennis players. Fowler (1961) compared 10 outstanding athletes with 10 junior varsity athletes in such sports as football, basketball, and wrestling, and found that certain traits differentiated the two groups. Since his between-sport comparisons were nearly identical, and the personality differences that he found were related to performance levels within each sport, Fowler concluded that the degree of involvement has more bearing on personality formation than does type of sport. Even major league baseball players, as La Place (1954) reports, are distinguished from minor league players in some personality traits.

Johnson, Hutton, and Johnson (1954) administered projective personality tests to 12 outstanding athletes from different sports, and compared the results with test norms. The champions were readily distinguishable as a unique group on the basis of personality characteristics, including:

1   Extreme aggression
2   Uncontrolled emotions
3   High anxiety
4   High self-assurance
5   High levels of aspiration
6   A strong need to achieve

Thus it appears that superior athletes can be typified even though there are differences between individual superior athletes. Some researchers in this area, notably Kane (1965), feel quite strongly about the relationship of athletic achievement to dimensions of personality. He states:

> Personality ratings on traits of aggression, dominance, persistence, drive, confidence, and general extroversion have been found to go most often with success in athletic skills. . . .
>
> A process of selection on personality grounds begins to work as the highest levels of athletics achievement are reached. From among the stable, dominant, tough-minded extrovert youths who are physically gifted there emerge at the top those who are less outgoing and more sensitive.
>
> Over the years the unique forces of the competitive athletics environment effect changes on the athlete's personality. In particular the development of greater subjectivity and self analysis may result from constant competitive crises [p. 772].

With better measuring devices and techniques, consistently applied over a wide range of athletes from various sports, perhaps greater agreement in experimental results will occur. Personality tests are currently being administered to a number of professional teams. It can be hoped that the results will provide greater insight into the nature of the players and will help predict later behavior in given situations.

The potential help to the coach of knowing the personality of a performer has yet to be realized. As research is only beginning, confusion and contradiction must be expected. With the development of more sophisticated instruments and better experimental designs, the application of personality evaluation to sports shows great promise. It will be to the coach's advantage to keep abreast of the experimental results in this area as they are reported in scientific journals.

## PERSONALITY DATA AND THE COACH

Perhaps some day the coach will select athletes not only according to demonstrated skills and physical characteristics but according to personality traits as well. If two players have similar ability, the deciding factor may be the presence in one of them of a desirable combination of personality traits known to be associated with success in a given sport.

When traits can be ascribed with a reasonable degree of confidence to athletes in a particular sport, or in certain events or positions in a sport, statistical analysis will be able to predict the probability of a person's being a member of a team, participating in an event, or holding a position. Athletes whose personalities are most like those of, say, successful baseball catchers, will be described as such through discriminant function analysis. With a computer, individual personality profiles can be compared with the established normative profile of the group. The degree to which an individual profile is compatible with the group profile would be used to increase the likelihood of success by allowing appropriate selection.

The implications are great. All that is needed are sensitive, accurate personality-assessing instruments, and data that consistently support the notion of profile dissimilarities between athletic groups and between skill levels within a sport. Although Rushall (1970) ". . . has strong reservations as to the importance of personality to athletic performance" (p. 172), he nevertheless suggests that statistical techniques be used to differentiate among members of teams. He recommends, "For coaches who believe certain behavioral characteristics are essential for performance this method [discriminant function] appears to be an aid in selection procedures" (p. 172).

## PERSONALITIES OF COACH AND TEAM

It is well known that we tend to select friends and judge them according to our own value systems and personalities. We like to see in other people the kinds of traits we admire in ourselves. Do coaches therefore tend to select athletes who possess similar qualities to their own? Although conclusive research evidence is lacking, it does appear that an aggressive football coach tries to pick aggressive players. A conservative basketball coach, on the other hand, may select players who are exceptionally alert, composed, and calculating.

One psychologist working with athletic teams told me that his preliminary research reveals that coaches select athletes whose personalities coincide with their own. In cohesive, successful teams, the coach and players have similar traits, according to his data. Thus it may be that selection by similarity leads to closer bonds within the team and to a greater probability of achievement. Other data from this psychologist indicate that losing teams are typically represented by dissimilarities between coach and athletes in personality profiles. It will be interesting to see some published research on this matter.

From another vantage point, it appears that coaches and athletes agree on the personality traits of the "ideal" coach, according to Hendry (1969) who compared swimming coaches' estimations of the "ideal" coach with estimations by international-caliber junior swimmers. Hendry writes:

> It would seem that top coaches and these junior swimmers have similar views of the "ideal" coach stereotype: An outgoing, dominating, stable individual, highly intelligent and conscientious; realistic, practical, confidently secure, a man willing to break with tradition, make his own decisions, and very self-sufficient. The kind of man, from the swimmers' point of view, that they could lean on in competitive crises; the kind of man, from the coaches' point of view, who could organize and control the swimmer. Hence the similar construction of stereotype, perhaps for differing reasons [p. 304].

The swimmers and coaches in the preceding study were a select group. Whether the same results could be found in athletes of different skills, of different ages, and in other sports remains to be seen.

## PERSONALITY AND TYPE OF SCHOOL

Not only may various sport groups display dissimilar personalities, but it has been reported that college football players from various kinds of colleges differ to some degree in personality (Kroll & Petersen, 1965). Church schools, state colleges, universities, and private schools apparently attract students with particular and unique profiles. The degree to which personality influences choice of school versus the extent to which it is modified while the individual is at the school is naturally impossible to determine accurately. Nonetheless, the possibility exists that particular types of schools are associated with athletes who display unique personality characteristics.

Furthermore, the personality traits of players on winning and losing college football teams have been distinguished, as revealed by analysis of "sister schools," i.e., two schools that are comparable except in win-loss records. (Discussion and references are given in Chapter 9.)

At the present time such data are more informative than directive. If more evidence supports the idea that there is a relationship between type of school and athletes' personalities, perhaps coaches will be hired according to numerous criteria including the degree of consistency of their value structures with those of the school. Athletes may be offered scholarships by colleges with which their personalities and value systems are compatible. However, such talk is only speculative as yet. There is food for thought, however, and actions based on thought are generally more productive than those that are unpremeditated.

## TACTICAL ADVANTAGES

No discussion of the psychological aspects of sport would be complete without reference to tactical maneuvers employed in athletic competition. The coach and the athlete attempt to outguess, outmaneuver, and out-think their opponents. The superior athletes and superior teams are not necessarily the ones who have the best motor skills or the most ideal physical characteristics. Strategy and tactics often make the difference between winning and losing.

This psychological aspect of sport is quite intriguing. Man is pitted against man and team against team not only with regard to motor skills and physical proficiency, but also with regard to psychological skills. The psychological factor operating in sport is called "gamesmanship." How does one gain a psychological advantage over an opponent? In a sense, we are talking about the type of situation encountered in a poker game, in which the player with the best cards is not always the winner. The poker player's personality, in terms of his mannerisms, style of playing, and ability to bluff, contributes to his success. The same is true in athletic competition.

Psychological warfare is demonstrated in many sports and in various ways in each sport. The things coaches say to newspapermen about forthcoming contests may affect the performance of the opponents (as well as the performance of their own team members). The first score in a basketball game or football game, or a good attempt by a javelin thrower or pole vaulter, is of great psychological advantage. Franz Stampfl (1955), in his book on track and field, gives insight into psychological advantages in certain tactics.

In basketball, stealing an opponent's dribble or passing at a crucial time may change the psychological tide of the game. Walt Frazer, all-star guard with the New York Knickerbockers, has repeatedly demonstrated the demoralizing effect a theft can have on opposing teams, and his actions also reinforce his own playing ability and raise the morale of his team. An article in *Newsweek* (December 15, 1969) described Frazier as follows:

> Other Knicks have suggested that Frazier is so quick he can snatch flies out of midair and steal hubcaps off moving cars, and those cracks also please him. "There's nothing better than stealing the ball," he says. "That screaming and cheering makes me jingle inside. Sometimes when I click with a few steals early in a game, that noise makes me feel like I can do anything. Sometimes I want to guard that whole team by myself" [p. 66].[1]

One help in planning effective tactics is knowing the strengths and weaknesses of the opponent. The impact of any move geared to upset the opponent psychologically is dependent upon corresponding weaknesses. A football or basketball team whose members are always spirited and talking may beef up their own morale while upsetting their opponents. A "mean" pitcher can unnerve batters. A base runner with a reputation for stealing and sliding with his spikes high can have similar effects on the infielders who have to cover the bases. In tennis, certain strategies are effective against some adversaries, and other strategies are called for against different opponents.

Any move made by an opponent can be met by a countermove. Appropriate tactics include the skilled execution of movement patterns as well as any other actions that might bring some sort of an advantage. Sport is much more than a physical interaction between human beings. The intellectual processes contribute to the total concept of the highly skilled athlete, the winning athlete, or the winning team.

## PSYCHOLOGICAL INJURIES

Due to the nature of competitive sports, where activity is spirited and behavior aggressive, physical injuries are not at all uncommon. The danger involved in some athletic events leads to a probability of bodily harm. Sadistic and masochistic tendencies on the part of some competitors may partially explain other injuries. The intensive training for conditioning and in preparation for athletic competition and the call to push oneself as

---

[1] Copyright Newsweek, Inc., December 15, 1969.

far as possible also result in certain physical and emotional hardships and stresses on the body. Lately, however, serious thought has been given to the possibility that a number of so-called "injuries" sustained in athletics are caused more psychologically than otherwise. That is to say, the athlete may make unconscious attempts to injure himself in order to resolve internal conflicts.

It is well known that some people are accident- and injury-prone; they experience a greater number of mishaps than the average person. They may be more reckless and careless, or other factors may be involved. Certain athletes have histories of repeated injuries or slow recovery from injuries. In some cases the injuries are identifiable and real; in other cases trainers and doctors cannot verify the athletes' claims. Psychiatrists have made case studies of both situations and have determined that particular incidents have had psychological origins.

Some athletes evidently fear defeat, and others, surprisingly enough, fear success. Some athletes participate because they unconsciously want to get hurt, for reasons that differ in as many ways as there are athletes who have such fears. For example, a second-string athlete who finally has the opportunity to play may be afraid: he hurts himself and thus becomes a hero. As a benchwarmer, he was secure; as an injured hero, he is pampered and conjoled. An example of this case might be the boy who wants to play, be on a team, and be looked up to, but who has poor abilities.

In competitive athletics, a certain amount of aggressiveness is needed for success. The athlete who participates on a purely voluntary basis will probably have a certain degree of aggressiveness. When participation is involuntary, is caused by family or peer pressures, for example, internal conflict is likely. Moore (1967) writes that ". . . athletic injuries or slow recovery from the same may result in psychological conflict between passivity and aggressivity" (p. 319). He states that injury provides an escape mechanism for the player who thinks he is going to lose. Physical injury allows him to save face, for without being really beaten by an opponent, he gains the sympathy of his coach, his team, and the spectators.

According to Moore, a number of psychiatric cases exemplify the inability of athletes to stand success. Such athletes deliberately try to fail, and their symptoms are extremely difficult to treat. Ogilvie & Tutko (1967) have described the athlete who fears success: "Success can only mean added responsibility and added responsibility can only mean more anxiety, thus a socially acceptable way-out is a physical pain or injury" (p. 1). They claim that such injuries are psychological in nature, and that the pain complained of by the athlete is hypochondrial.

For the coach, psychological injuries of this sort are a severe problem. How can they be accurately diagnosed? How can they be treated? Moore suggests that an alert coach might be able to predict potential dangers, and he also suggests that the following situations may lead to psychological injury:

(1) Gross disproportion between athletic ability and willingness to be aggressive.
(2) Disproportion between father and son as to athletic ability and expression of aggression.
(3) Lack of adequate control of aggression.
(4) Fear of injury.
(5) A history of multiple injuries.
(6) Concealment of minor injuries.
(7) Exaggeration of injuries.
(8) Inability to tolerate success.
(9) Omnipotent feelings of invulnerability. [Pp. 322–323.]

Ogilvie & Tutko recommend that the coach accept the athlete and his pains but give him no extra consideration. When the athlete can feel that he is accepted as an individual no matter what the outcome of his performance, his pains will diminish. When the coach confronts an athlete who appears to have a psychological injury, he realizes more than ever before that part of his role is to be an amateur psychologist.

SUMMARY

The meaning of the word "personality" has been altered through the centuries, and even now, there is little agreement on a satisfactory definition. One's personality is usually thought of as the characteristic way he behaves. It reflects both hereditary and environmental influences. Personality research on sport and athletes has only recently been undertaken with a reasonable degree of sophistication and meaning. Clinical psychologists, growth and development psychologists, psychiatrists, and physical educators interested in sport psychology have contributed to the current state of knowledge.

*Personalities of athletes and nonathletes*  In general, athletic groups and nonathletic groups have been distinguished in certain personality traits. Differences in evaluative instruments, samples, statistics, and the like, from study to study, make it hard to obtain agreement on the specific dissimilarities of such groups. Researchers disagree about whether there are adequate data at the present time to characterize the personality of the "typical" athlete.

*Personality changes due to athletic experience*  Anything an individual experiences in life can affect his personality. Because of a dearth of longitudinal studies, no clear picture emerges of the effect on personality of participation in sports. Obviously, meaningful experiences should have a desirable effect on personality.

*Personality comparisons of various sport groups*  Comparisons of athletes in different sports and comparisons of athletes in team sports with athletes in individual sports have yielded some personality distinctions and some disagreements.

*Recreational and activity interests and personality*  There seems to be some relationship between personality and activity interest, as researchers have usually detected differences in personality traits between various physical activity groups.

*Physical fitness and personality*  Students who are physically fit and unfit have been distinguished in some personality traits.

*Personality of the superior athlete*  Although some researchers have had little success in differentiating champion from average athletes, others have developed a personality profile of the superior athlete.

*Personality data and the coach*  In the future, with improved data-collecting devices and with research indicating a greater association of variables, it is possible that athletes may be selected for team membership, position, event, or situation partly on the basis of personality.

*Coach and team personalities*  Preliminary evidence indicates the probability of a cohesive team and a greater chance of success when the personalities of the athletes are compatible with the personality of the coach.

*Personality and type of school*  Athletes on winning and losing teams and on teams from different types of schools have different personality profiles.

*Tactical advantages*  Sports is filled with situations in which tactical maneuvers have psychological overtones. Such maneuvers can overcome other limitations.

*Psychological injuries*  Athletes who have internal conflicts may so fear winning or losing that they unconsciously harm themselves or imagine they are injured in order to avoid the consequences of winning or losing.

## REFERENCES

Allport, Gordon W. *Pattern and growth in personality.* New York: Holt, 1961.

Booth, E. Personality traits of athletes as measured by the MMPI. *Research Quarterly,* 1958, **29,** 127–138.

Carlson, B. Robert, & Kroll, Walter. Discriminant function and hierarchical analysis of karate participants' personality profiles. *Research Quarterly,* 1967, **38,** 405–411.

Cattell, R. B. *The scientific analysis of personality.* Baltimore: Penguin, 1965.

Cooper, Lowell. Athletics, activity and personality: a review of the literature. *Research Quarterly,* 1969, **40,** 17–22.

Cortés, Juan B., & Gatti, Florence M. Physique & propensity—for achievement, sex, politics, aggression, religion, crime, esthetics, economics, sociality. *Psychology Today,* 1970, **4,** 42–44, 82–84.

The dazzling Knicks. *Newsweek*, December 15, 1969. Pp. 64–67.

Flanagan, Lance. A study of some personality traits of different physical activity groups. *Research Quarterly*, 1951, **22**, 312–323.

Fowler, William H. A comparative study of evaluative attitudes of outstanding varsity athletes and junior varsity athletes. Unpublished master's thesis, Springfield College, 1961.

Gedda, Luigi, Milani-Comparetti, M., & Brenci, G. A preliminary report on research made during the games of the XVIIth Olympiad, Rome, 1960. In Jokl, E., & Simon, E. (Eds.), *International research in sport and physical education*, Springfield, Ill.: Charles C Thomas, 1964.

Gold, Marvin. A comparison of personality characteristics of professional and college varsity tennis and golf players as measured by the Guilford-Martin Personality Inventory. Unpublished master's thesis, University of Maryland, 1965.

Gorsuch, H. R. The competitive athlete and the achievement motive as measured by a projective test. Unpublished master's thesis, The Pennsylvania State University, 1968.

Harlow, Robert G. Masculine inadequacy and compensatory development of physique. *Journal of Personality*, 1951, **19**, 312–323.

Harris, Dorothy V. Comparison of physical performance and psychological traits of college women with high and low fitness indices. *Perceptual and Motor Skills*, 1963, **17**, 293–294.

Hendry, L. B. A personality study of highly successful and "ideal" swimming coaches. *Research Quarterly*, 1969, **40**, 299–304.

Ibrahim, Hilmi. Recreational preference and personality. *Research Quarterly*, 1969, **40**, 76–82.

Johnson, Warren R., Hutton, Daniel C., & Johnson, Granville B. Personality traits of some champion athletes as measured by two projective tests: the Rorschach and H-T-P. *Research Quarterly*, 1954, **25**, 484–485.

Kane, John E. Personality profiles of physical education students compared with others. In Antonelli, F. (Ed.), *Proceedings of the 1st International Congress of Sports Psychology*. 1965. Pp. 772–775.

Kistler, Joy W. Attitudes expressed about behavior demonstrated in certain specific situations occurring in sports. *Proceedings of the National College Physical Education Association for Men*, 1957, **50**, 55–58.

Kroll, Walter. Sixteen personality factor profiles of collegiate wrestlers. *Research Quarterly*, 1967, **38**, 49–56.

Kroll, Walter, & Crenshaw, William. Multivariate personality profile analysis of four athletic groups. Paper presented at the 2d International Congress of Sport Psychology, Washington, D.C., 1968.

Kroll, Walter, & Petersen, Kay H. Study of values test and collegiate football teams. *Research Quarterly*, 1965, **36**, 441–447.

Lakie, Wiliam L. Personality characteristics of certain groups of intercollegiate athletics. *Research Quarterly*, 1962, **33**, 566–573.

La Place, John E. Personality and its relationship to success in professional baseball. *Research Quarterly*, 1954, **25**, 313–319.

Meyers, Carlton R., & Ohnmacht, Fred W. Needs of pupils in relation to athletic competition at the junior high school level. *Research Quarterly*, 1963, **34**, 521–524.

Moore, Robert A. Injury in athletics. In Slovenko, Ralph, and Knight, James A. (Eds.), *Motivations in play, games and sports*. Springfield, Ill.: Charles C Thomas, 1967.

Ogilvie, Bruce C. What is an athlete? *Journal of Health, Physical Education, and Recreation*, 1967, **38**, 48.

Ogilvie, Bruce C. Psychological consistencies of competitors. *Journal of the American Medical Association*, 1968, **205**, 780–786.

Ogilvie, Bruce C., & Tutko, Thomas. When is pain real? Unpublished dittoed paper, San Jose State University, 1967.

Olson, Edward D. Identification of personality differences among male tennis players. Unpublished doctoral dissertation, Ohio State University, 1966.

Peterson, Sheri L., Weber, Jerome C., & Trousdale, William W. Personality traits of women in team sports vs. women in individual sports. *Research Quarterly*, 1967, **38**, 686–690.

Richardson, Deane. Ethical conduct in sport situations. *Proceedings of the National College Physical Education Association for Men*, 1962, **66**, 98–103.

Riddle, Lynne. Relationships between physical education activity preference, socioeconomic status, and personality needs of freshman and sophomore college women. Unpublished doctoral dissertation, Syracuse University, 1968.

Ruhling, Robert O. A comparative study of introversion-extroversion in selected varsity and intramural athletes using the composite MMPI introversion-extroversion scale. Unpublished master's thesis, University of Maryland, 1966.

Rushall, Brent S. Some practical applications on personality information to athletics. In G. Kenyon (Ed.), *Contemporary psychology of sport: Proceedings of the 2d International Congress of Sports Psychology*. Chicago: The Athletic Institute, 1970, 167–173.

Schreckengaust, V. J. Comparison of selected personality variables between women athletes in individual sports and women athletes in team sports. Unpublished master's thesis, The Pennsylvania State University, 1968.

Singer, Robert N. Athletic participation: cause or result of certain personality factors? *Physical Educator*, 1967, **24**, 169–171.

Singer, Robert N. Personality differences between and within baseball and tennis players. *Research Quarterly*, 1969, **40**, 582–588.

Slusher, Howard. Personality and intelligence characteristics of selected high school athletes and nonathletes. *Research Quarterly*, 1964, **35**, 539–545.

Sperling, Abraham P. The relationship between personality adjustment and achievement in physical education activities. *Research Quarterly*, 1942, **13**, 351–363.

Stampfl, Franz. *Franz Stampfl on running*. New York: Macmillan, 1955.

Thune, John B. Personality of weightlifters. *Research Quarterly*, 1949, **20**, 296–306.

Tillman, Kenneth. Relationship between physical fitness and selected personality traits. *Research Quarterly*, 1965, **36**, 483–489.

Werner, Alfred, & Gottheil, Edward. Personality development and participation in college athletics. *Research Quarterly*, 1966, **37**, 126–131.

# CHAPTER FOUR

# Personal Factors and the Athlete

$A$lthough much can be done to train an athlete for specific goals, his personal qualities will be of great importance in determining achievement. Genetically transmitted physical, intellectual, and temperamental characteristics and the way these characteristics interact may predispose a person to a likelihood of success in a given sport. Characteristics and abilities are general personal features while the skills resulting from their presence in desirable qualities and quantities are associated with proficiency in particular sports. Can these factors be identified?

In order for an athlete to excel in his sport, whatever it may be, certain general qualities should appear. Unique personal qualities associated with success in a specific athletic endeavor should be present as well. However, an important consideration is that personal qualities help to determine achievement potential, but proficiency can occur in spite of apparent shortcomings. Certain personal factors can be associated with success, but there are so many exceptions that predictions of athletic success from personal assets are questionable, to say the least. Nevertheless, the attempt in this chapter will be to identify physical, motor, sensory, intellectual, and emotional characteristics that are seemingly associated with athletic achievement.

One method of determining factors related to athletic success is to compare athletes with so-called "nonathletes" or to compare subgroups of athletes with each other. Differences between groups indicate that one or more variables may be associated with a given person. Many studies may be found in the literature in which this procedure has been employed.

A second research technique is to compare better and worse athletes within the same sport in order to determine their differences in personal attributes. More studies of personality differences are appearing, but few investigations contain analysis of the personal qualities discussed in this chapter.

It is extremely difficult, and perhaps an injustice, to try to isolate attributes. A person's performance is typically the product of the interaction of many variables. Since there is an even greater difficulty in trying to identify the ideal combination and interaction of factors related to success in sport, the plan here will be to report on research which has attempted to isolate personal characteristics. Discussion will, therefore, center around artificial categories such as body build, motor abilities, intellectual attributes, emotions, and sensory factors. The relative importance of heredity and experience in determining desirable traits in these areas, and in determining ultimate achievement in sport, should be understood first. The reader might very well review the material on this topic in Chapter 2 as a preliminary to this chapter.

## BODY BUILD

People have analyzed each others' physical appearance for centuries. Individuals have been classified and typed, and their body compositions have been determined. Categories have been formed on the basis of casual observations, photographic analysis, skinfold and body girth measurements, and more scientific techniques in recent years. Regardless of the classification technique, the coach and the athlete are both interested in knowing whether a particular body build is associated with athletes in a given sport. If such an association were definitely discovered, an athlete could select the activity which was most compatible with his body type, i.e., the one in which he had the best chance of success. A coach could select team members on the basis of numerous criteria, one of which would be body build. If the probability of achievement were known to be less with the presence of a given body type, the coach would not want to waste countless training hours. This is the direction in which the speculation runs. What does the research indicate?

Most body typing, especially using the *somatotyping technique* in which people are rated on their relative degrees of endomorphy (obesity), mesomorphy (muscularity), and ectomorphy (thinness), has been done with swimmers and track and field athletes. Investigators who have examined Olympic athletes have been able not only to generalize across the body builds of all Olympians and specific sport groups, but across athletes in various events in track and field and swimming as well. In other words, the "typical" athlete in a short-distance track event has been found to possess a somatotype dissimilar to that of the long-distance track man. Different builds are associated with Olympic swimmers and with college swimmers.

There is, however, a great variability of body builds in any sport or event. The implication from the research is that particular body types are best suited for specific activities, but are not necessary conditions and will not ensure proficiency. Overall, in terms of probability of success in a wide range of activities, the ectomesomorph (lean and muscular) build is most desirable.

### Differences between Sports

Some anthropometric studies have attempted to identify the particular body types that are likely to lead to success in selected sports and in particular positions within sports. Certain body builds can probably be associated with success at playing different football positions. In an attempt to investigate this hypothesis, Carter (1968) determined the somatotypes of the entire 1964 San Diego State College football team (35 lettermen). Table 4-1 contains a breakdown of the football players by position: mean

TABLE 4-1   Means, differences between means, and $t$ ratios, for San Diego State football lettermen according to playing group

| Group | Statistic | Height (in.) | Weight (lb.) | First component | Second component | Third component |
|---|---|---|---|---|---|---|
| Offensive backs N = 12 | Mean | 71.83 | 193.17 | 4.46 | 5.46 | 2.25 |
| Defensive backs N = 5 | Mean | 71.40 | 182.00 | 3.90 | 5.50 | 2.70 |
| | Difference | 0.43 | 11.17 | 0.56 | −0.04 | −0.45 |
| | $t$ ratio | 0.47 | 0.97 | 1.49 | −0.15 | −1.23 |
| Offensive linemen N = 10 | Mean | 74.40 | 227.20 | 5.05 | 5.70 | 1.85 |
| Defensive linemen N = 8 | Mean | 72.44 | 217.63 | 5.13 | 5.75 | 1.68 |
| | Difference | 1.96 | 9.57 | −0.08 | −0.05 | 0.17 |
| | $t$ ratio | 2.66* | 1.04 | −0.10 | −0.15 | 0.57 |
| Backs N = 17 | Mean | 71.70 | 189.88 | 4.29 | 5.44 | 2.38 |
| Linemen N = 18 | Mean | 73.52 | 222.94 | 5.08 | 5.70 | 1.75 |
| | Difference | −1.82 | −33.06 | −0.79 | −0.26 | 0.63 |
| | $t$ ratio | −3.36* | −4.75* | −3.16* | −1.06 | 2.17* |
| Total N = 35 | Mean | 72.6 | 206.9 | 4.70 | 5.52 | 2.06 |
| | SD | 1.92 | 25.95 | 0.82 | 0.72 | 0.88 |
| | Range | 67.5–77.0 | 154–262 | 3–6 | 4½–7 | 1–3½ |

* $t$ ratio significant at or beyond the .05 level.

*Source:* J. E. Lindsay Carter. Somatotypes of college football players. *Research Quarterly*, 1968, **39**, 476–481. P. 478.

statistics for height, weight, and components of endomorphy, mesomorphy, and ectomorphy; and *t* tests for significance of the difference between means. In somatotyping, a person can be rated from 1 to 7 in any component, with the higher number indicating a greater presence of that component. It can be observed in the somatocharts in Figure 4-1, taken from a paper by Carter (1969), that most of the football players fall in the endomorph-mesomorph category. Indeed, the average player had a component rating of 4.70–5.52–2.06.

Differences were noted between backs and linemen, and the unique size of the players as a group when compared to the average college population was pointed out. When compared with norms, the San Diego team was at the 91st percentile in height and at the 94th percentile in weight.

Body type in relation to success in track and field has been the object of intense investigation by Tanner (1964). He somatotyped 137 track and field athletes, classified by event, in the 1960 Olympic Games. Differences in body type were found according to event. Some of the events and their corresponding somatotypes are as follows:

| | |
|---|---|
| Discus, javelin, shot and hammer throwers | 3–6–2 |
| Sprinters | 2½–5½–3 |
| Runners | 2½–4½–4 |
| Middle- and long-distance runners | 2½–4–4 |
| High jumpers | 2–6–2 to 2–3–6* |

* The most successful high jumpers registered higher than 4 in mesomorphy.

Carter has done perhaps the most intensive investigation into the relation between body build and sport. Summarizing much of his work in the paper he delivered in Czechoslovakia (1969), he concluded that:

1. "Champion" performers at various levels of a sport exhibit similar patterns of body size and somatotype, with the patterns tending to become narrower with increasing levels of performance.
2. "Champion" performers from many different sports show considerable differences in body size and somatotype; however, some sports show overlapping patterns.
3. In answer to the question "Do athletes differ from non-athletes?" we can only infer that they do, largely on the negative evidence that certain somatotypes are not found in groups of champion athletes [p. 3].

In Figure 4-1, the uniqueness of each group's body build may be seen. Carter feels that there is little or no overlap among the following groups of male athletes: football players, track and field throwers, distance runners, gymnasts, basketball players, wrestlers, weight lifters, and nonathletes. On the other hand, considerable overlap in build is found among swimmers, track and field athletes (excluding throwers), basketball players, golfers, boxers, rowers, and baseball players. A comparison of various women's groups shows much overlapping, although track and field athletes, ballet dancers, and gymnasts appear to be fairly distinct in body build characteristics.

Carter suggests that "selecting the right somatotypes to train can save the coach and athletes considerable time and frustration" (p. 4). It is true that levels of nutrition, motivation, opportunity, and training conditions can alter many outcomes. But one cannot argue with the premise that "Physical activities that place a premium on strength, power, speed, or endurance tend to limit successful participation to the somatotypes that are best suited, or best developed, to fulfill the physical requirements of the activity" (p. 4).

Kroll (1954) did an analysis of the physiques of 36 varsity wrestlers from four Big Ten schools. The average somatotype rating for the wrestlers was 3–5–4, indicating a trend toward ectomorphy-mesomorphy. Kroll compared his data with other data collected on weight lifters and concluded, "It seems as if the wrestling type is sufficiently different from the weight-lifting type to suppose the existence of different body types being characteristic of each sport" (p. 309). The complete data obtained on the wrestling subjects are presented in Table 4-2. The concept of the short-legged, bulky-muscled physique was rejected; rather, these wrestlers possessed body characteristics identified with agility.

Hirata (1966) has collected interesting data on the various participants in the 1964 Olympics in Tokyo. The ages, heights, and weights of 435 males and 722 females were recorded, and the groups were compared by event. In addition, an $F$ index (stout-lean index) was formulated. A higher $F$ index is associated with a higher ratio of stoutness to leanness. In Table 4-3, the data are classified by sporting event, and the gold medalist and his characteristics are differentiated.

Beisser (1967) explains very well what reservations are needed about predicting sport success from physical characteristics. He developed case histories of athletes associated with different sports. A psychiatrist, he delved deeply into the underlying behavior of his athlete patients, who had come to him for treatment and thus do not represent a random sample. In discussing a certain basketball player, Beisser notes that the physical demands of any sport may be quite specialized. One reason why the patient

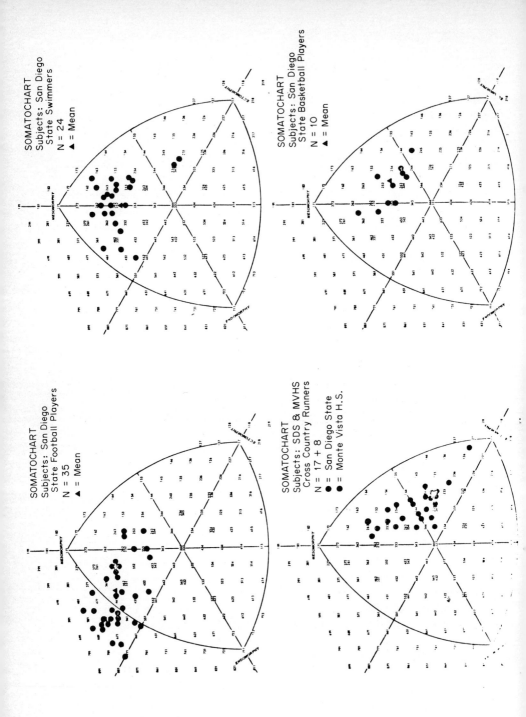

SOMATOCHART
Subjects: San Diego
State Swimmers
N = 24
▲ = Mean

SOMATOCHART
Subjects: San Diego
State Basketball Players
N = 10
▲ = Mean

SOMATOCHART
Subjects: San Diego
State Football Players
N = 35
▲ = Mean

SOMATOCHART
Subjects: SDS & MVHS
Cross Country Runners
N = 17 + 8
● = San Diego State
● = Monte Vista H.S.

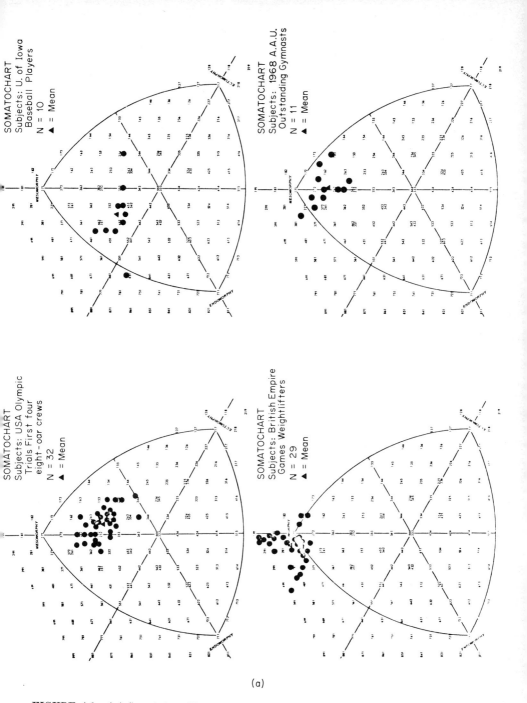

(a)

FIGURE 4-1    (a) Somatotype distributions of eight groups of male athletes. Ratings by
the Heath-Carter method.

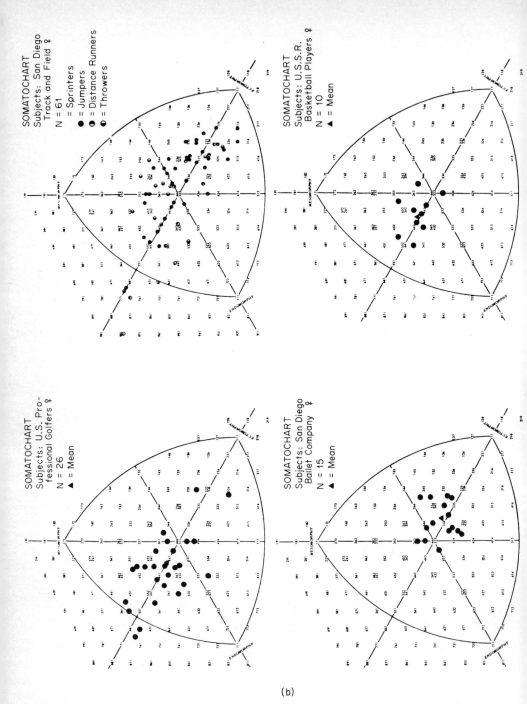

(b) *Somatotype distributions of four groups of female athletes. Ratings by the Heath-Carter method. (*SOURCE: *J. E. Lindsay Carter. Somatotype characteristics of champion athletes. Paper presented at the Anthropological Congress, Praha-Humpolec, Czechoslovakia, 1969. Pp. 7–9.)*

TABLE 4-2  Summary of anthropometrical measurements taken on Big Ten wrestlers

| Measure | Mean | |
|---|---|---|
| Height | 68.8 | inches |
| Weight | 160.3 | pounds |
| R.P.I. | 12.867 | |
| Chest breadth | 11.36 | inches |
| Ankle girth | 8.46 | inches |
| Chest depth | 7.96 | inches |
| Hip width | 11.2 | inches |
| Skeletal index | 131.7 | |
| Gluteal girth | 34.55 | inches |
| Calf girth | 13.61 | inches |
| Biceps | 12.27 | inches |
| Thigh | 19.86 | inches |
| Muscular index | 134.6 | |
| Cheeks (fat mm.) | 14.34 | mm. |
| Abdomen | 14.46 | mm. |
| Hips | 14.91 | mm. |
| Gluteals | 20.94 | mm. |
| Front thigh | 17.29 | mm. |
| Rear thigh | 17.29 | mm. |
| Adipose index | 152.20 | |
| Residual weight | 25.06 | pounds |
| Shoulder width | 15.85 | inches |
| Chest normal | 35.3 | inches |
| Chest deflated | 32.55 | inches |
| Chest inflated | 36.71 | inches |
| Arm span | 71.36 | inches |
| Abdominal girth | 29.36 | inches |
| Vital capacity | 313.27 | cubic inches |
| V. C. residual | 24.059 | cubic inches |
| Strength: | | |
|     Right grip | 122.6 | pounds |
|     Left grip | 114.45 | pounds |
|     Back lift | 429.1 | pounds |
|     Leg lift | 540.4 | pounds |
|     Total strength | 1190.0 | pounds |
| Endomorphy | 2.74 | |
| Mesomorphy | 5.01 | |
| Ectomorphy | 3.823 | |
| Height/abdominal thickness | 9.35 | |
| Ht. × 100/6 × transverse chest | 103.64 | |
| Leg length/trunk length | 1.6979 | |
| Crural ratio | 1.191 | |
| Arm span/height | 1.0373 | |
| Upper arm/forearm | 1.189 | |
| Bust height/height | .47076 | |
| Shoulder width/hip width | 1.4175 | |

*Source:* Walter Kroll. An anthropometrical study of some Big Ten varsity wrestlers. *Research Quarterly*, 1954, **25**, 307–312. P. 310.

**TABLE 4-3** Physique, age, height, and weight of Olympic athletes according to event

*Female*

| | Average | | | | | Name | Medalist | | | | | |
|---|---|---|---|---|---|---|---|---|---|---|---|---|
| | No. | Age | Height | Weight | F index | | Country | Record | Age | Height | Weight | F index |
| **Athletics** | | | | | | | | | | | | |
| 100m | 43 | 22.3 | 166.0 | 56.2 | 23.14 | Tyus | USA | 11.4 | 19 | 170 | 61 | 23.2 |
| 200m | 42 | 23.1 | 166.0 | 57.0 | 23.18 | Mcguire | USA | 23.0 | 20 | 173 | 59 | 22.5 |
| 400m | 22 | 24.0 | 167.0 | 57.5 | 23.14 | Cuthbert | AUS | 52.0 | 26 | 169 | 57 | 22.8 |
| 800m | 25 | 24.2 | 167.0 | 56.0 | 22.98 | Packer | GBI | 2.01.1 | 22 | 169 | 56.5 | 22.7 |
| 400R | 84 | 23.1 | 165.7 | 56.7 | 23.23 | Poland | | 43.6 | | | | |
| 80H | 31 | 24.5 | 168.6 | 60.8 | 23.33 | Balzer | GER | 10.5 | 26 | 171 | 60 | 23.0 |
| High jump | 24 | 23.2 | 172.0 | 62.2 | 23.02 | Balas | RUM | 1.90 | 28 | 184 | 72 | 22.7 |
| Long jump | 32 | 24.0 | 167.8 | 58.2 | 23.08 | Rand | GBI | 6.76 | 24 | 172 | 59.5 | 22.6 |
| Shot put | 16 | 25.8 | 173.0 | 82.0 | 25.03 | T. Press | URS | 18.14 | 27 | 180 | 100 | 25.8 |
| Discus throw | 21 | 26.6 | 174.0 | 76.0 | 24.47 | T. Press | URS | 57.27 | 27 | 180 | 100 | 25.8 |
| Javelin throw | 15 | 24.4 | 169.4 | 68.0 | 24.09 | Penes | RUM | 60.54 | 17 | 186 | 94 | 24.5 |
| Pentathlon | 22 | | 170.6 | 63.7 | 23.32 | I. Press | URS | 5246 | 25 | 168 | 74 | 25.0 |
| **Swimming** | | | | | | | | | | | | |
| 100F.S. | 39 | 18.4 | 167.2 | 60.1 | 23.42 | Fraser | AUS | 59.5 | 27 | 178 | 68 | 23.0 |
| 400F.S. | 31 | 17.9 | 163.5 | 56.0 | 23.45 | Duenkel | USA | 4.43.3 | 16 | 170 | 61 | 23.1 |
| 200B. | 25 | 18.8 | 168.3 | 62.8 | 23.59 | Prozumen-schikova | URS | 2.46.4 | 16 | 168.5 | 71 | 24.6 |
| 100B.F. | 30 | 18.4 | 167.0 | 59.6 | 23.47 | Stouder | USA | 1.04.7 | 16 | 173 | 61 | 22.8 |
| 100B.S. | 29 | 18.9 | 167.3 | 60.0 | 23.39 | Ferguson | USA | 1.07.7 | 17 | 173 | 61 | 22.8 |
| 400I.M. | 20 | 19.1 | 164.0 | 60.2 | 23.70 | Devarona | USA | 5.18.7 | 17 | 168 | 61 | 23.5 |
| 400R. | 50 | 18.5 | 166.0 | 58.6 | 23.43 | U.S. | | 4.03.8 | | | | |
| 400M.R. | 48 | 19.0 | 167.2 | 60.3 | 23.47 | U.S. | | 4.33.9 | | | | |
| Spring D. | 17 | 20.3 | 161.0 | 54.2 | 23.60 | Engel | GER | 145.00 | 17 | 157 | 54 | 24.1 |
| High D. | 20 | 20.0 | 160.7 | 54.0 | 23.53 | L. Bush | USA | 99.80 | 17 | 160 | 52 | 23.4 |

| | n | age | ht | wt | | Name | | Perf. | | | | |
|---|---|---|---|---|---|---|---|---|---|---|---|---|
| Gymnastics............ | 102 | 22.7 | 157.0 | 52.0 | 23.73 | U.R.S. | | 380.890 | | | | |
| Ind................ | | | | | | Caslavska | CZS | 77.564 | 22 | 160 | 55 | 23.7 |
| | | | | | | Latinina | URS | 19.599 | 30 | 163 | 52 | 23.0 |
| | | | | | | Caslavska | CZS | 19.449 | 22 | 160 | 55 | 23.7 |
| | | | | | | Astakhova | URS | 19.332 | 28 | 167 | 56 | 23.0 |
| | | | | | | Caslavska | CZS | 19.483 | 22 | 160 | 55 | 23.7 |
| Volley ball......... | 59 | 24.0 | 170.8 | 65.0 | 23.51 | Japan | | | | | | |
| Fencing............. | 58 | 27.0 | 165.0 | 59.0 | 23.76 | Hungary | | | | | | |
| Canoeing K1....... | 12 | 25.1 | 165.4 | 63.5 | 24.17 | Khvedosink | URS | 2.12.87 | 28 | 164 | 69 | 25 |
| K2....... | 18 | 24.9 | 165.8 | 61.3 | 23.88 | Germany | | 1.56.95 | | | | |
| Equestrian sports..... | 13 | | 167.0 | 56.0 | 22.87 | | | | | | | |

*Male*

Athletics
| | n | age | ht | wt | | Name | | Perf. | | | | |
|---|---|---|---|---|---|---|---|---|---|---|---|---|
| 100m.............. | 70 | 24.5 | 175.0 | 71.4 | 23.67 | Hayes | USA | 10.0 | 22 | 183 | 86 | 24.2 |
| 200m.............. | 65 | 24.9 | 177.0 | 70.2 | 23.35 | Cars | USA | 20.3 | 22 | 191 | 84 | 23.0 |
| 400m.............. | 54 | 24.8 | 178.0 | 70.0 | 23.25 | Larrabee | USA | 45.1 | 26 | 186 | 77 | 22.9 |
| 800m.............. | 48 | 25.0 | 178.3 | 67.7 | 22.96 | Snell | NZL | 1.45.1 | 26 | 179 | 80 | 24.1 |
| 1500m............. | 50 | 25.4 | 176.2 | 64.0 | 22.86 | Snell | NZL | 3.38.1 | 26 | 179 | 80 | 24.1 |
| 5000m............. | 56 | 26.9 | 174.5 | 62.7 | 22.85 | Schul | USA | 13.48.8 | 27 | 184 | 66 | 22.0 |
| 10000m............ | 43 | 27.7 | 172.7 | 62.0 | 22.90 | Mills | USA | 28.24.4 | 26 | 180 | 70 | 22.9 |
| Marathon.......... | 74 | 28.3 | 170.3 | 60.8 | 23.09 | Abebe | ETH | 2.12.11.2 | 32 | 177 | 61 | 22.2 |
| 110H.............. | 37 | 25.3 | 183.1 | 75.1 | 23.15 | Jones | USA | 13.6 | 26 | 178 | 73 | 23.5 |
| 400H.............. | 39 | 24.8 | 180.3 | 73.0 | 23.13 | Cawley | USA | 49.6 | 24 | 183 | 75 | 23.1 |
| 3000H............. | 31 | 26.9 | 172.8 | 63.5 | 23.15 | Roelants | BEL | 8.30.8 | 39 | 174 | 58 | 22.2 |
| 400R.............. | 115 | 25.1 | 176.2 | 70.0 | 23.46 | U.S. | | 39.0 | | | | |
| 1600R............. | 110 | 24.7 | 178.7 | 70.7 | 23.19 | U.S. | | 3.00.7 | | | | |

# TABLE 4-3 Continued

Male

| | Average | | | | Name | Medalist | | | | | | |
|---|---|---|---|---|---|---|---|---|---|---|---|---|
| No. | Age | Height | Weight | F index | | | Country | Record | Age | Height | Weight | F index |
| 20K.W. | 27 | 28.3 | 175.8 | 66.5 | 23.12 | Matthews | GBT | 1.29.34.0 | 30 | 185 | 73.5 | 22.7 |
| 50K.W. | 40 | 29.4 | 175.0 | 65.3 | 23.05 | Pamich | ITA | 4.11.12.4 | 31 | 183 | 74 | 23.0 |
| Decathlon | 26 | 26.3 | 183.2 | 83.5 | 23.88 | Holdorf | GER | 7887 | 24 | 182 | 90 | 24.7 |
| High jump | 24 | 23.5 | 186.2 | 77.7 | 22.98 | Brumel | URS | 2.18 | 22 | 184 | 75 | 22.9 |
| Long jump | 37 | 25.7 | 179.5 | 71.6 | 23.17 | Davies | GBI | 8.07 | 22 | 189 | 82.5 | 23.1 |
| Triple jump | 28 | 26.7 | 178.8 | 70.4 | 23.20 | Szmidt | POL | 16.85 | 29 | 183 | 76 | 23.2 |
| Pole vault | 26 | 25.9 | 179.0 | 72.7 | 23.34 | Hansen | USA | 5.10 | 24 | 183 | 75 | 23.1 |
| Shot put | 24 | 26.4 | 190.2 | 105.5 | 24.98 | Long | USA | 20.33 | 24 | 193 | 118 | 25.5 |
| Discus throw | 29 | 27.9 | 189.1 | 102.3 | 24.73 | Oerter | USA | 61.00 | 28 | 193 | 118 | 25.5 |
| Hammer throw | 26 | 29.3 | 182.5 | 96.5 | 25.10 | Klim | URS | 69.74 | 31 | 187 | 103 | 25.1 |
| Javelin throw | 25 | 26.0 | 183.0 | 83.4 | 23.99 | Nevala | FIN | 82.66 | 24 | 178 | 80 | 24.3 |
| Swimming | | | | | | | | | | | | |
| 100FS | 56 | 21.2 | 180.0 | 74.8 | 23.43 | Schollander | USA | 53.4 | 18 | 182 | 75 | 23.2 |
| 400FS | 51 | 20.2 | 179.6 | 74.3 | 23.46 | Schollander | USA | 4.12.2 | 18 | 182 | 75 | 23.2 |
| 1500FS | 33 | 18.4 | 178.0 | 72.7 | 23.50 | Windle | AUS | 17.01.7 | 19 | 184 | 74 | 22.8 |
| 200BR | 30 | 21.5 | 175.2 | 73.5 | 23.95 | Obrien | AUS | 2.27.8 | 16 | 182 | 80 | 23.7 |
| 200BF | 32 | 19.7 | 174.8 | 72.7 | 23.85 | Berry | AUS | 2.06.6 | 19 | 178 | 80 | 24.3 |
| 200BS | 32 | 20.8 | 182.0 | 75.8 | 23.26 | Graf | USA | 2.10.3 | 22 | 198 | 91 | 22.7 |
| 400I.M. | 24 | 19.8 | 178.4 | 73.0 | 23.48 | Roth | USA | 4.45.4 | 17 | 184 | 84 | 23.9 |
| 400R | 55 | 21.0 | 179.2 | 74.0 | 23.44 | U.S. | USA | 3.33.2 | | | | |
| 800R | 69 | 20.5 | 180.5 | 76.0 | 23.51 | U.S. | | 7.52.1 | | | | |
| 400M.R. | 68 | 20.9 | 179.0 | 74.5 | 23.50 | U.S. | | 3.58.4 | | | | |
| Spring D. | 23 | 22.8 | 170.2 | 65.6 | 23.73 | Sitzberger | USA | 159.90 | 19 | 177 | 70 | 23.3 |
| High D. | 31 | 23.2 | 169.8 | 66.4 | 23.90 | Webster | USA | 148.58 | 26 | 175 | 68 | 23.3 |

| Event | n | Age | Height | Weight | | Winner / Country | | Result | | | | |
|---|---|---|---|---|---|---|---|---|---|---|---|---|
| Water polo | 96 | 26.5 | 182.2 | 82.1 | 23.81 | Hungary | | | | | | |
| Basket ball | 186 | 25.3 | 189.4 | 84.3 | 23.16 | U.S.A. | | | | | | |
| Volley ball | 116 | 26.2 | 183.8 | 79.0 | 23.32 | U.R.S. | | | | | | |
| Soccer | 261 | 24.9 | 172.3 | 69.3 | 23.77 | Hungary | | | | | | |
| Hockey | 232 | 26.8 | 173.0 | 69.2 | 23.71 | India | | | | | | |
| Gymnastics | 122 | 26.0 | 167.2 | 63.3 | 23.86 | Japan | | 577.95 | | | | |
| Ind. | | | | | | Endo | JBN | 15.95 | 27 | 161 | 58 | 24.1 |
| | | | | | | Shakhlin | URS | 19.625 | 32 | 172 | 70 | 24.0 |
| | | | | | | Cerar | YUS | 19.525 | 25 | 172 | 71 | 24.1 |
| Canoeing | | | | | | | | | | | | |
| Kayak 1 | 15 | 27.4 | 178.1 | 75.8 | 23.75 | Peterson | SWE | 3.57.13 | 20 | 185 | 75 | 22.8 |
| 2 | 25 | 25.8 | 177.2 | 75.0 | 23.75 | Sweden | | 3.38.54 | | | | |
| 4 | 38 | 26.1 | 178.0 | 76.0 | 23.82 | U.R.S. | | 3.14.67 | | | | |
| Canadian 1 | 10 | 23.6 | 179.7 | 76.6 | 23.66 | Eschert | GER | 4.35.14 | 23 | 176 | 73 | 23.7 |
| 2 | 19 | 25.4 | 178.0 | 77.3 | 23.94 | U.R.S. | | 4.04.65 | | | | |
| Yachting | | | | | | | | | | | | |
| 5.5 M. | 42 | 30.9 | 178.0 | 78.6 | 24.10 | Australia | | 5981 | | | | |
| Dragon | 57 | 37.1 | 174.0 | 74.0 | 24.18 | Denmark | | 5854 | | | | |
| Star | 27 | 34.3 | 178.8 | 79.8 | 24.09 | Bahama | | 5664 | | | | |
| Finn | 29 | 30.1 | 178.5 | 79.6 | 24.10 | Germany | | 7638 | | | | |
| Flying D | 38 | 30.5 | 177.0 | 75.2 | 23.86 | New Zealand | | 6255 | | | | |
| Cycling | | | | | | | | | | | | |
| 1000 T.T. | 25 | 22.0 | 174.7 | 72.1 | 23.85 | Sercu | BEL | 1.09.59 | 20 | 180 | 76 | 23.6 |
| Scratch S. | 29 | 23.4 | 173.2 | 70.7 | 24.00 | Pettenella | ITA | | 21 | 178 | 73 | 23.5 |
| 2000 Tandem | 13 | 24.1 | 175.0 | 73.8 | 23.98 | Italy | | | | | | |
| Ind. Purs. R. | 76 | 24.4 | 175.3 | 68.3 | 23.40 | Daller | CZS | 5.04.75 | 24 | 184 | 82 | 23.7 |
| Road Race | 127 | 24.3 | 173.5 | 68.4 | 23.58 | Netherlands | | 2.26.31.19 | | | | |
| Ind. | | | | | | Zanin | ITA | 4.39.51.63 | 24 | 174 | 74 | 24.2 |
| Shooting | 256 | 32.6 | 172.5 | 73.5 | 24.28 | | | | | | | |
| Modern Pent. | 39 | 26.8 | 179.0 | 72.0 | 23.33 | | HUN | 5116 | 29 | | | |

# TABLE 4-3 Continued

## Male

| | | Average | | | | | Medalist | | | | | |
|---|---|---|---|---|---|---|---|---|---|---|---|---|
| | No. | Age | Height | Weight | F index | Name | Country | Record | Age | Height | Weight | F index |
| Equestrian sports...... | 131 | 30.3 | 173.0 | 67.0 | 23.49 | Menichelli | ITA | 19.450 | 24 | 162 | 60 | 24.2 |
| Weight lifting | | | | | | Hayata | JPN | 19.475 | 24 | 160 | 58 | 24.2 |
| Bantam............ | 29 | 27.2 | 157.0 | 56.4 | 24.50 | Endo | JPN | 19.675 | 27 | 161 | 58 | 24.1 |
| Feather........... | 21 | 28.5 | 160.7 | 60.3 | 24.49 | Yamashita | JPN | 19.600 | 26 | 165 | 60 | 23.8 |
| Light............. | 30 | 27.5 | 164.0 | 68.2 | 24.89 | Vakhonin | URS | 357.5 | 29 | 156 | 58 | 24.8 |
| Middle............ | 22 | 25.7 | 169.5 | 76.8 | 25.14 | Miyake | JPN | 397.5 | 25 | 154 | 60 | 25.5 |
| Light heavy....... | 21 | 27.2 | 171.0 | 82.0 | 25.52 | Baszanowski | POL | 432.5 | 29 | 165 | 67 | 24.7 |
| Middle heavy...... | 16 | 27.1 | 172.0 | 90.5 | 25.90 | Zdrazila | CZS | 445.0 | 23 | 169 | 75 | 25.0 |
| Heavy............. | 17 | 29.2 | 178.0 | 116.0 | 27.22 | Plyukfeider | URS | 175.0 | 36 | 172 | 83 | 25.4 |
| Wrestling (free) | | | | | | Golovanov | URS | 487.5 | 26 | 172 | 90 | 26.1 |
| Fly............... | 18 | 24.8 | 159.0 | 54.0 | 23.64 | Zhabotinsky | URS | 572.5 | 26 | 190 | 157 | 28.4 |
| Bantam............ | 18 | 25.9 | 164.0 | 58.5 | 23.69 | Yoshida | JPN | | 23 | 161 | 56 | 23.8 |
| Feather........... | 17 | 27.6 | 168.0 | 64.5 | 23.80 | Uetake | JPN | | 21 | 165 | 61 | 23.8 |
| Light............. | 20 | 25.0 | 171.0 | 71.0 | 24.30 | Watanabe | JPN | | 24 | 160 | 65 | 25.2 |
| Welter............ | 21 | 26.0 | 173.0 | 79.0 | 24.75 | Dimov | BUL | | 28 | 170 | 70 | 24.3 |
| Middle............ | 17 | 26.4 | 180.0 | 87.5 | 24.66 | Ogan | TUR | | 31 | 170 | 73 | 24.6 |
| Light heavy....... | 15 | 28.4 | 180.0 | 95.0 | 25.41 | Gardjev | BUL | | 28 | 175 | 87 | 25.3 |
| Heavy............. | 13 | 28.6 | 182.0 | 102.5 | 25.75 | Medved | URS | | 27 | 187 | 97 | 24.6 |
| Wrestling (Greco Roman) | | | | | | Ivanitsky | URS | | 24 | 189 | 106 | 25.1 |
| Fly............... | 13 | 27.3 | 158.0 | 53.0 | 23.76 | Hanahara | JPN | | 24 | 159.5 | 57 | 24.2 |

| | | | | | | Name | Country | | | | |
|---|---|---|---|---|---|---|---|---|---|---|---|
| Bantam | 11 | 25.8 | 162.0 | 60.0 | 24.25 | Ichiguchi | JPN | 24 | 162 | 62 | 24.5 |
| Feather | 18 | 28.7 | 164.5 | 64.5 | 24.28 | Polyak | HUN | 32 | 170 | 63 | 23.4 |
| Light | 14 | 26.7 | 170.0 | 70.0 | 24.15 | Ayvaz | TUR | 26 | 170 | 70 | 24.3 |
| Welter | 13 | 28.5 | 175.0 | 79.5 | 24.55 | Kolesov | URS | 26 | 174 | 80 | 24.8 |
| Middle | 14 | 26.9 | 179.5 | 86.1 | 24.55 | Simic | YUS | 29 | 180 | 87 | 24.7 |
| Light heavy | 13 | 27.5 | 182.5 | 96.0 | 25.20 | Alexandrov | BUL | 22 | 173 | 90 | 25.9 |
| Heavy | 9 | 26.8 | 189.0 | 115.0 | 25.94 | Kozma | HUN | 25 | 198 | 135 | 26.0 |
| Judo | | | | | | | | | | | |
| Light | 23 | 25.1 | 169.0 | 68.0 | 24.20 | Nakatani | JPN | 23 | 165 | 67 | 24.6 |
| Middle | 24 | 24.7 | 174.2 | 77.5 | 24.40 | Okano | JPN | 20 | 171 | 80 | 25.2 |
| Heavy | 11 | 26.9 | 182.0 | 94.2 | 25.08 | Inokuma | JPN | 26 | 196 | 87 | 25.6 |
| All weight | 7 | 27.8 | 187.0 | 104.5 | 25.25 | Gelsink | NLD | 30 | 173 | 120 | 25.2 |
| Boxing | | | | | | | | | | | |
| Fly | 20 | 21.9 | 161.5 | 51.0 | 22.98 | Atzor | ITA | 22 | 158 | 51 | 23.5 |
| Bantam | 35 | 22.0 | 163.5 | 54.0 | 23.10 | Sakurai | JPN | 23 | 164 | 54 | 23.1 |
| Feather | 27 | 22.0 | 166.5 | 56.5 | 23.23 | Stepashkin | URS | 21 | 157 | 51 | 23.6 |
| Light | 34 | 24.0 | 169.5 | 61.0 | 23.35 | Grudzien | POL | 25 | 168 | 60 | 23.3 |
| Light welter | 33 | 23.6 | 172.5 | 64.5 | 23.28 | Kulej | POL | 24 | 167 | 63 | 23.8 |
| Welter | 26 | 24.4 | 174.5 | 67.5 | 23.31 | Kaspezyk | POL | 25 | 168 | 67 | 24.2 |
| Light middle | 23 | 24.4 | 175.0 | 69.5 | 23.61 | Lagutin | URS | 26 | 180 | 71 | 23.1 |
| Middle | 17 | 25.4 | 177.0 | 74.5 | 23.77 | Popenchenko | URS | 27 | 176 | 75 | 24.0 |
| Light heavy | 18 | 27.5 | 181.0 | 81.0 | 23.94 | Pinto | ITA | 21 | 178 | 81 | 24.4 |
| Heavy | 13 | 25.2 | 186.5 | 87.5 | 23.82 | Frazier | USA | 20 | 180 | 89 | 24.9 |
| Fencing | | | | | | | | | | | |
| Foil group | 73 | 27.5 | 176.3 | 70.2 | 23.40 | U.R.S. | | | | | |
| Ind. | | | | | | Franke | POL | 29 | 176 | 68 | 23.3 |
| Epee group | 77 | 29.3 | 179.6 | 73.6 | 23.39 | Hungary | | | | | |
| Ind. | | | | | | Kriss | URS | 24 | 175 | 69 | 23.5 |
| Sabre group | 56 | 24.8 | 176.0 | 71.8 | 23.65 | U.R.S. | | | | | |
| Ind. | | | | | | Pezsa | HUN | 29 | 190 | 82 | 22.9 |
| Rowing | 357 | 25.0 | 186.0 | 82.2 | 23.60 | U.S. | | | | | |

Source: Kin-Itsu Hirata. Physique and age of Tokyo Olympic champions. Journal of Sports Medicine and Physical Fitness, 1966, 6, 207–222. Pp. 216–219.

selected basketball was his height, which was 6 feet, 7 inches. Beisser writes further:

> Similarly, one finds certain unique physical requirements in all sports. Thus, football players must be strong and rugged, with the ability to withstand hard physical contact. Linemen are generally bulky, while backfield men have to be more agile. In track, runners must be lean and shot-putters strong and hefty. But within most sports, fortunately, there is a place for athletes of all sizes and nearly all physical differences. We usually take particular notice of the athlete who does not seem to fit his sport, such as a 150-pound football player, a short basketball player, or a fat tennis player. With exceptions such as these, it can be assumed that the factors which determined the selection of a particular sport were more psychosocial than physical [p. 143].

## Differences between Races

The exceptional success of black athletes, especially in certain sports, has led to speculation on racial differences in anatomy, physiology, body composition, and abilities. Social psychologists have studied early play activities of black and white children, particularly as these experiences relate to socioeconomic level; it has been found that children in lower socioeconomic groups (into which category a large proportion of blacks fall) tend to show greater motor development and to be more active than their counterparts in higher socioeconomic groups. Some physiologists, anthropologists, and anatomists are interested in the possibility that racial differences in body build might help to explain why a racial group sometimes appears to be superior in a particular athletic event.

For example, swimming is notorious for its lack of black champions, and there is substantial evidence to indicate that whites have greater buoyancy than blacks. But there is an alternative explanation for the lack of outstanding black swimmers: the situation may have come into being because black children do not have access to swimming water, as a result of discrimination at beaches and pools or simply a lack of beaches and pools near their homes.

In track, basketball, football, boxing, and baseball, on the other hand, there are numerous outstanding black athletes. Is this due in part to body composition? One must always consider the influence of sociocultural factors, such as those mentioned above with regard to swimming. However, research does show that Negroes, in comparison to whites, have a greater specific gravity (less fatty deposit, hence poorer buoyancy), lower vital capacity, smaller skin folds, heavier and denser skeleton structures, and longer arms and legs. Physical characteristics, then, might account for a greater probability of success in some sports and a lesser probability in others.

In an experiment conducted by Burdeshaw (1968), it was found that Negro women have relative difficulty in learning to swim. Although the black subjects scored significantly higher than the white subjects in a test of motor ability, the whites were better in swimming performance and buoyancy. This seems to bear out the possibility of a physical explanation. Again, blacks may be expected to excel at power events on land. In a study of Olympic athletes, Tanner (1964) found that Negroes had longer arms and legs, denser and heavier bones, narrower hips, and slenderer calves than whites competing in the same track and field events. Black athletes were observed by Tanner to have a better power-to-weight ratio, and he offered this physical explanation for their success in power events, notably the sprints.

Ferguson (1967) tested 20 white varsity track athletes from Oklahoma State University and 20 black varsity track athletes from Langston University. He campared them in reaction time, movement time, and time in the 60-yard dash. The black athletes demonstrated faster reaction and movement times; but when these data were subjected to statistical analysis, they did not reveal significant differences between the black and white athletes. The black athletes did, however, have a significantly faster average time for the dash (.26 seconds).

Racial differences in success in various athletic events are, of course, due to numerous complex factors; body constitution may be one of them. A person with a particular body build is most apt to succeed in an athletic event where that type is usually successful. However, the contribution of such variables as personal motivation, socioeconomic status, opportunities, and sociocultural influence is not to be discounted. The coach should keep in mind that, regardless of color, each athlete has similar basic needs and drives, and each must be treated with respect. Furthermore, the coach should realize that each athlete must be evaluated as an individual, on the basis of his own performance. It would be a serious mistake for the coach to prejudge his athletes on a basis of statistical generalizations, since any particular athlete may or may not fall into the expected pattern. For practical purposes of selecting and training a team, then, it may probably safely be said that the coach would do well to disregard statistics concerning physical racial differences and base his decisions, instead, on his own experiences with his own athletes.

## PHYSICAL AND MOTOR MEASURES

Each sport makes different demands on the athlete, but certain fundamental attributes are necessary for reasonable achievement in a variety of activities. Some of the more important of these attributes are strength, endurance, flexibility, speed, accuracy, and coordination. These general qualities may be described more specifically, according to the movements in the tasks associated with particular sports.

Strength is needed to hit a golf ball for distance, to lift a weight, to throw a shot, to grab and hold on to a rebound in basketball, to strike a baseball with force, and to block a man in football. Endurance is associated with continual hitting of a golf ball or a baseball, with running, with repetitious jumping and lifting of weights, and in general, with repetitious practice over a period of time. The athlete must have enough strength and endurance to persist at practice, which is a prerequisite for acquisition of skill. Extra flexibility in some sports, i.e., of the wrist in golf (for example, Wiren, 1969), of the trunk in gymnastics, and of parts of the body in swimming, is associated with good performance.

"Speed" may refer to quickness of overall bodily movement over a short or long distance. It is also associated with specific parts of the body in a limited space. Furthermore, a speed component—commonly referred to as "reaction time"—is present before movement can be observed, in response to a stimulus event. Response speed may be self-initiated or may be elicited at the instigation of predictable or unpredictable stimuli in different athletic events. Accuracy is measured in terms of goals scored and targets hit. Speed and accuracy in movement are necessary components of many sport skills.

The most difficult term to explain is "coordination." Essentially, it has to do with effective usage of the musculature in performing sequential movements in predetermined spatial and temporal patterns. Coordination is thus reflected in many types of acts. The ability to organize and execute appropriate movement patterns is the essence of proficiency in activity. It is greatly dependent on the presence of the physical elements discussed already: strength, endurance, flexibility, speed, and accuracy. Naturally, the extent to which any of these or other factors influence a given performance will depend on the activity or skill to be performed.

For readers who are interested in a more sophisticated analysis of the dimensions underlying human performance, the efforts of Fleishman provide meaningful data. After extensive testing of thousands of subjects, he has isolated a relatively small number of abilities that account for performance in various laboratory tasks. He classifies them in two categories, physical proficiency and psychomotor:

| *Physical Proficiency*[1] | *Psychomotor Factors*[2] |
|---|---|
| Extent flexibility | Control precision |
| Dynamic flexibility | Multi-limb coordination |
| Static strength | Response orientation |
| Dynamic strength | Reaction time |
| Explosive strength | Speed of arm movement |
| Trunk strength | Rate control |
| Gross body coordination | Manual dexterity |
| Gross body equilibrium | Arm-hand steadiness |
| Stamina | Wrist-finger speed |
| | Aiming |
| | Finger dexterity |

It should be emphasized that the psychomotor factors established by Fleishman are the result of performance on laboratory tasks. The extent to which these factors underlie athletic performance has yet to be ascertained. Nevertheless, we may conjecture that the physical proficiency items are most associated with athletic events requiring primarily strength and endurance, with only a minimum of intricate, coordinated movement patterns. Psychomotor factors are probably more related to athletic skills that involve refined activity.

The number and nature of the variables underlying achievement in many sports or even within one sport awaits scientific documentation. In most cases, however, on the basis of observation and experience, we can make fairly good educated guesses about what these important abilities are.

## SENSORY FACTORS

In many activities, the appropriateness of a response is determined by its effectiveness. The mere act means little unless it is temporally and spatially timed to the onset of a stimulus. A beautiful swing of the bat is beautiful only if a productive output occurs. A jump shot is effective only when it can be made in a game as well as in practice. The basketball player quickly makes a decision in response to a momentary opening, and makes appropriate adjustments in his sensory inputs and perceptual interpretations

[1] E. A. Fleishman. *The structure and measurement of physical fitness.* Englewood Cliffs, N. J.: Prentice-Hall, 1964.

[2] E. A. Fleishman. Development of a behavior taxonomy for describing human tasks: a correlational-experimental approach. *Journal of Applied Psychology,* 1967, **51,** 1–9.

of the distance the shooter is from the basket, the distance the defensive man is from the shooter, the feel of the ball, and the equilibrium of the body while shooting.

Input, therefore, and having the best means of receiving input, will greatly determine the nature of the performer's output. Our receptacles for information about ourselves and the environment are common to all of us. The senses usually mentioned are vision, hearing, taste, equilibrium, proprioception, and touch. In the world of sport, taste plays no role in performance. Hearing, with the exception of responding to starting signals, is involved only slightly in athletic performance. That leaves the visual, equilibrium, proprioceptive, and tactile senses to play a critical role in acquisition of motor skills.

The impairment of any sense receptacle can lead to inappropriate body movements. Poor vision in a sport such as baseball causes inferior performance. In numerous cases on record, athletes in the sports in which vision plays a crucial role in determining output improved in performance when their visual problems were recognized and rectified. When infection or damage is present in the inner ear and body balance becomes disoriented, the execution of a wide assortment of tasks may be interfered with. Balance is one of the abilities displayed by the gymnast doing a routine, the basketball player shooting a hook and landing in a good position, the football back darting through the line and cutting in and out as he goes down a field, the bowler as he releases the ball, and the golfer as he follows through.

In addition, the sense of awareness of one's body parts in relation to his whole body is associated with achievement in motor tasks. The terms "kinesthesis" and "proprioception" refer to this sense. Many athletes are coached to "feel the act"; that is, they are encouraged to be aware of the changing positions of the body parts, and their relations to each other, as they progress through an intricate skill. At highly skilled levels, these acts become routine and seem to operate at a subconscious level, but for the learner, kinesthetic awareness can be an important facet of the learning process.

Some interesting data have been collected on the relative contributions of spatial orientation (visual sense) and kinesthesis at various stages of learning a motor task. Fleishman & Rich (1963) determined the relationships between spatial-visual ability and kinesthetic ability, on the one hand, and achievement in a motor task, on the other hand. Changes in the relative importance of these factors were noted with successive practice trials. Vision was much more important than kinesthetic sensitivity in the first few trials, but the two factors reversed in importance by the last few trials. The correlations, presented in Table 4-4, are not very high, and are therefore indicative of trends rather than highly meaningful relationships.

TABLE 4-4   Correlations of spatial and kinesthetic tests with successive trials of two-hand coordination task performance

| Two-hand coordination trial | Aerial orientation | Kinesthetic sensitivity |
|:---:|:---:|:---:|
| 1 | .36* | .03 |
| 2 | .28† | .19 |
| 3 | .22† | .15 |
| 4 | .19 | .15 |
| 5 | .08 | .10 |
| 6 | .07 | .09 |
| 7 | .09 | .23† |
| 8 | −.05 | .28† |
| 9 | −.02 | .38* |
| 10 | .01 | .40* |

\* $p < .01$.

† $p < .05$.

*Source:* Edwin A. Fleishman & Simon Rich. Role of kinesthetic and spatial-visual abilities in perceptual-motor learning. *Journal of Experimental Psychology,* 1963, **66,** 6–11. P. 8. Copyright 1963 by the American Psychological Association and reproduced by permission.

Closely related to the kinesthetic sense is the tactile sense. Changes in pressure on the skin need to be distinguished in a sport such as wrestling. Changes in offensive and defensive maneuvers have to be detected quickly in order for appropriate responses to be shown. Sensitivity to touch is associated also with the feel of a basketball while passing. The sense receptors responsible for detecting changes in pressure stimuli are closely related to those that are responsible for detecting changes in movement stimuli.

*Reaction Time*

In the sports world, movement times are daily referred to as being representative of reaction time, but in actuality, an athlete's "reaction time" is only the time it takes him to initiate a response to the onset of a stimulus. The "movement time" is the time from the actual beginning of a response to its conclusion. The batter's reaction time is the time that elapses between his first sight of the moving ball and the beginning of the swing. The sprinter's reaction time is the time between the sound of the gun and the initiation of body propulsion. Published event times in swimming and track, for example, actually include both reaction times and movement times.

Reaction time is so brief and so subtle that it can only be accurately measured in a laboratory, not in an athletic situation. Still, it is such an integral part of so many athletic tasks that it is often taken for granted. Reaction time studies are plentiful in the literature of psychology. Among the problems investigated have been sex and age differences; the effect of such variables as time of day, practice, fatigue, and motivation; and differences among various stimuli. (Reactions to auditory or tactile stimuli are usually found to be slightly faster than reactions to visual stimuli.)

A number of investigators have compared athletes with so-called "non-athletes," and the results are invariably the same: athletes have faster reaction times and limb movement times than nonathletes. Therefore, quick responses are associated with athletic success. In some sports, better performances are related to faster reaction times. The batter with a fast reaction time has more time to wait and study the pitched ball before he commits himself. Since reaction time is not usually benefited by practice, some people think that fast reaction time is primarily hereditary or "natural." A person with quick reactions, ideal body dimensions and characteristics, and various other abilities is naturally well suited for achievement in athletics.

Some interesting data have been collected by Cureton (1951) on the reaction times of various groups of champion athletes to different stimuli. Subjects for the study were the 1948 Danish gymnastic team, 1948 U.S. Olympic swimmers and divers, and U.S. track and field champions. It can be seen in Table 4-5 that the reactions of the groups were faster to stimuli in the following order: visual and auditory, auditory, and visual. The more information there is, the better the performance. The track and field athletes responded fastest, while the swimmers and divers were slowest of the three groups tested. Cureton points out, though, that the swimmers and divers were faster than a group of nonathletes.

TABLE 4-5    Average reaction time of groups of athletes to different stimuli

|  | | *Average reaction time* | | |
|  | *N* | *Visual* | *Auditory* | *Visual and auditory* |
|---|---|---|---|---|
| Danish gymnasts.................... | 15 | .320 | .286 | .281 |
| Track and field champions............ | 15 | .274 | .267 | .259 |
| Swimming and diving champions...... | 23 | .321 | .313 | .303 |

*Source:* Thomas K. Cureton. *Physical fitness of champion athletes,* Urbana, Ill.: University of Illinois Press, 1951. P. 101.

TABLE 4-6    Kinesthetic and visual reactions of various athletic groups

| Group | Kinesthetic reaction-time mean (ms) | Visual reaction-time mean (ms) |
|---|---|---|
| All groups | 145.89 | 200.47 |
| All athletes | 139.93 | 194.84 |
| Wrestlers | 130.12 | 188.28 |
| Baseball | 139.24 | 189.08 |
| Football | 139.48 | 197.32 |
| Basketball | 150.88 | 204.68 |
| Nonathletes | 157.62 | 211.72 |

*Source:* James J. Wilkinson. A study of reaction-time measures to a kinesthetic and a visual stimulus for selected groups of athletes and non-athletes. *Proceedings of the National College Physical Education Association for Men,* 1959, **62**, 158–161. P. 161.

Other reaction time data, with different athletic groups, have been reported by Wilkinson (1959). Equipment was constructed in a laboratory for measuring both kinesthetic reaction time and visual reaction time. The college subjects selected for the study were 50 nonathletes and 100 athletes (25 wrestlers, 25 football players, 25 basketball players, and 25 baseball players).

Keep in mind that a lower reaction time, as measured in hundredths of a second, demonstrates better performance. The data collected are tabulated for comparison purposes in Table 4-6. It can be seen that: (1) as is usually found, reaction time was shorter to a kinesthetic or tactile stimulus than to a visual stimulus for all groups; (2) the athletes performed faster than the nonathletes; (3) for both kinesthetic and visual reactions, the wrestlers displayed the best times. The basketball players and the nonathletes had significantly slower times than the other groups. In thinking of the repertoire of responses required in each sport, and the nature of the participants, perhaps it is not too surprising that the order of performances, from best to worst, was wrestlers, baseball players, football players, and basketball players.

Reaction time in certain track and swimming events is especially important. The time elapsed between the sound of the gun and the initiation of movement may determine the winner. The highly skilled performer depends upon various cues which facilitate concentration and decrease reaction time. In the case of the sprinter and the swimmer, the question is whether reaction time is faster when the athlete concentrates upon the sound of the gun or upon the movement to be made. Henry (1960) has compared reactions when subjects are under sensory sets (concentrating on the stimulus sound) with those obtained under motor sets (thinking of the appropriate movement). Most subjects had faster reaction and movement times when they concentrated upon the sensory set rather than the motor set. The implications of this research are that most athletes should focus primarily on the stimulus rather than the movement.

### Vision

Visual acuity, depth perception, color recognition, and peripheral vision are aspects of vision that influence athletic proficiency. Obviously, poor vision should be remedied with appropriate glasses or contact lenses. Athletes, especially those in activities which require excellent vision, should have thorough eye examinations regularly.

Even though peripheral vision, of all the aspects of vision, has been of most interest to coaches, very few studies on this topic appear in the literature. Generally speaking, the research bears out the premise that athletes have better depth perception than nonathletes. In many team and individual sports, athletes must be able to see players or projectiles at either side without turning their heads. Basketball, hockey, and soccer players have the most need for excellent peripheral vision. Outstanding athletes in these and other sports seem to have the knack of seeing objects and other athletes on either side of them without turning their heads. The athlete can develop this ability by practicing looking ahead while attempting to detect free teammates on either side to whom he can pass the ball. He must also see opponents as they approach from the rear and sides.

Stroup (1957) compared two groups of college students, one consisting of varsity basketball players and the other of nonathletes, in peripheral vision, and found that the basketball players had a wider field of vision than the nonathletes. In a study of high school students, Dembowski (1968) also found that basketball players have better peripheral vision than nonathletes. Figure 4-2 shows that the athletes displayed an average peripheral vision of

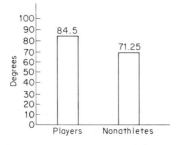

FIGURE 4-2   *Peripheral vision of basketball players as compared with nonathletes. (*Source: Michael Dembowski. A comparison of the peripheral vision of high school varsity basketball players and non-athletes.* Your* Challenge, Toledo* University, 1968,* **3**, *3–7. P. 5.)*

84.5 degrees and the nonathletes had an average peripheral vision of 71.25 degrees. Even basketball players with glasses had better peripheral vision than nonathletes with glasses.

Another evidence of the association of athletic greatness with superb peripheral vision is provided by John McPhee (1965). McPhee writes about Bill Bradley, the former outstanding Princeton basketball player who is presently playing professional ball with the New York Knickerbockers, that Bradley sees 195 degrees in the horizontal while looking straight ahead; usually, 180 degrees is considered perfection. Bradley sees 70 degrees straight down, more than 5 degrees past perfection. He also sees 70 degrees upward, whereas the average person can see only 47 degrees upward. McPhee writes that Bradley does have one weakness: he cannot see behind himself.

It is not surprising to find that athletes in the sports in which depth perception is an essential component do have good depth perception. Also, more skillful players show better depth perception than less skilled ones. The study by Graybiel, Jokl, and Trapp (1955) supports these statements: 30 tennis players had considerably better depth perception than 122 football players.

### Kinesthesis

Awareness of muscles, joints, and tendons and information about what occurs during movement is provided by the kinesthetic sense. We know that this sense is important in motor performance. No matter how it is tested, and there are many ways of testing it, in general people who demonstrate outstanding skill in motor activities seem to have a good kinesthetic sense.

But there is no one general kinesthetic sense. Kinesthesis is highly specific to the area of the body being tested and to the nature of the test. In many sport situations, movements are executed so quickly that kinesthetic feedback cannot occur. In fact, an attempt at conscious organization of the movements so as to take advantage of the kinesthetic sense can impede execution of a series of rapid movements. Nevertheless, the presence of the kinesthetic ability and kinesthetic sensitivity seems to be associated with motor skill. Perhaps this ability could be developed further with practice in sport skills in which it is desirable to heighten the feeling of movement. Such practice would involve paying deliberate attention to and concentrating on the parts of the body during the act.

### Equilibrium

Many of the statements made about kinesthesis are also true of balance. Indeed, tests of balance are often used as tests of kinesthesis. As with kinesthesis, there is no one general sense of balance. Balance is highly specific to the manner in which it is tested, and it can be tested in many ways.

When a person attempts to stand perfectly still without swaying, he is practicing static balance. More dynamic forms of balance are shown in walking on a narrow rail; standing on one foot without falling; maintaining a teeter-totter board in a horizontal position; hopping from object to object; and performing an assortment of athletic skills, finishing each in a correct position. Many factors contribute to variability in motor performance, but it seems logical to think that the sensitivity of body equilibrium may be one of the main factors.

Generally, people do not think about maintaining balance in most motor activities (the exception is in balancing stunts, as in gymnastics), but take the ability to balance for granted. In many motor tasks and in such skills as pitching a baseball, balance is a prime requisite for good control. Little wonder that balance plays such an important role in achievement.

Athletes have shown a tendency to score higher on balancing tests than nonathletes. For example, Singer (1970) tested seven different groups of male athletes, a group of female athletes, and a group of male nonathletes. The nonathletes performed least well on the stabilometer, an instrument used for measuring dynamic balance. The data from this study are shown in Figure 7-2. The athletic groups scored dissimilarly, and an explanation of this occurrence also appears in Chapter 7. Slater-Hammel (1956) found that varsity athletes perform significantly better on a balance test than either physical education majors or liberal arts majors.

If balancing ability is to be improved when it is needed in an athletic situation, it should be practiced in the kinds of tasks that closely simulate the situation. A stabilometer, which is essentially a teeter-totter board, provides the kind of balancing experience associated with water skiing and gymnastics. Hopping actions, such as those tested by the Bass Stepping-Stone Test, are similar to the cutting movements a football player makes. Naturally, any disturbances in the mechanisms of the semicircular canals, the cerebellum, the visual perception of motion, the proprioceptors in the muscles and joints, or other mechanisms involved in equilibrium will result in awkward movements. A medical examination can reveal whether balancing difficulties are due to medical problems.

## THE PERCEPTUAL MECHANISM

The senses are the means for receiving information, while the perceptual mechanism is the interpreter, or translator, of this input. The sense apparatus must be perceptive enough and functionally operational enough to receive the "true" signals, but the perceptual process must make sense, must organize the inflow of messages. During or after this activity, responses are initiated, terminated, or moderated.

Although we typically refer to athletic skills as "physical" or "motor" skills, in reality nothing could be further from the truth. The batter does not merely physically swing at the ball; he perceives its speed, its accuracy, and the nature of its flight before deciding whether to swing. The quarterback perceives the distance the end is from him and the relative positions of the defensive linemen and backs, and then throws the ball to the point where it will be caught. The golfer must judge the distance to the hole, the nature of the wind currents, the lie of the ball, and the potential roll of the ball, and must swing with such considerations in mind. How the athlete perceives the situation greatly determines his behavior.

Many psychological and neurophysiological theories have been advanced to explain the perceptual process. Various aspects of perception have been examined intensively by different researchers. In order to understand how and what someone perceives, consideration must be given to his past experiences, present expectancies, personality, motivation, and a host of other factors. It is evident that since these dimensions vary from person to person, perceptions of the same situation by different people will also vary. Selective attention and figural aftereffects are two of the more interesting perceptual phenomena associated with sport.

### Selective Attention

If we stop to think about it, we quickly realize that at any given moment many environmental stimuli are impinging upon our systems. Fortunately, we do not react to all of them. If we did, we would be in a constant state of hyperactivity, most of it meaningless. In the athletic situation, the same circumstances exist. Many stimuli are present that can be potentially reacted to, but acquisition of skill is associated with the process termed "selective attention."

The perceptual mechanism acts as a filter system. When the human organism receives a number of cues simultaneously, it processes them in order of importance. A novice usually overresponds; his perceptual process is not selective enough. With experience and skill, he learns to detect and identify the stimuli most important and most revelant to successful performance. Not only does the superior athlete block out unnecessary cues and attend to the important ones, he can handle a number of the relevant ones almost simultaneously.

The basketball player is a good example. While dribbling the ball to the basket, he alternates his attention from control of the ball, to awareness of near opponents and teammates, to the basket, to the possible shot. His accurate perception of the entire situation leads to the correct response for that circumstance. If he decides to shoot, he must concentrate on the target. At this point, he selectively disregards inappropriate stimuli; attends to the most important stimuli, the ball and the basket; and shoots.

The coach's role, a necessary one, is to guide the perceptual process of the athlete. On one hand, the variety of important cues that appear in a given situation should be stressed. The athlete must learn to sense the possible combinations of events that can occur at one time, and must then develop the motor acts necessary for skilled execution. He must also develop the ability to make decisions immediately and with desirable consequences.

Once a decision is made, the athlete's concentration for the moment must be applied to that activity. Not that the superb athlete thinks through the act as he does it; not at all. His response is so well learned that it unfolds as if automatic and at a subconscious level. However, the quarterback must begin to concentrate on the receiver the moment he has decided to throw the football to him. The basketball player must concentrate on the rim of the basket as he shoots. For that moment, other stimulus cues are disregarded. Coaching and personal experience hasten the selective attention process.

### Kinesthetic Aftereffects

The psychological benefits derived from following a set routine before performance are difficult to distinguish from the actual physical benefits. Eating a particular pregame meal that may contain no nutrients known to be especially valuable to athletic achievement may still result in outstanding athletic performance. The athlete probably performs better because he *thinks* he will perform better, because he believes the particular meal helps to increase his output.

The practice of swinging a weighted bat before hitting is common in baseball. Can the batter really swing the regulation bat faster as a result of this ritual, or does he merely think he can? The use of weighted shoes to improve jumping and running and weighted balls to improve throwing are other examples.

In psychological research, aftereffects have been observed under a number of conditions. After one sees and concentrates on a curved line, a straight line appears to curve the other way. Prolonged satiation with a stimulus results in perceptual distortion. Aftereffects have been produced in the visual, auditory, and kinesthetic senses. A regulation bat *seems* lighter (kinesthetic aftereffect) after swinging a heavier bat. The little research that has been done is inconclusive about the value of this procedure in increasing bat swing. The impression of greater speed may be illusory.

The residual effects of the satiation are greatest immediately following the experience. If preperformance conditions produce perceptual distortions, it should be determined whether such altered judgments are good or bad for the performance. Evidently, kinesthetic perception in tasks can be easily distorted by engaging in certain previous tasks. The kinesthetic after-effect of weighted practice creates the impression of extra speed or strength in the performance that follows. It may indeed produce stronger or quicker movements, it may have no effect, or it may create new learning problems that would lead to the conclusion that such practice is undesirable.

## INTELLECTUAL ATTRIBUTES

At one time, the term "intelligence" was mainly associated with the IQ score. The realization of intelligence potential was measured by grades received in academic classes. With increasing knowledge and a broader perspective on the human organism, however, we have come to realize that there are many types of "mental" intelligence and that there are also other forms of intelligence. Some kinds of intelligence are demonstrated in creative and abstract thinking, in remembering, in problem solving, in rote learning, and in forming judgments. Intellectual, or cognitive, behaviors are demonstrated in the classroom, and in the traditional concept of intelligence, academic grades constitute intellectual attainment. In research, where an attempt has been made to correlate various human characteristics, intelligence is usually represented by academic grades or IQ. It could be very well argued however, that there are also a social intelligence, a motor intelligence, and a mechanical intelligence. None of the forms of intelligence are necessarily related to each other.

There is a very large body of literature on the relationships of various human dimensions. There are discrepant results, many concepts, and, in general, much speculation. Let us examine some of the issues.

### Intelligence, Motor Performance, and Physical Characteristics

The extent to which human abilities and physical characteristics are interrelated is of practical and theoretical concern. Throughout history, some leading philosophers and psychologists have emphasized a division between mind and body, and others have emphasized the unity of mind and body. There are probably few people today who would attempt to claim that mind and body are separate, and yet, the degree to which cognitive, affective, and motor abilities and physical characteristics interrelate within a human being has not been ascertained.

Questions often asked by interested scholars and laymen alike include:

Does the child who has high intellectual abilities also have superior motor abilities? Is a person's size, i.e., height, weight, or body build, related to intelligence factors or to athletic skills? If a person displays superior skill in one type of task, will he be likely to do the same with other tasks? And, finally, will performance in certain types of perceptual-motor tasks correlate better than others with academic achievement?

There are diverse viewpoints on the relationship between maturational and achievement variables. At one extreme are psychologists such as Olson (1959) who support the organismic approach. This theory proposes a coherence of all aspects of a child's growth patterns. Studies in which Olson has been involved show remarkably high correlations among various factors. The child's organismic age, as proposed by Olson, consists of the average of seven variables: height, weight, grip strength, reading age, carpal age, mental age, and dental age. His data indicate that increments in growth in all these are essentially the same, and that physical and mental growth rates yield similar patterns.

Other psychologists have been critical of this assumption, and have charged that there is too much individuality in growth patterns and that the various ages are too independent for the organismic concept to be true. Experimentally, many researchers have found little relationship between physical development and academic achievement. Perhaps the difficulty lies in the attempt to relate purely physical characteristics to intellectual success. There have been some recent contentions that tasks which require motor coordination and high degrees of perceptual and cognitive involvement are more highly related to academic achievement. Some researchers have obtained apparent success in utilizing coordination and balance tasks as predictors of the intellectual achievement of preadolescent children.

The interrelationship of perceptual-motor and intellectual variables appears to be most evident in children of preschool age. Tests of abilities indicate that achievement is more specific in older children. That is to say, individual abilities are more closely related in infants than in adults. Maturation is associated with an organizing and a differentiating process, and what people become interested in, learn, and practice causes differences in ability in assorted skills.

There has been too much research to cite it here, but the indication is that there are positive but low relationships between intellectual and motor abilities. Bright children, in the genius category, are generally taller and heavier than average children, and retarded children are usually smaller in stature and poorer in motor skills than normal children. College or high school subjects have been utilized in most investigations in which intelligence was compared with motor ability, and distinctions on intelligence tests are smaller with such subjects than when an entire population is used.

In the "normal" population there is little justification for expecting a relationship between intelligence factors and physical characteristics (height, weight, strength, and the like). The typical athlete is in the so-called "normal" range of intelligence. Although his athletic skills are superior, there is no reason to expect that his other personal attributes will be better or poorer than normal.

## *Athletes and Academic Achievement*

Anyone even remotely connected with sports realizes that the athlete's commitment is deep. He devotes a large amount of time and energy to practice and other matters associated with his sport. Since many of these hours could have been spent studying, there is little wonder that the academic achievement records of athletes are sometimes questioned. Many people expect the athlete's scholastic record to be lower than the nonathlete's, and others believe that the athlete possesses inferior intellectual potential. The research does not support either claim.

Some evidence supports the idea that the scholarship attainment of athletes is lower, but the majority of research projects indicate little academic difference between the groups, and there are even indications that athletes make better grades than nonathletes. It should be pointed out here that investigators have usually taken isolated groups of subjects; have differed in their interpretations of "athlete," "nonathlete," "academic performance," and "intelligence"; and in general have not taken account of many variables that might have influenced their results. Such limitations in the research confuse and confound the issue.

Some of the more recent studies, however, have shown a greater sensitivity to these problems. Winter (1968) paired 39 junior high school athletes with 39 nonathletes as closely as possible on the basis of school, course selection, intelligence, social and economic backgrounds, somatotype, height, and weight. Academic achievement, as measured by academic grade averages, was compared between and within the groups during two semesters. No significant differences in grade averages were found between the groups during either semester or within either group between the two semesters of the study. Participation in athletics, it was concluded, did not affect academic performance.

The matched-pair technique was also employed by Klingbeil (1967); 222 college freshman athletes were paired with college freshman nonathletes from the University of Wisconsin in composite score in the American College Testing Program Examination (ACT), high school rank, and the particular school or college of the University in which the student initially registered. The academic potential of the two groups was measured by a few tests and was determined to be comparable. No difference in academic scholarship was found between grant-in-aid athletes and nonathletes, though when the athletes were studied further, the academic achievement and qualifications of different sport groups were found to vary.

The results of a recent investigation, initiated by two University of Oregon sociologists, indicate that participation in sports has a positive effect on academic achievement. Schafer & Armer (1968) claim that many negative beliefs about sports are unfounded and unjustified. They write, "Not only does participation in sports generally seem to have little or no effect on a student's scholarship, but it seems to actually *help* certain students academically—especially those students from the poor and disadvantaged groups that usually have the most trouble in school" (p. 21). Schafer & Armer examined the high school records of boys from two unidentified midwestern high schools for three years. Of the 585 boys studied, 164 were athletes, and these were matched with 164 nonathletes. Many variables were considered, and some of the findings are as follows:

1  Athletes obtain better grades than nonathletes. The students were divided into subgroup classifications according to such criteria as high and low IQ, college-bound and work-bound, high achievers and low achievers, and white-collar families and blue-collar families. More than half the athletes in each category exceeded their matches in grade point averages. If anything, the gap is greatest between athletes and their matches in the "lower" categories. The authors write, "The boys who would usually have the most trouble in school are precisely the ones who seem to benefit most from taking part in sports" (p. 25).

2  More participation in sports is related to better scholastic success. Fifty-two percent of the less active athletes received higher grades than their nonathlete counterparts, but 60 percent of the more active athletes exceeded their matches.

3  Participation in sports keeps boys in school. More athletes than nonathletes expected to go to college, and almost five times as many nonathletes dropped out of school before graduating. Schafer & Armer conclude, "Athletics fosters rather than interferes with the educational goal of sending a maximum number of youth to college" (p. 61).

There are many reasons why the athlete's academic performance may be as good as, if not better than, that of the nonathlete, in spite of the energies and time he spends on athletics. The individual athlete may have a high motivational level, a strong need to achieve. Second, he may make better use of his time. Third, it is possible that athletes are graded more leniently.

Fourth, the necessity to stay eligible for athletic competition may elicit a greater concern about grades. Fifth, the special attention and encouragement athletes receive from coaches, guidance counselors, and others, might make the difference. Finally, the possibility of deriving future benefit from athletics, playing on college or professional teams, may be a motivation. No matter what the reasons, the important thing is that athletes do well in school.

## EMOTIONS

Everyone constantly experiences familiar situations and new ones. The environmental stimuli place a person in a state of arousal; his homeostasis is disturbed. Emotions, as a consequence or in anticipation of experiences, are accompanied by internal chemical and physiological changes and sometimes by outward behavior. Many emotions are hereditary; others are learned. Such terms as "stress," "anxiety," and "tension" are used to represent emotional states. There are distinct differences in the patterns of responses invoked by each such state, as well as a good deal of overlap, but we need not be too concerned with technicalities in this book. Since emotions have such a strong effect on human behavior, what will serve our purpose best is to understand how emotional stress affects performance.

The skills, or mechanical aspects, of a sport are practiced over and over, but in competition, skills are subject to outside influences. The athlete works under conditions that are highly stressful, and the extent to which he can be stimulated and yet remain in control of his movements will determine his output.

In determining the level of tension for each endeavor which will produce optimal results, consideration must be given to the anxiety level that the athlete normally operates under and also to the nature of the task. An extremely aroused state serves more productive ends in relatively uncomplicated skills, involving primarily strength and endurance. In more refined activity, when the body needs to be under control at all times, a moderately aroused state is needed. Competition in athletics makes unusual demands on an athlete's resources. Little wonder that the highly proficient athlete is one who demonstrates not only superb skills but also emotional control under all sorts of circumstances. In fact, his skill reflects his emotional behavior in part.

Rarely if ever is a person not emotionally involved to some extent in any activity which he performs, and since people are unique, they are affected differently in similar situations. Nevertheless, general conclusive statements are emerging from the research that indicate expectations when certain factors are present. After reviewing these problematical areas, we will turn to particular aspects of sport in which the coach may need to be sensitive to the emotional disturbances of athletes in relation to competition, and may need to be aware of possible remedies.

### General Considerations

The skill level of the athlete has an important effect on the relationship between emotion and the acquisition of skill. In general, it appears that stress hinders the early learning process but does not interfere with or may be beneficial in the later stages of skill development. The implication is that athletes learning skills for the first time should learn them under relatively stress-free conditions for more productive results, but that, as learning progresses, stress may help to improve performance.

The nature of the learner, and more particularly, his anxiety level, is also important in determining how much stress should be present in the learning situation. The complexity of the task and the anxiety level of the person interact to produce interesting performance expectancies. With a complex task (the kind athletes usually have to learn), the expectation would be that highly anxious people would tend to perform less well under stress than less anxious people. This phenomenon has been observed by a number of researchers. In Carron's study (1968) the less anxious group performed better on a stabilometer under stress than the highly anxious group early in the learning stages.

The implications are that the coach should determine the anxiety levels of his athletes. The Taylor Manifest Anxiety Scale (MAS) is typically used in research. It is easily administered, quickly completed, and easily scored. In competition, athletes who score extremely high or low in anxiety should be placed in situations which will allow them to perform the types of skills best suited to their temperament. Anxiety-level data can also help the coach to have a better understanding of the learning and performance problems of certain athletes.

A third consideration is the optimal level of emotions in a given situation. Too much stress reduces the athlete's perceptual efficiency. Naturally, when the perceptual mechanism is continually operating, as in team sports, the extent of the stress should not be so great that behavior becomes disorganized. A low level of anxiety, however, can serve as a general alerting mechanism, allowing the athlete to distinguish environmental cues more effectively; his attention increases and his performance is improved.

Finally, disruptive emotions may impair or improve performance. In other words, the athlete's performance may be better or worse than usual because of an emotional disturbance. Another possibility is that facilitating and disrupting motivational and emotional reactions may balance out and produce no observable effect upon performance.

## Competition Considerations

The athlete's emotional state before competition may very well determine his performance level. Many athletes report concern before the contest; such worry is natural but serves no constructive purpose. Too much worry results in anxiety or fear, and the outcome is certain to be harmful to athletic productivity. As mentioned before, however, a certain amount of anxiety acts to prepare the athlete for competition.

A study completed by Lampman (1967) supports the value of a slight rise in anxiety before competition. Members of the University of Florida varsity swimming team were given an anxiety test before the season and another approximately an hour before competition. It was concluded that a rise in anxiety before competition improved performance, and that performance was better if the athlete's premeet anxiety level was at least equal to or slightly above his preseason anxiety level.

The coach is naturally concerned about "getting the team up" for a contest. Many variables, including the importance of the contest and the pep talk given by the coach, can affect the different levels of emotion experienced by the athletes before the contest. When and how to start building a team up for a contest are difficult questions to answer, especially because people respond differently to a particular motivational technique. The inspirational type of speech is fine for those who need to be pushed, but sensitive athletes who are already operating at a high level of emotion may require a different approach, perhaps even a sedative type of talk by the coach. The best suggestion that can be made to the coach is to take a general approach in addressing the team, one that he feels suits the situation. Athletes whose emotional tendencies are different from those of the team should be confronted by the coach on an individual basis. Not everyone should be handled alike, nor should every similar situation be approached in the same way. The same consideration should be given to half-time pep talks, in those sports where half-times exist.

The highly skilled person is of course less affected by emotionally arousing stimuli than the person of average skill. Previous experiences in similar situations have "conditioned" the outstanding athlete, and his well-learned skills are unlikely to be disrupted in stressful situations. Therefore, pep talks and other similar coaching techniques are usually of minimal value for exceptional athletes. They probably know how to "get themselves up" for the contest, which is one of the reasons why they are labeled "superior."

Thus far we have treated aspects of the pre-event situation. What of the coach's approach in the beginning of a season? Postman & Bruner (1948) report an experiment in which subjects were confronted with a completely hopeless task. As a result, they displayed frustrated behavior, did not appear to benefit from previous experiences, and constantly gave incorrect responses. The analogy is that if the season appears to be hopeless to the coach and the athletes, losing will be encouraged. A winning attitude should prevail, for a defeatist attitude will logically end in defeat. The same holds true before any contest. The prospect of winning should always be presented in a realistic manner, in order to encourage the athletes to have a desirable psychological "set."

During the contest, the nature of the tasks should reflect the amount of tension an athlete expresses. Throwing a projectile for distance or running a race demands the mustering of a large amount of emotional resources. Shooting a foul shot, hitting a golf ball, or bowling requires low-keyed emotional states. The nature of the event dictates the desirable emotional operating level of the athlete.

Indirectly, the results of Vizard's thesis (1967) indicate how much resistance to stress skilled athletes possess. Success in the first attempt of the one-and-one basketball foul shot was compared with success in the first attempt of the two-shot free throw. Data from a high school tournament and a college tournament were analyzed. No differences in first-shot comparisons were noted under either free-throw condition, nor were there differences between high school and college athletes. Further analyses of foul-shooting success were made, comparing differences in score between two teams for a given half of a basketball game and relating this to the success in shooting. (That is, was the shooting better when the score was close or when one team was farther ahead?) However, the findings were difficult to interpret because of the presence of other variables.

The best preparation for a stress is experience with that particular stress, as research indicates that resistance to stress is not a generalized quality. The stress associated with the contest and the spectators is best minimized by continued experience. Athletes should have opportunities to perform in contests as often as possible so that they may reach a somewhat stress-resistant state.

After a contest, various emotions are displayed, depending on the athlete's personality, on what happened during competition, and on the outcome of the contest. The coach has more to do after defeat or poor personal performance than after victory. His approach to the athletes after a disappointment is extremely important in their adjustment process. Once again, as was the case with the pre-event approach, he may give general talks to the team and may also talk with individual athletes on a personal basis.

## STALENESS

For lack of a better term, "staleness" is used to describe the state an athlete sometimes finds himself in after a long and intensive training program. His skills do not develop, and they may even appear to deteriorate. He feels depressed, tired, and frustrated. Staleness due to overtraining is not unusual.

The batter goes into a slump and does not reach base safely in a number of consecutive turns at bat. Why? This phenomenon is difficult to explain, and yet it does occur. Some batters are able to overcome the situation by staying in the lineup; others have to be benched. The high-level pressure of the activity and the prolonged intensity of the practice sessions may contribute to a breakdown of response patterns. Rest and a change in activity schedules may bring about improvement.

The coach should be on the lookout for the athlete who is working himself to a point of diminishing returns. The zealous and highly motivated athlete is an asset to the team, but by overpracticing and overtraining, he may do himself and the team more harm than good. The athlete needs to be paced and even rested if necessary. Fortunately, staleness is a reversible process for most athletes, and the recovery rate is extremely high.

## EXPRESSION

Athletes become involved in sports for varied reasons, each of which has certain values and meets particular needs. One of two fundamental instincts, according to Freud, is the urge to be aggressive. In the emotionally healthy person, aggressive tendencies are sublimated and channeled into socially acceptable directions. Competitive sports appears to be an ideal avenue for expressing aggressive feelings.

According to some psychiatrists, sport can relieve natural hostilities and aggressiveness. Presumably, anxiety is decreased and tension is lessened as a result of participation in sports. Although these claims are difficult to substantiate objectively, sport does seem to have value as an outlet for athletes and spectators. Learning to control aggressive tendencies in sports competition can transfer over to situations in daily life.

Thus, with regard to aggression, the athlete's conceivable personal gains from athletic competition are twofold. On the one hand, athletics provides a means of expressing aggressive tendencies in a controlled and acceptable way, and on the other hand, sport can teach the athlete ways of coping with other situations that arouse his aggressive tendencies.

## FORM

Because of unique differences in personality and body type, people express themselves in unlike ways. In the learning of athletic skills, standards or guiding principles have been developed for ideal execution, which are based on kinesiological, anatomical, physiological, psychological, and mechanical evidence as well as common sense. Yet, many times athletes are told to conform to one standard or "ideal" technique in their practice of a given skill without consideration to their physiological and anatomical limitations and differences.

Trying to make everyone conform to one technique is an error in judgment. To have athletes strive to use an "ideal" way of executing tasks and to understand the processes involved is more desirable. Each person must adapt and adjust his means of skill execution according to the limitations of his body framework. Furthermore, one's emotional temperament and other aspects of his personality are reflected in his performance. Past experiences will promote or hinder the learning of a skill.

By observing and critically analyzing the form of outstanding athletes, we can determine certain points that should be emphasized during performance of an act. There may be observable dissimilarities in the performance of champions, and usually some movements are irrelevant to the purpose of the task, though the more important features of the act are fairly consistent from athlete to athlete. The coach should be aware of these major elements in the performance of a skill, and should encourage their development during practice. Modifications must be allowed where necessary, however; many attributes contribute to skilled performance, and an athlete can succeed even if his form does not emulate that of a superior athlete.

One of the hazards of professional sports is the impact the athletes have on younger, would-be athletes attempting to master skills. Young athletes do not possess the motor abilities or physical characteristics of professional athletes, and imitation, if carried too far, can be a source of frustration. On the other hand, the superior athlete serves as a model and provides the aspirant with ideas and techniques. A reasonable attempt at copying performance, with modifications according to the young person's abilities, will have rewarding and beneficial outcomes.

One final word might be offered on the athlete's style of performance. Some express themselves in such a way that they are considered "showboats," and others are quite reserved in their behavior. The coach's responsibility is to determine what harm or good can come of extreme expressiveness. The effects on the athlete, team, fans, and other concerned groups must be considered. The actions of the athletes, in skill execution and general behavior, often reflect the guidance of the coach.

SUMMARY

Every person possesses certain qualities and characteristics that set him apart from others. In Chapter 3, it was shown how personality is reflected in one's unique way of behaving. In this chapter, many personal features have been referred to that not only contribute to individual differences but also help to describe the superior athlete. A number of the personal factors described are primarily determined by hereditary factors; others are most influenced by environmental experiences. Regardless, certain personal assets of the athlete can prepare him to meet training regimens and competition with a greater probability of success. This is certainly the case with body build, for it has been found that certain body types are well suited for particular activities. They increase the probability of success, but are not necessary conditions.

*Differences in body build and sport*   Anthropometric techniques have led to the distinguishing of the "average" athlete in a given sport and even in a particular event or position in that sport. There are a number of exceptions to the rule, however.

*Physical and motor measures*   Certain degrees of such qualities and abilities as strength, endurance, flexibility, speed, accuracy, and coordination need to be present for athletic achievement. Such factors are usually not generalized but rather are developed in relation to the specific movements of the tasks associated with a particular sport.

Output mechanisms are important, but sources of input reception need to be considered as well. The receptacles of information, the senses, should be in good working order. Poor sense apparatus can lead to incorrect perception and inadequate performance.

*Reaction time*   Faster reactions are associated with athletes than with nonathletes. Quickness in initiating a response is invaluable in a number of sports situations.

*Vision*   Athletes typically have better peripheral vision than nonathletes, and athletes engaging in sports in which greater depth perception is needed display even better peripheral vision than the usual athlete.

*Kinesthesis*   Athletes generally also possess a keener kinesthetic sense than nonathletes, no matter how it is measured. But there is no one general kinesthetic sense.

*Equilibrium*   Balance, too, is not a general ability. There are many forms of balance skill, but athletes' balance is usually superior to that of nonathletes.

The senses provide the means of receiving information, and the perceptual mechanism is the source of interpretation. In many sport situations, the perceptual process operates at rapid speed and is, in a sense, responsible for the consequent actions. How and what is perceived usually reflects a certain type of behavior on the part of the individual. Of the many interesting aspects of the perceptual process, only two were discussed in this chapter.

*Selective attention*    The superior athlete disregards unimportant stimuli and attends to the relevant ones in performing his skills.

*Kinesthetic aftereffects*    Prolonged satiation with a certain stimulus results in a perceptual distortion; for example, swinging a heavier bat makes a lighter one seem to move faster. The merits of deliberately causing such an illusion in sport have yet to be determined.

Intelligence has been the subject of much study and still has not been adequately defined. Nevertheless, determining the intellectual and academic status of athletically gifted students can be helpful.

*Intelligence, motor performance, and physical characteristics*    When correlated, these factors generally yield positive but low relationships in the "normal" population.

*Athletics and academic achievement*    The academic performance of athletes is usually found to be equal to or better than that of nonathletic students.

Skills demonstrated in competition reflect perfection in mechanical execution and also an ability to control one's emotions to a desirable degree. Stress, tension, and anxiety are emotions usually associated with sports situations. The outstanding athlete can use his emotions as they interact with stressful competitive conditions to elicit excellence in performance.

*General emotional considerations*    In the learning of a skill, stress is generally a hindrance during the early stages, but at later stages, it does not hinder or may facilitate performance. A highly anxious person usually has more difficulty learning a complex task than a less anxious person. There is an optimal level of emotions for any given situation.

*Competitive emotional considerations*    A slight upward trend in anxiety before competition is beneficial to performance. In attempting to motivate the team, the coach should consider individual differences in temperament. A highly skilled person is little affected by emotionally arousing stimuli. The coach should encourage a winning attitude to prevail, for the expectation of ultimate loss will probably result in frustrated behavior and losing. During a contest, the nature of the tasks should reflect the amount of tension an athlete expresses. The best preparation for a stress such as the presence of spectators is experience with that particular stress, for resistance to stress is not a generalized quality.

*Staleness*    Poor performance due to overpractice, overtraining, and too much tension can usually be remedied by a rest or a change of pace.

*Expression*    Sometimes the athlete's tendency to be aggressive can be relieved and controlled by participation in competitive sports.

*Form*    Although there is a "standard" form for executing most acts, the athlete should perform in a manner that is consistent with his physiological and anatomical limitations. Not all athletes should be expected to perform in the same manner.

REFERENCES

Beisser, Arnold R. *The madness in sports.* New York: Appleton-Century-Crofts, 1967.

Burdeshaw, Dorothy. Acquisition of elementary swimming skills by Negro and white college women. *Research Quarterly,* 1968, **39**, 872–879.

Carron, Albert V. Motor performance under stress. *Research Quarterly,* 1968, **39**, 463–468.

Carter, J. E. Lindsay. Somatotypes of college football players. *Research Quarterly,* 1968, **39**, 476–481.

Carter, J. E. Lindsay. Somatotype characteristics of champion athletes. Paper presented at the Anthropological Congress, Praha-Humpolec, Czechoslovakia, 1969.

Cureton, Thomas K. *Physical fitness of champion athletes.* Urbana, Ill.: University of Illinois Press, 1951.

Ferguson, Don P. Racial comparisons and relationships of reaction time, body movement time, and sixty yard dash performance. Unpublished master's thesis, Oklahoma State University, 1967.

Graybiel, A., Jokl, E., & Trapp, C. Russian studies of vision in relation to physical activity and sports. *Research Quarterly,* 1955, **26**, 480–485.

Henry, Franklin M. Influence of motor and sensory sets on reaction latency and speed of discrete movements. *Research Quarterly,* 1960, **31**, 459–468.

Hirata, Kin-Itsu. Physique and age of Olympic champions. *Journal of Sports Medicine and Physical Fitness,* 1966, **6**, 207–222.

Klingbeil, Jerrold L. Athletic participation and the academic success of college freshmen. Unpublished master's thesis, University of Wisconsin, 1967.

Kroll, Walter. An anthropometrical study of some Big Ten varsity wrestlers. *Research Quarterly,* 1954, **25**, 307–312.

Lampman, James Joseph. Anxiety and its effect on the performance of competitive swimmers. Unpublished master's thesis, University of Florida, 1967.

McPhee, John. *A sense of where you are.* New York: Farrar, Straus & Giroux, 1965.

Olson, Willard C. *Child development.* Boston: Heath, 1959.

Postman, Leo, & Bruner, Jerome S. Perception under stress. *Psychological Review,* 1948, **55**, 315–323.

Schafer, Walter E., & Armer, J. Michael. Athletes are not inferior students. *Trans-Action,* 1968, **6**, 21–26, 61, 62.

Singer, Robert N. Balance skill as related to athletics, sex, height, and weight. In G. Kenyon (Ed.), *Contemporary psychology of sport: Proceedings of the 2d*

*International Congress of Sport Psychology.* Chicago: The Athletic Institute, 1970. Pp. 645–656.

Slater-Hammel, A. T. Performance of selected groups of male students on the Reynolds' Balance Test. *Research Quarterly*, 1956, **26**, 347–351.

Stroup, Francis. Relation of playing ability to peripheral vision. *Research Quarterly*, 1957, **28**, 72–76.

Tanner, J. M. Physique, body composition and growth. In Jokl, E. & Simon, E. (Eds.), *International research in sport and physical education.* Springfield, Ill.: Charles C Thomas, 1964. (a)

Tanner, J. M. *The physique of the Olympic athlete.* London: G. Allen, 1964. (b)

Vizard, Thomas C. The effects of increased emotional pressure on foul-shooting performance in college and high school basketball tournaments. Unpublished master's thesis, University of Massachusetts, 1967.

Wilkinson, James J. A study of reaction-time measures to a kinesthetic and a visual stimulus for selected groups of athletes and non-athletes. *Proceedings of the National College Physical Education Association for Men*, 1959, **62**, 158–161.

Winter, Robert B. A comparative study of the academic achievement of junior high school athletes and non-athletes. Unpublished master's thesis, Pennsylvania State University, 1968.

Wiren, Gary. Human factors influencing the golf drive for distance. Paper presented at the annual convention of the American Association for Health, Physical Education, and Recreation, Boston, Mass., 1969.

# CHAPTER FIVE

# Social Factors and the Athlete

Athletics typically demands competition and cooperation among participants. Rarely, if ever, is the athlete completely alone and independent. He is part of a group or team, and he must conform to certain policies and adjust to the personalities of teammates and coaches. At the same time, he attempts to maintain a degree of individuality and independence which will help him to be more proficient than other performers.

Individual and team performances are somewhat dependent on the relative contributions of many social factors. Group cohesion, personal identity, the presence of certain attitudes and values, reactions to others, and performance in front of an audience are some of the athletic situations in which social factors operate. Social factors that act on and are related to achievement in athletic performance are difficult to measure and therefore hard to identify in specific situations. Much of our knowledge in this area is speculative or has been suggested by research but not strongly confirmed. Nevertheless, the influence of human beings and social settings on human performance must be sought and identified as well as possible.

It is therefore the purpose of this chapter to attempt to isolate and discuss social variables that may affect the output of athletes. These sources of variability in performance are not strangers to us. Unfortunately, however, they are usually treated with vague generalizations in books, with the result that they seem almost meaningless. It is hoped that this chapter will provide some sorely needed clarification. It will include material relevant to the group and its effective functioning; individual emotional reactions in social environments associated with athletic competition; and responsiveness to the presence of an audience.

## GROUP INTERACTIONS

Whether a sport is individual, dual, or team according to its competitive design, a number of athletes are involved. In every sport group a certain number of athletes find a place. The total number is dependent on (1) limits set by schools, conferences, or organizations; and (2) how many persons are interested in and capable of filling available positions.

The people in any athletic group come together for reasons that they have in common—skills, talents, and interest in a particular sport—as well as for dissimilar reasons. These dissimilar reasons are sometimes subtle and difficult to determine, as they may range from a desire for personal glory to a wish to help the team win. Sometimes such motivational factors are apparent to the athlete and others; at other times they are repressed and disguised. Whatever their reasons, people have been brought together to form a group or team under the leadership of a designated director, the coach. What is the composition of the group?

Within any formed group there is a certain amount of interpersonal attraction, or *cohesiveness*. The group, defined sociologically, is not merely a gathering of people. Rather, it is a collection of people who have a common goal and who interact in an attempt to reach this goal. Since the degree of cohesiveness in a group may ultimately determine the quality and effectiveness of its performance, an optimal amount of cohesiveness is desirable. There are ties within a group which can result in formation of primary groups and secondary groups. A "primary group," as usually referred to, is one with a considerable degree of unity and social interaction, while a "secondary group" is usually one formed with the intent of fulfilling an expressed purpose, and in which social values are held to a minimum. Cratty (1967) writes, "The most successful groups, it seems, are those whose members know each other well enough to be tolerant of their strengths and weaknesses, can communicate effectively, and have a leadership pattern appropriate to the task performance, but whose primary orientation is toward the specifics of the task rather than toward social interaction as an end in itself" (p. 41).

If this is true, the implications in the formation of an athletic team and its objectives are fairly clear. Socialization and fraternization are of some importance, but specified tasks and goals may be of greater relevance in attaining team victories. Indirect confirmation of these ideas is provided by Fiedler (1954), who administered a forced-choice questionnaire on interpersonal relationships to high school basketball players. He found that players on effective teams can distinguish between the teammates with whom they can and cannot cooperate, whereas players on ineffective teams perceive their teammates as similar. The implication is that ineffective teams are more socially oriented and effective teams contain players who become hostile toward less skillful players. For them, winning is a more important objective than having friendly relations with teammates. Fiedler concludes that the group that shows definite preferences among teammates is most likely to perform effectively. Such a group is task-oriented and is usually more successful for this reason.

There are other considerations in group or team productivity. Darley, Gross, & Martin (1952) list the following contingencies:

1   The extent to which the goal is accepted by the group
2   The previous group experiences at success and failure
3   The use of differential skills within the group
4   The acceptability of the leadership of the group and leadership persistence
5   The abilities and special skills of the members

The size of the group and the type of communication within it are other variables that may influence its performance. Personal dislikes and over-reactiveness to other team members will hamper group communication. In research involving manual or laboratory-type tasks, performance yields of individual persons and of groups of various sizes have been compared. The largest group in such studies is usually a four-man team. Weyner & Zeaman (1956) found that the greater the number of subjects in such a group, the better the performance level. As measured on a motor task, a group of four did better than a group of two, and a group of two in turn performed more effectively than one person alone.

However, we can only speculate on what the results would be if larger groups were compared in a similar manner. Groups that become too large are unwieldy and incohesive. Leadership must be more authoritarian in larger groups in order to reach objectives. The individual members are less important in their own eyes in larger groups and tend to contribute less to the overall performance of the group.

In many sports, the number of athletes on a particular team and the number of team members who can play at any one time in a contest are rigidly fixed by the regulations. Therefore, the achievement of each athlete is a function of such restrictions.

Naturally, within every group certain people gain more respect and admiration than others. It is unusual for every team member to gain equal recognition. Research (Kleiner, 1960) indicates that a member of a group becomes more attractive to the group when his acts are responsible for reduction of the threat of loss of status for the group. The stronger the threat of loss of status, the greater the person's attractiveness to the group. These statements are certainly borne out in athletics. The outstanding performer and the athlete who is turned to in "clutch" situations are of great value to the team. The more an athlete can diminish the probability of a loss, the more attractive he is to the team members.

On the other hand, a member who demonstrates behavior in conflict with the group's interests will affect the attitudes of the team as a whole. In an experiment by Rosenthal & Cofer (1948), the subjects were given a dart-throwing test in which group scores were the only concern. Attitude scales and level-of-aspiration scales were administered. Control and experimental groups were formed, the experimental variable being the use of a "plant" who showed no interest in the project, and it was found that the plant had a detrimental effect on his group. Aspiration levels in this group were not agreed upon, and the inability of the members to concur increased with the number of trials under the experimental condition. The results of the study reinforce the coach's natural feelings toward athletes who demonstrate undesirable attitudes: they can undermine the emotional climate of the group. Such athletes should be reckoned with quickly: their attitudes must change or dismissal from the team may be advisable.

Obviously, individuals with complex and different personalities are found in any team. This makes it hard for interaction between them to lead to productive experiences and the realization of mutual goals. The coach has the task of organizing and structuring the group. He determines goals and means of achieving them, usually with the assistance of others. Unfortunately, organizational or institutional pressures sometimes direct the coach to win the game, without regard to the personal considerations of the team members. In such a case, athletes must be treated in a rigid and authoritative manner; methods are standardized and relationships are far too distant. The shame of the matter is that, in educational institutions, student-athletes are supposed to be gaining an "education" through their athletic experiences, and presumably, this education goes beyond the development of athletic skills, physical fitness, and competitive attitudes.

It has been written elsewhere that personal identity is meshed with group identity. A person's worth must be proved to himself as well as to the group. A sensitive and intelligent leader sees to it that the group has purpose and direction and that each member knows his role and can play a part in achieving objectives. Every athlete is treated with respect and dignity, and is dealt with on a personal basis. The group's performance and behavior will reflect such treatment.

With regard to teaching skills to the group, drill, like any other form of teaching, must be executed properly to be effective. With inexperienced or young athletes, simple drills are advocated. Drills must be meaningful, and they are useless from a practical point of view if they are dazzling, intricate, and only superficially beneficial. Skills are being taught that will be applied in competition, and therefore the coach should not hurry through drills, for it is the quality, not the quantity, that counts.

## COMPETITION AND COOPERATION

Cooperation among members of a group must be fostered, and qualities associated with being a "good" competitor must be emphasized. Communication and cooperation among team members allow goals to be more easily reached. Working together serves to facilitate the achievement of objectives and is also a motivating force, for people often perform better in a group than alone.

Competitive situations, many of which are "natural," others contrived, also raise motivational levels. The coach wants to build up the cooperative and competitive tendencies of the individual athletes so that the team may function effectively. These goals are quite realistic and consistent with the demands of society; thus, in this sense, as in others, athletics is indeed a preparation for life. Man's natural environment contains numerous situations in which competitive behavior and cooperative behavior are needed. As one famous sociologist-anthropologist (Mead, 1961) has pointed out, many factors in a given culture determine the relative amount of emphasis on and the nature of competition and cooperation. Economic conditions, natural inclinations, social structure, education, and the current status of technology, are among the determining factors.

Competition and cooperation are conditioned by the *total* social picture, and the goals of individuals are culturally determined. Competition and cooperation are not opposites, but are two processes that work together to assist the individual in reaching his goals. A basketball game involves competition with the opponent and cooperation with the referee and the other team in obeying the rules and in putting on a "show" for the spectators. Cooperation is also, of course, needed among members of the same team. Cooperative attitudes are a function of increasing age; that is, with maturity, or sometimes with special training, children learn to cooperate better. The coach who deals with young people might do well to consider the problems a child has in learning to cooperate, and might show patience and at the same time use techniques that can help the child to learn to cooperate.

Competitiveness is a more natural urge, though children must also, to a certain extent at least, learn to compete. Still, rivalries between youngsters sometimes have to be controlled. With age, competitive feelings become more channeled for most people, and cooperative ventures increase. The desire to compete or cooperate (or both) may be determined by the discrepancy between level of achievement and desired goals. The manner in which goals may be best attained will dictate the approach taken toward these goals. In team sports, if the goal of all members is winning, maximum cooperation is more than likely to be displayed and personal sacrifice and teamwork are usually displayed. When personal glory and status are at stake, however, competition may be directed not only against the opponents but also against team members who are a threat to this achievement.

Much evidence indicates that there are motivational advantages in working with or against someone rather than working alone. When athletes practice in pairs or larger groups, they assist each other, and their motivation is increased or sustained. Competing against another, against norms, or against one's previous record can be an incentive. In fact, it is usually found that competition leads to higher motivation and performance than cooperation. The least desirable condition, in most cases, is training by oneself. Although superior athletes possess the dedication and psychological endurance necessary, the average athlete does not.

The countless hours of practice the young athlete puts in pay large dividends in later years, as indicated by the following accounts of the early years of two great basketball players. Bob Pettit, a professional all-star for many years with the St. Louis Hawks, writes (1966):

> I would get home from school and shoot baskets from 3:30 to 5:30. Then I would have dinner and do my lessons and by 7:30, I was out shooting baskets again. With light from a couple of window lamps, which I placed on the window sill facing the backyard, I was able to practice a few hours at night.
>
> You would be surprised how far you can go with constant and regular practice. It turned me into the leading scorer on my church league team, which may not sound like much, but only a year before I couldn't hold a basketball properly [p. 11].

Of Bill Bradley, a former college star at Princeton, now an outstanding player in the National Basketball Association for the New York Knickerbockers, it has been written (McPhee, 1965):

> On the inside of his bedroom door he had a basketball net, and when the weather was bad outdoors he would get down on his knees—he was six feet three when he was in the eighth grade—and play against boys his own age, two at a time. Conditions outside had to be pretty unsavory before that happened, though; he and his friends played around the outdoor basket in gloves, if necessary, and at night, under floodlights. Gradually, Bradley's back yard evolved into a basketball court nearly as good as Princeton's. "Our yard wasn't for the purpose of raising grass," his father recalls. "There was no grass in it at all." This was because they had a macadam surface put over it, flat and smooth, around the steel pole supporting a fan-shaped backboard, whose hoop was exactly ten feet above the ground [p. 75].

It is interesting to note that Pettit emphasizes that he practiced in solitude, while Bradley evidently spent his time primarily in competition with others. Both, however, were extremely motivated and determined to become outstanding basketball players. Similar accounts are given by superior athletes in other sports. Competition with other athletes or with one's own previous performances will usually improve performance. Competition does not always bring out the best in everyone, however; so-called "good" and "bad" competitors have been identified, and are described below. Many techniques have been suggested to encourage feelings of competitiveness in athletes who do not develop them unaided, and if the athlete's motivation is not already operating at a very high level, these innovations may inspire the additional efforts desired.

There is always the danger that intense and extended competition may have harmful emotional effects, and furthermore, the stress of competition may impede the learning of skills. Careful consideration of particular situations involving both cooperation and competition may help the coach to have a better understanding of the complexity of the problem. Some variables in such situations could be the age of the athlete, his skill level and athletic status, his goals, and the nature of the tasks to be learned. Relative emphasis should be placed on cooperative and competitive attitudes according to these and other criteria.

## COMPETITIVE ABILITY

One problem faced by every coach, regardless of sport, is the development and demonstration of good competitive ability. Nothing is more frustrating to the coach, and to the athlete himself, than the athlete who appears to have great potential, whose practice is excellent, and who then performs in mediocre fashion in the contest. A good competitor often exceeds practice performance in the contest, but a poor competitor may be variable, and his contest scores may be lower than his practice scores. Ever since the beginnings of athletic competition, speculation has surrounded the mysterious person called "the poor competitor." Recently, however, greater insight has been attained into this type of athlete, and distinctions have been made between good and poor competitors.

Two of the leading, if not the only, researchers in this area are Arnold Beisser (1967) and Francis Ryan (1958). Evidently, having a positive attitude is much more important in winning than heretofore realized. The athlete must overcome many psychological obstacles as well as physiological ones in order to win. Ryan has attempted to identify the psychological factors that differentiate good and poor competitors, as designated by track and field coaches. In this way, as shown in Table 5-1, he has associated certain personality characteristics with the good competitor. As indicated below the table, significant differences in the responses of the two types of athletes were found on all questions except the first. The responses to item 4 were in

TABLE 5-1    Coaches' ratings of good and poor competitors

| Item | | Responses | "Good" | "Poor" |
|---|---|---|---|---|
| 1 | What time of the day does he (did he) usually come to practice? | Earlier in the day than most men | 11 | 12 |
| | | About the same time as most | 43 | 38 |
| | | Later than most | 3 | 6 |
| | | Other | 0 | 4 |
| 2 | Does he work hard in practice? | Lazy—needs to be pushed | 1 | 5 |
| | | About average | 4 | 19 |
| | | Hard worker | 50 | 32 |
| | | Other | 2 | 2 |
| 3 | When he talks about future performance, is he shooting for | The next meet? | 40 | 23 |
| | | Late season? | 2 | 3 |
| | | Some eventual performance? | 10 | 28 |
| | | Other? | 5 | 6 |
| 4 | After a poor competitive showing, does he blame | Conditions, officials, etc.? | 2 | 10 |
| | | Himself? | 44 | 38 |
| | | Both? | 1 | 10 |
| | | Other? | 10 | 2 |
| 5 | Is he considered | A lone wolf? | 1 | 18 |
| | | Very friendly? | 42 | 12 |
| | | About average? | 13 | 28 |
| | | Other? | 1 | 2 |
| 6 | Does he seem to be happy? | Usually in good spirits, has plenty of belly laughs | 31 | 16 |
| | | Smiles easily, but seldom laughs heartily | 24 | 29 |
| | | Seldom smiles or laughs | 1 | 15 |
| | | Other | 1 | 0 |
| 7 | Does he tend to be | The life of the party? | 15 | 9 |
| | | About average? | 35 | 25 |
| | | Very quiet? | 7 | 21 |
| | | Other? | 0 | 5 |
| 8 | Does he make sense in his conversation? | Always rational and coherent | 46 | 15 |
| | | About average | 10 | 32 |
| | | Conversation sometimes seems strange and hard to follow | 1 | 12 |
| | | Other | 1 | 1 |
| 9 | Does he follow coaching instructions well? | Usually follows instructions well without comment | 43 | 19 |
| | | Follows instructions well but often with comment | 14 | 16 |
| | | Usually makes out a case for doing something different | 0 | 21 |
| | | Other | 0 | 4 |

TABLE 5-1   Coaches' ratings of good and poor competitors (*Continued*)

| Item | Responses | "Good" | "Poor" |
|------|-----------|--------|--------|
| 10  Does he learn easily? | Learns well | 47 | 13 |
| | An average learner | 8 | 31 |
| | Has great difficulty in learning some things | 2 | 14 |
| | Other | 0 | 2 |
| 11  Does he talk easily? | Communication good | 48 | 23 |
| | About average | 9 | 23 |
| | Difficult to talk to | 0 | 13 |
| | Other | 0 | 1 |
| 12  Is he popular with his teammates? | Well liked | 48 | 14 |
| | About average | 7 | 30 |
| | Unpopular | 1 | 15 |
| | Other | 1 | 1 |
| 13  What is his reaction following a good competitive performance? | Likely to make another good performance the following week | 51 | 0 |
| | Likely to make an average performance the following week | 4 | 21 |
| | Likely to fall off badly in the next meet | 1 | 29 |
| | Other | 1 | 10 |

*Note:* Distributions of responses on each item for good and poor competitors were compared by means of the chi-square technique. With the exception of item 1, differences were significant at less than the .01 level of confidence.

*Source:* Francis J. Ryan. An investigation of personality differences associated with competitive ability. In Bryant M. Wedge (Ed.), *Psychosocial problems of college men.* New Haven, Conn.: Yale University Press, 1958. Pp. 117–118.

the opposite direction to that expected, according to Ryan, but the responses to 11 of the 13 questions were as expected. In concluding his report he writes, "Differences in competitive ability represent relative differences in freedom to achieve or to express aggression" (p. 122).

Ryan has described the differences that he distinguished between the types of competitors:

*1*  Good and bad competitors possess different emotional abilities to accept high-level athletic achievement.

*2*  When the normal or good competitor competes badly, he may be a temporary victim of overanxiety, but the poor competitor demonstrates "feebleness of effort, almost a kind of paralysis" (p. 125).

*3*   The good competitor shows warm friendship with opponents, but not during competition. The poor competitor likes an atmosphere of friendliness and he does not get angry or bitter.

*4*   The poor competitor is self-condemning—he constantly berates himself. He is not constructive enough, is fearful of error, and takes a negative approach. He demonstrates an "emotional inability to accept achievement" (p. 131).

*5*   After competition and a bad performance, the poor competitor is in good spirits, but the good competitor is difficult to live with.

These observations provide much insight. Although there is danger in generalizations, Ryan does provide food for thought with his data and observations, and the inferences that can be drawn from them. He remarks, "The responsibility of the mature coach to the poor competitor is a complex matter, involving both value judgments and considerably more knowledge than is now available" (p. 139).

Beisser, from a different vantage point, has also made considerable perceptive comments on athletes (1967). As a psychiatrist, he has been able to delve more penetratingly into the problems of athletes. Ways of competing and the context in which competition occurs (team sport, individual sport, etc.) are greatly dependent on the psychological events of a person's past, according to Beisser. Early childhood family encounters are often reenacted in athletic competition.

One of the main features of successful competition in sports is that aggressive tendencies are channeled toward winning. Beisser states that the poor competitor generally fears aggression, whereas the good competitor has less fear of it. To be able to compete successfully, one must be able to express aggression in an acceptable manner. Many psychological factors can have an effect on attitudes and ultimate performance. Beisser discussed the unconscious forces in the psychological factors which tend to inhibit or prevent the athlete from achieving the logical goal of sport-winning. He also stresses the importance of having the experience of winning. "A player must get the feel of winning before he can be successful. If he has the physical talent and skill there is a psychological obstacle which must be overcome" (1967, p. 170).

The athlete has many hidden fears about why he does not do well in competition despite his apparent capabilities. The coach must somehow assist him in developing a favorable psychological attitude. The athlete has to depend on the coach, and therefore the coach must be strong, protective, and understanding.

## RELATIONSHIPS BETWEEN INDIVIDUAL AND TEAM PERFORMANCE

One of the more prominent problems in sport is selecting the athletes who will represent the team in competition. Though many criteria are available and have been employed, it might be wise to discuss at this point the relationship between achievement in skills performed alone and achievement in a team context. In other words, if we could designate a team score and an individual score, what would be the association between the two?

The limited research on this topic has been completed on laboratory-oriented tasks, and the findings are in agreement. In these experiments, people are tested on their performance when working alone and in pairs, and the findings are that group or team performance is not dependent on individual scores. Individual skill alone cannot be used to predict success in a team task, for other factors operate and interact in a team. Even when the tasks are similar, achievement in group performance cannot be predicted with any degree of confidence from individual performance.

In sports situations, very often individual "star" performers are placed together, as a starting unit in basketball or as the number-one doubles team in tennis. Perhaps this is not a desirable procedure. We often assume that the outstanding individual performer will automatically fit in well in a team context. Cratty (1967) wisely observes:

> Essentially, the ability to anticipate a teammate's movements and to integrate one's actions with another individual on the team is probably as important as individual skill in a sport such as basketball. In activities such as tennis doubles this quality probably assumes even more importance [pp. 37–38].

Implications that a coach may draw from these comments and from the research are (1) that individual accomplishments are not necessarily related to accomplishments in a team contest and (2) that if team performance is the ultimate goal, much practice should occur in a team situation.

## MORALE AND SPIRIT

The terms "morale" and "spirit" are used often, and often interchangeably, in the context of athletics. Although they are difficult to define precisely, we would probably generally agree on their general meanings and implications. The problem posed by the coach is not how to define morale but rather how to develop and maintain it.

Morale is typified by a feeling of acceptance, and by a feeling of confidence that one's actions contribute to the goals of the team. If morale is high, the athletes' needs are satisfied, and a general feeling of well-being prevails. The members of the group agree on goals and ways of achieving them, and are actually able to make progress. In athletics, as contrasted with other groups in which the goals may be unclear and possibly conflicting, the major objective is winning. Athletic group or team members therefore usually have a fairly high morale simply because of their shared objective. Morale is further enhanced when *all* members of the group contribute in some way to the achievement of the goals.[1] Some of the more important elements associated with morale are examined below.

First of all, the members of the group need to have a *common goal*. In athletics, the goal is winning, and each team member is encouraged to contribute. This requires the team members to be interested in one another, to be willing to make sacrifices when necessary, and to have a strong concern for the welfare of the team. Personal or vested interests must play a secondary role. How often have we witnessed the quarterback intent only on breaking passing records? The end playing each game to add to his record of most passes caught? The back adding up the yardage for personal glory? How high can morale be on the team that contains such players? Cooperation among team members is a necessity.

Second, appropriate leadership can upgrade morale. Aspects of leadership will be treated at some depth a little later in this chapter, and it is sufficient here merely to call attention to the importance of the *right kind of leadership* for the particular group under its particular set of circumstances. No one leader is able to build morale under all conditions. A social distance is needed between coach and athlete, but interpersonal relations are also essential.

Third, *interaction* among team members and between them and the coach should be considered. Ideally, all members of the team have the opportunity to contribute to the goal in some way. In wrestling, all individual match scores count for the team total. During the week before each match, wrestlers in a particular weight class compete vigorously for the right to represent the team. They also give helpful tips to each other by suggesting cer-

[1] Books on industrial psychology provide a wealth of information on group dynamics and work output. The coach who reads them and reflects on similarities between work situations and athletic situations is apt to gain much insight into the management of a team. An excellent source is Milton L. Blum & James C. Naylor, *Industrial psychology*. New York: Harper & Row, 1968.

tain maneuvers and encouraging every member to improve. In a team sport such as football or basketball, the necessity of mutual assistance and interaction among the members is obvious. Each player is dependent on the others, and the possibility of victory depends on a concerted effort by the team to maximize individual strengths.

Finally, the *incentives* the coach gives his team members will greatly determine their feelings. If his incentives are specific and are too much oriented toward the success of the individual athlete, the team's morale will go down. This happens often in basketball, where the emphasis is on scoring, and the high scorer stands to gain personal prestige. Other qualities, such as ball handling, rebounding, and defense, must also be encouraged so that players whose forte is one of these qualities, will also feel important. No matter what the attributes of the individual players the prime incentive for participating in athletics should ideally be the good of the team as a whole.

## ATTITUDES AND VALUES

Much psychological terminology is confused, and such words as "attitudes," "values," "opinions," "beliefs," "traits," and "concepts" are no exception. Once again, though, we need not be overly concerned with semantics. Since social psychologists have varied in their interpretations of attitudes and values, and one author has listed 23 distinct definitions of the term "attitude" (Rhine, 1958), there is no reason to expect to resolve the issue in this brief section. The following explanation, however, is offered as one about which there is some mutual understanding and agreement. Values and attitudes are interrelated. A "value" appears to be a concept, or an abstract idea, and an "attitude" is less general and usually refers to a feeling about a specific thing. Values provide direction for attitudes, which in turn predispose one to activity. A person evaluates something as good or bad; he is for it or against it. His behavior is accounted for by his feelings and his state of reactivity to a particular aspect of his surroundings. Attitudes and values are formed early in life, are enduring and persistent, but can be modified. A "value system" comprises various separate attitudes.

The nature of people's values and their consequent attitudes toward other people, toward situations, and toward their environment as a whole is important to other members of society. When athletes are involved, the interest is of greater magnitude than usual. Athletes and coaches are constantly in the public eye, both during competition and at other times. Their behavior reflects their attitudes, and the public has come to expect acceptable social expressions from people involved in athletics. This may be an unrealistic expectation, but nevertheless, the opportunity to develop high standards of social conduct is popularly associated with organized athletics. Are athletes indeed among the most idealistic of American youth? Is athletics really the developing grounds for such qualities?

Savage (1929) is quite cynical about the situation. He writes about the lack of intellectual challenge for athletes at the collegiate level:

> Their [athletes'] governance has been delivered utterly into the hands of older persons, whose decisions are made with little reference to the benefits that the reasoning processes involved might confer upon younger minds. Most inter-collegiate contests entail little independence of judgment on the part of players, whether in preparation or in actual participation. At every turn, our college athletes and managers are mechanized into automatism, and our athletes and managers are puppets pulled by older hands. What intellectual challenge inter-collegiate sport might afford has given way before the forces of commercialism [p. 309].

On morals and conduct his words are equally pessimistic and depressing, although he does express hope:

> In the field of conduct and morals, vociferous proponents of college athletics have claimed for participants far greater benefits than athletics can probably ever yield, and in attempting to evaluate these supposed benefits, have hailed the shadow as the substance. The workings of commercialism have almost obliterated the non-material aspects of athletics. And yet such qualities as loyalty, self-sacrifice, courage, and, above all, honesty, can be more readily and directly cultivated through the activities and habits of the playing field than in almost any other phase of college life. What, therefore, is needed is not one set of moral and ethical standards for sports and games, and another for all other phases of college life, but a single set of standards so sincerely valued that by taking thought they can be made operative in life's every aspect. The transfer or spread of training implied is as much the affair of the academic teacher as of the coach or the director of physical education. It must begin with a diminished emphasis upon the material benefits of college athletics and a sincere resolution to substitute other and more lasting values for those that now are prized [p. 310].

Savage describes the challenge to athletics as follows:

> The prime needs of our college athletics are two,—one particular and one general. The first is a change of values in a field that is sodden with the commercial and the material and the vested interests that these forces have created. Commercialism in college athletics must be diminished and college sport must

rise to a point where it is esteemed primarily and sincerely for the opportunities it affords to mature youth under responsibility, to exercise at once the body and the mind, and to foster habits both of bodily health and of those qualities of character which, until they are revealed in action, we accept on faith.

The second need is more fundamental. The American college must renew within itself the force that will challenge the best intellectual capabilities of the undergraduate. Happily, this task is now engaging the attention of numerous college officers and teachers. Better still, the fact is becoming recognized that the granting of opportunity for the fulfillment of intellectual promise need not impair the socializing qualities of college sport. It is not necessary to "include athletics in the curriculum" of the undergraduate or to legislate out of them their life and spirit in order to extract what educational values they promise in terms of courage, independent thinking, cooperation, initiative, habits of bodily activity, and, above all, honesty in dealing between man and man. Whichever conception of the function of the American college, intellectual or socializing agency, be [adopted], let only the chosen ideal be followed with sincerity and clear vision, and in the course of years our college sport will largely take care of itself [pp. 310–311].

It is interesting to remember that these words were written in 1929. Have times changed?

Three fairly recent studies shed some light on the subject. Kistler (1957) found that a high percentage of college students had what might be considered as unsportsmanlike attitudes in sport situations. A finding that stands out is that college men who had previous varsity experience showed poorer attitudes about sportsmanship than nonvarsity athletes.

Richardson (1962) developed an instrument to measure sportsmanship and administered it to 233 students from 15 schools. As the data were not analyzed statistically, the results are presented with reservation. Those who had not won their letters had a higher degree of sportsmanship than those who had. Football players scored lowest in sportsmanship of all the teams represented; baseball players, basketball players, and track and field athletes scored highest. Of all the athletes, subsidized athletes (the better ones?) demonstrated the poorest sportsmanship attitudes. An overwhelming number of all the respondents approved of breaking rules if they would not be caught or penalized.

In the third research project, Lakie (1964) formulated a competitive attitude scale and collected data on 220 varsity athletes in different sports and from various types of schools. Statistical analysis revealed that none of the sports or schools represented in the study were distinguished by the findings of the inventory. A higher score represented more of a "win-at-any-cost" attitude toward athletics, and the mean scores of the football groups at the various colleges were generally higher than those of the other five groups studied. In general, the responses of groups indicated that they bordered on being undecided or approving of the "win-at-any-cost" attitude.

There appears to be some inconsistency between the values approved by society and those believed in by athletes. Perhaps the idealistic values of society are unrealistic and impractical for the athlete who must compete for victory. Maybe the athletes who are most highly acclaimed become so because of the attitudes they hold. It is possible that coaches encourage such attitudes, or it may be that the athletes come to the team with their value systems already fairly well established. No matter what their source, it appears that the attitudes of many athletes toward sportsmanship would not be looked upon with favor by a society which expects high standards of ethical and moral behavior.

The setting of the athletic contest lets the participant experience activities and relationships that can be extremely meaningful to him. Although we have presented the negative side of the picture thus far, much could be written in favor of the potential of athletics in developing better citizens. The following article by Singer is indicative of popular thought on the problem.

---

## STATUS OF SPORTS IN CONTEMPORARY AMERICAN SOCIETY[2]

Robert Singer

The status of sports and athletics has been subject to much debate ever since the early and late Athenian periods (776–355 B.C.), and possibly even before then. The Olympic games, begun in 776 B.C., and supposedly representative of the highest in ideals and athletics, had to be finally dissolved in 394 A.D. because the Games were no longer games. Athletics of the period, once the symbol of the highest achievement, had been degraded, misused, and made worthless with the decadence of the great Greek civilization.

Many years passed before sports and athletics were again to come to the attention of people. Interest grew slowly in the nineteenth century. The first intercollegiate competition (rowing) occurred in America in 1852. This was followed by baseball (1857), football in the 1860's, and others soon after. The Olympics were renewed in 1896 in Athens, and the United States was represented at this event.

[2] Reprinted from *The Physical Educator*, 1966, **23**, 147–149.

At the turn of the century intercollegiate football became so unmanageable that the Intercollegiate Athletic Association (I.A.A.) was formed in 1905. Five years later, the name of the Association was changed to the National Collegiate Athletic Association (N.C.A.A.), and this Association still exists, exerting powerful control over intercollegiate competition in practically all sports.

It is interesting that the Greeks, as well as contemporary civilizations, have found sports productive of evil as well as good, pleasure and dissatisfaction. In general, it has been and is a source of controversy. Whereas the Olympics had to be dissolved in the olden days, and athletics practically forbidden throughout the Dark and Middle Ages, modern sports, under the guidance and with the assistance of many controlling bodies, notably the N.C.A.A., A.A.U., N.A.I.A., and the N.F.S.H.S.A.A., have won a new height of acclaim and attention at the present time. Because of the publicity, emphasis, and control of sport, the situation has become as distasteful to some people as it is popular with others.

The limitations and assets of sport should be realized by coaches, players, spectators, educators, family, and the public in general. Weaknesses must be overcome and controversial areas ironed out. Many people are not aware of the contributions of sport to the total development of the participants. These, too, must be acknowledged and used for effective promotion of a program of athletics.

Let us look at some of the assets of sport and the contribution it makes to the quality of American living. Since sport is subject to criticism some of these objections will be presented as well.

## Assets of sports

1. *Sports provide the more athletically gifted people with a means of developing their skills even further.* The educational system of our country is supposed to offer a program which encompasses the needs and interests of all the students. There are programs for physically handicapped youngsters, and those individuals low in physical fitness and/or motor ability are provided with additional assistance. The need for sports as an outlet for the gifted cannot be denied.

2. *Nowhere in education can a student's values be more directly influenced than in the keen competition of sport.* One of the primary roles of education is to inculcate values and morals in students so that they will lead more useful lives. A coach who maintains a high sense of values can exert a beneficial influence on his team members. Daily practice sessions and actual contests produce close contact between coach and players and create situations with rich educational implications. Honesty, the ability to win

and lose graciously, fair play, ethics, leadership, spirit, etc.,—these are a few of the many character traits which can and should be developed in each player under the guidance of the coach.

3. *Personal relationship was one of the four objectives of education set down by the Educational Policies Commission in 1938. Sports,* with special reference to team sports, *have a major role to contribute to this goal.* Boys (or girls) have to play together, to be together, think together—they have to be an organized unit if the team is to function best. Transfer from the sport's situation may possibly carry over to many transactions in life.

4. *An athletic event which represents a particular school will tend to create spirit in that school.* Call it a spirit of nationalism, if you will. The contest not only involves and arouses the students of the schools or colleges involved, but also residents of the town, city, and even state. People take pride in their team. The team is a sort of "common ground" for many persons of all ages with diversified interests and vocations. The athletic contest brings out the feelings of people: their spirit, enthusiasm, and pride.

5. *Finally, sports will better develop the physical fitness of the participants.* A strong body, functioning maximally along with an active and stimulated mind, is the ideal condition for which most of us strive. Through conditioning practices, athletes have the opportunity to develop themselves beyond a mediocre state.

## Liabilities of sports

1. *The present role of athletics* in our society *has resulted in an overemphasis on recruiting of athletes in many colleges and universities throughout the land.* In many cases, academic standards are lowered for their benefit and illegal monetary rewards are given to these prodigies. The situation reached such a bleak point in the collegiate ranks in 1948, that the N.C.A.A. was impelled to enforce the "Sanity Code." Although it was not officially in effect long, due to loud protests, recruiting measures became more realistic and less objectionable. However, every so often, violations are uncovered and colleges are penalized by the N.C.A.A.

2. *There are many who feel that the role of sports in our society has completely grown out of hand.* There is too much idolization of athletes, too much glamorization of sports events, and, in general, just too much interest in sports to the neglect of cultural and academic pursuits. Although sports have always been accepted as a phase of physical education, physical educators are questioning the validity of such a unity. There are those who feel that big time collegiate sports today are an entirely separate entity from physical education.

3. *Many athletes are spoiled, coddled, overpraised, and glorified.* Their value is overemphasized to society and to themselves. When they are

through playing, what contributions will they be able to make to society without their footballs and basketballs? Will they be able to step down from their pedestal and accept a life of reality?

4. *Too much time is taken for athletics and not enough for academic pursuits.* Athletes receive a very narrow education. The time spent for practice and actual contests leaves little for other endeavors. In addition to this time, the emotional tone of sports is such as to affect individuals for a certain period preceding and following the events. Players invariably think about the contests. They become psychologically prepared for them, and afterwards, reflect on important aspects and situations, replay them mentally, with a result that the dreamed outcome is better than the actual one. This situation will also detract from the attention needed for academic work.

5. *Lastly, America has become a country known for its spectators.* The emphasis on sports elevates a few to the sacrifice of many. The onlookers receive a vicarious thrill from watching others perform: they do not express or develop themselves physically or mentally. Varsity teams control the usage of the best equipment and facilities while the general student body is either allowed to find time before and after practice (usually inconvenient times) or is not permitted at all to use the same equipment and facilities.

## Personal reflection on the controversy

The pros and cons of sport can be debated forever and more can be added to the list proposed above. Contributions of sport potentially counter balance by far its liabilities. Educated, dedicated, and interested coaches have the final say in the benefits sport may offer to all concerned. Communication with the athletes, student body, faculty, and community is the important thing. The values and ideals of the coach can either elevate the stature of sport or degrade it to such a point that it becomes a Roman spectacle. Coaches primarily create the image. They influence the physical, mental, emotional, and social growth of the boys possibly more than any other individual besides the family.

Some of my feelings on the present status of sport coincide with Huizinga, a German philosopher, who wrote *Homo Ludens: Man the Player*. He believes that play is natural; there is a certain element of play behind war, music, art, and everything created and performed by man. However, he wonders what happened to the play element in sport. Rules and strict control has increased, enjoyment for the participants has decreased, and sport has changed to become a business.

I, too, wonder where the play and fun element has gone in sport. Too much emphasis, too much control, too much leadership, too much attention —where can sport go from here?

*Conclusion*

Once again the burden of solution rests on the shoulders of the coach. He can return these elements to sport. He is responsible for and capable of presenting sport to the players and spectators in a manner socially desirable, within proper perspective, and in such a manner that the value of sport is unquestioned. He should not allow pressure to be cast on him by individuals who have no concern for the welfare of the athlete but only to increase the economic and public status of the school. Above all, the coach's ethics and intentions should be such that he is beyond reproach.

Competition, cooperation, enjoyment, mind and body development,— these are the major potential contributions of sport to the participant. *Are you, the coach, considerate of these factors or is your only concern winning?*

---

Finally, any discussion of attitudes should refer to the attitudes held by the athlete and coach toward the contest. The "winning attitude" is mentioned often in popular journals and books. Thinking positively and confidently is a great asset in reaching victory. Feelings of nervousness and anxiety before competition are common to all athletes, whatever their levels of proficiency or years of experience. This emotional state indicates the importance of the contest to the participant and is associated with being "up" for the contest. The athlete's frame of mind before competition may very well determine his performance.

## SPORTSMANSHIP

Any discussion of attitudes and values in athletics naturally leads to the role of sportsmanship before, during, and after competitive activity. "Sportsmanship" has been defined as "honest rivalry" and the "graceful acceptance of results." Unfortunately, athletic codes of sportsmanship have become so hackneyed and generalized as to be unrealistic in today's society. When winning is important and emotions run high, consistently ideal social behavior is apparently difficult.

When the athlete has trained hard and has played to win, should he be expected not to be bitter in defeat or boastful in victory? When the athlete has exhausted himself physically, mentally, and emotionally for a long period of time in pursuit of the ultimate goal—to prove he is superior to his opponent—what kind of behavior can and should be expected of him? When the athlete takes advantage of opportunities that arise in the contest to interpret rules to his own advantage, is he cheating, behaving immorally, or "making his own breaks"?

Many educators claim that sportsmanship and other desirable values can and should be taught through athletic experiences. Others are quite critical of the job that is being done. Keating (1965) is especially critical of the actions of basketball coaches which encourage disrespect and contempt for authority. He asks, "Are emotional outbursts during the course of the contest, public expressions of disgust, and outrage, verbal abuse and ridicule, coincident with the goals of the educational institution which serves as sponsor of the contest?" (pp. 302–303). Keating writes further, "In his public exhibitions of emotional self-indulgence the coach is unwittingly initiating the destruction of public confidence [in the officials]" (p. 304).

Sportsmanship is open to interpretation, especially with respect to its application to and demonstration in sports. The moralist has one viewpoint, the pragmatist another. The issue is the discrepancy between expected and actual behavior. Very few people would encourage the coach to teach his players to use unethical practices, to deliberately break rules, to cheat, and to act out their emotional instability. Ideally, the athlete should be able to play hard but fairly. It must be realized, however, that the social conduct and athletic performance involved in playing hard will not always be in conformity with a strict code of ethics.

## LEADERSHIP

Considering how much is said and written about leadership, it is amazing how little is really known about (1) the kinds of personal characteristics that lead to effective leadership and (2) the techniques one might employ to become a good leader. Whenever a group, defined as two or more people, is interacting, a leader may emerge. In athletic teams, there is the appointed leader, the coach, and there may be one or more athletes who also become leaders in their own right.

Although it is true that "good material" can "make" a coach, we have special respect for the coach who consistently gets results better than might have been expected of his team. The good coach has certain skills to use in dealing with people. What is the nature of the effective leader? Why and how do certain athletes emerge as leaders of the group?

First of all, we must realize that leadership is a function of the interaction between a *unique personality* and a *situation*. A person who is a leader will control the group, subtly or with power. His will directs the behavior of others. Presumably, the leader has been appointed or elected because of his apparent or implied ability to help solve the group's problems and help it to reach the desired objectives. Ideally, the same person would be appointed or elected from the group. Since every condition demands different talents to solve different problems, leadership is fairly specific to the task. That is, because a person emerges as a leader of the soccer team does not mean he will necessarily become a leader in other athletic situations, in time of war, or in social crisis. Similar circumstances probably require similar leadership abilities. Whenever the group or the situation changes, it is conceivable that the leader will also change.

For instance, in a study in which 36 college men were observed without their knowledge as they worked in pairs and quads in solving various tasks, different leaders emerged for the intellectual tasks and the manual tasks (Carter, Haythorn, & Howell, 1950). The behavior of the leader has also been found to vary with the size of the group. Leading larger groups is more demanding, and it has been demonstrated that leaders of larger and smaller groups do possess certain characteristics that distinguish between them (Hemphill, 1950). Research in industry indicates that the amount of consideration (for those under them) and amount of structure (ability to define group roles in relation to goals and ability to initiate activity) that supervisors have are related to the effectiveness of groups. Coaches might be successful more often if they paid more attention to *consideration* and *structure*.

But basically, it has not been too rewarding to attempt to identify traits that differentiate leaders from followers. On this matter, Fiedler (1969) writes:

> People who become leaders tend to be somewhat more intelligent, bigger, more assertive, more talkative than other members of their group. But these traits are far less important than most people think. What most frequently distinguished the leader from his co-workers is that he knows more about the group task or that he can do it better. A bowling team is likely to choose its captain from good rather than poor bowlers, and the foreman of a machine shop is more likely to be a good machinist than a poor one.
>
> In many organizations, one only has to live long in order to gain experience and seniority, and with these a position of leadership [p. 39].

Thus it becomes apparent that personality is only a part of what makes a leader. Other considerations, according to Fiedler are age, socioeconomic level, education, experience, and being in the right place at the right time. Figure 5-1 illustrates many conditions and personal characteristics which may help to determine whether a person becomes a leader. The figure serves to emphasize the complexity of the matter, for many variables may theoretically interact to produce a leader.

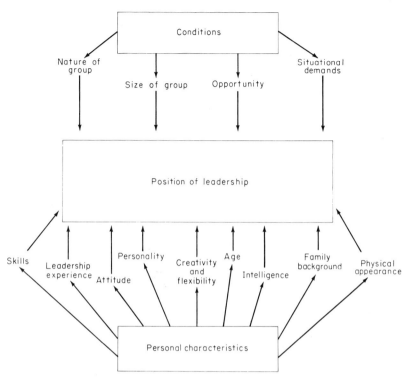

FIGURE 5-1   *Conditions and personal characteristics influencing the acquisition of a position of leadership.*

In the military, industry, athletics, and elsewhere, there have been attempts to decide what type of leadership is most effective. Two different but not necessarily mutually exclusive forms of leadership have been identified: (1) the autocrat and (2) the democrat. The autocratic coach makes all the decisions for the team, is task-oriented, and directs the team as much as possible. His goal is to win, to achieve. He takes all the responsibility for the results of his efforts. On the other hand, the democratic coach is group-oriented and method-centered, and provides the structure for group participation in decisions affecting the group. Winning is important to him, but so is the method of achievement. Fiedler (1969) states that the research has not shown one type of leader to be consistently better than the other. Each is successful in some situations but not in others. His own research demonstrates that autocratic leaders perform best in situations in which they have either a great deal of power and influence or no influence over the group members. Democratic leaders are most effective in situations in which they have a moderate influence over the members of the group.

Therefore, each coach must analyze his own situation and his own personality in order to determine how to approach the responsibilities of a leadership position. Typically, though, the coach is in a position in which numerous decisions have to be made, many of them quickly, and group discussions may cause delay. Therefore, he would probably generally have to be fairly autocratic. If he is well liked and respected by the group, the semi-autocratic method should be quite effective, all other things being equal. An important thought to remember is that no one style of leadership or one type of person can represent good leadership under all conditions.

Anyone can be a leader if he analyzes his own strengths and weaknesses, picks the right situation in which to emerge as a leader, and works at becoming a leader. As far as the coach is concerned, a relevant consideration is that the players must believe in his decisions. The athletes should understand and share the coach's philosophy. Vanderburgh (1956) suggests the importance of psychologically conditioning the team and goes on to say, "Success or failure depends not only on individual physical ability but, to a great extent, on good attitude and the acceptance of team strategy" (p. 42).

Consideration should also be given to leadership, status among one's peers, and athletic ability. A tremendous amount of evidence indicates a close association between physical prowess and status within a group when children and adolescents are involved. Athletic talents are recognized by youth as being extremely important. When the age and importance of physical prowess in males and females are compared, one might expect the curves drawn in Figure 5-2 to represent the situation theoretically. Up to early adulthood, the athletic skills of the male play an important role in determining his level of acceptancy and prestige within a heterogeneous group. Emphasis on such skills then diminishes. When the group is more homogeneous —for example, a baseball team—amount of skill is one of a number of factors that help to determine the leader.

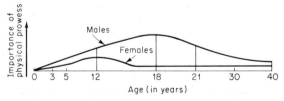

FIGURE 5-2 *The relationship of physical prowess to status, as a function of age.* (Source: *Bryant J. Cratty. Social dimensions of physical activity. Englewood Cliffs, N.J.: Prentice-Hall, 1967. P. 56. Copyright 1967 and reprinted by permission of Prentice-Hall, Inc.*)

Are successful leaders—coaches and captains—born or made? Is achievement due to certain abilities or traits or to varying combinations of both? Evidently, from the discussion presented thus far, to a great extent a leader is made, for leadership is dependent on developed personal qualities and their interaction in particular situations. No one basic pattern of traits serves to represent all leaders. Different circumstances in different areas—the military, for example—require different leadership characteristics. Think, if you will, of the type of leader who might be successful in war but not in peacetime. A particular coach, likewise, may succeed in one situation and not another. Teams representing higher versus lower socioeconomic players, various regional locations, varying school and community pressures, and different institutional levels (high school, college) are examples of situations in which one coach may succeed and another may not. The situation and the person must be matched in order for leadership to be successful.

## FAMILY

Although relationships between coach and athlete are explored and written up extensively, the athlete and his family interactions are ignored. Yet, families have a strong influence on the interests and attainments of their members. This influence is due both to genetic factors and to parental encouragement. Patterns of activity are somewhat similar within given families, and body types of children are moderately correlated with those of their parents. The probability that a person will select a particular sport and succeed in it is enhanced by a predisposition in inherited body characteristics to achieve in certain sports, and by family encouragement provided in various ways.

An athlete may participate in a given sport for many reasons. Some of these have been expressed by Boyle (1963): ego involvement, need to compete, poor physical endowments that are overcome as a result of competitive spirit, and the like. Boyle quotes a psychiatrist, Stephen D. Ward, who offers another plausible hypothesis, that the athlete's drive stems from infancy. Every new physical achievement is greeted by the mother's expression of love and approval. The mother's approval and reinforcement of participation in certain kinds of activities will serve as encouragement for the child to continue in his efforts. The father actually plays a minor role in the early formation of the child.

Sometimes there may be antagonism between the athlete and his family. Not all athletes conform easily to the demands of competition. The family has to adjust emotionally to the athlete's periods of sulkiness, exuberance, temporary losses in appetite, and other expressions of the tension he is under. If this sort of thing is carried to extremes, he should be encouraged to drop out of competition. Sport and competition are dear to the athlete, and because of his physical, mental, and emotional involvement, it is not unexpected that his behavioral patterns at home might be inconsistent and at times contrary to his parents wishes.

There is also danger that a parent, typically the father, may be too pre-occupied with the son's accomplishments. He may expect too much of the boy and drive him too hard. Antagonism occurs when the coach and the father have different expectations of the athlete. The father may want the son to become an individual star and gain in personal stature while the coach wishes the athlete to merge with the team for the good of the entire team. Thus the athlete is frustrated because of the conflicting demands made on him.

These and other family considerations are offered by Dolan (1967). Dolan talks about the "Plimsoll Point," an intolerable state which a person reaches as a result of terrific frustration, high motivation, and strong out-side pressures. When the athlete is continuously bombarded with advice and direction both at home and at school, the Plimsoll Point is bound to be reached. Such a situation should be straightened out as soon as it is observed, possibly by confrontation of the involved parties.

Fathers are usually quite devoted to their athlete sons. Dolan warns about the effects of the overprotection or indifference or rejection shown by the father to his son. He also describes how mechanisms of adjustment—projection of blame to other team members, rationalization, and repression—are employed by the parents of the athlete. Becoming acquainted with the parents of the team members may be helpful to the coach, and may afford insights which will help him to understand the thoughts and actions of the athletes.

It is interesting to note that first-born children differ from later-born children within a family in a number of ways. Personality characteristics are usually predictable when first- and second-born children are compared in adolescent or adult years. For example, there is a tendency for the first-born to find pain aversive and to avoid activities of a punishing nature.

Nisbett (1968) examined this hypothesis with regard to participation in dangerous sports. Birth-order information was obtained from the college files of over 2,000 Columbia University students enrolled in 1963, from 110 Pennsylvania State University students, from 384 Yale University students, from the New York Giants professional football team, and from the New York Mets baseball team. Table 5-2 clearly shows the predicted birth-order effect. The consistent pattern for all samples indicates that first-borns are less likely than second-borns to participate in dangerous sports. First-

TABLE 5-2  Ratio of first borns to second borns as a function of athletic participation

| | Columbia | | Pennsylvania State | | Yale | | Professional teams | |
|---|---|---|---|---|---|---|---|---|
| | Students who play dangerous sports (college) | Students who do not play dangerous sports | Students who play dangerous sports (in high school) | Students who do not play dangerous sports | Students who play dangerous sports (in high school) | Students who do not play dangerous sports | Football | Baseball |
| Ratio of first borns to second borns......... | .510 | .603 | .560 | .660 | .508 | .581 | .600 | .727 |
| N ................................... | (192) | (1,583) | (25) | (53) | (124) | (260) | (15) | (11) |

Source: Richard E. Nisbett. Birth order and participation in dangerous sports. Journal of Personality and Social Psychology, 1968, **8**, 351–353. P. 352. Copyright 1968 by the American Psychological Association and reproduced by permission.

borns are apt to play in activities in which there is a low risk of injury. These findings are in agreement with other recent research that demonstrates that first-borns have a greater fear of physical harm and perhaps are more sensitive to pain.

McIntyre (1959) has undertaken one of the few studies of the socioeconomic backgrounds of the families of athletes. The athletes represented football, basketball, wrestling, and gymnastics at Pennsylvania State University. From questionnaire returns, it was determined that football players were dissimilar to athletes in the other three sports, in that the majority of the football players came from a lower socioeconomic background. (The urge to use sport as a means of elevating one's social status is discussed in the next section.)

Loy (1969) has begun to analyze questionnaire returns from UCLA graduate athletes on the nature of the families of athletes. Some of the preliminary findings are as follows:

1   Athletes with foreign-born fathers: soccer players, 60 per cent; wrestlers, 43 per cent; tennis players, 31 per cent; gymnasts and trackmen, 29 per cent; football players, 26 per cent; baseball players, 23 per cent; swimmers, 22 per cent; and basketball players, 19 per cent
2   Athletes whose fathers did not complete high school: about 50 per cent of wrestlers, football players, and baseball players
3   Athletes whose fathers were blue-collar workers: about 50 per cent of wrestlers; 33 per cent of baseball players, trackmen, and football players; 16 per cent of basketball players; and 13 per cent of swimmers and tennis players

## SOCIAL MOBILITY AND STATUS

Sport has been the vehicle on which many athletes have risen from a lower socioeconomic class. Members of minority groups, lacking opportunities in many aspects of our society, have historically struggled for and obtained status in athletics. Unfortunately, in some cases, the individual is exploited for his talents and given pseudo-status; there are many black and Puerto Rican athletes who are successful on the playing field, but who experience discrimination when buying a house, for example.

According to Boyle (1963), most popular sports in the United States have arisen among upper-class families. The upper class imports a sport, typically from England, and the middle class then takes it over and popularizes it. Nevertheless, studies have shown that wealthier families have a tendency to participate in different activities from poorer families. Various reasons can be offered to explain this practice. Economic factors, available resources, personal needs, and the like are plausible explanations. Beisser (1967, p. 143) writes that "Each sport . . . has its own social connotation." In his case studies, "The tennis player and the golfer were influenced by the possibility of elevating their social positions through the sport. So, too, was the boxer, but it was the only sport available to him as a Negro in the geographical area where he lived."

Interesting information on the boxer has been reported by Weinberg & Arond (1952). Data were collected by reading firsthand literature, by personal experience, and by interview with 68 professional boxers, 7 trainers, and 5 managers. It was found that professional boxers typically represent lower socioeconomic classes. During the course of the twentieth century, certain ethnic groups have been more substantially represented than others in the boxing world; e.g., Italians, Irishmen, Jews, Puerto Ricans, and Negroes, in that order. The ethnic composition prevalent in boxers at a given point in history reflects the ethnic shifts in the urban lower socioeconomic levels. Weinberg & Arond, on the basis of their data, state that boxing leads to increased social status for the participants. And, as might be expected, successful boxers serve as models for youth.

Not every athlete, however, has a strong hope that participation and success in athletics will result in improved social status. Many psychological, sociological, and physiological factors operate and interact to influence activity choices and outcomes. Sport is a center of our social scene today; athletes are acclaimed for their feats and receive extensive recognition. Increased status and upward social mobility are natural in such a situation.

There is sufficient evidence to indicate that the middle-class person usually has a higher motivation for achievement than the lower-class person. This observation is especially true of academic pursuits and job aspiration. The higher need to achieve in the middle class can be explained by a number of factors, many of which are discussed by Rosen (1958). Besides available opportunities in the culture, and the physical and intellectual characteristics of the middle-class person, Rosen states, "There may be psychological and cultural factors which affect social mobility by influencing the individual's willingness to develop and exploit his talent, intelligence, and opportunities" (p. 496).

If such thoughts and the data obtained in a number of studies pertain to athletics, then the coach should be interested in the social class of the athletes on his team. Motivation to perform and to experience success may vary greatly with a person's socioeconomic background. Although it is true that many people rise from lower social classes due to intense desire and motivation, many more feel little hope and therefore maintain a generally low level of aspiration, with little urge to strive for goals and less expectation of attaining them. Perhaps such people need to be approached in a somewhat different manner than do middle-class people. They need to learn to set realistic goals and to raise their motivation for achievement in order to perform successfully.

Athletes' personal motivation and satisfaction are much influenced by whether the coach deploys his athletes in an honest manner. Fair treatment and the placement of athletes in positions that suit their skills and their worth to the team help to inspire those who are used to being rejected in society. But the status given to the athlete should be real. When an athlete is "used" for his talents, resentment will ultimately prevail, and team morale will be undermined.

The relationship of high school participation in athletics to certain status measures has been researched by Rehberg & Schafer (1968). Nearly 800 Pennsylvania high school students served as subjects in this study. High educational expectations and participation in athletics were generally found to go together. The investigators conclude:

> These data have shown that a greater proportion of athletes than non-athletes expect to enroll in a four-year college, even when the potentially confounding variables of status, academic performance, and parental encouragement are controlled. This relationship is especially marked among boys not otherwise disposed to college, that is, those from working-class homes, those in the lower half of their graduating class, and those with low parental encouragement to go to college [p. 739].

Rehberg & Schafer report that their data strongly show that interscholastic athletics is one channel for upward mobility (assuming that desire to go to college is an example of upward mobility).

A number of studies have been completed that, in one way or another, deal with success after college graduation as related to participation in athletics. Invariably, the findings are consistent. Former University of Minnesota athletes have been found to earn higher incomes than former nonathletes (Schrupp, 1953). Data from former Iowa State University subjects indicated that there was a positive relationship between the extent of participation in athletics and financial success (Thisted, 1933). Participation in athletics at Purdue University has been shown to be a strong factor in social mobility (Annarino, 1951). The postcollege success of athletes has been demonstrated in a number of studies and in a variety of ways. In one investigation, Partch (1963) studied graduates from San Diego State College from 1936 to 1940, comparing the success of athletes and nonathletes, as determined by elevation in social class, or social mobility. Analysis of the data indicated that the athletes came from a lower socioeconomic level than the nonathletes, but after 23 to 27 years had attained the same social class level. Partch concluded: "Of the lettermen, 69.7 percent were classified as climbers, 27.6 percent were listed as static, and 3 percent were identified as decliners. Of the non-lettermen, 56.8 percent could be called climbers, 40.5 percent as static, and 2.7 percent as decliners" (p. 39). It appears that intercollegiate athletic participation has a favorable effect upon social class, and hence upon success, in the years after graduation.

## HANDLING INDIVIDUAL ATHLETES

In essence, "coaching athletes" refers to the particular type of understanding and treatment given to the individual members of the team. Each person has different problems. To neglect these problems would be to go against the best interest of the team. The coach usually formulates general training rules and procedures at the beginning of a season, but situations invariably arise which are not covered by the rules. Furthermore, exceptions to rules may be desirable in certain cases.

To be sensitive to the unique differences and problems of each athlete requires great feeling and perception by the coach. In the university, in industry, in the military, or on a team—whenever a person is part of a larger functioning unit—personalized consideration results in increased motivation. To discuss all the problems a coach or any leader might be confronted with would be impossible. Let us, however, discuss some that are prominent.

### Group Acceptance and Social Integration

The cohesiveness of any unit depends greatly on the acceptance of each member by every other member. Inevitably, a few people in any group are initially rejected for any one of a number of reasons, but members of a unit can become "closer" with time, mutual experiences, and the attainment of shared objectives to a reasonable degree. Social integration in turn leads to increased team productivity.

Why some people become outcasts is open to speculation in some cases and entirely understandable in other cases. Trapp (1953) has identified possible subgroup formations within a college football team but, more importantly, has attempted to study social integration in the squad during the season. Personal distance ballots (on which the social distance at which each member holds every other member is recorded) were taken throughout the season. It was found that the social integration within the squad improved progressively during the football season. The team demonstrated greater unification; the various subgroups merged together. Furthermore, the college in Indiana which was represented in this study was undefeated and had only one tie game. The increased social integration may have led to the winning record, the record may have led to better integration, or, the two processes may have been mutually reinforcing.

### Dating

Every coach arranges a regimen that he feels will help to fulfill his and the team's objectives, and the regimen always includes regulations concerning social activity. Two extreme policies are possible: (1) the Spartan way of life, in which curfew hours and extracurricular activities are carefully scrutinized, and (2) complete freedom, in which the athlete moderates his own after-practice hours.

Since no research has been done on this exact problem, a common-sense, though unoriginal, approach is the best available. First of all, in the ideal physical state, one would be able to learn and perform athletic skills with a high degree of proficiency. Acceptable training procedures include maintaining the body in an optimal state of health, and therefore, social activity should not be excessive during the athletic season. The athlete requires a suitable sleeping period and time for relaxation in order to be prepared mentally, emotionally, and physically for practice and competition. Whether a statement of policy about specific sleeping hours, dating hours, and other evening activity is necessary probably depends on the age and maturity of the athletes, the philosophy of the coach, and the importance associated with winning. Coaches in situations where dramatic emphasis is placed on winning usually require the most rigid training programs of their teams.

If the primary emphasis is on the well-being of the athletes, however, many of the usual or "normal" activities of people of the athletes' age should be allowed and even encouraged. Dating is a socially acceptable activity, and if it is suppressed, more problems may arise than will be resolved. Thus we see that a second consideration is that in the ideal psychological state, the athlete would have the desire to learn and perform well. This condition is most likely to occur when athletes are permitted healthy outlets, such as dating. The athlete who has a strong motivation to achieve, who is sincerely dedicated to bettering himself and the team, will not need many restrictions and penalties. His common sense and good judgment will prevail in tempering his personal activity. The ideal goal is for the athlete to become a self-regulating organism, one who needs few restrictions from external sources. If athletics is to be an educational and meaningful experience, the athlete should understand how he can best assist the team to reach its objectives, and his actions should reflect this understanding and his personal commitment.

### The Married Athlete

Other factors than those studied by Trapp can have an effect on the athlete's relationship with the other team members. The married college athlete poses certain problems not associated with single athletes. As college students now marry more frequently than they used to, the married college athlete is no longer the rarity he once was. Although his responsibilities are different from those of the single athlete, he should still be able to follow training regulations set forth by the coach.

The psychological effects that marriage may have on athletic performance are of major concern. The author does not know of any research that has been undertaken on this subject, but one may conclude that some married athletes perform better, some worse, and others the same in comparison to their performances when single. However, if the experience of the author were true of all athletes, then it would be recommended that athletes not marry until after they had been graduated from school or at least were no longer eligible for teams (the number of years an athlete can play on a high school or college team is restricted by rules). As a junior in college, the author scored an average of 19 points in basketball games and was a conference first-team all-star. As a married senior and captain of the team, his performance fell woefully, and his motivation seemed to diminish as well.

Fortunately, this is not the case with all married athletes. Adjustment to marriage is a personal matter, and the role and importance of athletics in the context of marriage varies from athlete to athlete. The effects of marriage on performance in athletics are unpredictable. When the effects seem to be negative, the coach can attempt to determine the causes and help the married athlete through the troublesome period.

## Discrimination

Many people feel that athletics has been relatively free from prejudice, and to some extent this may be true on the surface; but a more penetrating examination reveals the presence of discrimination and prejudice as serious as in many other institutions in our society. Discrimination, even on a minor scale, can never be condoned. It must always be a source of latent bitterness, a potential tinderbox—both destructive and paradoxical in athletics, which demands selfless cooperation. This point has been alluded to a number of times in this chapter in the discussions of morale and spirit, group interactions, social mobility and status, and group acceptance and social integration. A cohesive unit is one that works together. Feelings of superiority or inferiority because of racial background or religious affiliation are detrimental to cohesion and morale.

Berelson and Steiner (1964) have done an excellent review of research findings concerning discrimination and prejudice in general. Some of the findings are relevant to our understanding of interactions between the coach and the team and within the team. First of all, it is estimated that only 20 to 25 percent of the adults in the United States are generally free of hostile attitudes toward minority groups (Berelson & Steiner, 1964, p. 501). People usually do not realize how prejudiced they are; they have a tendency to underestimate the strength of their feelings. In many cases, prejudiced people demonstrate a remarkable ability to rationalize their feelings.

Prejudice tends to be generalized to, although not necessarily equally directed toward, various groups. In other words, a person who is prejudiced against one ethnic group is probably prejudiced against all groups other than his own, although perhaps to different degrees. Prejudice and discrimination are usually learned within the family and home environment, because parents' attitudes are often emulated by their children (Berelson & Steiner, 1964, p. 502).

Studies in industry and elsewhere show that when ethnic or racial groups meet on a personal basis and with a common task at hand, prejudices lessen. It would appear, then, that athletics can serve to further understanding and cooperation between various represented groups. On the other hand, direct competition between members of groups may cause more prejudice to develop. For example, if a black man were competing against a white man for the fifth spot on a basketball starting team, prejudices might be heightened. A white football team playing against a black football team might be an illustration of another situation in which prejudices could increase.

Whenever a minority group improves its status, it is placed in further conflict with the majority group. For instance, Jews in America were not very much discriminated against when they were thought of as part of the working class a number of years ago, but when they began to compete with Protestants for professional and other higher-level positions, they became more of a threat, and discrimination therefore increased. Negroes, Chinese, and other groups are more acceptable if they "know their place" and do not attempt to elevate their status in American society. Because man's natural tendency is to improve his lot, especially if he feels he can attain his goals, tensions between majority and minority groups have been heightened. There is a tendency for people to value their own ethnic group highly and to stereotype and look down upon other ethnic groups, especially those with lower status.

A sensitive, intelligent coach will undoubtedly be aware of the factors that may contribute to, or work against, the smooth functioning of a team whose members belong to different ethnic groups. Self-analysis can help give the coach insight into his own prejudices. Analysis of team members and the groups they represent, their families, and their socioeconomic levels, will help him anticipate possible discrimination and prejudices within the team. Further, the coach should learn about the community where he works, and interact with its people. Talks with various community leaders will indicate local concerns, interests, and problems related to discrimination, and how these might affect, or be affected by, athletics. Tensions can be more readily eased before they become too intense.

Of particular concern today is the black athlete, who typically has an increasing sense of identity, who has been the object of discrimination and suppression for many years, and who is often blessed with superior motor skills and talents. The black athlete in these times usually feels that he is misunderstood and discriminated against by whites. These objections are typically unacceptable to whites, who deny that such practices exist. In the ideal situation, of course, all teammates are treated as equals by the coach and are respected for their human qualities and potential contributions to the team. But when there are intense competitions for team positions or dramatic contests with other teams, when the athletes and coaches are from different majority and minority ethnic groups, and when each person has his own degrees of prejudices toward various groups, feelings of prejudice can come to the surface. One situation to avoid is competition among the few black members of a team for one position. If there are only five black athletes on a football team, and three of them are competing for one available spot as a result of the encouragement of the coaching staff, there is every reason for bitterness.

The black athlete's call for black coaches is not at all unwarranted, for the black coach is symbolic; positions in society that were once exclusively white are now opening up to blacks, and when the prestigious title of "coach" is given to a black man, the morale of Negroes in general is raised. Furthermore, the black coach is apt to be sensitive to black athletes' problems and to communicate effectively with them. No matter how he tries, it is often difficult for the white coach to gain the confidence of the black athlete, especially in these confused times when the philosophies of "separatism" and "integration" are competing within both races.

To those who feel that sport has been especially kind to the black athlete, Boyle's book (1963) is recommended, as it contains an excellent chapter on the history of black baseball players. It is true that sport has helped many minority groups and has done much for the black man, but Boyle describes the problems, atrocities, and indignities suffered by black baseball players. How it feels to be a black baseball player is described, and a better understanding of the bitterness of the black athlete is revealed to white readers.

The black athlete is currently asking why he is in such demand. Is he being "used" for his skills? Are both black and white athletes "used," or is it particularly the black man who finds himself in such a position? Is the black athlete respected for being himself, as a person of worth and dignity, who can contribute much to society? Questions like these are being raised by the black athlete, and these questions must be dealt with by both black and white coaches.

Al McGuire, coach of Marquette University's basketball team, has been

quite successful in molding a winning team out of one white and four black
starters. His philosophy is to allow his players to behave as individuals.
McGuire was quoted in *Newsweek* (March 1, 1971, p. 96) as follows: "They
do my thing when they're playing, and they can do their own things when
they're not. There's something called individual dignity here." McGuire
demonstrates sincerity and sensitivity, as when he remarked, "I may not
agree with everything the blacks say on campus. But, hey, at least it's
occurred to me that they could be right and I could be wrong." Evidently,
McGuire's approach to coaching has produced successful relationships between coach and athletes and impressive records for the team. He percep-
tively suggests that "you can't treat a kid who grew up knife-fighting in
Harlem the way you treat a blond, four-letter man from Christ Lake,
Wisconsin." Blacks and whites may have to be handled in different ways in
order to bring out the best performance. Rules, which once were set rigidly
for all team athletes, may have to be modified and made flexible. If, as
McGuire suggests, "too many coaches are running plantations," black athletes have a right to be upset. Coach McGuire recognizes the concerns of his
athletes and attempts to deal with them promptly in a straightforward
manner.

For any coach, talking over problems and meeting them with frankness
and flexibility will help the team's morale and improve its performance. It
should be remembered that the black athlete's responsibilities in contemporary society typically go far beyond competing in sport. He may have
internal social, personal, and political conflicts that need to be resolved. In
such a situation understanding and communication are called for—not rigid
control, aloofness, and strict rules.

In one of the few studies of prejudice and athletes, Ibrahim (1968) administered two tests to measure prejudice against Negroes and Jews. The
subjects were white athletes and white nonathletes at Whittier College in
California. The results indicated that both athletes and nonathletes were
generally (1) tolerant of blacks, (2) tolerant of Jews, and (3) not rated as
prejudiced, according to norms of the scales used. This was, however, ad-
mittedly an unrepresentative group: students at Whittier usually come from
high-income families and an area of the country not especially noted for
segregation. The question, then, whether participation in sports diminishes
feelings of prejudice is still unanswered.

The extent to which sport has helped the Negro is questioned in a series
of provocative articles written by Jack Olsen which appeared in five parts
in *Sports Illustrated.*[3] Those in control of sport feel that they have helped

---

[3] The articles appeared on the following dates: Part 1, July 1, 1968 (pp. 12–27);
Part 2, July 8, 1968 (pp. 18–31); Part 3, July 15, 1968 (pp. 28–43); Part 4,
July 22, 1968 (pp. 28–41); Part 5, July 29, 1968 (pp. 20–35).

the black to overcome severe disadvantages, but Harry Edwards, assistant professor of sociology at San Jose State College and leader of the black athletic rebellion, bitterly observes that "black students aren't given athletic scholarships for the purpose of education. Blacks are brought in to perform. Any education they get is incidental to their main job, which is playing sports" (Part 1, p. 16). Although many Negro athletes have been enabled through sport to obtain college degrees, many of them never come close to a degree. Their previous experiences have not, typically, prepared them for college life. They received watered-down courses that permit them to remain eligible to compete but accomplish little else for them.

Personal interviews with many top-flight college and professional black athletes reveal discontent, disappointment, and anguish caused by the "system." Olsen reports that numerous black athletes undergo severe social problems, e.g., feeling against dating between blacks and whites on campus, poor relationships between coaches and athletes, and personal indignities. Stacking certain positions and specifying quotas for blacks on a team may be a fairly common practice on many college teams. An analysis of many colleges and universities noted for their athletic successes reveals startling similarities with regard to the recruitment and treatment of black athletes.

According to Olsen, there are many more tensions between blacks and whites on the same professional athletic team than most people realize. He writes, "Instead of ameliorating the tensions between the races, pro sport is sometimes more likely to inflame them" (Part 4, p. 34). Furthermore, many blacks feel that they must be significantly more skilled than whites on the same team in order to play, and that they are underpaid compared to whites. Once their playing days are over, white athletes have many opportunities which are not open to black athletes. This material certainly does not support the contention that the sports world provides some sort of haven for Negroes. Rather, it exposes common, prominent practices in sports and suggests a new look at the treatment of black athletes and a greater sensitivity to their problems.

### Training Rules and Absence from Practice

Every team operates within a framework of rules and policies. From both a psychological and a practical point of view, guidelines are necessary to define the mode of operation. We all need to know our boundaries as well as our freedoms. Assuming that training rules are acceptable according to various criteria, what does one do with the rule violator?

Presumably, training rules that are well established and that support the mutual objectives of the coach and members should not be abused. Exceptions may be made in extenuating circumstances, but the general rule of thumb is that violators should be penalized, even if it means dropping them from the squad. The same rules should apply to everyone, even the "star," for making exceptions to rules on the basis of status will lower the morale of the team. The importance of applying the same rules to all athletes cannot be underestimated.

Respect for the team, the rules, and the man who developed the rules should lead to a minimal amount of rule breaking. Attendance at regularly scheduled practice sessions is one important rule that should be stressed. Latenesses, absences, or poor attitudes should not be tolerated, for permissiveness in such matters will undermine the team's morale. The coach may attempt to determine the causes of such activity, but the athlete should be made to take the consequences of his actions.

### Hair

At one time hair length and style posed no problem to the coach. He dictated to his athletes the physical appearance expected of them, and his wishes were immediately obeyed. However, times change. Currently, many young people are questioning all rules imposed in our society by adults. And styles of hair and dress are quite different from what they were a few years ago. Considering these factors, the coach is now confronted with issues which never before existed. The coach's ultimatum—"Do this because I tell you so, and if you don't like it, get off the team"—no longer suffices. In fact, the moral and legal issues of such rules are being submitted to the courts for settlement.

Sideburns, beards, and long hair were almost nonexistent in the sports world about 10 years ago. Clean faces and crew cuts were in. Hair today may symbolize youths' disillusionment, antiestablishment feelings, personal experimentation, self-identity, symbolism, or desire to be part of the "in group." However it is interpreted, hair is a battlefield in society, schools, business, and sports. The following commentary (Joseph, 1970) depicts the confrontation between the athletics establishment and long-haired athletes.

> Last year's official entry card of the Pacific Southwest National Open Tennis Tournament, for example, included a paragraph that read: "All boys are required to be clean-shaven and have short haircuts." Questioned about this, the tournament director explained: "We're trying to keep this game fine. We don't want boys coming in here looking like hippies. We want them to have a nice trim, and we're not ashamed of it. I think it's time people took a stand on this."
>
> Such an enlightened bastion of liberalism as Stanford University kicked a record-breaking sprinter off the track team because he wouldn't cut his hair. (He was from Britain and had worn it long all his life.) Two Purdue runners were dropped from the track team when they refused to shave off moustaches.

(They were later reinstated by an athletic affairs committee that overruled the coaches.) When Oregon State football coach Dee Andros ordered one of his players to shave off a Van Dyke beard and moustache last spring, nearly two-thirds of the black students enrolled there—including 17 athletes—threatened to leave the campus.

Andros defended his action vigorously. "It is essential for team morale and unity," he told the *Los Angeles Times,* "for each individual player to conform to the rules and regulations set up for the rest of his teammates. I guess I'm the old-fashioned sort; I've always liked the Jack Armstrong, all-American-boy type of athlete. Although I believe in human rights and in individual rights, when we become a member of an organization or a team, there are certain things we must all give up. No individual can be put before the team."

When the *Times* polled other coaches for reaction, Notre Dame's Ara Parseghian put it even more vehemently. "Wearing a beard or moustache," he said, "doesn't make anyone like the scum that populates Haight-Ashbury. But it *does* give an empathy or sympathy for a movement that is certainly the direct opposite of what we strive for in college football, which is goal-oriented."

Added USC coach John McKay: "We don't really keep our players from growing their hair long. If they do, all that happens is we make them play without helmets. I like a little conformity on our team. If we permit our players to grow long hair, what is the next step? What else do we permit? . . . I like long hair. My wife has it. I don't want people with long hair to get angry with me. But you have to have certain standards to have a country, to do anything."

Not all coaches share these views. Pete Newell, former athletic director at the University of California and now general manager of the San Diego Rockets, took a different tack. "A coach," he said, "now has to be more aware of social changes and adjust to them. What was true three or four years ago is not necessarily true now. Sure, it's a voluntary act when an athlete goes out for a team. It's something he has chosen to do. He is responsible for the rules of the scholarship and the coach's rules. If he doesn't like them he has the choice to say, 'thanks but no thanks.' But it's a two-way response. Coaches are vulnerable if they put rules on a team that are contrary to accepted, normal modes of dress. Times change. What wasn't acceptable before is acceptable now—meaning long sideburns, beards, and long hair. It is mandatory that a coach recognize these changes" [pp. 30–31].

Coaches disagree about what hair length should be allowed, although most of them probably prepare guidelines that require shaven faces and relatively short haircuts. What may be of minor concern to the coach, however, can be a real issue for the athlete. Social pressure or a feeling that identity and independent thinking are threatened can result in a vigorous rebellion. No one can tell a coach how to "run his ship," and certainly whether to make liberal allowances or to enforce restrictions is a matter for the individual coach to decide. He should, however, at least be sensitive to changes in society and to the problems of youth. Training rules that were acceptable in 1950 are not necessarily appropriate for the 1970s. Either the coach must modify his rules accordingly, or else he had better be in such a respected and revered position of control that his dicta will go unchallenged.

### Dismissals

Although many of the coach's decisions are difficult, none is more painful than dismissing an athlete from the team. The grounds for this action are an individual matter with each coach. Ideally the situation will not arise if clarification of objectives, training rules, and channels for communication between coach and athlete are specified early in the season. Still, there can be no guarantees that an athlete will not do something that would warrant his dismissal from the team.

It is important for team morale that rules be maintained except in unusual cases, and an athlete should be dismissed from the team where such action is warranted, no matter what his status on the team. This decision has traditionally come from the coach, but in more and more institutions of learning, student hearing boards are being formed to evaluate cases and recommend disciplinary actions. A group of students is elected to serve on the board, which may or may not also include faculty members. The principle employed here is that students should be involved in decisions about discipline. Another possibility is that the coach might have a three-man committee, elected from the team, to hear the cases of team members charged with rules violations or inappropriate behavior. Such a committee makes recommendations to the coach, and he in turn of course makes the final decision. The age and maturity of the athletes determine whether formation of such a committee would be desirable.

### Newsmen and Communications Personnel

Thus far we have talked only about handling the people directly involved with the team—the coach and the athletes. Other people, however, have more than a passing interest in the team. Some, such as newsmen and radio and television commentators, make a living by informing the public of news about the team. These people report events in both objective and subjective fashion. Words and actions in the sports world result in newspaper print. Because their activities make news, the coach and athletes always have to be on the alert and on their best behavior. News in sports is of interest to a great number of people. Many communications people therefore go beyond the typical observed events to report "human interest" stories. The personal lives of athletes are no longer private, but become everyone's business. Comments made in interviews have to be guarded and tactful, for words spoken in a heightened emotional state may be regretted later.

An article by Francis (1967) can give the reader insight into the nature of various kinds of sportswriters. The sportswriter interacts with many people and strives to make an image for himself among them. The amount of newspaper space devoted to sport indicates its importance in contemporary society. Therefore, many types of sportswriters develop, and Francis says that they are motivated to achieve in one of the following categories:

1  Reporter (an objective writer)
2  Huckster (an events advertiser who does favors for people and gets the inside dope in return)
3  Informant (one who writes the "real dope," the scoop)
4  Analyst (one who critically examines every aspect of the contest)
5  Dramatist (one who exaggerates every feature of the contest)
6  Instructor (one who describes situations for laymen)
7  Influencer (one who writes without power and responsibility)

For the most part, it probably pays to deal honestly and fairly with all representatives of the news media. Although some coaches claim they thrive on "bad press," and deliberately maintain a running feud with newsmen, probably more gains for the team in general will be made where there are cordial relations. It would even make sense for the coach and his team members to discuss methods of handling reporters. When all the people who work with the team and the communications people most connected with it become well acquainted, interaction between them and the team personnel can become harmonious and beneficial to the team.

Newsmen and television and radio reporters can be good public-relations men for a team. Their words can ignite a spirit in the team itself, in the school, and in the community. Favorable commentary also helps to increase the support of fans and is beneficial for recruiting purposes. Just as the coach must learn how to deal with athletes on an individual basis, he is also responsible for handling communications people in a manner that is in the best interests of the team and school.

### School and Community

The coach's relationships with people in the school and the community are also important. The coach and his squad do not live in a vacuum. Much of what they do, during and outside competition, affects many other people. The team is often a focal point of excitement, interest, and spirit in the school, and many community people also support the team. The coach is obliged to communicate effectively with all these people. If he speaks at school and local functions, is active in the school and community in various projects, and in general does the best job possible, most people will probably be satisfied with him. The psychological value for the team of gaining widespread fan support at the home contests cannot be overestimated. The process is circular and mutually beneficial. The team plays well and wins; the fans are enthusiastic and excited, and they turn out in mass numbers and vocally support their team; the team feels encouraged and is influenced to win again.

### Psychological Approach of Sports Recruiters

The skill and experience of the coach can be very effective, but talented athletes make it easier for him to get good results. At the college and professional levels of sport, there is keen competition for the best athletes. Since outstanding athletes help to contribute to a winning team, and because of their scarcity and the resultant competition for their services, college recruiting is now recognized as "big business."

Recruiting high school athletes for a college team is extremely time-consuming and difficult. Why does an athlete choose one college over another? The location of the campus, the athletic program and opportunities, the academic possibilities, and the advice of family and friends are some of the many factors that enter into his decision. The recruiter can also be important. His personality and ways of dealing with people have a strong effect on how well he can "sell" the school he represents. He must be able to gain immediate insight into the athlete and his family so as to use a convincing approach. Any good salesman is basically honest but knows how to sell his product. His mannerisms should be pleasant and agreeable to the candidate and his family, and physical appearance and attire are important also.

Once the recruiter has made a good impression, other satisfied "customers" can help to convince the athlete. Athletes who received similar promises and have seen them realized will speak highly of the coaches and the college. Word of mouth spreads quickly and can be damaging or helpful. Little things may have a big effect. Meeting a former great athlete of the college may impress the potential enrollee to a great extent. Personal attention and treatment given to the athlete and his family may make the difference. The recruiter's concern is to get to know people as well as possible in the brief time he spends with them. The honesty, perceptiveness, and warmth of the sports recruiter will pay dividends in the long run for the team.

## SPECIAL CONSIDERATIONS

Besides the problems discussed thus far, there are other sociocultural aspects of athletics that need to be recognized and analyzed. Professional athletics has a tremendous influence on the public, as attested by its growth, the number of spectators at contests, its prevalence as a topic of conversation, and television, radio, and newspaper coverage. How and to what extent does professional sport affect young athletes? The current growth and development of women's sports parallels in some cases the direction men's athletics has taken. What are the cultural implications? Athletes at all ages are often looked upon as leaders. To what extent should they attempt to influence the sociopolitical atmosphere of an institution? Is athletics to be valued along with intellectual, social, and political activity at an institution of learning? Finally, does sport provide a release of hostility or an increase in aggression as far as the spectator is concerned? These are some of the situations and questions discussed below.

### *Effect of Professional Athletics*

There is little doubt that professional athletics affects the eating, television viewing, reading, and conversational experiences of many people. To know about sports and to identify with a team is important at all socioeconomic levels. In fact, it might be called the "in thing." Little wonder, then, that many children and adolescents aspire to be professional athletes. The anticipation of fame and money is a great motivation.

Especially, young people of various ethnic and racial groups identify with professional athletes of the same background, who serve as an inspiration. Youngsters who live in deprived areas and have limited means of expression sometimes develop hope for increased social status through athletics. Professional athletes influence the playing habits and social habits of the would-be athletes of tomorrow.

Professional sport has encouraged participation and provided motivation for many youths. It has encouraged people to devote a large amount of leisure time to spectatorship. It has given direction to competition in institutions at various levels of learning but at the same time has helped to create strict rules, all-out competition, and a feeling that there is less fun associated with school athletics than there once was. It is at once an evil and a blessing. Sport provides a therapeutic, physical, emotional, and psychological outlet for numerous people; and yet, it also drains energies which might be devoted to other things.

The school athlete learns how to develop and maximize his skills by watching the professional athlete in action, but attempts at emulation can also result in frustration when the young athlete cannot successfully copy his model's style. The influences of professional sport on the young athlete are many and varied, and if these influences are kept in proper perspective, they can work to the advantage of young athletes.

### Development of Women's Interscholastic Contests

For many years our society condemned women for participating in "men's games." Only such activities as swimming, diving, gymnastics, and fencing were considered acceptable means of expression for women. They were not supposed to sweat, to build firm muscles, or to compete with, or possibly beat, their male counterparts. That times have changed is a gross understatement.

Girls and women at all levels of schooling are now competing in a wide range of activities. Organizations are being formed; tournaments are held at local, state, regional, and national levels; and the female sex is demonstrating its prowess in basketball, golf, volleyball, badminton, and a host of other activities. Since 1969, an annual schedule of national intercollegiate athletic championships for college women has been held. The controlling body for these new championships is the Commission on Intercollegiate Athletics for Women, established in 1966 by the Division for Girls and Women's Sports (DGWS) of the American Association for Health, Physical Education, and Recreation. The purpose of the Commission is to provide more college women with an opportunity for competition at the national level. In some states, such as Iowa, girl's basketball games have radio coverage and are attended by many dedicated and spirited spectators. Participation in and audience for women's athletics have dramatically increased in the last few years. It has been reported that interscholastic athletic programs for girls were in effect in 41 states in 1968 (JOHPER, 1970).

The organizations that control women's competition are attempting to avoid the pitfalls and yet reap the benefits of men's athletics. Scholarships, extent of tournaments, type of control, and general direction are some of the problems that have to be resolved. In 1968, the Executive Council of the DGWS clarified its position on intercollegiate participation for women, recruitment, and scholarships. The Council does not approve of athletic scholarships nor of recruiting: "Participants in the school sports program should be students first and athletes second" (JOHPER, 1970, p. 69).

But there is no doubt that with extensive training, dedication, and motivation, and with public acceptance and approval, the female athlete can develop sport skills that closely resemble men's skills in a variety of activities. How much she should be encouraged to devote her time and energies to such a goal is difficult to say. Nonetheless, sports for women are here to stay. In some respects, they are going "big time." An evaluation of the implementation of such plans will have to wait a few years until programs are better established, and until the personal effects and resultant practices are more apparent. It will also be interesting to see what effects, if any, women's programs may have on men's sports.

*Athletic versus Intellectual, Social, and Political Activity on Campus*

Any school or college offers a variety of activities to its students. Such activities sometimes compete for recognition and importance, but at other times there is no conflict. On any campus there are some who would condemn athletics as being intellectually stultifying and generally worthless. Others would come to the defense of athletics, claiming it as important in the total well-being of participants and audience as intellectual, social, and political events.

Whether the emphasis on a campus should be on intellectual matters or on meaningful experiences depends on one's viewpoint. Judging by campus patterns throughout the country, most students, faculty members, and community members enjoy and want a campus that encompasses a variety of events, as long as a reasonable degree of excellence is maintained. Outstanding entertainment, enlightening speakers, and successful athletic teams are the types of events that make campus life something more than merely a series of courses and library assignments. To some students, extracurricular activities turn out to be more personally meaningful than the prescribed academic program.

When an athlete of stature participates in other forms of campus activity, he usually becomes a focal point. His political beliefs, for example, may influence a considerable number of other students. The athlete, in terms of personal convictions, principles, and need for expression, is no different from anyone else. He should be allowed and even encouraged to express his beliefs when a cause arises about which he feels strongly. Although a typical coach might tell the athlete to mind his own business, it must be remembered that an athlete's education and personal growth do not begin and end in the gymnasium or on the athletic field. To become educated means to experience many things—to learn how to live effectively within oneself and in society. Involvement in many activities broadens a person's perspective and helps him to reach this broad objective of education.

*Effect of the Contest on Spectators*

It has already been established that many people are involved in a given athletic contest. Some researchers have attempted to determine the effect of an audience on a person's performance, but fewer investigations have been concerned with the impact a contest might have on the spectator. Evidently watching an athletic contest meets certain needs. The situation permits the spectator to project himself into the sport. He lives vicariously through the athlete, and the athlete's successes and failures are the spectator's experiences also.

Since the more popular sports in our society have aggressive and hostile elements, spectators' identification with the athlete and the contest can lead to problems. Crowd disorders, especially in foreign soccer games, are notorious. Crowds must be controlled and their expressive tendencies tempered, or the consequences can be serious. There are two schools of thought about the effect of athletic competition on spectator behavior. One is that aggressive sports tend to encourage and produce aggressive tendencies in the fans, but the opposing view is that observing violent activity serves as an emotional release and decreases the aggressiveness of the spectator.

In a study of the effects of sports on spectators, Turner (1970) determined the elicited aggression of spectators before and after certain athletic contests. One spectator group viewed a football game, a basketball game, and a wrestling match; a second group viewed the basketball game and the wrestling match; and a third viewed only the wrestling match. The following conclusions were drawn:

> Football and basketball spectator situations increase the *frequency* of an individual's elicited aggression.
> Football and wrestling spectator situations do not increase the *intensity* of an individual's elicited aggression [p. 327].

Since these are isolated contests, it is possible that the nature of any one of them might produce differential results. The meaningfulness of the contest, the extent and nature of the crowd, and the nature and outcome of the contest may differ from situation to situation, and their effects on spectators may therefore also differ.

Kingsmore (1970) collected data from a number of contests. One group watched wrestling contests, another watched basketball games, and a third was a control and watched no competitive events. The subjects who served as spectators for an event in the experiment were selected because they had previously attended that activity. Pregame tests, postgame tests, and neutral-condition tests were compared. Kingsmore reports that the wrestling spectators showed less extrapunitive aggression (aggressive tendencies channeled outside the person) and no significant differences in total aggression and intrapunitive aggression (self-punishing tendencies) between pre- and post-match scores. The basketball spectators showed no differences on any of the three measures of aggression. The basketball and wrestling spectators displayed less intrapunitive aggression after the contests than the control group did under neutral conditions. This finding is interesting considering that the three groups of subjects did not differ on pregame test scores and scores under neutral conditions.

Changes in emotion are difficult to detect with written tests. It is agreed, though, that the athlete is not the only one who experiences the contest. The spectator is very much a part of the activity. For both the athlete and the fan, it is healthy to express feelings outwardly. And, for both parties, it is a question whether the results of these experiences are to sublimate or reduce aggressive impulses, to have a catharsis, or to heighten aggressive tendencies. There is some argument, at least in theory, that viewing aggressive activities is likely to increase aggressive tendencies. Further research along the lines laid out by Turner is needed before definite conclusions may be reached.

## SOCIAL FACILITATION (EFFECT OF SPECTATORS)

As long ago as 1897, Triplett attempted to determine the effects of an audience on motor performance. Subjects performed a reel-winding task and performed in bicycle races, and were found to be influenced in various ways by the presence of others. The investigator concluded that in general, the bodily presence of an audience seemed to liberate latent energy and stimulate the performer to greater effort.

Even today, however, it is difficult to make general statements about the influence of an audience on performance. A survey of the research, in which an assortment of tasks and diverse samples of subjects have been tested under widely different circumstances, permits the conclusion that some people's performance is impaired because of emotional upset at the presence of an audience, whereas others' performance may be improved, and still others may not appear to be affected at all.

There are two possible approaches to the problem: (1) to compare the effects of working in pairs or triads, where assistance may be offered, with the effects of performing alone in front of a crowd, and (2) to study the subjects and tasks involved. The interest in this book is naturally in research on athletes and sports skills. Since, unfortunately, the entire area of social facilitation has been poorly researched, to attempt to describe only experiments that are relevant to sport might be unwise. A broad description of the research and a discussion of the implications it can have for sport will be more meaningful.

In theory, it is conjectured that the presence of an audience elevates the arousal state of the individual performer, so that responses that are dominant in his repertoire of responses will tend to be emitted. A beginner (the learner of a new skill) should, according to this theory, demonstrate inappropriate responses in the presence of spectators. Well-learned skills, in which correct responses are dominant, should be aided or not affected in the social situation. Perhaps this is why the so-called "better" athletes perform more effectively with spectators watching; their performance has been socially facilitated.

Research on various motor tasks—not athletic skills, for none have been studied or observed under realistic situations—appears to support this theory. In an early experiment, Travis (1925) used a pursuit rotor apparatus to test eye-hand coordination in tracking. Each subject received 20 trials a day until his learning curve had leveled off for two days. On the next day, after the supposed maximum performance had been reached, an audience of from four to eight people was introduced. Performance scores with and without the audience were compared. An 81.8 percent improvement on the average was noted for performance with the audience. Evidently, once reasonably high skill in a task has been reached, social facilitation occurs.

One of the outstanding qualities of the successful athlete is his ability to perform, and perform well, before numerous spectators. Whereas lesser athletes would find their performance of athletic skills hampered under the pressure and stress of having an audience, superior athletes either appear to be oblivious to their environment during a contest or do better than in practice.

Some people feel that athletes can generally perform any skills well before a crowd, but if the theory discussed above holds true, the performance of newly acquired skills should not be enhanced by the presence of spectators, even if the subjects are athletes. The theory was upheld in an experiment undertaken by Singer (1965). Sixteen Ohio State University athletes from a variety of sports and sixteen nonathletes learned how to balance on a stabilometer. All the subjects were given 10 trials to learn the task with only the investigator present. The next day, they were allowed three more trials alone and three trials before a group of passive spectators. The three trials in the presence of others actually resulted in generally poorer performances than on the trial immediately preceding, which was executed without the audience. In addition, the nonathletes performed better than the athletes on two of the three trials performed in front of the spectators. Data for each trial are presented in Table 5-3 and illustrated in Figure 5-3. A number of factors may help to account for the performance of the athletes. The theory of specificity of situations appears to be verified by the inability of the athletes to perform a motor skill well in front of a small

TABLE 5-3  Means and standard deviations of athlete and nonathlete groups with and without the presence of spectators

| Group | | First day (practice trials) | | | | | | | | | | Second day | | | | | |
| | | 1 | 2 | 3 | 4 | 5 | 6 | 7 | 8 | 9 | 10 | Without spectators | | | With spectators | | |
| | | | | | | | | | | | | 1 | 2 | 3 | 4 | 5 | 6 |
|---|---|---|---|---|---|---|---|---|---|---|---|---|---|---|---|---|---|
| Athletes...... | $\overline{X}$ | 19.88 | 17.63 | 15.40 | 13.38 | 12.78 | 11.16 | 7.84 | 8.19 | 7.31 | 7.28 | 7.97 | 5.66 | 5.31 | 6.50 | 4.97 | 5.69 |
| | s | 4.46 | 4.98 | 4.26 | 4.63 | 5.83 | 4.98 | 4.79 | 5.30 | 3.57 | 4.70 | 4.71 | 3.43 | 3.71 | 4.10 | 3.31 | 4.73 |
| Nonathletes.. | $\overline{X}$ | 19.75 | 14.00 | 12.60 | 9.00 | 8.78 | 8.03 | 7.75 | 5.78 | 6.78 | 4.66 | 10.03 | 5.22 | 5.66 | 4.25 | 3.81 | 2.78 |
| | s | 4.44 | 4.72 | 5.21 | 4.97 | 5.24 | 4.62 | 5.37 | 5.06 | 4.71 | 3.85 | 3.21 | 2.45 | 3.82 | 4.05 | 3.28 | 2.20 |

Source: Robert N. Singer. Effect of spectators on athletes and non-athletes performing a gross motor task. Research Quarterly, 1965, **36**, 473–482. P. 478.

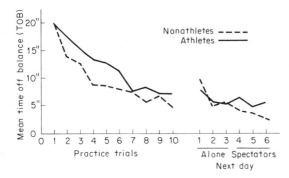

FIGURE 5-3 *Performance comparison between athletes and nonathletes alone and in the presence of spectators.* (Source: *Robert N. Singer. Effect of spectators on athletes and non-athletes performing a gross motor task.* Research Quarterly, *1965,* **36,** *473–482.* P. 477.)

audience even though they had successfully executed other motor skills before crowds on many previous occasions. Another possibility may be that athletes are more sensitive to an audience than nonathletes are, and that they feel uncomfortable demonstrating a skill at which they are not extremely competent.

The presence of an audience in sports is an interesting social phenomenon. It creates conflict: an audience is needed, and yet its presence arouses fear and other emotions. In a detailed analysis of the effect of an audience on performance, consideration should be given to (1) the size, familiarity, composition, and arrangement of the audience; (2) the anxiety level, temperament, and general personality of the performer; and (3) the past successes and failures of the performer in front of an audience.[4] Unfortunately, such a detailed analysis is not within the scope of this book.

In conclusion, however, it can be said that performance usually fluctuates more under stress than in practice. Second, with practice and familiarization with the situation of performing a particular skill in front of an audience, performances tend to improve, and the effects of previous bad experiences in front of a crowd are usually overcome. The athlete must be coached to avoid noticing the audience, as concentration on the events in the contest will improve his performance.

SUMMARY

Social variables, as they relate to sport and interact with the athlete and his performance, have been discussed and analyzed in this chapter. An athlete's output is contingent upon numerous social influences. One of the first

[4] These and other factors are discussed in depth in H. C. Hollingworth. *The psychology of the audience.* New York: American Book, 1935.

responsibilities of the athlete is to learn that he is part of a functioning unit, a group.

*Group interactions*    A "group," defined sociologically, is a cohesive unit, brought together for common reasons and shared objectives. For a group or team to be effective, the goals and tasks of the individual members must be specified; although interpersonal relationships are important, they should not reach a point where they obscure individual goals and specified tasks for the group. Leadership must be effective; communication channels must be open; and the size of the group should be reasonable for the goals at hand.

*Competition and cooperation*    Both these factors operate in typical athletic situations; both serve to elevate motivation and improve performance. There should be relative emphasis on cooperative and competitive attitudes according to various criteria associated with the nature of the athlete and the sport.

*Competitive ability*    Good and poor athletic competitors can be distinguished according to various behavior and personality variables.

*Relationships between individual and team performances*    Individual skill alone cannot be used to predict success in a team task. If team performance is the ultimate goal, much practice should occur in the team situation.

*Morale and spirit*    Morale is improved when a common goal exists; when effective leadership is present; when group interactions occur; when the members of the group feel accepted and confident, and believe their contributions to the goal are worthwhile; and when the team's goals are actually being achieved.

*Attitudes and values*    There appears to be some inconsistency between the values approved by society and those advocated by athletes. The "winning attitude," thinking positively and confidently, is a great asset in achieving victory.

*Sportsmanship*    The athlete is often in conflict between the expectations of society and the pressures of athletic competition. The coach can sometimes help him to find a reasonable compromise.

*Leadership*    Leadership is an interactional function of an individual's unique personality and the situation. No one style or one type of person represents good leadership under all conditions.

*Family*    Interaction among the athlete, the family, and the coach is important, for if family pressures are antagonistic to the athlete's and coach's goals, situations that are intolerable to the athlete may result.

*Social mobility and status*    Athletics provides a vehicle for social mobility, although the middle-class person usually has a higher motivation for achievement than the lower-class person.

The coach is faced with many individual problems when he attempts to mold a group of athletes into a functioning, cohesive unit. His recognition of and sensitivity to athletes' personal problems and attempts to resolve them satisfactorily are most desirable. Some problems that he may encounter are as follows:

*Group acceptance and social integration*    Generally, team members tend to become more friendly with one another as time goes by, but the coach should look out for the few people who continue to be outcasts.

*Dating*    The athlete has normal urges and interests and should be allowed to express them as other people of his age do. Ideally, the athlete should regulate his own extracurricular activities according to the potential contribution he wishes to, and can, make to the team.

*The married athlete*    The effects of marriage on athletic performance appear to vary from person to person. Some married athletes perform better, some worse, and others the same.

*Discrimination*    Much evidence is now available on the nature and extent of discrimination. The coach should make every attempt to treat all men as equals, to understand racial issues, and to be sympathetic to athletes of all ethnic groups.

*Training rules and absence from practice*    Society can function only within a framework of rules, and the same is true of the team. Rules should be developed, and penalties for violation should be understood and applied where necessary.

*Hair*    Hair length and style can become an issue between athletes and coach in this era in which youths are questioning authority and searching for identity. Training rules should be realistic and appropriate and should take into account fads and changes in society.

*Dismissals*    Rules must be maintained, and where warranted, an athlete should be dismissed from the team for the good of the morale of the team.

*Newsmen and communications personnel*    These people should be treated honestly and tactfully, for they can be good public relations men for the team. What they write about the team may affect morale and ultimate performance.

*School and community people*    Such people have a stake in the team, and their support must be garnered however and whenever possible.

*Psychological approach of sports recruiters*    The market for college athletes is quite competitive, and the coach needs outstanding athletes to form a superior team. The recruiter plays an important role in the eventual success of the team.

Special consideration should be given to other forces that may influence the athlete as well as to people who are affected by him. Although such relationships can only be expressed in a general way, they need to be expressed and realized.

*Effect of professional athletics*    Professional athletics has been shown to have positive and negative influences on young athletes and on society in general.

*Development of women's interscholastic contests*    Women's athletic competition is becoming highly organized and structured. Some of the problems involved are recruiting, rules, scholarships, and formation of a policy on athletic competition that is educationally sound.

*Athletic versus intellectual, social, and political activity on the campus*    A campus should have a variety of activities to satisfy the needs of various people, the prime requisite being that the activities represent a reasonable degree of excellence.

*Effect of the contest on spectators*    Both the spectator and the athlete experience the contest; for the spectator, it can provide a means of releasing emotions and projecting himself.

*Social facilitation (effect of spectators)*    The audience also has an effect on athletes. On the basis of theory and research, it can be expected that the performances of highly skilled athletes will be enhanced or unchanged by the presence of others. Specific aspects of the audience, the event, and the athlete must be considered in order to make accurate predictions of performance level.

## REFERENCES

Action highlights of council meeting. Girls and Women's Sports Column, *Journal of Health, Physical Education, and Recreation*, 1969, **40**, 69–70.

Annarino, Anthony A. The contribution of athletics to social mobility. Unpublished master's thesis, Purdue University, 1951.

Beisser, Arnold R. *The madness in sports*. New York: Appleton-Century-Crofts, 1967.

Berelson, Bernard, & Steiner, Gary A. *Human behavior: An inventory of scientific findings*. New York: Harcourt, Brace & World, 1964.

Boyle, Robert H. *Sport—mirror of American life*. Boston: Little, Brown, 1963.

Carter, L., Haythorn, William, & Howell, Margaret. A further investigation of the criteria of leadership. *Journal of Abnormal and Social Psychology*, 1950, **45**, 350–358.

Cratty, Bryant J. *Social dimensions of physical activity*. Englewood Cliffs, N.J.: Prentice-Hall, 1967.

Darley, J., Gross, N., & Martin, W. Studies of group behavior factors associated with the productivity of groups. *Journal of Applied Psychology*, 1952, **36**, 396-402.

Dolan, Joseph P. Parents of athletes. In Slovenko, Ralph, & Knight, James A. (Eds.), *Motivations in play, games and sports.* Springfield, Ill.: Charles C Thomas, 1967.

Fiedler, F. E. Assumed similarity measures as predictors of team effectiveness. *Journal of Abnormal and Social Psychology,* 1954, **49**, 381–388.

Fiedler, F. E. Style or circumstance: the leadership enigma. *Psychology Today,* 1969, **2**, 38–43.

Francis, Roy G. The sportswriter. In Slovenko, R., & Knight, J. A. (Eds.), *Motivations in play, games and sports.* Springfield, Ill.: Charles C Thomas, 1967.

Hemphill, John K. Relations between the size of the groups and the behavior of "superior leaders." *Journal of Social Psychology,* 1950, **32**, 11–22.

Ibrahim, Hilmi. Prejudice among college athletes. *Research Quarterly,* 1968, **39**, 556–559.

Joseph, Newton. A victory for youth? The great hair hassle. *Today's Health,* published by the American Medical Association, March 1970, **48**, 30–33.

Keating, James W. Character or catharsis. *Catholic Educational Review,* 1965, **63**, 300–306.

Kingsmore, John M. The effect of a professional wrestling and professional basketball contest upon the aggressive tendencies of the spectator. In G. Kenyon (Ed.), *Contemporary psychology of sport: Proceedings of the 2d International Congress of Sports Psychology.* Chicago: The Athletic Institute, 1970. Pp. 311–315.

Kistler, Joy W. Attitudes expressed about behavior demonstrated in certain specific situations occurring in sports. *Proceedings of the National College Physical Education Association for Men,* 1957, **50**, 55–58.

Kleiner, R. J. The effects of threat reduction upon interpersonal attraction. *Journal of Personality,* 1960, **28**, 145–155.

Lakie, William L. Expressed attitudes for various groups of athletes toward athletic competition. *Research Quarterly,* 1964, **35**, 497–503.

Loy, J. Social background, college experience, and present status of college athletes. Unpublished paper, University of California, Los Angeles, 1969.

McIntyre, Thomas D. Socio-economic backgrounds of white male athletes from four selected sports at the Pennsylvania State University. Unpublished master's thesis, Pennsylvania State University, 1959.

McPhee, John. *A sense of where you are: a profile of William Warren Bradley.* New York: Farrar, Straus & Giroux, 1965.

Mead, Margaret. *Cooperation and competition among primitive peoples.* New York: McGraw-Hill, 1961.

Nisbett, Richard E. Birth order and participation in dangerous sports. *Journal of Personality and Social Psychology,* 1968, **8**, 351–353.

Olsen, Jack. The black athlete. *Sports Illustrated,* July 1, 1968, pp. 12–27 (Part 1); July 8, 1968, pp. 18–31 (Part 2); July 15, 1968, pp. 28–43 (Part 3); July 22, 1968, pp. 28–41 (Part 4); July 29, 1968, pp. 20–35 (Part 5).

Partch, Andrew F. A comparative study of varsity lettermen and non-lettermen graduates of San Diego State College from 1936 through 1940. Unpublished master's thesis, San Diego State College, 1963.

Pettit, Bob. *The drive within me.* Englewood Cliffs, N.J.: Prentice-Hall, 1966.

Rehberg, Richard A., & Schafer, Walter E. Participation in interscholastic athletics and college expectations. *American Journal of Sociology,* 1968, **73**, 732–740.

Rhine, R. J. A concept formation approach to attitude acquisition. *Psychological Review,* 1958, **65**, 362–370.

Richardson, Deane. Ethical conduct in sport situations. *Proceedings of the National College Physical Education Association for Men,* 1962, **66**, 98–103.

Rosen, Bernard C. The achievement syndrome: a psychocultural dimension of social stratification. In Atkinson, J. W. (Ed.), *Motives in fantasy, action, and society.* Princeton, N.J.: D. Van Nostrand, 1958.

Rosenthal, D., & Cofer, C. N. The effect on group performance of an indifferent and neglectful attitude shown by one group member, *Journal of Experimental Psychology,* 1948, **38**, 568–577.

Ryan, Francis. An investigation of personality differences associated with competitive ability; and Further observations on competitive ability in athletics. In Wedge, Bryant M. (Ed.), *Psychological problems of college men.* New Haven, Conn.: Yale University Press, 1958.

Savage, Howard J. *American college athletics.* New York: Carnegie Foundation, 1929.

Schrupp, Manfred H. The differential effects of the development of athletic ability of a higher order. *Research Quarterly,* 1953, **24**, 218–222.

Singer, Robert N. Effect of spectators on athletes and non-athletes performing a gross motor task. *Research Quarterly,* 1965, **36**, 473–482.

Thisted, M. N. A study of the relationship between participation in college athletics and vocational success. *Research Quarterly,* 1933, **4**, 5–20.

Trapp. William G. A study of social integration in a college football squad. *Proceedings of the National College Physical Education Association for Men,* 1953, **56**, 139–141.

Travis, L. E. The effect of a small audience upon eye-hand coordination. *Journal of Abnormal and Social Psychology,* 1925, **20**, 142–146.

Triplett, Norman. The dynamogenic factors in pacemaking and competition. *American Journal of Psychology,* 1897–98, **9**, 507–533.

Turner, Edward T. The effects of viewing college football, basketball, and wrestling on the elicited aggressive responses of male spectators. In G. Kenyon (Ed.), *Contemporary psychology of sport: Proceedings of the 2d International Congress of Sports Psychology.* Chicago: *The Athletic Institute,* 1970, Pp. 325–328.

Vanderburgh, Bill. Physical and psychological conditioning for competitive basketball. *Journal of Health, Physical Education, and Recreation,* 1956, **27**, 42.

Weinberg, K. S., & Arond, Henry. The occupational culture of the boxer. *American Journal of Sociology,* 1952, **57**, 460–469.

Weyner, Norma, & Zeaman, David. Team and individual performances on a motor learning task. *Journal of General Psychology,* 1956, **55**, 127–142.

# CHAPTER SIX

# Practice Factors and the Athlete

Thus far it has been shown that many variables interact to produce the skilled athlete. Genetic factors, personal development, and experiences are all important. The coach's role in development of the athlete's accomplishments is far greater than has been suggested up to this point, however. The coach has the power to vary environmental and learning conditions, and the athlete can benefit when the coach makes good decisions about such external controls.

There are general learning procedures, or principles, which are applicable to many people. Therefore, in this chapter and the next two, as we consider what is best for the group, or the so-called "average" person in the group, the tendency will be to present data in the form of group means or averages. Respect for individual differences will also be maintained, particularly under certain selected topics.

There are many factors which the coach can vary to facilitate the learning process and to enhance performance. He designates practice sessions in terms of number, length, and spacing over a given number of days. A particular practice period is organized around the skills and maneuvers to be learned and practiced, and time is allocated for each. Motivational factors are introduced. Certain techniques raise the level of performance; others lower it. Concepts of transfer of training are employed: drills to transfer to game skills, practice to transfer to the actual contest, practice cues and aids to transfer to better performance, and related skills and techniques to transfer to each other. Attention to and discrimination of the appropriate environmental events can improve performance. Finally, the degree of retention of skills once learned is the result of many variables, at least some of which can be manipulated by the coach.

Unfortunately, there has been very little experimental research on the learning of athletic skills, and researchers' lack of interest in this area is probably one of the leading reasons for this. Therefore, it has been necessary to apply principles from the psychology of learning, which have been based upon studies primarily concerned with fine motor skills and verbal learning, to the learning of athletic skills. There is, however, an obvious hazard in applying the principles of one experimental area to an apparently related one.

The coach as manipulator of environmental variables and learning situations plays an important role in attaining the shared objectives of the coach, athlete, and team: better performances lead to high skill levels, which lead to winning.

## PRACTICE SESSIONS

The coach faces two fundamental problems with regard to practice sessions. First, he must organize the content of each period and how much time will be spent on each aspect. Second, the number and spacing of practices in a given week or month must be planned. Physiological factors which will determine, to a large extent, the nature of the practice sessions include the physical nature of the skills to be practiced and their possible fatiguing effects on the performers; the effects of temperature and humidity; the athletes' physical condition; and how soon after the practice day the contest will occur (allowance must be made for body rest, recovery, and preparedness).

Other sources have quite adequately covered such physiological conditions, and the concern of this book is with the psychological reasons for selecting certain practice schedules. The reasons should be consistent with the results of psychology-of-learning investigations and therefore with "laws of learning." Practice procedures are suggested below on the basis of psychological findings alone, and no attempt is made to suggest modifications in them because of physiological factors. It is assumed that the application of anything suggested here will be tempered by the findings of other sciences as well as by common sense.

### The Practice Periods

Psychologists working in this area have been primarily occupied with comparing the results of continuous practice with those of spaced practice. "Massed practice" or "continuous practice" refers to the practicing of a task without any rest pauses or with rests of short duration, whereas "distributed practice" or "spaced practice" refers to practices divided by rest intervals or intervals learning alternate skills. Does continuous practice lead to more effective skill acquisition and retention than practice broken up by spaced rest periods? Is it better to practice a task with very little interruption for rest, or is rest beneficial to learning and performance? What are the optimum intervals between practice periods?

As long ago as 1932, a famous psychologist, probably the founder of modern sports psychology, offered his views on coaching in general and on the nature of the practice period in particular. Coleman Griffith, in *Psy-*

*chology of Coaching,* wrote that there is a proper and favorable length for a practice period. For most tasks (including basket shooting, batting, serving, and punting) the limit is approximately 20 minutes, and continued practice of any one skill beyond this limit without sufficient rest leads to ineffective repetitions.

Although the above comments appear to be based more on common sense than on established fact, Griffith did report a study which demonstrated the effectiveness of a varsity basketball practice period interrupted by short intervals of complete relaxation. Two groups were formed: group A shot baskets continuously for an hour; group B shot three minutes, relaxed two, for an hour. The next day the procedures were reversed. The results of the investigation indicated that although both groups shot about an equal amount of time, the men averaged 15 percent more baskets when shooting with frequent rest periods than when shooting steadily.

The issue of massed versus spaced practice is not new by any means. Studies in the literature of psychology can be found as early as 1885. Mohr, in the May, 1960, edition of *Research Quarterly,* reviewed 45 studies and found that 40 favored distributed practice. However, she noticed that the evidence specifically from physical education was far too scanty to uphold the belief that distributed practice in athletics would have a more favorable outcome than massed practice. Massed versus distributed practice is one of the areas in which physical educators and coaches have accepted the conclusions psychologists have drawn from studies using mazes, puzzles, rotary pursuit tasks, and nonsense syllables.

Of the many studies which are found in the experimental literature, the vast majority have demonstrated the immediate superiority of distributed practice over massed practice using a wide range of learning materials and methods. As to the optimal rest interval between learning trials, wide variations are found depending on the task employed. Little difference between continuous and space practice has been found in eventual retention, although distributed practice seems to lead to slightly better retention.

Figure 6-1 contains data on varying conditions of massed and distributed practice on the pursuit rotor. Notice the effect of each condition on performance. Distributed practice throughout the experiment resulted in excellent achievement, and merely changing one group's schedule from massed to distributed practice in the terminal stages of practice yielded equally good performance. The massed-practice group demonstrated a performance curve similar to that of the group whose schedule was changed from distributed to massed practice. Before the final performance, all groups rested, and there was very little difference in performance among the groups, indicating that inhibiting effects of massed practice are temporary.

The learning curves in Figure 6-2 are also interesting to observe. Once

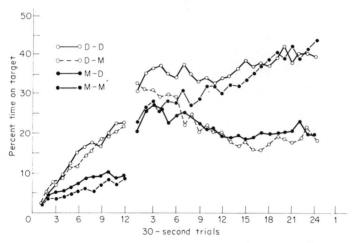

FIGURE 6-1  *Performance curves for groups practicing under vary-ing combinations of massed and distributed practice. (*Source: *M. R. Denny, N. Frisbey, & J. Weaver. Rotary pursuit performance under alternative conditions of distributed and massed practice.* Journal of Experimental Psychology, *1955,* **49**, *48–54. P. 49. Copyright 1955 by the American Psychological Association and reproduced by permis-sion.)*

again, the apparatus employed was the pursuit rotor. The massed-practice group was given 18 trials a day with two-second breaks between trials, and the distributed-practice group also had 18 trials but took 1½-minute breaks between trials. On each succeeding day of the study, the distributed-prac-tice groups began at a lower performance level than they ended the day before, whereas the massed-practice group began higher. Increase in per-formance following a period of no practice, a phenomenon typically ob-served following massed practice, has been termed "reminiscence." During practice on each day, the gap in performance between the two groups widened. Both groups were provided with the same type of distributed prac-tice on the last day. It is apparent in Figure 6-2 that there were very few differences between the groups on the final day (trials 90 to 108).

As Gagné & Fleishman (1959) point out, the inhibiting effect of massed practice does not affect what is learned. The concentrated learning of a motor skill by the massed-practice technique may not be inefficient even though its effect on immediate performance appears to be detrimental, for Gagné & Fleishman find that when a period of rest is allowed, perform-ance levels recover. The massed-practice method apparently exerts its effects on immediate performance rather than on the learning process itself.

On the other hand, a number of researchers and coaches believe that rest

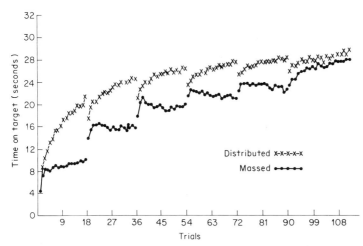

FIGURE 6-2   *The effects of distributed and massed practice on the learning of a motor skill. (Source: J. M. Digman. Growth of a motor skill as a function of distribution of practice. Journal of Experimental Psychology, 1959, **57**, 310–316. P. 94. Copyright 1959 by the American Psychological Association and reproduced by permission.)*

periods are appropriate when the athlete is showing signs of fatigue, since he may practice incorrect response patterns if he is overtired. The more complex the task, the greater the danger, and of course it is difficult to unlearn movement patterns with flaws that have been continuously practiced.

It cannot be safely assumed that the experimental results reported earlier will always be obtained with every skill, for more research on practice of athletic skills is needed before any conclusions can be reached. However, it is obvious that, at worst, concentrated practice does have an eventual effect that is almost as good as the effect of distributed practice. Furthermore, the diminished immediate return from massed practice need not be considered prohibitive.

### Administration of Practice Periods

Practice sessions for most sports are usually daily occurrences. However, thought has been given to concentrating practice on certain days and skipping practice on others or shortening the length of the periods but having more periods, perhaps two a day.

One reason for having more frequent but shorter football practices during hot, humid August weather is readily apparent from a consideration of such physiological factors as fatigue and heat exhaustion. But what of the psychological rationale for organizing practice?

A summary of the research would lead one to conclude that the most effective learning occurs in relatively short practice periods distributed over longer periods of time. Research in this area has been done primarily on college subjects learning a variety of verbal and motor tasks, not on superior or even average athletes learning to perfect their skills. Younger athletes, not so expert as older performers, might do better with brief but frequently repeated sessions because of (1) their youth and the short attention span associated with youth and (2) their skill level, which will be developed only in later years to high degrees of proficiency.

Crawford et al. (1947), in a study of aerial gunnery, used 221 students being trained for the Air Force. When ammunition was distributed over many training missions, the percentage of target hits was as much as five times better than when all the ammunition was fired on one mission. The investigators concluded that the distribution of rounds and number of missions was directly related to terminal proficiency in aerial gunnery.

Lashley's early study (1915) is one of the few investigations of athletic skills. He studied the acquisition of high skill levels in archery. The subjects were divided into five groups, each of which ultimately made 360 attempts at the target and each of which was provided with one-day rest intervals. Each group, however, shot a different number of arrows per day: 5, 12, 20, 40, or 60. During the first 180 attempts, little difference in accuracy between the groups was noted, but later it was determined that a wider distribution of practice resulted in higher proficiency. For example, the 12-shot-a-day group improved 47 percent while the 60-shot-a-day group improved 29 percent over initial scores. Lashley's results have been generally borne out in many subsequent studies under a wide range of experimental conditions.

In LaLone's study (1967), two groups of subjects were taught how to snow ski over a four-week period. One group had one-hour practice sessions four days a week; the other group had two-hour practice sessions two days a week. The first group was found to be more effective in developing the skill of snow skiing.

Many basketball coaches appear to agree with these findings in their approach to basketball practice sessions. Sauter (1959) recommends that coaches make practices as enjoyable as possible and remove all drudgery. He writes that practice sessions which are brief and snappy are important in the schedule. Bee & Norton (1942) make the point that coaches often become so enthused about practice that the players are overworked. They recommend short, brisk practice sessions and variation in activities in such a way that rest periods are included.

The studies described above and others point to the desirability of spreading practice over a longer period of time, e.g., four months instead of four weeks. Unfortunately, the time the coach has available for practice is restricted. Even under these conditions, however, more frequent and shorter practice should yield better performances.

Another consideration in the administration of practice sessions is the amount of practice of a skill per week needed to maintain effective levels. In strength development, for instance, it is popularly believed (e.g., Goldenberg, 1961) that three days of training a week is as productive as five days. Evidently, the two extra days of training do not add measurable differences in strength. The usual assumption about athletic skills is the more practice, the better, but this is not necessarily true. In a given period of time, say a week, there may be an optimal amount of practice for a given task; less would be detrimental, but more would be wasted.

If Murphy's study (1916) is any indication of what to expect, the results of practice in motor skills may very well be similar to those of strength training. The girls in this study threw the javelin in 34 practice periods. One group practiced five times a week, a second group three times a week, and a third group only once a week. From the results of the study, Murphy concluded that the different distributions of practice yielded about the same levels of performance. Therefore, he favored three times or one time a week over five times a week.

The preceding investigation gives food for thought. Although it is doubtful that high skill levels could be maintained in once-a-week practice, there is a possibility that some athletes overpractice a skill. Perhaps the excess time could be best used in practicing other skills or techniques. The decision is left to the coach, for there is not enough research in this area to make conclusive statements possible.

## PRACTICING FOR PERFECTION

Mere practice by itself seldom leads to the attainment of high skill levels. Many factors must be emphasized by the coach if learning is to progress in a somewhat orderly and desirable way. Within each practice session, the coach must be aware of these factors in order to impart such information to the athlete. These considerations for the facilitation of the learning process generally hold true from person to person, whether swimmer or golfer, basketball player or tennis player, athlete or nonathlete. They affect the learning of written materials as well as motor skills.

### Intent to Learn

The learner must be intent on learning, desirous of accomplishing the tasks set before him. In other words, motivation is extremely important in the learning of skills. Routinely going through an act without the intent of bettering oneself with each execution is a waste of time. When the athlete has a purpose, he learns from experience, striving to improve with every performance whether in practice or in actual contest.

The wish to excel may occur because of one or a combination of many variables, but it should be present. Associated with the intent to learn are a receptiveness to suggestions, advice, and guidance; motivation, dedication to the task; and a willingness to undergo sacrifices. If the athlete has these qualities and the necessary abilities, accomplishment will occur. Many limitations have been overcome by athletes with a strong intent to succeed, as every coach has observed.

### Meaningfulness

The meaningfulness of the skills to be learned in practice is yet another consideration. This meaningfulness implies that not only must the skills and the routines employed for practicing them actually be significant, but they must also be perceived as such by the learner. In other words, the learning experience should be meaningful as viewed by both the coach and the athlete.

The athlete should understand the purpose behind what he is told to do, for purposeful activity yields more favorable results. Fortunately, most motor executions make sense to the athlete who has an intent to achieve. If athletics in general were not meaningful to him, his performance endeavors would not last very long. Nonetheless, communication between coach and athlete must be carried on constantly to ensure that the coach's directions to the athlete be construed as purposeful. Therefore, instructions and desired outcomes should be clear, realistic, relevant, and attainable.

### Readiness

The developing of skills may be thought of as similar to building with blocks. One stage must be reached before the next can be handled effectively. As the athlete comes to be regarded as superior, he accomplishes more complex tasks, especially in stressful situations. It is important to remember that he did not reach his skilled status overnight. At each different level of achievement, he is ready to learn tasks appropriate to that level. The sensitive coach realizes that readiness is an individual matter, and his expectations of and direction to the learner are consistent with the readiness of the learner.

Readiness includes the capacity to handle certain responsibilities and is usually dependent on past experiences, maturity, growth and developmental factors, and a favorable attitude toward the activity to be learned. The most effective learning occurs when the skills to be learned are within the range and experience of the athlete but just beyond his present capabilities, forcing him to strive upward.

## Attention

During the process of acquiring a skill, the athlete often has a problem of focusing on the appropriate stimuli. In any given situation, there are a multitude of stimuli present, and the skilled performer can extract and concentrate on only the most relevant of these cues. Stimulus selectivity occurs with experience and direction. The athlete learns which cues in the situation are of primary importance, disregards or scans others, and thereby responds in an appropriate, skilled manner.

Isolating too few stimuli can be dangerous, however. A basketball player, when in the act of shooting, may be able to concentrate on only one item, the shot. He may lack the flexibility to note the defensive man's position in relation to him by adjusting the release of the ball or passing to a teammate in a better position to score. With experience and direction, however, the player can learn to concentrate on specific details but at the same time be flexible in his approach. The exclusion of inappropriate stimuli is a momentary thing, for that which is irrelevant one second may be quite relevant the next. In general, however, the learner must be taught to concentrate on certain stimuli, to become less aware of the many stimuli that surround each situation.

Giving attention at the wrong time to the wrong stimulus may of course have a detrimental effect on performance. For example, the long-distance runner may plan to run a particular race in a predetermined manner and may practice accordingly, planning to kick hard at a given point in the last lap. However, in the actual race, if the crowd cheers and excites him, he may start his kick too soon. Reacting to the wrong stimulus (the spectators instead of the race strategy) may cause him to lose the race when he tires during the final seconds.

Attention may be viewed from another aspect. During practice sessions, an obvious responsibility of the coach is to sustain the motivation, interest, and attention of the athletes. Benington & Newell (1962) recommend that practice schedules be changed on a daily basis, for they believe that variety in drills is absolutely necessary to maintain enthusiasm among the players. Anything a coach can do to elevate and maintain the alertness of the athletes during practice will pay dividends at later dates.

## Conditions

Research findings seem to imply that practice conditions should resemble actual contest conditions as much as possible. The ability to transfer skills from one situation to another depends on the similarity between the situations and skills to be employed. In other words, there appears to be a great amount of specificity in athletes' achievements, as shown in example after example. Many basketball players can perform well when shooting by themselves or under pressured practice, but in the actual game, they may be unable to demonstrate the talents that seemed so outstanding. Many boys can play a wonderful game of half-court or three-man basketball and yet do not possess the knack or desired combination of abilities to play a five-man, full-court game satisfactorily.

Basketball coaches indicate that they do indeed believe that practice shooting conditions should simulate game conditions. Howell (1958) writes that basketball drills should be competitive and should occur under game-like conditions whenever possible. He states that free-throw shots should be made competitive and can be best learned by practicing under simulated game conditions. While Johnny Bach (1958) was head basketball coach at Fordham University, he split his practice sessions into time periods, the longest of which was devoted to scrimmage. He did this because he believed that his athletes learned and worked best when practicing under game conditions.

Numerous coaches have reported that it is best to stop scrimmage or call fouls during scrimmage so that the players can experience free-throw shooting while fatigued and under stress. Leavitt (1955) says that free-throw shooting is more influenced by the type of practice used than by the style of the player's shot. He also indicates that the best time to practice foul shooting is after running drills or during scrimmage, when the player is slightly fatigued.

The skills that will be required in the game, then, should be the ones practiced, and the practice should occur in gamelike situations. Many skills are typically called for in the actual contest, and practice sessions should include as many of these as possible. In other words, there should be a variety of practice material. Wolfle (1951, p. 1272) states, "Practice materials should vary in as many dimensions as possible and over approximately as wide a range as will the situations to be encountered when the learning is to be applied." Also, the nature of practice sessions should be varied, because prolonged and monotonous practice yields diminishing returns.

In the research literature concerned with speed and accuracy, it has been usually determined that performance in the emphasized variable will become more proficient. Since many acts require both speed and accuracy, in most situations the rule might be to emphasize both during practice. If responses are slowed down in order to gain practice in accuracy, say in the fencing lunge, additional work will have to be done later in order to learn to strike the target accurately at optimal speed. Even initially, in fact, movements might well be practiced at regular speeds at the expense of accuracy. With this approach, accurate movements eventually become established along with the high speeds of execution. If movements are practiced at slow speeds in order to gain accuracy, however, almost totally new response patterns will have to be learned when ideal speeds are called for. The process of acquiring skill will probably take longer in the latter situation than in the former.

An additional thought about the nature of practice is offered here. It should not contain sloppy and mediocre performances; the actual contest requires all-out performance, and practice sessions might well simulate this condition. Practice should reflect the best the athlete has to offer, for excellence is something that emerges gradually, not overnight.

### Importance

Under the best conditions, practice is necessary if perfection in performance is to occur. It provides a situation in which the learning processes can be activated—hence the occurrence of learning. Although practice does not always bring about improvement, and certainly at high skill levels practice effects are barely noticeable, the coach should always strive to create circumstances that best promote effective learning during practice.

Although one can learn from reading, hearing of, and viewing materials, athletic skills are best learned by physical activity. Study after study indicates that motor performance can be improved by mentally rehearsing activity, reading the movement patterns, listening to instructions and directions, watching films, and the like. These means, however, are usually found to be not nearly as influential on the learning of motor skills as direct practice.

### Overpractice

Perhaps one of the most urgent concerns of coaches is to determine how much time should be devoted to the practicing of each skill and each play to ensure proper execution. It is evident that numerous repetitions of complex acts are a necessity in order to reach mastery. But just how many repetitions and how much time need be prescribed? What should be the practice criterion of proficiency that is acceptable to the coach?

Determining total practice time is extremely important, for neither the athlete nor the coach has an endless source at his disposal. Efficiency in terms of the maximal returns from a minimal input is the goal. In psychological studies of the benefits of overlearning, the number of trials it takes the subject to reach a criterion is recorded. It then becomes possible to observe the effect of additional trials. Invariably in these studies, when subjects overlearn, that is, receive additional trials, they show higher achievement on the task at hand. More practice does result in better performance, as shown in Table 6-1.

The necessity of adequate initial learning, when later retention is the goal, has been well established in the research literature. When a skill is well learned, it is well retained. Conversely, partially mastered skills are forgotten more easily. Coupled with knowledge on overlearning, this information suggests that the coach consider immediate and long-range objectives. The coach must evaluate the number of skills and strategies to be mastered by the athletes in terms of their relative importance. Considered in connection with time limitations and individual differences in achievement, the situation is difficult to resolve. But certainly, once he confronts the situation, the coach will learn which skills, techniques, plays, and strategies in the particular situation need the most practice.

## WARMUP

For many people, warmup is an implied function of practice. "Warmup" may be defined as (1) a practice period immediately before the actual contest, (2) all the practice sessions preceding the contest, or (3) a special designated period for prescribed activities which occurs in the beginning stages of every practice meeting or contest. The nature of warmup is such that it might include general body exercises (calisthenics) not specifically related to the movement patterns required in the particular sport, or it might consist of specifically related activities. Athletes also have been known

---

TABLE 6-1    The effects of overlearning on retention

| Recall delayed | *Mean number of words recalled after* | | |
| | *No overlearning* | *50% overlearning* | *100% overlearning* |
| --- | --- | --- | --- |
| 1 day............................ | 3.10 | 4.60 | 5.83 |
| 7 days........................ | 0.20 | 1.30 | 1.65 |
| 14 days........................ | 0.15 | 0.65 | 0.90 |
| 28 days........................ | 0.00 | 0.25 | 0.40 |

*Source:* Adapted from W. C. F. Krueger. The effects of overlearning on retention. *Journal of Experimental Psychology*, 1929, **12**, 71–78. P. 74. Copyright 1929 by the American Psychological Association and reproduced by permission.

to warm up by the use of diathermy, hot showers, massage, mental rehearsal of the physical activity, and the like.

Due to increasing controversy over the use of varied warmup techniques before athletic competition, much research has been conducted within the past decade. The actual benefits of warmup have been investigated, and the relative effects of warmup conditions on different types of physical activities have been compared. Merely through observation and personal experience, it would appear to most people that athletes in a wide variety of sports would require some activity before competition. Gymnasts go through warmup rituals. The football team undergoes prescribed drill before the game. Tennis players stroke the ball for a number of minutes before they begin their match.

Whether the need for or belief in warmups is physiological or psychological in nature is not easy to ascertain. Certainly it could be argued that if warmup enhances performance, in many athletic situations the delay between warmup and actually performing in the contest is so long as to negate any potential worth in the preliminary activity. The football team exercises, returns to the locker room, and reappears on the athletic field ready to play about 20 minutes later. Also, many players do not get into the game until the second, third, or fourth quarters; what good is pregame warmup to them?

## Physiology

Probably the two most accepted reasons for the use of warmups lie in the prevention of muscular injuries and in the promotion of better motor performance. Laboratory evidence supports the warming up of the muscle to an optimal state (1) to increase the speed of contraction, (2) to decrease blood viscosity and increase blood supply to the area, and (3) to reduce tearing of or other injury to muscle fibers. As to the first two reasons, which really imply an increased preparedness and readiness for activity and supposedly better performance, evidence is conflicting. Research on the hypothesis that warmup reduces athletic injuries is quite difficult to undertake. This hypothesis has always been an accepted belief, and hence an accepted procedure, because it makes sense, but its truth has not yet been substantially documented.

## Performance

Consider, for example, the conflicting results of the following two experiments. De Vries (1959) used swimmers on the University of Southern California swimming team as subjects in attempting to determine the value of various types of warmups on swimming times in 100-yard events. Each man swam under the conditions of (1) no pretrial warmups, (2) swimming warmup, (3) hot shower warmup, (4) calisthenic warmups, and (5) massage warmups. It was found that as a group, the swimmers made significantly better time after warmups than without any warmup. However, in a breakdown of events (freestyle, dolphin, breaststroke, and backstroke, all compared according to type of warmup procedure), inconsistent results were obtained. The investigator therefore calls for an individual approach to warmup methods.

Karpovich & Hale (1956) conducted two experiments dealing with warmup prior to performance. After massage, digital stroking, or running exercises, college track men were tested for time in the 440-yard dash. No significant difference in performance effects was noted between the warmup methods. Also, when performance was recorded on the bicycle ergometer after no warmup and after warmup similar to the tested activity, no difference in results was observed.

An examination of the research may help to determine why the results in these and other studies have been so conflicting. One explanation may be that various types of performance events have been the subjects of the studies. Events involving different qualities—strength, or endurance, or speed, or accuracy—may be affected differently by warmup techniques. Another possibility may be that some of the numerous types of warmups tested may be more effective than others for specific activities.

Generally speaking, most investigations have been conducted on track men and swimmers, and the data have variously supported or denied the value of warmups. Warmup might be more beneficial, however, for events involving accurate movements or fast and accurate movements, than for activities, such as track and swimming that are performed at a more physical and mechanical level. There is more room to improve in complex skills than in simple ones. An actual physiological basis for the use of warmups to improve motor performance has yet to be satisfactorily determined, however.

There is a possibility that warmup places people in a *psychological* state of readiness for competition. Perhaps warmup releases tension and provides the athlete with additional confidence. People often perform better when they think they are supposed to. After taking some worthless drug or foodstuff or going through some pregame ritual, very little physiological effect on performance can really be expected, but if the athlete expects positive effects, his performance yield may become higher. The supposedly nutritious pre-event steak is ingrained in the minds of many athletes, and has been for centuries, as a preparation for the event, and yet, physiologists have known for years that steak has very little physiological effect on athletic performance. The prime source of the energy needed in endurance events is carbohydrate, not protein.

The nature of the sport and its associated tasks is one consideration in the use of warmup procedures, and the skill level of the athlete is another. How warmup affects performers at various levels of skill in an assortment of activities is a mysterious web that should be unraveled. The value of warmups may be greater for some athletes than others, and may be more psychological than physiological or vice versa for certain people. In two leading books dealing with the physiology of exercise, Karpovich (1965) questions the widespread usage and acceptance of warmups, and de Vries (1966) supports the practice of warming up. If the coach is confused, he has a right to be. Perhaps he might like to do his own experimentation.

*Types*

As mentioned earlier, many types of techniques have been used as warmups. General activity, otherwise known as "unrelated warmups," supposedly places the cardiorespiratory system and general musculature in an optimal state of readiness for the event. Calisthenics best exemplifies this type of warmup. On the contrary, "related warmups" contain the movement patterns required in the contest skills. There appears to be more logic, if warmups are to be used, in using related warmups than unrelated warmups; and related warmups are most widespread in practice. Diathermy, massage, and hot showers are less utilized as warmups in practical situations. The physiological basis for the use of such techniques may be questioned, especially in the case of massage. E. A. Müller, the renowned German physiologist, has done much research on the relationship of massage to performance. He states that massage before performance when the athlete is in a resting state should not be expected to be of benefit (Müller, 1965). The function of massage is not to increase the oxygen supply to the muscles but to assist in quick removal of the accumulating fatiguing acids in the working muscles. Therefore, when the athlete is tired and there is a rest period, massage can be effective in speeding up natural muscle recovery.

The mental processes may be deliberately activated to serve as a basis for warmup before competition. "Mental practice," also called "conceptualization," "mental rehearsal," and "imagery," is the thinking through of an act without any observable physical movements. As a practice technique, substantial research confirms the hypothesis that mental practice results in higher motor achievement than when there is no practice, either physical or mental. As a warmup before an actual contest, its benefits are difficult to ascertain, but many athletes claim that they visualize contest conditions and, in one form or another, go through mental practice.

As an example, Jean-Claude Killy, the famous French skier and perhaps the world's best, was interviewed about his methods of practice and other factors that contributed to his success. It is said that after actual practice on a given slope, he runs the race in his head beforehand, eyes shut, timing himself with a stopwatch; that he traverses the entire slope, geographical landmarks and all, in detail—mentally.

The effect of hypnosis on athletic performance has also been a subject for conjecture. Certain athletes attempt to put themselves into a semitrance, a form of self-hypnosis, as if to talk themselves into better performances through concentration and deliberation for a designated time period. Some athletes primarily involved with power events, such as throwing the shot, admit to and swear by this routine, but it has yet to be questioned or supported by research.

Hypnosis can also be employed to determine the effects of warmup, as in a study reported by Massey, Johnson, & Kramer (1961). The subjects performed with and without warmups, but in a hypnotic trance at all times, so that they did not know whether they had warmups before the recorded performance. The findings were interesting in that no differences were observed between warmup and no warmup. No injuries or muscle soreness were reported by the subjects.

Another type of warmup is the overload practice. Coaches can readily think of examples in different sports: the baseball player swinging a weighted bat before batting, the track man running in weighted shoes, the jumper wearing weighted shoes or weights attached to his body, the pitcher throwing a weighted ball, and so on. The obvious intention of these practices is to allow the batter to whip the regulation bat around faster, the runner and jumper to run faster and jump higher with standard equipment, the pitcher to throw a regulation baseball faster.

There have been only a few investigations of the merits of such practices, and the results are conflicting. For example, in one study (the data of which are illustrated in Figures 6-3 and 6-4), throwing with a weighted baseball transferred over to increased throwing velocity with a regulation ball, but the effects on accuracy were obscure and difficult to estimate.

In an investigation completed by Brose (1964), the subjects were 21 candidates for a college freshman baseball team. One group practiced with leaded baseballs (10 ounces), a second exercised on a wall pulley (which had a resistance of 10 pounds), and the third was the control, practicing with regulation baseballs (5 ounces). Following practice, each group threw 20 regulation baseballs at a target 35 feet away. The performance scores, as represented by velocity and accuracy, indicated little difference among the groups. However, when these post-test scores were compared with initial test

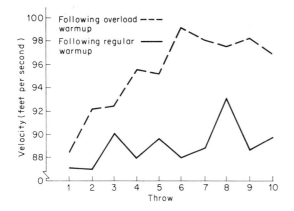

FIGURE 6-3 *Comparison of ball velocity by throw before and after warmup.* (Source: *W. D. Van Huss, L. Albrecht, R. Nelson, & R. Hagerman. Effect of overload warm-up on the velocity and accuracy of throwing.* Research Quarterly, *1962,* **33**, *472–475. P. 473.)*

scores (before training began), the two overload-practiced groups improved significantly, whereas the control group did not improve.

In another study, laboratory-designed, speed of elbow flexion was tested immediately before and after the application of selected levels of overload (Nelson & Lambert, 1965). Elbow flexion speed was found not to increase as a result of the overload warmup. An interesting sidelight on this study, though, is that heavier loads caused sensations of greater speed. The movements, as a result of the overload application, felt faster to the subjects, indicating the presence of kinesthetic illusions. Do athletes who warm up with weighted equipment improve their performances, or do they just think they do? Further research is needed before conclusions can be drawn.

## IMPROVEMENT AS A RESULT OF PRACTICE

In discussing aspects of motor learning it sometimes becomes apparent that many phenomena cannot be described in terms of group behavior. How and why individual performances change during practice is the subject of this section. In order to understand the learning process, the coach must be aware of the factors associated with practice and improvement, including prediction of ultimate achievement from early success, changes in abilities associated with early and late success, and variability in performance.

### Prediction of Achievement from Early Success

In any group of people, some can be classified as "fast learners" and "slow learners" of any given task. Because of previous experiences, devel-

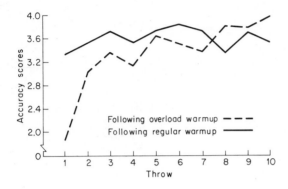

FIGURE 6-4 *Comparison of accuracy by throw before and after warmup. (Source: W. D. Van Huss, L. Albrecht, R. Nelson, & R. Hagerman. Effect of overload warm-up on the velocity and accuracy of throwing. Research Quarterly, 1962, **33**, 472–475. P. 474.)*

oped capacities, and present abilities related to the particular skill, some people are able to learn faster than others. However, ultimate proficiency in a skill is not necessarily related to early relatively successful attempts.

Investigations in this area are conducted by observing the status of subjects on initial trials of a task and comparing their achievement relative to other subjects in later, culminating trials. The statistical procedure usually employed is the correlational $(r)$ technique, which determines the relationship between any two variables, with scores from the same subjects used as the data for both variables. In the example above, we would want to know whether subjects who performed well in the beginning stages of learning also performed well at advanced stages of learning, and vice versa. The correlation coefficient $r$ indicates the relative status of individuals within a group on any two performance measures.

An $r$ never exceeds +1.00 or −1.00. The higher the correlation, the more positive the relationship. As $r$ approaches .00, no meaningful relationship exists, and a high negative correlation indicates an inverse relationship between two variables; i.e., one increases as the other decreases. Very generally speaking, a correlation from .00 to +.30 or .00 to −.30 demonstrates little or no relationship; from .30 to .60, a moderate relationship; and approaching 1.00, a high correlation.

It should be reemphasized here that a person is not typically an overall fast learner or a generally slow learner. Rather, achievement in each task is obtained in varying speeds and at different levels for each individual. For example, Woodrow (1940), who has done extensive research in the area, has found that there is no indication of a general learning ability or a general improvement factor. After testing subjects in widely different test performances, he concluded that no one general factor is associated with rate of improvement. Coaches would do well to bear this concept in mind in terms of expectations of achievement in skills across many athletes.

There is a fairly good indication that only a very small relationship exists between initial success and later proficiency in the learning of new tasks. In research concerned with beginners learning psychological laboratory tasks, prediction of skill attainment from initial performance in general is poor. The estimate of learning ability in these tasks should probably extend from one-quarter to one-half of the days or trials of practice. The coach usually comes in contact with people of a certain amount of talent and skill, and highly skilled people yield relatively stabilized performances; that is, there is less chance of change in their relative status within a group.

The point is, however, that some do and will improve faster than others. Even with the more skilled, performance in the first practice session is not sufficient to predict ultimate attained skill. A sport comprises many skills, and improvement in one skill may not make the person a better athlete. Rather, a person's success in a sport is probably determined by the interaction of many factors, which add up to a demonstration of talents consistent with the team's needs and the coach's expectations.

*Ability Patterns in Performance*

The studies cited below seem to provide further support for the concepts of the specificity of skills and the difficulty of predicting end achievement from early proficiency in any skill. Buxton & Humphreys (1935) attempted to measure the relative achievement of 50 male subjects in four laboratory motor tasks before and after practice. If there were a factor of general motor skill, the intercorrelations should have been high, and if end performance were reflected in the operation of a general factor, the terminal correlations could be expected to be greater than the early ones. In fact, however, the pretask practice intercorrelations ranged from .08 to .40, with an average $r$ of .25. After practice, the correlations were lower, ranging from $-.02$ to .39, averaging .16. No one ability operated to provide consistent initial success across the tasks for the subjects, nor did one ability determine ultimate achievement in these skills.

Research on the acquisition of proficiency in particular skills has provided some explanations of why some athletes reach higher skill levels than others and why there is difficulty in predicting later levels of achievement. Fleishman is well known for his work with psychomotor tasks and the underlying human abilities associated with performing well in them. There are implications from his findings about skill acquisition in athletics.

In one study (Fleishman & Hempel, 1954) in which subjects learned a complex motor task, the factors that were related to achievement at various stages of practice were isolated. Through the statistical procedure called "factor analysis," an extension of the correlation method, it was found that the task was more complex in the initial part of the practice and less complex with the continuation of practice. Seven factors were related to early success, but only three significant factors were isolated in the later stages. Furthermore, the abilities related to achievement were dissimilar at the different stages of practice. The authors state, "It is quite conceivable that the abilities contributing to individual differences in earlier stages of skill attainment . . . may be somewhat different than those contributing variance at more advanced and terminal levels of proficiency" (p. 251). In other words, the coach may expect different abilities to be important in different phases of learning a skill. Once these are ascertained for a particular skill, they should be emphasized when pertinent to the athlete's stage of development.

Researchers are attempting to isolate and predict factors necessary to high levels of proficiency in complex psychomotor tasks. It can be hoped that the same will be done with athletic skills. In another study, Fleishman (1957) attempted to determine the abilities involved in early and late stages of proficiency in seven psychomotor tasks. Once again it was observed that a change in abilities contributed to proficiency as training continued. The level of importance of some abilities increased, of others decreased. For example, in the discrimination reaction time task, spatial orientation and response orientation were important in early success. Later in practice and with increased levels of skill, speed of arm movement was most important. Similarly, the abilities related to achievement in swimming, golf, football, or basketball are probably also somewhat dissimilar at various points in skill development.

## Variability in Performance

Even to the most casual observer there appears to be an instability in the performance of individual athletes from practice session to practice session and even within sessions. With increased skill, performance levels become more predictable. That is, the athlete is more consistent in his output as he acquires skill; fluctuations in internal states and external situations have less impact on his performance.

Variability in human performance, the relationship of initial status to final status, and the relationship of performances in successive trials can be observed in ways other than those mentioned thus far. Research and data from performance on laboratory-type tasks are given below, and the association with athletic skills is evident. In these studies, one aspect of the nature of individual differences is pointed up, and it serves as a warning to the coach not to treat all athletes the same and not to expect similar performances under all conditions.

One way to observe variability in performance is to require subjects to learn a task during a number of trials and then to analyze all possible trial correlations. A comparison between test trials invariably indicates progressively lower correlations between the first trial and successively remote trials. Also, the most recent adjacent trials yield progressively higher correlations. As learning occurs, the abilities that are specific to the task are most important to the skill at hand. Later trials correlate more highly with each other as important factors become isolated and more limited in number, resulting in more consistent performances from person to person.

As an example, let us examine the data presented in Table 6-2. The correlations of trial 1 with each succeeding trial (top horizontal row) steadily decrease. The correlations in the lowest diagonal row, representing correlations of succeeding pairs of trials, consistently increase. These correlations are in general higher than those usually found in research of this nature, but they nevertheless exemplify the predictable direction of such correlations.

In attempting to predict final achievement, accuracy in prediction is poorer for complex skills in which many variables enter into the picture. Also, the longer the period of practice between initial and final testing, the better the chance that final status will have little relationship to early success. When people are learning a new skill, they are rather equal in performance, but with practice, a greater variability in their performances is noted, as some will improve greatly, some very little. In addition, with more practice, people's performances become more stable, and there is less relative change within the group. In Table 6-2, for example, the lowest diagonal row of correlations increases with the more recent adjacent trials.

An analysis of the acquisition of skill through learning trials reveals significant changes in the relationships among abilities both in different

TABLE 6-2    Intertrial correlations for a two-hand coordination test

| Trial | 1 | 2 | 3 | 4 | 5 | 6 | 7 | 8 |
|---|---|---|---|---|---|---|---|---|
| 1 | | .79 | .77 | .74 | .73 | .71 | .71 | .70 |
| 2 | | | .87 | .87 | .84 | .82 | .82 | .82 |
| 3 | | | | .91 | .89 | .87 | .85 | .86 |
| 4 | | | | | .91 | .88 | .86 | .88 |
| 5 | | | | | | .89 | .90 | .90 |
| 6 | | | | | | | .93 | .93 |
| 7 | | | | | | | | .94 |
| 8 | | | | | | | | |

*Source:* M. B. Jones. Practice as a process of simplification. *Psychology Review,* 1962, **69**, 274–294. P. 276. Copyright 1962 by the American Psychological Association and reproduced by permission.

tasks and within the same task at different stages of practice. The implications for the coach are that with more practice initial performances are less predictive of final achievement. Practice makes people less alike; they usually begin a new task with somewhat similar performances but then display greater differences with practice. Furthermore, practice causes one's performance to become less variable. The reasons for these outcomes have been discussed and other possible explanations offered elsewhere in this book.

In summary, not only are certain abilities needed for skilled performance, but these abilities apparently change in importance during practice as skill is acquired. Also, more factors are associated with initial achievement than are associated with practice in the final stages. Research has demonstrated that initial proficiency is related to final success in simple motor skills, but there is little indication of such a relationship in complex motor skills. In other words, if a person scores high relative to the group in early trials on complex motor skills, there is little assurance that he will do likewise on later trials. Further research on the effects of practice is needed, specifically pertaining to individual differences on various trials, various tasks, and growth and developmental factors.

## FATIGUE

Throughout this century, physiologists and psychologists have attempted to define and explain fatigue, with little success. Many attempted interpretations only confuse the issue, with the result that experimental work has been minimal and difficult to apply to motor learning.

Evidently, fatigue can be associated with tired feelings, physiological changes in the body, and a worsening in performance. To some people, fatigue is the opposite of rest: energy expenditure places the organism in an unbalanced state (nonhomeostasis), resulting in internal chemical changes in the body, which in turn encourage a disinclination to do work. Fatigue is also associated with poorer work output and decreased efficiency in effort.

Fatigue may be primarily induced locally or generally. That is, one may continually contract the elbow flexors and ultimately bring about a temporary decrease in the possibility of moving that limb, or he may exercise arms, legs, and trunk simultaneously and feel the more generalized effect of fatigue. It is important that the coach who is employing warmup techniques prepare the athlete for the contest either specifically or generally without extending the treatment to the extent of impairing performance.

Physiological fatigue and its symptoms and limits are somewhat easier to investigate and define than is psychological fatigue (if indeed these two states exist independently of each other).[1] Many people equate mental fatigue with psychological fatigue, although the difficulty, if not impossibility, of separating the mental from the physical is obvious. One can become fatigued from reading too much, playing too much handball, driving a car too long, or typing for a continuous stretch of time. The effects of each of these fatigues is such as to have a general overall influence on the body.

For the purposes of this book, let us accept Bartlett's interpretation of "fatigue," presented by Haider & Dixon (1961), as

> the term used to cover all those determinable changes in the expression of an activity which can be traced to the continuing exercise of that activity under its normal operational conditions and which can be shown to lead, either immediately or after delay, to deterioration in the expression of that activity, or more simply to results within the activity that are not wanted [p. 235].

Notice that in this definition, the effects of fatigue may be felt immediately or for some interval following the activity. Of particular concern to the coach is whether learning under conditions of apparent fatigue is inhibited or whether, as in the case of massed practice, performance is merely temporarily depressed, which would be an indication that learning was effectively occurring all the time. The coach is often confronted with the problem of having to determine the point at which time spent in practice begins to have diminishing returns. Naturally, if fatigue causes the practice of incorrect responses and sloppy movements, the coach should terminate the session.

However, on many occasions the athlete is in a moderately tired state and the coach must make a decision about the wisdom of introducing new skills to be learned or having the athlete continually practice old skills. Although there has been no research in athletic situations, implications may be drawn from laboratory-learned motor tasks. Is learning hampered under conditions of fatigue? Let us review experiments done by Phillips and by Nunney, and compare the results.

In Phillips' study (1962), the subjects were tested on a stabilometer and on the Rho test, which measures speed of arm movement. Basically, the design was as follows:

Test → fatiguing exercise → continued practice → test again three days later

---

[1] Various parameters (physical, mental, and emotional) of fatigue are identified and explained in S. Howard Bartley. *Fatigue: mechanism and management.* Springfield, Ill.: Charles C Thomas, 1965.

Three groups of subjects were formed: (1) a control; (2) a heavy exercise group that was fatigued by a step-up task; and (3) a local exercise group, which was fatigued by an arm-cranking task. It was found that all groups showed a significant learning improvement on the motor tests that were given three days after the designated experience. With only one exception,[2] there were no differences in performance among the groups.

Nunney (1963) formed five groups of 20 male college students each. Four experimental groups were fatigued in various ways on a treadmill or ergometer, and the fifth group, the control, was given no fatiguing task. Immediately after being fatigued, the groups were given one trial on a star-tracing task, and 10 minutes later, their rotary pursuit performance (tracking a moving disc with a stylus) was recorded. The four experimental groups were observed to be significantly worse than the control in star tracing, whereas no differences in rotary pursuit scores were noticed.

It is evident from the data provided in both of these studies that fatigue has an immediate depressant effect on performance. During supposed conditions of fatigue, however, people still learn. After the symptoms of fatigue have passed, learning is observed as a function of practice, even if the practice occurred when the subjects were fatigued. In these and a few other investigations, it might be argued that the subjects were not exhausted but simply fatigued. Results might be different with exhausted subjects.

Nevertheless, there is reason to believe that learning can still occur in the moderately tired state the athlete usually reaches near the end of practice. A worsening of performance may be only temporary, as in the typical massed-practice study, and therefore, when time is exceptionally important and practice sessions need to be extended, the athlete may be able to learn new skills when he is moderately fatigued. The coach should take a common-sense approach and should attempt to determine when fatigue has reached the extent that attention and learning have fallen off, movements are hampered, and practice is worthless. He should also keep in mind that going too far can be dangerous in some activities, such as polevaulting, diving, and gymnastics.

To practice under conditions of semifatigue skills that have already been learned may help athletes to prepare for their contests. Training under conditions similar to those of competition—for example, foul shooting when tired, in the late stages of a basketball game—could be helpful, although there has been no research on this specific problem. It would seem, however, that if skills are to be used in a rested state they should be practiced in a rested state, and vice versa. Since, in most contests, skills are used by ath-

---

[2] The only exception was the heavy-exercise and control groups on the Rho test, and in this case there was no difference between these two groups.

letes in a relatively fresh condition at the beginning and in a tired condition at the end, it may be that practice conditions should simulate this situation as closely as possible. Activity does not have to be curtailed whenever athletes are on the verge of becoming tired. Once again, the coach must use his discretion.

## SUMMARY

When planning practice sessions, the coach must consider the potential impact of many variables on the learning process.

*Practice periods*    For immediate high levels of performance, some distribution of practice in the various skills is suggested. As to retention and later performance, little difference has been found among continuous practice, practice spaced with varying rest intervals, and practice of alternate skills.

*Administration of practice periods*    Shorter practice periods spread over a longer duration of time are probably more effective than longer practice periods held during a brief time interval.

*Intent to learn*    The athlete must want to learn and succeed.

*Meaningfulness*    The learning experience should be meaningful from the viewpoint of both the coach and the athlete.

*Readiness*    Skills to be learned should be within the range and experience of the athlete (at his point of readiness) but at a level which forces him to strive upward.

*Attention*    Attention to the appropriate stimuli and a disregard for irrelevant cues enhance learning.

*Conditions*    Practice conditions should simulate contest conditions as closely as possible.

*Importance*    Practice is necessary for high skill levels to be reached.

*Overpractice*    Overpractice results in better-learned and hence more effectively retained skills.

*Warmup*    Warmup may assume many forms, and the research results are contradictory about its benefits. In most cases in which warmup is shown to be effective, warmups that are directly related to the sport are favored over other types. Performances involving complex and precise movements probably benefit more from warmup than do gross physical acts. The psychological implications of warmup should not go overlooked.

*Improvement as a result of practice*    Achievement in various athletic tasks is an individual matter, for there is no general learning ability or general improvement factor. In beginning stages of learning, there is little relationship between initial success and later proficiency. Abilities needed for achievement in motor performance change in nature and number as skill is acquired. There is more variability between individual performances later in practice as well as more consistency in each performance.

*Fatigue*   When fatigue results in the practice of incorrect responses and sloppy movements, practice sessions should be terminated. In moderately fatigued states, as in massed practice, immediate performance may suffer but long-term performance may be improved. Practice of skills in a tired state similar to that in the actual contest may prove to be an effective training technique.

## REFERENCES

Bach, J. Situation play practice. *Scholastic Coach*, 1958, **28**, 10–11.

Bartlett, F. C. Psychological criteria of fatigue. *Symposium on fatigue*. London, 1953. Cited by Haider, M., & Dixon, N. F. Influence of training and fatigue on the continuous recording of a visual differential threshold. *British Journal of Psychology*, 1961, **52**, 227–237.

Bee, C., & Norton, K. *The science of coaching.* New York: Ronald Press, 1942.

Benington, John, & Newell, Pete. *Basketball methods.* New York: Ronald Press, 1962.

Brose, Donald E. The effect of overload training on the velocity and accuracy of baseball throwing. Unpublished master's thesis, University of Maryland, 1964.

Buxton, C. E., & Humphreys, L. G. The effect of practice upon intercorrelations of motor skills. *Science*, 1935, **81**, 441–442.

Crawford, Meredith P., et al. Psychological research on operational training in the continental Air Forces. Army Air Forces Aviation Psychological Program Research Reports, No. 16, 1947.

de Vries, Herbert. Effects of various warm-up procedures on 100-yard times of competitive swimmers. *Research Quarterly*, 1959, **30**, 11–20.

de Vries, Herbert. *Physiology of exercise.* Dubuque, Iowa: Brown, 1966.

Fleishman, E. A. A comparative study of aptitude patterns in unskilled psychomotor performances. *Journal of Applied Psychology*, 1957, **41**, 263–272.

Fleishman, E. A., & Hempel, Walter E., Jr. Changes in factor structure of a complex psychomotor test as a function of practice. *Psychometrika*, 1954, **19**, 239–252.

Gagné, Robert M., & Fleishman, E. A. *Psychology of human performance.* New York: Holt, 1959.

Goldenberg, Joseph. A general progressive weight-training course for all athletes. *Scholastic Coach*, 1961, **31**, 40–41.

Griffith, Coleman R. *Psychology of coaching.* New York: Scribner, 1932.

Howell, Fred E. Basketball drills; make them competitive. *Athletic Journal*, 1958, **38**, 29–36.

Karpovich, Peter V. *Physiology of muscular activity.* Philadelphia, Pa.: Saunders, 1965.

Karpovich, Peter V., & Hale, Creighton. Effect of warming-up upon physical performance. *Journal of the American Medical Association*, 1956, **162**, 1117–1119.

LaLone, Patricia Anne. The effect of two distributions of practice on the acquisition of skill in snow skiing. Unpublished master's thesis, Pennsylvania State University, 1967.

Lashley, K. S. The acquisition of skill in archery. *Papers from the Department of Marine Biology of the Carnegie Institute of Washington, 7,* 105–128, 1915.

Leavitt, B. Foul shooting. *Scholastic Coach,* **25,** 18, 1955.

Massey, Benjamin H., Johnson, Warren R., & Kramer, George F. Effect of warm-up exercise upon muscular performance using hypnosis to control the psychological variable. *Research Quarterly,* 1961, **32,** 63–71.

Mohr, Dorothy R. The contributions of physical activity to skill learning, Part II. *Research Quarterly,* 1960, **31,** 321–350.

Müller, E. A. Physiological methods of increasing human physical work capacity. Paper presented at University College, Dublin, April, 1965.

Murphy, Herbert H. Distribution of practice periods in learning. *Journal of Educational Psychology,* 1916, **7,** 150–162.

Nelson, Richard C., & Lambert, Ward. Immediate after-effects of overload on resisted and nonresisted speeds of movement. *Research Quarterly,* 1965, **36,** 296–306.

Nunney, Derek N. Fatigue, impairment, and psychomotor learning. *Perceptual and Motor Skills,* 1963, **16,** 369–375.

Phillips, William H. The effect of physical fatigue on two motor learning tasks. Unpublished doctoral dissertation, University of California, Berkeley, 1962.

Sauter, Waldo. Guiding principles for the beginning basketball coach. *Athletic Journal,* 1959, **40,** 58.

Wolfle, Dael. Training. In Stevens, S. S. (Ed.), *Handbook of experimental psychology.* New York: Wiley, 1951.

Woodrow, Herbert. Interrelations of measures of learning. *Journal of Psychology,* 1940, **10,** 49–73.

CHAPTER SEVEN

# Learning Factors and the Athlete

$C$ertain concepts or areas of study are particularly associated with the psychology of learning. Each area has been the subject of entire books representing extensive research and theoretical speculation. Crucial to any discussion of learning is an understanding of the terms "motivation," "reinforcement," "transfer," and "retention." Although their technical and theoretical definitions are not commonly known, these terms are used widely, and many people have a general idea what they mean. The purpose of this chapter is to make them more understandable and to investigate ways in which the concepts behind the terms and the evidence from relevant research may be put to effective use by the coach.

It is not easy to make general statements about these terms or about many of the other variables described in this book. The coach must always make allowance for the nature of the athletes (age, sex, past experience, and other characteristics), the nature of the task (simple or complex, motor or cognitive), and the environmental conditions that affect the learning experience. However, once such factors are understood as they interact with the variable being studied or practiced, more precise predictions of behavior may be made with confidence.

At the heart of all learning situations must be a concern for the most desirable form of motivation. How to reinforce ideal responses and increase the probability that they will occur is also important to the coach. Principles of transfer inform us when, according to laws of probability, the most effective transfer may be expected to occur from skill to skill, concept to concept, and situation to situation (from practice to contest, for example). Finally, that which has been learned must be retained if practice is to be at all meaningful.

## LEARNING

The coach and the athlete are dedicated to the same goal: for the athlete to learn the appropriate skills and strategies as efficiently and effectively as possible. A well-learned skill is performed well when it counts—in the contest. Thus, a certain degree of relationship exists between how an act is performed and how well it has been learned, but to equate learning and performance leads to certain problems.

"Learning" and "performance" are not interchangeable terms. The method used to determine what learning has taken place is inference from performance. When relatively permanent changes in behavior have occurred as a result of experience or practice, learning has taken place, but temporary increases or decreases in performance are associated with such factors as warmup, fatigue, and time delay between practices. Many variables may cause fluctuations in performance, leading to an untrue indication of learning status. Well-learned skills, however, are somewhat resistant to such variables.

The athlete who receives the highest esteem has repeatedly practiced skills and has developed appropriate strategies. Continual practice under ideal conditions (discussed in the remainder of this chapter and in Chapter 8) leads to a permanent increase in motor behavior. This is the first step. Game or contest situations require further adaptive behavior. The athlete learns how to adjust to the pressure within the contest, to the crowds, and to the realization that every action is meaningful.

The adjustment from practice to contest conditions is easier for some athletes than others. In addition to previous learning experiences and level of skill, personal emotional factors come into play. Some athletes operate at a higher level of anxiety than others. The effect of stressful situations differs, of course, from athlete to athlete, and the results are variations in performance. The best learning of sport skills, then, is associated with superior athletes, whose superb performance is somewhat resistant to the differing conditions under which they perform from contest to contest.

Two suggestions for helping the athlete to learn more effectively can be extrapolated from learning theory, which unfortunately is not used often enough as a guide to teaching. The first is about the response: the skill to be learned should be *repeated in as similar a manner as possible during each execution.* From the time the golfer addresses the ball until he finishes the swing, his stance and every movement pattern should be consistent each time the same situation appears. Any slight deviation in the response pattern may have unexpected and undesired outcomes.

The second suggestion concerns the nature of the stimulus. Theoretically, if the stimulus and the response were both exactly the same every time, consistency in performance could be expected. Unfortunately, strictly interpreted, the stimulus is probably never the same from situation to situation. "Stimulus situation" refers to all conditions, both outside the athlete and organismic. Some examples of changing situational stimuli for the basketball player are how far he is from the basket, whether he is moving or stationary while shooting, the distance of the defensive player from the shooting position, the score of the game, and the size and reactions of the crowd. Some organismic stimuli representative of internal fluctuations are relative states of fatigue, temperature changes, chemical reactions to specific stressful conditions, and tension.

Since situations constantly change, it can be theoretically proposed that much practice of correct responses in many possible situations will promote greater proficiency. The skilled athlete is one who acts appropriately regardless of the situation. The person who has learned his responsibilities well can adjust to unpredictable or unexpected circumstances. The athlete's stage of development becomes apparent in performance. And learning is greatly facilitated by motivated performance.

## MOTIVATION[1]

To paraphrase an old saying, "You can take an athlete to the game, but you can't make him play." Physical attributes, skills, and abilities have a strong effect on outstanding performance, but the *ideal* level of motivation for the given task must also be present if the athlete is to demonstrate superior skill. The emphasis on the word "ideal" is intended to imply that "the more the better" does not apply to motivation. This point will be elaborated upon later.

But what is motivation? By definition, "motivation" deals with variables that incite or direct a person toward activity, and ultimately toward a specific goal (Atkinson, 1964). Some situations are generally motivating to most people; other situations elicit responses specific to and compatible with individual personalities. Saying it another way, on the basis of research, certain behavioral reactions can be predicted when certain motives are present, but it must be remembered that the human organism's reactions are also influenced by previous experiences, present expectancies, and other individual differences. Each athlete needs to be considered on an individual basis, to determine what certain motivational techniques will work best for him. The ensuing discussion will deal with motivational methods that have been shown to be generally beneficial or relatively more beneficial than others, and also with considerations of individual difference.

The importance of motivation to the athlete is described by Roger Bannister (1955) in relation to his own experiences: "Racing has always been

---

[1] A book recently published in this area that is recommended to the reader is Ralph Slovenko, & James A. Knight (Eds.), *Motivations in play, games and sports,* Springfield, Ill.: Charles C Thomas, 1967. It contains numerous articles written by people with diverse professional backgrounds and personal interests, and one is especially suggested: The role of the coach in motivation of athletes by Thomas A. Tutko & Bruce C. Ogilvie.

more of a mental than a physical problem to me" (p. 210). Many athletes have the physical abilities and developed skills to be outstanding, and yet do not possess the motivation to drive themselves to the necessary point. When morale and the will to succeed are high, and motivation is intense, tremendous feats can be accomplished in strength and endurance performance events. Of course, too much desire may hamper performance in events requiring complex movements. The athlete who thinks too much is in danger of lessening his performance. Many factors are related to proficiency, and too much mental and physical effort may reduce efficiency in activities that depend more on coordination, agility, balance, and the like than on strength and endurance. Not only, then, is motivation a personal matter, but it needs to be considered in the nature of the activity as well.

### "Material" versus "Ideal" Rewards

The urge to participate and succeed in athletics is basic to skilled performance. Reasons for involvement in athletics, as diverse as they may be from person to person, can be classified as either "materialistic" or "ideal." No athlete's reasons can fit into one category alone, and the degree of emphasis is the important concern.

There is no doubt that anticipated and obtained rewards are important motivations. The successful athlete receives money, status, and other materialistic rewards. Fulfillment of his immediate needs is represented by success, his name in print, and radio interviews, or for younger athletes by the reward of a candy bar, a pat on the back, or a better course grade. The best description of a person whose motivations are materialistic is that he performs not for enjoyment and freedom of expression but rather for recognition.

On the other hand, a person who undertakes an activity for the best reasons—because of a true love of the activity—demonstrates intrinsic motivation. He views the activity as being genuinely worthwhile; the very nature of the activity makes him want to participate and excel.

Any type of reward, materialistic or ideal, will probably have a positive effect on development of skill. Whether one form of personal reward is more effective than another is a moot question.

It is difficult to ascertain a person's specific reasons for playing on or coaching an athletic team, and as a consequence, research in this area has been virtually nonexistent. Rationally speaking, though, we may expect that the person's own view of his reasons will serve as a motive. Each person determines for himself what rewards are meaningful, though he is no doubt influenced by societal factors. It is important to recognize that different rewards are more or less effective as incentives for different people.

In our culture, the athlete who performs for the sake of the activity itself rather than for materialistic gain or glory is looked upon with greater favor. Intrinsic motivation is thought to have a more sustaining effect on motivation, hence on performance, and in turn on learning, and to be therefore more desirable. The assumption is that extraneous rewards maintain peak motivational levels for a shorter period of time. Such beliefs and assumptions, however, are primarily speculative, as researchers have not yet been able to design studies that would determine the facts.

## Setting Goals

When an athlete learns skills or performs them in a contest, his personal intentions and goals have an extremely important effect on his output. How he thinks he will do, and how and to what extent he is motivated to achieve are immediate determinants of his performance. It is not surprising that coaches have usually overlooked the conscious influences upon performance, for researchers have done likewise. The influence of the athlete's attitude toward his immediate task has often been underrated.

The athlete's experience in an activity—his successes and failures—affects his goal level (also called "level of aspiration"), which in turn affects the level of performance. Reasonably high goal levels result in better performance. Since a certain amount of success raises one's level of aspiration, and repeated failure lowers it, the coach should try to develop practice situations that tend to favor successes rather than failures for his athletes. In basketball, for example, if the same inadequately equipped defensive player frequently plays opposite the star offensive player in practice sessions and is repeatedly made to look foolish, his level of aspiration will deteriorate. However, if the same defensive player practices in situations that enable him to acquire skills and techniques that lead to more and more successes, his level will improve accordingly.

The level of aspiration is involved in a circular process. Success usually raises the level of expectancy and causes an improvement in performance. The level of expectancy is a personal matter: one golfer's level may be a score in the high 80s, another's in the low 70s. In this case, the appraisal of goal expectancy is qualitative, and success is determined on an individual basis. Success is quantitatively assessed when a cutoff point is introduced—say, when all those who shoot below 80 make the team and above-80 shooters do not. Both qualitative and quantitative situations occur in sports. In basketball, either the ball goes in the basket or it does not; "almost" does not count. In the tennis contest, however, winning is a relative matter and can occur in spite of a poor performance.

Previous experiences of achievement in related tasks serve to elevate the goal in the task at hand. Schiltz & Levitt (1968) administered a modified form of the Iowa Revision of the Brace Test, a test of motor educability, to fifth- and sixth-grade boys, and placed high achievers and low achievers in separate groups. All subjects were then given a simple motor task requiring small blocks to be moved from one board to another as quickly as possible. Students who had scored higher on the Iowa Brace Test set higher goal levels for themselves in the blocks task than did students who had scored lower. Evidently, the process of setting goals is a generalized phenomenon, and previous athletic achievements result in higher levels of aspiration in new motor skills than were expected.

The effect of conscious intention on behavior or performance is more prevalent than might be imagined. Even when we least expect it, goals may operate in a subtle way to shape outcomes. Locke (1968), who has done much research on task motivation, gives the following examples of "unintentional" performances that might be explained in terms of conscious intent:

> (1) For example, in returning an opponent's shot in tennis, an experienced player is not consciously aware of his footwork, back-swing, or grip, but only of the intent to approach and return the shot. In such cases as this, the action leading to the goal has become automated through extended practice; each response automatically sets off the next in sequence. However, it should be recognized that the behavior sequence as a whole must still be triggered by a conscious intent (e.g., as "to return the shot" or "win the point" in the example above). Once the initial intent is abandoned, action ceases, e.g., if the tennis player suddenly decides not to try to return a shot, the usual action sequence will not occur.
>
> Furthermore, automated behavior of this type is initially learned consciously and intentionally. This is true of any series of skilled goal-directed movements or actions taken by man (though such actions will involve physiological activities of which he may never be aware introspectively).
>
> (2) A second category involves behavior in which a different end occurs than is intended due to error or lack of ability. For instance, one could try to return a tennis shot but hit the net instead. The behavior would be consciously initiated but the outcome would be imperfectly correlated with the intended outcome due to lack of knowledge or ability. Such behavior is usually described as "accidental." Clearly concepts other than conscious intent are required to explain accidents, but it should be recognized that accidents often involve very small deviations from the intended outcome (e.g., as when a tennis shot goes out of bounds by an inch). Thus conscious intent would be one factor in the explanation of the action sequence as a whole [pp. 159–160].

These acts and others, as Locke states, are originally set in motion by some goal.

Directions given by someone else can also have an effect on a person's intentions of accomplishment. The coach often helps to set the level of achievement of his athletes by (1) not saying anything; (2) making negative criticisms; (3) giving positive qualitative directions such as "Do your best"; and (4) giving positive quantitative directions such as "Try for a golf score of 72" or "Try for a bowling score of 180."

The latter two types of incentives will be the concern here. One might think that it would not make a difference which of the two approaches was used, but research by Locke and others has repeatedly demonstrated that specific hard goals (a goal of 72 for the golfer who normally shoots in the high 70s would be an example) produce better performance levels than easier, qualitatively assigned goals ("Do your best"). The implication is that the coach should provide external incentives relevant to the status of each athlete. A hard goal for one person is not necessarily hard for another. Specific, hard, and reasonably attainable goals apparently have a stronger influence on output than the general encouragement given to all athletes.

## Need to Achieve

Since motivation is associated with a state of arousal to satisfy a need and reach a goal, an examination of all contributing factors would be in order. Unfortunately, motivation is so complex and involved that such an examination would be outside the scope of this book. Furthermore, much of our knowledge of motivation is speculatory even though entire books have been devoted to its theoretical aspects.

The discussion of personality in Chapter 3 included the relationship of certain traits to success in athletics. One such trait is the need to achieve. Many biological and psychological drives operate within the person to initiate some activity. The act is performed because it is apparently instrumental in the attainment of the goal of these motives (Atkinson & Reitman, 1958). The expectation that a certain kind of act will help us reach a certain kind of goal is reinforced by actual attainment of such a goal. A direct relationship is found between the achievement motive and performance when the cues surrounding the situation arouse an expectation that performance of an act will help in attaining the goal.

The need to achieve influences the goals that are set within a sport. Presumably, a higher need to achieve in a sport results in greater activity (practice, dedication, competition) directed toward reaching the desired status. A person with a high achievement motive does not necessarily start out hoping to accomplish either easy or difficult tasks. In fact, Atkinson, Bastian, Earl, & Litwin (1960) found that subjects who had a high need to achieve in shuffleboard initially selected intermediary distances to shoot from. All subjects could choose freely from among a number of distances.

With success or failure, the distances they selected changed. It becomes apparent that the level of the achievement motive can be used to determine the nature of the arousal state within the person and to predict the goal that will be set.

The athlete with a high need to achieve probably sets a goal for himself that is reasonably difficult to attain. Because he needs to achieve, he does not set hopelessly unattainable goals. The person with a low achievement motive, however, is more unpredictable in his goal setting. No matter what motives interact to influence the setting of goals, a need to achieve must be present, though it may be latent or concealed.

### Optimal Level of Motivation

Two frequently uttered directions, both intended to improve performance, are (1) "Try harder," and (2) "Relax, you're too tight." How do we resolve these apparently contradictory but inspirational directions? Different situations require different levels of motivation, and individual consideration must also be given to the athlete's unique personality. Athletes who try too hard may be as unsuccessful as those who do not try hard enough.

In an athletic contest, we usually attempt to goad others on to better performance by yelling, screaming, and encouraging greater output, but too much motivation in certain situations may be detrimental to performance. The results of too little motivation, on the other hand, are equally detrimental. For every situation or task, there is an optimal level of motivation. Both low motivation and extremely high motivation can cause a breakdown in performance. For a complex act like catching a baseball on the run in the midst of an eighth-inning tournament tie game, a theoretical middle level of motivation is most desirable. Where low motivation exists, the player will get a poor jump on the ball and fail to catch it. Where there is too much motivation, the player may try too hard and as a result drop the ball. Where there is an ideal level of motivation, the player can catch the ball, if nothing else prevents his catching it.

The complex tasks which are common in sport are performed most effectively, then, under relatively low motivation. "Low motivation," however, is not to be understood as meaning "no motivation." The drawing in Figure 7-1 demonstrates the theoretical relationship between motivation and the complexity of the act. Associated with increased motivation is increased tension (psychological and muscular). Too much motivation, hence too much tension, is destructive to the performance of an athletic skill. Performance is best when motivation is high, but not too high. In acts in which strength and power are the primary factors, motivation must be extremely high, but

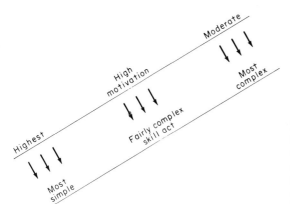

FIGURE 7-1 *The relationship between ideal level of motivation and the complexity of the act. Many sport skills fall in the "fairly complex" category and therefore require reasonably high motivation.*

when finesse and finer motor coordination are the essence of the act, lower motivation is preferable. An example is the motivation the weight lifter needs as contrasted to that the golfer needs.

The anxiety level of the individual athlete also has an effect on the ideal level of motivation. Highly anxious people have a tendency to do less well on complex tasks but better on simple tasks than less anxious people. Emotions, task complexity, and performance may theoretically interact in the following manner: The learning situation encourages the emission of dominant responses. In simple tasks, the correct responses are dominant, and thus are facilitated by increased motivation or anxiety. Many more types of responses can occur in complex tasks, however, and in the early stages of learning of complex tasks, incorrect responses are dominant over correct ones. Heightened motivation or anxiety would therefore be disruptive to the learning situation.

### External Comments

When interest is shown in the person, his motivation is heightened. A coach's comment during or after performance corrects, adjusts, or approves the execution of an act, and also stimulates performance. The comment increases the athlete's knowledge about the results of his performance (see Chapter 8), and also represents a form of motivation provided from an external source.

It can be seen, then, that the coach's remarks may be both directive, in that they may help the athlete to improve his performance, and incentive, in that they may help the athlete to develop a more favorable attitude. A person usually tries harder when someone he cares about acknowledges his performance. Positive and constructive comments by the coach can serve as a *reward* (discussed above) or as *reinforcement* (discussed below), but, disregarding the distinction between these two terms, the coach's positive, constructive comments on the athlete's performance are beneficial from a directive and an incentive point of view. Frequent and immediate remarks are most favored for both purposes.

### Competition

The athlete is, among other things, a competitor. It is difficult to improve one's athletic status without wanting to improve on past performance and to overcome the opposition. In Chapter 5 the section on Competition and Cooperation deals with the nature and effects of such behavior, which is natural and is also encouraged by society. All that is necessary here is to point out the motivational aspects of situations in which competition is encouraged.

When the competitive urge decreases, performance also wanes. Competing with one's previous record or with another athlete helps to maintain or increase the competitive urge. A decrease usually comes not in the contest but rather in practice sessions. Many coaches have developed their own techniques for introducing motivation into practice sessions, thereby acknowledging the importance of maintaining the competitive feeling during practice.

Depending on the sport, competition can pit the athlete against himself or against a group. An early study by Sims (1928), undertaken in a classroom situation, sheds some light on the relative effect of each on the competitive urge. Sims formed two groups, one in which a person competed with himself and others of similar ability, the other in which the individual as a member of a group competed with another group. A third group, a control, received no motivation at all. In one task (substituting digits for letters), during 12 learning trials, the control group improved 102.2 percent, the group-motivated group improved 109.9 percent, and the individual-motivated group improved 157.7 percent. In another task (concerned with reading improvement), the control group improved 8.7 percent, the group-motivated group advanced 14.5 percent, and the individual-motivated group advanced 34.7 percent.

If these results were applicable to athletic circumstances, the implication would be that competing with oneself was more effective than competing with a group. It may be, however, that athletes who participate in team sports would be more likely to be affected by group competition, and if so, competing with a group would be as effective as individual competition. Furthermore, there is an element of self-involvement and personal competition in all team sports.

TABLE 7-1    Characteristics of good and poor competitors

| | Percentage* | |
| Characteristics | Good competitors | Poor competitors |
|---|---|---|
| Is a hard worker............................... | 50 | 32 |
| Is very friendly................................. | 42 | 12 |
| Is always rational and coherent.................... | 46 | 15 |
| Usually follows instruction well without comment..... | 43 | 19 |
| Learns well...................................... | 47 | 13 |
| Communicates well.............................. | 48 | 23 |
| Is well-liked.................................... | 48 | 14 |
| Is likely to make another good performance the following week....................................... | 51 | 0 |

*These data have been arbitrarily gleaned from Ryan's report and represent items that particularly distinguished groups. The figures represent the number of coaches who rated their good competitors and poor competitors on a particular item.

The characteristics of "good" and "poor" competitors, if they are indeed different, can provide meaningful data to coaches (see Chapter 5). The poor competitor often has suppressed emotional conflicts about competition; his problems are deep-seated and would be difficult to ascertain.[2] General observation of certain behavior of athletes, however, can permit the coach to designate poor and good competitors. Ryan (1968) has reported the results of a questionnaire study of track athletes; 57 coaches responded, and the information shown in Table 7-1 was among the results.

In the words of Ryan, "The 'good' competitor is not the tight-lipped, uncommunicative lone wolf. The 'good' competitor tends to be more conflict-free, less constricted, and better adjusted; in general, he is freer to express his aggression." More research is needed on the nature of competitive ability and on the role the coach might take in assisting the athlete to formulate a desirable attitude toward competition.

## Hawthorne Effect

Situations in which similar activity patterns unfold day after day require strong emphasis on the sustaining of motivation. When the athlete has high

[2] Interesting observations and case studies on athletes appear in Bruce Ogilvie & Thomas Tutko. *Problem athletes and how to handle them.* London: Pelham Books, 1966.

internal motivation, the problem is not serious. Unfortunately, constant, repetitious, and for some, boring routines are necessary in order to attain the highest levels of skill. If achievement and satisfaction are to result, skills must be constantly practiced.

Implications for sport may be derived from a classic early study at the Western Electric Company's Hawthorne Plant in Chicago. (Roethlisberger & Dickson, 1939). A series of studies, begun in 1924, were carried out for 15 years. The illumination in the working environment was changed in these studies, but the changes did not appear to make a difference in productivity : output rose whether illumination was increased or severely decreased. Industrial management and coaches have the same objective as that study : maximum effective output. In the research, productivity was high as long as environmental conditions continually changed. Variables could be introduced and removed, but the important consideration was not the nature of the particular environmental variable, but rather that change take place and that attention be given to the worker. The special attention and treatment given to the working situation and the worker evidently elevated motivation and increased performance output.

The Hawthorne effect can be observed in work situations which might normally be boring except for altered conditions and worker consideration. Personal attention can overcome the monotony of repetitive acts. Although athletic practice sessions can become routine, we can believe with some confidence that they are more stimulating than working on a factory assembly line or typing in an office. Still, the coach should always be sensitive to the nature of practice sessions and their effect on performance yield. Altering certain aspects of each session, providing unexpected circumstances, and varying the structure of a routine may enhance attention and increase motivation.

### Social Presence

One is more likely to be highly motivated in the presence of others, whether in terms of working in a group or performing in front of it, as has been pointed out in an earlier chapter. Team projects, especially when there is verbal interaction among the members, generally result in more favorable performance than isolated practice conditions.

Some skilled athletes tend to want to perform in front of others in order to demonstrate their proficiency and thereby gain acclaim. An audience also creates conflict, as it causes fear. Hence, motivation must overcome fear, and the effect on the skilled performer is usually to cause more concentration and better performance. Obviously, the influence of any audience or group depends on its size, arrangement, familiarity, and composition (Hollingworth, 1935). Past experiences and successes in front of an audience tend to lead to better performances in that situation. In most competitive athletic situations, audiences of varying sizes and characteristics are present. The ideal situation is one in which the optimal level of motivation operates as a result of the social condition and the nature of the activity. This is likely to happen with increased proficiency and more experiences with spectators.

Motivation to sustain and improve upon performance is usually greater when practice occurs in a social context than alone. Verbal encouragement, competition with others, and other factors in group situations have a positive influence on motivation.

## REINFORCEMENT

As every coach knows, one main objective of training the athlete to acquire high levels of skill is to encourage correctly executed acts and discourage poorly executed ones. The coach wants to "shape" the behavior of the athlete. The ideal behavior for which both coach and athlete strive may be more effectively attained when consideration is given to the consequences of each act. The concern in this section is the consequence of the nature and timing of the coach's comments on the athlete's performance.

The development of ideal behavior is aided by reinforcement. A "reinforcer" is any type of stimulus that maintains or increases the probability of an event occurring; it may constitute anything from an achieved goal (intrinsic reinforcer) to the remarks and expressions of an outsider (extrinsic reinforcer). The focus in athletics is on the relative effectiveness of extrinsic positive and negative reinforcement; or, to say it in layman's language, of praising good performance and criticizing poor performance; or, even more generally, of giving reward or punishment.

Reinforcement has been discussed in terms of motivation, feedback, and knowledge of results. It is the source of much theoretical involvement in the psychology of learning as well as terminology confusion, especially as it relates to such terms as "reward" and "punishment." Becoming embroiled in such issues would not serve our purposes, and therefore, we shall discuss only a generalized concept of reinforcement.

### Negative and Positive Reinforcement

The word "reinforcement" is usually interpreted as being of a positive nature. That is, a response is positively reinforced and strengthened by the occurrence of some stimulus event. The athlete executes an act in ideal form, the coach responds by commenting favorably, and the athlete then attempts to repeat the act. Positive reinforcement is satisfying; and, in fact, in the early 1900s the great psychologist Thorndike referred to the positive reinforcer as a "satisfier." We usually like to repeat activities that are satisfying to us, that provide pleasure rather than pain.

But there are also negative reinforcers. The implication here is that a response is somehow weakened and yet strengthened. This is the case, for the removal of the stimulus (negative reinforcer) given to an incorrect response increases the strength of the ideal response. If the athlete demonstrates an inappropriate act, the coach might tell him to do 30 push-ups as a punishment. In order to avoid the push-ups, the athlete attempts to do the act "right" at the next opportunity, and the correct response results in the elimination of push-ups. A negative reinforcer contains aversive characteristics which, of course, the person attempts to avoid. Thorndike referred to negative reinforcers as "annoyers."

Which is more effective in learning: negative or positive reinforcement? Research and common sense indicate that both techniques can effectively influence behavioral outcomes. In many instances, though, the better of the two is probably positive reinforcement. Positive reinforcers inform one when he is doing something right and encourage the continuation of activity in a specific direction. Unacceptable behavior is indicated by negative reinforcers, which do not teach the correct response and thus lengthen the learning process, at least theoretically, as a variety of activities may be attempted before the correct one is found.

On top of this, negative reinforcers also cause anxiety, which is associated with irrational and uncontrollable behavior. Furthermore, negative reinforcers imply failure, and failures are less meaningful than successes in improving performance. If possible, therefore, positive methods in reaching goals should be encouraged whenever possible. This concept is illustrated nicely in an article by Gary Wiren about teaching golf. The emphasis in the article is on the positive approach. It is much easier to constantly offer negative remarks and Wiren's approach to coaching is all too often neglected.

---

TEACHING GOLF: HOW IS YOUR APPROACH[3]

Gary Wiren

While teaching a university physical education golf class a few years ago, one of my pupils came to me before the period began and asked permission to let one of his friends, a member of our varsity golf team, help him with

[3] Reprinted from *The Physical Educator*, 1968, **25**, 51–53.

his swing. Since the group was large and it was not possible for me to devote a great deal of individual attention to each student, I readily okayed the request.

The student, whose name was Mark, and his well-skilled friend took a position at the end of the semi-circular turfed range and participated in the opening drills that are a part of most of my group instructional sessions. When it came time for each pupil to start hitting balls, I found myself positioned about midway through the group and within earshot of Mark and his newly acquired teacher. On the first shot Mark made a reasonably good swing "coming off it" slightly so that the ball's trajectory was lower than normal, but, all considered, not a bad start for the day.

"Don't lift your head up like that!" was the comment which came from his "coach." So, on the next shot Mark made a concerted effort to follow the instruction and focused his attention on "not lifting his head." Solid as a rock he kept it stationary behind the ball; but unfortunately his weight stayed to his right also, and the club dug far into the ground, sending both ball and turf an equally short distance ahead of him.

"You didn't shift your weight!" was comment number two from the newly-acquired assistant. Mark teed up another ball and paused, mentally preparing to do better. Sure enough, on the next shot the head stayed there and the weight shifted to the left, but the left arm shortened slightly at the elbow and the ball, having been "skulled," went skimming across the grass tops—a "worm burner," the students would call it.

"Don't bend your left arm. Keep it straight!" I overheard. By this time I was working closer to the pair and was becoming so absorbed in their private lesson that my other students were getting some pretty perfunctory treatment. Mark, growing annoyed with himself (because he knew he could hit it better than he had) quickly raked another ball into position, took a hurried grip and stance, swung a little more wildly than before, and connected with a strong shot which went sharply hooking across the range. "You regripped the club at the top!" was his friend's comment. "And don't hurry your backswing so fast."

There followed two or three more poor shots by Mark with brief admonitions from his friend. I could tell from Mark's reactions that he was becoming very frustrated. He was sincerely trying to think of all the things that he shouldn't do: Don't move head; don't keep weight back; don't bend left arm; don't hurry; don't regrip; and these thoughts were now reflected in his swing. Mark was beginning to resemble a herky-jerky automaton that was programmed for but one movement at a time. The semblance of good rhythm that he had displayed on his first swing was rapidly disappearing. When I finally reached the pair, Mark's varsity friend apparently had lost his patience as well, had resorted to the "watch and see the way that I do it method," and was hitting some effortless shots down the range far beyond

Mark's highest expectations. Mark did not recover during that class period, and his friend did not return to the next.

One might conclude that Mark's friend didn't know what he was talking about. But the interesting thing is that EVERYTHING THE VARSITY GOLFER TOLD MARK WAS TECHNICALLY CORRECT. Mark HAD, in fact, committed all of the mistakes that his friend had very keenly spotted. The fault was not in the observations but in the approach that was used to implement them. And that is what this article is all about.

How is your approach to teaching the golf swing? Included in the following pages are four suggestions for you to consider or reconsider in your approach to teaching golf.

*Teach one thing at a time*

When dealing with an individual student, either in a private lesson or a group situation, I have made it a personal practice to seldom attempt more than one fundamental change per teaching period. It is very hard, particularly when you are eager to help, to restrain yourself from "overteaching," that is, trying to accomplish too much at one time. This obviously was one of the faults in the method of Mark's varsity friend. He did not stick to a particular error. It is possible, of course, to make minor adjustments in a fundamental like grip or stance while still attempting another major improvement; but don't press ahead too quickly. It takes a great deal of patience to develop a fundamentally sound stroke. An overzealousness to learn the golf swing or to teach it in "a couple of lessons" is the side on which people most often err. It's an unfortunate mistake.

Some pupils seem to possess the uncanny knack of being able to violate every known fundamental of good form in a single swing of the club. It is fairly obvious that you must bring these people on very slowly, making one cautious improvement at a time. This may prove to be a bit laborious, as progress with this kind of pupil is extremely slow. The temptation to "overteach" comes not so often with these poorly skilled, however, but rather with the seemingly "natural golfer," the former athlete, or possessor of good motor skills. Obviously no one was ever really born a "natural golfer."

True, it is easier for some to learn than it is for others; but don't let a talented tyro tempt you into assuming too much about his kinesthetic or academic knowledge of the swing. Teach one fundamental at a time, and be sure that each fundamental has become a habit before moving ahead just as you did with the poorly skilled subject. The urge to teach just a little bit more, too prematurely, particularly with the good student, may insidiously creep into your approach, introducing confusion, and as a result, eat away at the sound foundation of fundamentals that you have started to build.

During each teaching session try to quit while you are ahead. You'll get ahead a lot faster.

### Be positive

The game of golf offers a wonderful workshop in the study of psychology. One of the most widely used "psych" gimmicks by the touring professional is the "be positive" state of mind. He tries to eliminate negative thoughts from the mind because they create fear (fear of going out-of-bounds, fear of missing a putt)—fear causes tension—tension produces bad golf shots— bad golf shots produce high scores—and high scores produce low incomes. This positiveness takes a great deal of time and experience to develop, but it can begin with early instruction.

For example, golf teachers could make it a policy in their teaching to be stingy with the use of the word "don't;" e.g. "don't bend your arm," "don't raise your head," "don't hit from the top,"—those very reproofs that Mark received from his friend inexperienced in teaching. Even when correct, negative comments fail to create a word picture of what *should* be done. The student, on the other hand, needs frequent positive reminders of what he is trying to do.

How many times have we witnessed a person miss a shot, then turn and ask, "What did I do wrong?" My stock answer to that query is, "I don't know what you did wrong, but here's what you should have done right." From this positive springboard begins the lesson.

### Allow for individual differences

A large number of the golf instructional books on the market are mis- nomers. They could well be encompassed under one title: *How It Feels To Me When I Play Golf,* by whomever the star might be. Now there is nothing wrong with writing a book about how you play golf, especially if you have become a success with your technique. Some golf books are well written and extremely helpful. But the reader must recognize that what works wonders for Hogan may mean misery for him.

There are several reasons for this—all encompassed under the term, "in- dividual differences." Body type, temperament, and physical attributes such as strength, flexibility, and balance, are just a few of these. For example, how can a man with below average strength take the compact swing advo- cated by Sanders and be able to move the ball any distance? Why can't the chronic slicer employ Nicklaus' open stance to produce longer tee shots? What does the woman with a history of back trouble do when Mickey Wright suggests she "turn it loose?" How do you interpret the Julius

Boros "effortless swing" to a highly strung ex-collegiate wrestler? Golf may be played with the hands by Byron Nelson, but what about the man who works out-of-doors and has developed a touch of arthritis in his fingers?

Some books describe techniques that many of its readers simply cannot perform. Is your approach to teaching flexible enough to recognize individual limitations and differences, or is your methodology so wooden as to require everyone to grip, stand, and swing alike? Granted, there are standard successful patterns in the swing. Yet, spending a Sunday afternoon watching the latest golf tournament should be proof enough that there is more than one style leading to golf greatness. The good teacher recognizes this.

### Keep it simple

Do you know what the sign of the "master teacher" is? It's simplicity. It is being able to take something which can be very hard and making it seem relatively easy. Tommy Armour said, "The most difficult thing about teaching golf is making the facts simple."

A classic story about teaching is the one involving the incomparable Bobby Jones and his Scottish pro, Stewart Maiden. Jones had arrived at Worcester, Massachusetts, to practice a few days prior to the 1925 U.S. Open. After the first day of hitting shot after erratic shot, he was beside himself trying to discover a cure for his sudden wildness. A hurried 'phone call was made to Stewart Maiden in Atlanta begging him to come up immediately on the next train. After a long ride, Maiden arrived the next day, came straight to the course and met Bobby, where they proceeded to the practice tee with two pails of practice balls in hand.

Jones, continuing his wildness, spraying shot after shot across the range until the two buckets were nearly empty. Maiden, in the meantime, remained completely silent. After Jones emptied the second bucket, Maiden turned abruptly to leave. In parting, he commented in his brusque Scottish way, "Why dintya tri itting it an yer bakswing?"

The bewildered Jones pondered the comment for a moment, slowed down his backswing, and began to rifle out the straight and true shots for which he was famous. Maiden had not confused Jones with detail, nor did he experiment on him by saying, "try this," or "try that." He singled out the crucial error, the critical point, and made that point known in a very simple way. Simplicity, that's the mark of the "master teacher." Jones went on to tie for first in that U.S. Open.

---

Assuming the desirability of positive reinforcers, a logical next step is to look for an effective way to implement them. Perhaps the most intriguing and meaningful approach is to shape behavior through a series of positive reinforcers. The "shaping" concept, developed by the outstanding psychologist B. F. Skinner, holds out much promise to teachers and coaches.

## Shaping Behavior

The process of learning a complex skill is delayed considerably if positive reinforcement is withheld until a task is performed with a high degree of accuracy and proficiency. The path to mastery of a skill is filled with many blocks. Each block is piled on the preceding one until ultimate goals are reached. At first goals are general and undefined; later they become more fixed and specific.

In applying the shaping concept to the learning of complex motor skills, we would at the beginning reinforce any activity that was in the correct direction. The youngster learning the hook shot in basketball will obviously not perform with precision and grace at the onset, but any movements that bear some resemblance to the hook shot should be reinforced. The positive aspects of the child's activity should be emphasized. Presumably, with reinforced practice, the act will become more skilled, and behavior will be shaped in the desired direction: from gross motor movement patterns to a hook shot. A series of successive approximations leads to refined movements.

The principles of reinforcement are used in programmed texts and teaching machines, which Skinner had much to do with publicizing. Reinforcement is the key to the acquisition of complex behavior. The learner always begins from the simple or general stage and gradually moves forward as he accomplishes tasks. Complex acts are built on a foundation of mastered simpler routines, and thus, with patience, tolerance, and reinforcement, behavior is shaped and goals are attained. The optimal quantity, quality, timing, and frequency of reinforcements are important and are discussed below. First a comparison of the relative merits of praise and critical commentary as used by the coach in dealing with his athletes is in order.

## Praise and Criticism

In the classroom environment, it is not difficult to determine the effects of praise and criticism on test achievement. The data from an early, classic study (Hurlock, 1925) are often cited as an example of the relative effectiveness of the two techniques. In this investigation, four groups of students were formed; one received praise; another received reproof; a third was ignored by the teacher, who was present in the room; and a fourth, the control, performed in a room with no teacher. The same problems were given to all students to solve. The data indicate remarkable trends. Although differences in group performance were small at first, dissimilarities were apparent by the end of the fifth day. The following conclusions were drawn: the most effective technique in improving performance is praise, followed first by criticism, and then by ignoring the student. Two things should be emphasized: First, criticism leads to performance nearly, but not quite, as good as that demonstrated as a result of praise. Second, the ignored group scored higher than the control group which was left alone in the room. Social presence is thus once again shown to serve as a motivator.

The coach is therefore encouraged to use praise more often than criticism, or as suggested throughout this book, to take a positive approach. Exceptional criticism, yelling, or threat of punishment may cause anxiety to the athletes, which may, of course, be disruptive to performance. In many situations, a combination of praise and constructive criticism, when appropriate, may work in synchronizing fashion to increase output.

Since people differ in temperamental makeup, individual reactions to general techniques are difficult to predict. Nevertheless, poorest incentives in school are thought to be obtained from public ridicule, reprimand, sarcasm, low grades, and additional assignments; private reprimands, however, are probably more effective. Friendly conferences and public praise are the most effective incentives. There is every reason to believe that these statements may be applicable to relationships between coach and athlete.

### Applications of Reinforcement

In considering how reinforcement might be applied most effectively, some applicable questions are: (1) How much reinforcement is needed? (2) What should be the nature or quality of this reinforcement? (3) What are the timing considerations, e.g., what is the optimal time after an act for presenting reinforcement? (4) What is the most beneficial schedule of reinforcement?

In answer to the first question, reinforcement can obviously be varied in amount—from greater to lesser degrees. The coach can follow the athlete's performance by enthusiastic complimentary remarks, by saying "Good," or by an acknowledgment such as nodding the head affirmatively. Or, for the younger athlete, a suitable reward may be a box of candy bars, or one bar, or one bite.[4] Much depends on the meaningfulness of these rewards to the

---

[4] Dr. Jim Counsilman, the successful swimming coach at the University of Indiana, is reported to give candy bars to his swimmers when they perform well in practice.

performer and on his ability to distinguish differential rewards. One athlete may respond well to any positive actions taken by the coach, but another may respond only to higher levels of reinforcement. Of course, self-motivated athletes may need little external reinforcement and may be able to find intrinsic motivation from reaching personal goals.

A number of classroom studies have shown that performance increased when the quantity of the reinforcement (or reward) was increased, but such results may be explained in terms of interacting and confounding experimental variables. In athletic situations, it is more than likely that small but frequent reinforcers are just as meaningful as larger ones, and of course they are also more practical to administer.

Quality is somewhat related to amount, however, in that the learner must be able to distinguish between levels of reinforcement. Probably the same things that have been said about amount could be said about the nature, or quality, of reinforcements. Interpretation of quality is an individual matter, and a reinforcer of a reasonable degree of quality may be as effective as one of high quality.

Delayed reinforcement may be less productive than immediate reinforcement. The knowledge-of-results aspects of reinforcement are associated with immediate insight and skill mastery, and are most beneficial when closely associated with the completed act. (See the section on Knowledge of Results in Chapter 8.) Most sports skills are self-reinforcing in that simply performing an act provides intrinsic reinforcement about the general acceptability of the performance. Where form is important, however, reinforcement is most helpful when it comes quickly and from another person. If a person must wait for reinforcement, especially when the delay is considerable, its effectiveness is weakened, and the directional, instructional, and motivational aspects of reinforcement have less impact on behavior. When the athlete has become conditioned to waiting for a reinforcer, however, problems associated with delay may be overcome.

The effectiveness of various ratios and intervals of reinforcement has been studied extensively with many forms of life. Usually a rat, chicken, or some other organism is placed in a state of deprivation and the experimenter reinforces certain behavioral patterns on an intermittent or a regular basis. The experimenter thus controls the responses of the subject. A single reinforcement affects behavior and a series of reinforcements affects it more, whereas the removal of reinforcement results in the extinction of that behavior. Animals in little cages can be controlled nicely in such fashion. But what of human beings?

It would appear that *intermittent* and *random reinforcements* produce responses most difficult to extinguish. The batter does not know the number of times at bat he will have before getting a hit, nor the number of consecutive hits he will make, nor the nature of these hits. These reinforcements occur in unpredictable variable fashion. A reasonable number of reinforcements (hits) helps to maintain a reasonable degree of motivation. The coach need not reinforce every "good move" made by the basketball player, but certainly intermittent and randomly assigned comments will serve the purpose: to sustain motivation and maintain or elevate performance.

## TRANSFER OF LEARNING[5]

Perhaps no phenomenon in learning is more important than transfer of training. The relationship between the present learning task and what has already been learned constitutes the general domain of transfer. The importance of such a concept can be understood by recognizing that almost all learned behavior is interrelated. Furthermore, after the early years, perhaps all learning is influenced by transfer.

It is difficult to conceive of learning a completely new skill. Every sport comprises basic underlying elements—throwing, kicking, running, jumping, twisting, and the like. How these movements are assembled and arranged is what makes activities unique. Even certain movements may be similar from sport to sport; the degree to which they are related and to which the athlete sees their relationship are reflected in the relative ease with which he acquires a new skill. Besides the transfer of skills and abilities from one situation to another, the coach hopes that skills and strategies learned in practice will be transferred to the contest. He hopes, further, that the study of films, charts, mechanical principles, and literature will lead to more successful motor executions. We could go on and on about intended and less obvious transfer situations in sport (many of which are discussed in Chapter 8), but the object of this section is simply to point out the scope of transfer.

The presence of certain conditions and personal experiences leads to a greater expectation of the occurrence of transfer. Such conditions and experiences will help or hinder the learner insofar as they represent positive or negative transfer. The influence of preceding activity may conceivably go in several directions. Aside from the learning of nonsense syllables or unusual laboratory tasks, in which little or theoretically no transfer from previous activity may take place, most if not all of the meaningful things we learn are in some way related to previously learned matter.

[5] The scope of transfer is much broader than this discussion. For easy reading on many aspects of transfer, the following source is recommended: Henry C. Ellis. *The transfer of learning*. New York: Macmillan, 1965.

*Positive and Negative Transfer*

Previous experience may aid or promote the learning of a newly introduced skill, a situation called "positive transfer," or it may impede or interfere with the learning of a new task, a situation called "negative transfer."
By the same token, a recently learned act may positively or negatively affect
previously learned related acts, as indicated by retesting. Usually some form
of interference, called "retroactive inhibition," occurs in the negative aspect
of this process.

In an industrial setting, Singleton (1957) studied the effect of previous
experience with sewing machines on the learning of a task that had some
similar features: experienced sewing-machine operators were compared
with novices. Briefly, on the portion of the task involved with stimulus
differentiation where no transfer was expected, the groups performed similarly. In the portion of the activity involved with response, similarities between previous experience and the task at hand enabled the experienced
group to show an advantage. Negative transfer has been reported by
Entwisle (1959), from an experiment in which drivers tried to relearn how
to drive motor vehicles after experiences with horse-drawn vehicles. (They
also tended to have more accidents while relearning than drivers without
experience in handling horse-drawn vehicles.)

In laboratory situations it is fairly easy to isolate tasks and compare
the influence of one on the other. Comparisons of common elements—stimuli
and responses—may be made, and consequences may be inferred from associations. The influences of sports skills on one another are far more complex, and the many factors related to achievement in them cause great
difficulty in predicting positive or negative transfer from skill to skill.

As an example, let us review a thesis by Diane Daniels at North Texas
State University on badminton and tennis, two sports that appear to be
quite related. Both involve rackets, projectiles, and nets; and the court lay-
outs, game strategies, body movements, and strokes are also similar. Such
similarities may facilitate or delay the learning of one sport after the learning of the other. For instance, the ability to hit a moving projectile over a
net with a racket is common to both sports. Experience in one sport should
positively affect this aspect of the other sport. However, a ball and a shuttlecock move at different speeds, the ball is usually hit on a bounce while the
shuttlecock never is, and the wrist is extremely flexible in badminton stroking but relatively firm in tennis stroking. Such factors may cause interference in learning, or negative transfer. Further similarities and differences between tennis and badminton could be enumerated. The same
approach could be used in comparing baseball and golf swings, different
swimming strokes, and certain basketball and volleyball skills. We know

that great similarities exist. The question is: To what extent does positive transfer operate as compared to negative transfer?

In Daniels' study (1968), two groups of women students served as subjects in the investigation of transfer of training and retroactive inhibition in selected tennis and badminton skills. The two groups learned the sports in opposite sequence, and the analysis revealed that neither positive nor negative transfer effects occurred, nor were retroactive effects observed when the skills were learned consecutively. We might speculate that the positive and negative aspects of the situation canceled each other out, resulting in minimal if not zero transfer. Another possibility is that the tests used were not sensitive enough to detect effects. Nevertheless, it can be seen that the same general conditions can contribute to both positive and negative transfer. The prerequisite is a similarity between situations. The effect of experience in one sport on the learning of the other is such as to reflect both positive and negative characteristics.

Certain conditions can encourage or impede transfer. In psychological terms, a situation in which an old (already learned) response is to be made to a new stimulus should result in positive transfer. Swinging a baseball bat, an experience well learned in a baseball context, will facilitate batting performance in a softball game or against a pitching machine. Timing is different in these situations, but the consequences will be better than when someone undertakes such a task with no previous batting experience.

When a new response must be made to an old stimulus, the possibilities of negative transfer are high. If a person has learned to swim the freestyle crawl very well with a flutter kick, and then is asked to learn a scissor or trudgeon kick, negative transfer may be expected. The stimulus condition, swimming in the prone position, is the same for the old response—the flutter kick—as for the new response—a different kick. The tendency to make the flutter kick must be weakened before the new kick can be strengthened. The most prominent cause of interference in transfer is competition between responses.

Fortunately, positive transfer is typically quite permanent while negative transfer is more transient. That is, the effects of negative transfer are temporary and are not too difficult to overcome. We can learn many things with a reasonable degree of rapidity due to the powerful influence of positive transfer. The important factor to be considered, as illustrated below, is that the learner understand the relationships between the skills he knows and those to be learned.

*Identical Elements*

The more closely two situations approximate each other, the more we might expect transfer to take place. At the other end of the spectrum, it was at one time thought that the transfer process was so general that matter taught in school would necessarily affect out-of-school situations. Formal logic was therefore taught in school in an effect to influence all thinking, and such difficult subjects as mathematics and Latin were taught in order to exercise and tax the brain and thereby develop its agility. These experiences, it was assumed, would enable one to function more effectively in all circumstances requiring "brain work."

The "formal discipline theory," as it was called, was not supported by research in the beginning of this century. No general mental factors were found. The success one had with one or more school subjects had little bearing on other activities. Training in a specific subject was found to be more effective than training in tasks that were supposed to transfer. Thorndike and Woodworth (1901) in a series of studies found that mental functions were independent and largely separate in many cases; but since they did find a small amount of transfer from training on allied tasks, an "identical elements theory" was proposed.

"Identical elements" are similar responses to stimuli that are the same in different tasks or skills. More nearly similar situations should naturally lead to greater transfer. Although there is no doubt that the formal discipline theory is too general and has no value, the identical elements theory may be too strict and rigid. The coach might do well to take into consideration the nature of the strategies and skills which each athlete has learned in the given sport as well as in other sports, in order to estimate the degree of transfer, hence learning, that may be expected when new skills are introduced. (Again, "new" refers to that which appears different to the athlete because he has not had specific practice in it. However, he might very well have experienced aspects of the skill before, in different contexts and different movement patterns. Both positive and negative transfer have an influence; the athlete does not begin at zero.)

### Similar Underlying Abilities

Thus far we have considered the formal aspects and relationships of stimuli and responses. The extent to which abilities common to a number of skills are developed will have a strong effect on success. (The terms "ability" and "skill" were explained and differentiated in Chapter 1.) Research indicates that ability in spatial orientation is important in the early stages of learning many motor skills, and that kinesthetic ability is important to success at later stages.

When similar spatial orientation is demanded in different sports, as in handball, squash, and paddle ball, the most transfer may be expected of learners in whom this ability is highly developed. Responses requiring movements that activate similar proprioceptors in sequence would fall under the general kinesthetic ability, and transfer to similar situations may be expected. Because many abilities and traits which are similar but not identical in different sports interact to affect ultimate performance, distinguishing abilities and indicating their relative contributions is no easy matter.

Another difficulty is the arbitrary manner in which abilities are measured. Kinesthesis or balance can be measured in many ways, and the results of the tests are usually positive but not high. The same can be said of the so-called "coordination tests." Perhaps satisfactory measures  ͡ ability have not yet been developed, or perhaps skill tests are being used to test abilities, and performance on such tests may be confounded by the interaction of dissimilar abilities.

The most that is possible at present is to conjecture that balancing ability, for example, is one of the abilities required for proficiency in such sports as gymnastics, water and snow skiing, wrestling, and basketball. This ability is used in dissimilar ways from activity to activity. The data in Figure 7-2 indicate that gymnasts and water skiers have much better balancing ability than other groups. This is as expected, for the balance demanded in these sports is quite similar to the kind of balance that is meas-

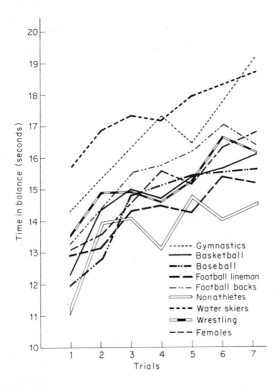

FIGURE 7-2 *Comparison of groups in balancing ability on the stabilometer. (Source: Robert N. Singer. Balance skill as related to athletics, sex, height, and weight. In G. Kenyon (Ed.),* Contemporary psychology of sport: Proceedings of the 2d International Congress of Sports Psychology. *Chicago: The Athletic Institute, 1970. P. 649.)*

ured on the stabilometer. Also, balance is probably a stronger component in proficiency in these sports than in most others. Since nonathletes did more poorly than all other groups on the task, it can be inferred that some degree of balancing ability is associated with participation in athletics.

## *Habits and Subskills*

Within a given sport, a number of skills are used. Skills can be divided into subskills and may be thought of as requiring an organized sequence of habits. As the subskills are learned and habits are formed, the skill is mastered. Subskills are often interrelated, which brings about a system of transfer situations.

In the elementary backstroke, arms and legs move in synchronized, similar movement patterns. Learning to move the arms correctly helps the swimmer to learn the correct leg movement. After learning to make a basketball lay-up from a stationary position with the preferred hand, transfer occurs to making a lay-up while dribbling to the basket. These are two examples, in different activities, in which subskills transfer positively to other subskills within the same sport. Well-learned acts that appear to have become habits are most likely to yield transfer effects.

Within a sport a number of skills may be interrelated. The overhand volleyball serve is similar in movement pattern to the arm movement in the spike. Similarities between sports exist as well; they may be obvious, or for some reason the learner may not be aware of them. The good coach or teacher can point out meaningful similarities in a manner that is helpful to the learner. For example, many learners have difficulty with the tennis serve, and yet it is quite like throwing a football or baseball, except that a racket is used. When the relationship is understood, the related skill may be learned faster and more easily.

Providing examples from sport to sport, skill to skill, and subskill to subskill serves a definite purpose—pointing out that the requisite movement patterns already exist in the athlete's repertoire. In fact, stimulus complexity rather than motor capacity is probably the problem in most motor skills (Gagné & Foster, 1949). A limited number of different movements are required in sports, but from isolated practice to unpredictable contest conditions, innumerable variations occur. Gagné & Foster state that motor skill tasks can be made more difficult simply by increasing the number and complexity of stimuli. They write, "Learning of motor tasks is largely a matter of learning perceptual relationships; the 'perceptual aspect' of the task is the thing which has the greatest effect on the learning of the motor skill" (p. 342).

Organized movements in most cases seem to be fairly easy to master at a reasonable level. Changing situations demand behavioral modifications, and the ability to apply appropriate responses thus becomes the major problem. The basketball jump shot is part of every player's arsenal today. Shooting it alone in practice is not difficult for the player; he can score a high percentage within a reasonable range from the basket. In the game, however, while moving around at varying speeds and playing against assorted defenses and under stressful conditions, the task seems to be completely different. Emotional and mental preparation for the variety of stimulus conditions that may be encountered reduces the complexity of the entire act.

### Learning to Learn

We have observed that in many instances the relative stimulus and response characteristics of two tasks are specified and transfer effects are predicted. In a sense, then, discussion has primarily focused on the specifics of transfer. There are, however, a few generalized circumstances in which transfer phenomena are observed. One such circumstance is referred to as "learning to learn."

Early studies of monkeys in problem-solving situations (Harlow, 1949) and humans learning lists of nonsense syllables (Ward, 1937) point to the interesting conclusion that after much experience and practice, *learning sets* are developed to handle similar types of learning situations. When lists of different nonsense syllables are given to subjects to learn, they show a gradual improvement in learning speed with each list. Such increased performance must be due to learning how to learn this kind of matter, for the syllable associations are different from list to list.

Just as a person learns to take essay tests and multiple-choice tests, or to solve problems, he also learns to master the common features of athletic skills. Experience in the tactics and strategies of the basketball fast break probably provides insight into an offensive attack in soccer. Learning how to play a court sport may be generalized to other court sports. Many problems, such as what tactics are effective, are similar from sport to sport, and they can probably be generalized more effectively across different sports by athletes with extensive experience.

### Bilateral Transfer

Another generalized transfer function is popularly referred to as "bilateral transfer." Limb performance on a task is improved as a result of practice on the same task with the opposite limb. Research indicates that bilateral transfer of strength, endurance, and skill does occur.

Slater-Hammel's experiment (1950) is a good demonstration of the phenomenon of bilateral transfer. Male college students were divided into two groups of 10 each. The experimental group received flexion and extension exercises of the preferred arm against a 14-pound resistance, while the control group rested. All subjects were pretested and post-tested in strength of the nonpreferred arm. The investigator found that the exercise program for one arm resulted in a significant improvement in the strength of the other arm.

Similar improvements in the performance of unexercised limbs have been observed under a number of conditions. Positive transfer occurs from one side of the body to the other. Besides the implications for overall skill development within a given sport, such as facilitated learning of basketball shooting with the nonpreferred hand following much preferred-hand shooting, the performance effects of injury to a limb may be minimized. Athletes who have one injured limb may practice skills and do exercises with the other limb to reap the benefits of bilateral transfer. The effects may be minimal, but they are certainly better than nothing at all.

### Speed and Accuracy

The question is often asked whether practice conditions during acquisition of a new skill should be such as to emphasize speed or accuracy. Many athletic skills demand both speed and accuracy. Should one be emphasized at the expense of the other during early learning stages?

The traditional practice has been to stress body control and accuracy while slowing down the speed of the body movement. Research and authoritative opinion, however, do not support the value of this procedure. On the contrary, two other conclusions become apparent: (1) a skill should be practiced the way it will be performed in the contest, and (2) if anything, speed should be emphasized rather than accuracy. Let us examine the meaning behind these statements.

If a skill demands both speed and accuracy, both should be emphasized in practice, because fast movement is unlike slow movement in form: after the athlete learns a skill at a slow speed he has to change his body control and adjust the movement to the fast speed. Further, in investigations of transfer effects, initial stress on speed promotes performance where both speed and accuracy are considered important, while accuracy gained at the expense of speed is lost when speed is increased.

Two studies are presented here as examples. Fulton (1945) trained one group of subjects for speed and another for accuracy in a motor skill. Later, both speed and accuracy were emphasized. Early emphasis on speed resulted in a high degree of transfer; stronger transfer was found in the speed-trained group than in the accuracy-trained group. Fulton remarks: "Therefore, movements such as tennis strokes, golf strokes, and hammer throws in which the accumulation of momentum is essential for effective performance would be particularly adversely affected by early emphasis on accuracy" (p. 52).

A recent investigation by Woods (1967) supports earlier findings. An attempt was made to determine the effect that varied instructional emphasis on speed and accuracy would have upon the learning of the forehand tennis stroke. Beginning high school tennis players were trained for five weeks, after which it was concluded:

> For a tennis skill which is deemed to require both ball velocity and ball-placement accuracy simultaneously, the most desirable results were obtained by equal and simultaneous emphasis on both the velocity and accuracy variables. The second most desirable results were obtained by beginning with velocity and terminating with accuracy. The least desirable results were obtained by initial emphasis on accuracy followed by velocity [p. 141].

Thus far in discussing transfer we have only dealt with the initial stages of skill acquisition and with considerations of speed and accuracy. What about the athlete who has gained reasonable success but suddenly develops problems? It may very well be appropriate in such cases to practice skills at a slower pace. Flaws that are not apparent at high speeds may become more noticeable at slow speeds. Then again, the flaws may occur only at high rates of speed, in which case films or videotapes of the performance can be of invaluable assistance.

## RETENTION

The goal of most learning situations is not only immediately successful performance but also the ability to perform in the same manner at later dates. The skills learned on Monday in practice should be remembered, and remembered well, in Saturday's contest. The retention, or remembrance, of written matter, concepts, skills, and the like is an important part of the learning process. The value of learning is often judged in terms of whether its effects are long-lasting.

"Retention" and "forgetting" are two opposing terms used to describe the same process in opposite ways. The more a person retains, the less he forgets, and vice versa. One of the criteria for successful coaching is related to the amount of material (skills, tactics, knowledge, etc.) that is retained by athletes at a maximum level for the desired period of time. The ultimate goal of both coaches and athletes is for the athletes to use what they have learned when the appropriate situations arise in future contests. Little wonder, then, that top consideration is given to practice techniques that may have favorable long-term results. Actually, of course, much of the material already discussed in this chapter, as well as in the immediately preceding and following chapters, suggests ways of improving learning and, at the same time, retention. A few additional ideas about retention are discussed below.

### Practice Conditions[6]

A review of the sections on Practice Sessions and Practicing for Perfection in Chapter 6 may be helpful at this point, for that material is germane to the practical aspects of retention of motor skill. For example:

1 Distributed practice results in retention as good as or better than massed practice. Perhaps distributed practice should be selected when there is a choice, to take advantage of any possible slight benefit it may offer.
2 Overlearning or overpractice leads to greater retention.
3 Matter that the learner perceives as meaningful is retained longer and better than meaningless matter.

We have noted in this chapter that (1) intermittent and variable reinforcements maintain motivation and performance levels for a longer period of time than other reinforcement schedules; and (2) positive reinforcement leads to more desirable long-range goals than does negative reinforcement.

Among the factors studied by Fleishman & Parker (1962), level of initial proficiency was cited as being most important in retention. This finding is unexpected, as other research has shown low relationships between initial and final achievement (reported in Chapter 6). The highest proficiency levels lead to the best retention. Another interesting finding in this study is that the amount of verbal guidance has no effect on retention of the skill. Other factors, such as length of time between initial learning and repeated performance, need to be considered, and it should be recognized that the nature of the intervening activity affects retention. These two factors are discussed below in detail.

[6] An excellent article that includes many considerations about retention in the learning of a motor task is Edwin A. Fleishman & James F. Parker. Factors in the retention and relearning of perceptual-motor skill. *Journal of Experimental Psychology*, 1962, **64**, 215–226.

*Nature of Learned Matter*

There is pretty good indication that not all types of subject matter are retained to the same degree. Motor skills are usually retained better than verbal materials (Leavitt & Schlosberg, 1944). Once a person has learned to swim, ride a bicycle, or hit a baseball, he will demonstrate a reasonable amount of skill after many years of no practice, but recalling poetry or history that was learned years before is often quite difficult. Naturally, a complicated maneuver in gymnastics or diving can remain in a highly developed state only with continual practice. However, reasonable facsimiles of the earlier performance can usually be shown after a fairly long layoff.

Forgetting usually takes place rapidly at first and then more slowly as time passes. Motor skills are usually remembered better than verbal matter at all stages of retention. In the study by Leavitt & Schlosberg (1944), the subjects were tested each week for 10 weeks. The motor skill was performed at a higher level of retention than the verbal material each time. It is true, as McGeoch and Irion (1952) point out, that "studies which make comparisons between perceptual-motor skills and verbal habits, however, have uniformly been unable to achieve comparability" (pp. 382–383). It is also true that there have been severe methodological handicaps in research dealing with the retention of verbal materials. Nonetheless, Adams (1967, p. 230) writes, "We all know from personal experience that the forgetting of continuous motor skills like ice-skating and riding a bicycle is trivial over long retention intervals of weeks, months, and years. These anecdotal observations are supported by controlled laboratory investigations. . . . The very high retention shown in [motor-response] experiments is a research challenge because the long-term retention of well-learned verbal responses (as well-learned is defined in laboratory studies) is so much poorer than of continuous motor responses." In the study by Fleishman and Parker (1962), three groups learned a motor task and then were retested—one group after an interval of 9 months, the second after 12 months, and the third after 24 months. Retention was almost perfect and about the same for the three groups, although the group tested after 24 months demonstrated slightly more forgetting than the other two. Whatever the explanation for this superior retention of motor skills, it is obviously of a nature to benefit coaches and athletes. Moreover, the importance of an activity and the pleasure connected with it, are also conducive to learning and retention of learning—a fact which also works to benefit those engaged in athletics.

Since meaningfulness and importance determine to a great extent how well matter is retained, we can assume that youths who are particularly fond of sports attach a great deal of significance to athletic skills and, as a consequence, are willing to practice these skills a great deal. Also, pleasant experiences are remembered longer (at least consciously) than unpleasant ones; evidently many people find sports and games rewarding and pleasurable, and remember the skills involved for a long time. The coach should therefore make learning situations and practice sessions as pleasant as possible.

The data collected by Meyers (1967) on retention of motor skills during various intervals of no practice are an illustration of resistance to forgetting over a 13-week period. Using a ladder-climbing task that involves balance, and after an initial test of 10 trials, five groups of subjects were retested after layoffs of 10 minutes, 1 day, 1 week, 4 weeks, and 13 weeks. The performance curves in Figure 7-3 and statistical analysis of the data indicate little or no loss of proficiency upon resumption of practice after a layoff period of up to 13 weeks. In fact, of the five groups, the 1-week rest group demonstrated the most forgetting. Thus, the general implication is a strong resistance to forgetting during at least a 13-week period.

## Reminiscence

In every type of learning situation the unexpected may happen. Such is the case when the first performance after a period of no practice results in higher levels than the levels attained during the last performance. Increase in performance, which is apparently a function of rest, has been termed "reminiscence." This phenomenon is by no means new, having been observed and studied on a wide range of learning materials throughout this century.

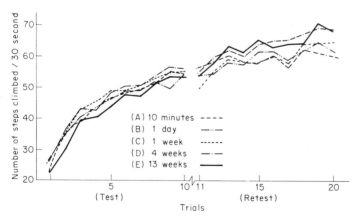

FIGURE 7-3 *Comparison of five groups in retention of a motor task following varying intervals of no practice.* (Source: *Judith L. Meyers. Retention of balance coordination learning as influenced by extended lay-offs.* Research Quarterly, *1967,* **38**, *72–78. P. 75.)*

Why should performance be better after a layoff? First, it should be pointed out that the usual experience is performance decrement. However, improved performance can occur, and different explanations have been offered. If it does happen, the task involved usually had not been previously well learned, for extremely well-learned skills do not show performance increments after periods of nonpractice. It is possible that the tendency to make incorrect responses may be weakened due to the passage of time and inactivity, and that correct responses may become more dominant, leading to greater proficiency.

Another possibility is more mental rehearsal of activities than is realized. Such rehearsal may occur during periods of no physical practice and may help to improve performance. Perhaps the most common condition in which reminiscence occurs is after massed practice of a skill. Continuous practice, without any rest pauses, typically results in fatigue, boredom, and poorer performance at the end of practice than during the middle stages. A day or a week of rest may allow the person to "recover," and his learning status, which was depressed under the conditions of practice, may be more truly represented under better circumstances—namely, the absence of fatigue and boredom.

### Competing Responses versus Disuse

Of particular theoretical concern is the reason why forgetting occurs with the passage of time. Although a number of theories have been advanced, the most convincing arguments are (1) the theory of disuse: that forgetting is a function of elapsed time and lack of practice; and (2) the theory of competing responses or retroactive inhibition: that interference from new learning causes performance decrements. Research indicates the theory of competing responses is more acceptable. In other words, not only time but also what occurs in that time determines retention of what has been learned. That may be one reason why verbal and written materials are so difficult to remember over a lengthy period of time; so much material is read that competing responses is the consequence. Many athletic skills, on the other hand, are unique to given sports and overpracticed; the number of potential competing responses is far fewer than with verbal and written material.

Another variable in the forgetting process is the role played by reinforcement. When reinforcement is first applied and then removed, it is only a matter of time until extinction occurs. "Extinction" refers to the elimination of the tendency to respond in a certain way. When reinforcement is omitted, an act is gradually eliminated from the repertoire. For example, a basketball player might have been a highly effective passer in high school.

On the college team, the coach or other players do not praise his passing talents, players drop his passes, and in general, individual scoring skills are placed at a high premium. Gradually, this player will probably begin to shoot more and pass less. Thus, reinforcement, period of disuse, and competing responses are all psychological variables to contend with in analyzing the process of retention.

SUMMARY

In this chapter, the phenomena most associated with the psychology of learning have been discussed. At the onset, performance and learning were compared and differentiated. Motivation, the urge to push toward some goal, was explained in terms of the following factors:

*Material versus ideal rewards*   Any sort of perceived reward in athletics motivates the athlete. Society assumes that the motivation of someone who participates in an activity for the love of it or for some other ideal will last longer than the motivation of a person whose chief incentive is materialistic gain. Probably anticipation of both types of rewards is present in most situations.

*Setting goals*   Past experiences in an activity are related to present goal levels, and these levels in turn affect performance. Specific hard goals are evidently more effective in raising performance output than easier and more general goals.

*Need to achieve*   Although many needs operate to initiate activity and provide it with direction and sustenance, the need to achieve is one of the more important. It influences the setting of goals and the quality and quantity of practice.

*Optimal level of motivation*   For every task and for every individual there is an optimal level of motivation. Complex tasks are performed best under fairly low motivation, for too much motivation may cause tension and low performance.

*External comments*   The coach's remarks to an athlete may be directive, reinforcing, or incentive. Frequent and immediate positive comments may motivate the performer.

*Competition*   The urge to compete with oneself or someone else heightens motivational levels. Certain behavioral characteristics of good and poor competitors can be differentiated.

*Hawthorne effect*   Making changes in environmental setting and the routines of practice sessions, and giving special attention to the athlete may increase his productivity.

*Social presence*   The presence of other people during a performance by the skilled athlete will have a positive influence on his performance.

Reinforcement can act as a motivation or can give the athlete knowledge of results. Any type of stimulus that maintains or increases the probability of occurrence of a response is a reinforcer. Some of the qualitative and quantitative aspects of reinforcement that must be considered in any type of learning situation are:

*Negative and positive reinforcement*    Positive reinforcement after performance has a more beneficial effect on future performance than negative reinforcement, though both are effective.

*Shaping behavior*    Through reinforcement, general behavior is shaped until specific goals are reached.

*Praise and criticism*    Praise, or the positive approach, is generally preferable to criticism.

*Applications of reinforcement*    Intermittent and irregular reinforcement schedules have been determined to be best, both practically and theoretically, in maintaining motivation and performance levels.

At the heart of learning is the concept of transfer. What the person has experienced always affects what is to be presently learned.

*Positive and negative transfer*    In positive transfer, previous experience promotes the learning of a new skill, and in negative transfer, previous experience interferes with the learning of a new skill. When a new stimulus calls for a response that has already been learned, positive transfer should result, but when a new response is to be made to a familiar stimulus, negative transfer will probably occur.

*Identical elements*    Similarity between stimuli and responses in two tasks results in the greatest amounts of transfer.

*Similar underlying abilities*    Common abilities demanded in a number of skills and the extent to which they are developed will influence success.

*Habits and subskills*    When the subskills of a particular activity are interrelated, transfer is facilitated. The relationships of movements, habit patterns, and subskills should be pointed out to the learner in order to encourage transfer from learned responses to newly introduced ones.

*Learning to learn*    With experience, learning sets are developed which enable the learner to handle similar types of learning situations with greater effectiveness.

*Bilateral transfer*    Performance of a task with one limb is improved as a result of practice on the same task with the opposite limb.

*Speed and accuracy*    These variables are involved in the execution of many motor acts, and the relative emphasis placed on each in practice should duplicate contest conditions insofar as possible. When this is not possible or when both are equally important, speed should be emphasized in the initial learning stages.

The effectiveness of a learning situation is often determined by what is retained. Little wonder, then, that some factors influencing later retention have been identified and analyzed. Retention is dependent upon a number of variables, among which are:

*Practice conditions*    Retention after distributed practice is better than or equal to retention after massed practice. Overlearning leads to better retention. Matter that the learner perceives as meaningful is retained longer and more effectively than matter that he believes is unimportant.

*Nature of learned matter*    Motor, or athletic, skills are usually remembered better than verbal materials.

*Reminiscence*    Improvement in performance is occasionally noted after a period of no practice.

*Competing responses versus disuse*    Forgetting may be due to a number of factors, but competing responses is probably the most important. The passage of time, lack of practice, and the elimination of reinforcement also encourage forgetting.

REFERENCES

Adams, Jack A. *Human memory*. New York: McGraw-Hill, 1967.

Atkinson, John W. *An introduction to motivation*. Princeton, N.J.: Van Nostrand, 1964.

Atkinson, John W., Bastian, J. R., Earl, R. W., & Litwin, G. H. The achievement motive, goal setting, and probability preferences. *Journal of Abnormal and Social Psychology*, 1960, **60**, 27–36.

Atkinson, John W., & Reitman, Walter R. Performance as a function of motive strength and expectancy of goal-attainment. In Atkinson, J. W. (Ed.), *Motives in fantasy, action, and society*. Princeton, N.J.: Van Nostrand, 1958.

Bannister, Roger. *The four minute mile*. New York: Dodd, Mead, 1955.

Daniels, Diane. Transfer of training and retroactive inhibition existent in the learning of a selected tennis and badminton skill. Unpublished master's thesis, North Texas State University, 1968.

Entwisle, D. G. Ageing: effects of previous skill on training. *Journal of Occupational Psychology*, 1959, **33**, 238–243.

Fleishman, Edwin A., & Parker, James F. Factors in the retention and relearning of perceptual-motor skill. *Journal of Experimental Psychology*, 1962, **64**, 215–226.

Fulton, Ruth E. Speed and accuracy in learning movements. *Archives of Psychology*, 1945, No. 300.

Gagné, Robert M., & Foster, Harriet. Transfer to a motor skill from practice on a pictured representation. *Journal of Experimental Psychology*, 1949, **39**, 342–354.

Harlow, H. F. The formation of learning sets. *Psychological Review*, 1949, **56**, 51–65.

Hollingworth, H. L. *The psychology of an audience*. New York: American Book, 1935.

Hurlock, E. B. An evaluation of certain incentives on school work. *Journal of Educational Psychology*, 1925, **16**, 145–159.

Leavitt, Harold J., & Schlosberg, J. The retention of verbal and of motor skills. *Journal of Experimental Psychology*, 1944, **34**, 404–417.

Locke, Edwin A. Toward a theory of task motivation and incentives. *Organizational Behavior and Human Performance*, 1968, **3**, 157–189.

McGeoch, John A., & Irion, Arthur L. *The psychology of learning*. New York: David McKay, 1952.

Meyers, Judith L. Retention of balance coordination learning as influenced by extended lay-offs. *Research Quarterly*, 1967, **38**, 72–78.

Roethlisberger, F. J., & Dickson, W. J. *Management and the worker—an account of a research program conducted by the Western Electric Company, Chicago.* Cambridge: Harvard University Press, 1939.

Ryan, F. J. Some aspects of athletic behavior. *Track and Field Quarterly Review*, December, 1968.

Schiltz, Jack H., & Levitt, Stuart. Levels of aspiration of high- and low-skilled boys. *Research Quarterly*, 1968, **39**, 696–703.

Sims, Verner M. The relative influences of two types of motivation on improvement. *Journal of Educational Psychology*, 1928, **19**, 480–484.

Singleton, W. T. An experimental investigation of sewing-machine skill. *British Journal of Psychology*, 1957, **48**, 127–132.

Slater-Hammel, A. T. Bilateral effects of muscle activity. *Research Quarterly*, 1950, **21**, 203–209.

Thorndike, E. L., & Woodworth, R. S. I. The Influence of improvement in one mental function upon the efficiency of other functions; II. The estimation of magnitudes; III. Functions involving attention, observation, and discrimination. *Psychological Review*, 1901, **8**, 247–261; 384–395; 553–564.

Ward, L. B. Reminiscence and rote learning. *Psychological Monographs*, 1937, **49**, No. 220.

Woods, John B. The effect of varied instructional emphasis upon the development of a motor skill. *Research Quarterly*, 1967, **38**, 132–142.

# CHAPTER EIGHT

# Training Factors and the Athlete

The psychologist views training as the practical application of the learning phenomena that are understood. The study of processes associated with learning is of concern to researchers and theorists, and its applications can be seen in industry, the military, and the gymnasium. Much that has already been said in this book could be repeated in this chapter, but emphasis will be placed instead on variables associated with training procedures.

The obvious intent of any training program is to reach short-term objectives in as small an amount of time as possible, with planned sequences of experience. It is unwise to proceed in a random manner when certain training programs are known to work. Coaches are primarily concerned with two types of training programs. The goal of the first is to develop athletes physically to the extent that they become physically capable of performing the desired acts. This development must not only reach an optimal level for execution of single acts, but must far surpass it in order that skills may be continually practiced. If athletes have great amounts of endurance, they can practice more and hence increase their learning of skills and their performance levels.

In the second type of training program, an attempt is made to apply learning principles and findings from behavioral research to "real" situations. For example, the coach attempts to structure practice sessions in a manner consistent with psychological advice on how to attain desired behavior outcomes in the most efficient manner.

As the first type of training program is the subject of many books and many articles in professional and popular journals, it is necessary here only to acknowledge the necessity for the physical development of the athlete to correspond to the demands of his sport. Let us therefore examine the psychological factors associated with training the athlete, where the intent is to improve skill levels to meet the demands of the tasks. In some kinds of training situations, the learner initially has very little appropriate skill development, but in athletics, this part of the training problem is nonexistent, as a systematic process of selection has eliminated applicants who do not have basic skills.

At this point, the reader might very well rebel against the term "training" and wish to substitute "education." For some reason, the public accepts and respects education but often views training as applicable to animals or unthinking humans. Actually, the objectives of both training and education are to modify behavior, and both are part of the instructional process. Instruction involves systematic, guided experiences similar to those of both education and training. However, there are differences between the two.

Generally speaking, education is concerned with individual differences, with long-range effects which are often not measurable. Training, however, encompasses teaching similar operations and expecting uniform outcomes, and includes less respect for individual changes. It would appear, then, that the coach is both a trainer and an educator. He works as perhaps no other teacher does in considering individual differences, but his goals are short-range and specific. There are more short-term goals in training programs, in a relative sense, than in education programs. In other words, people who are to be trained come to the program with a certain set of skills. The major objective is to influence them to attain a given level of skill at the end of a specified period of time:

*The training process*

*Stage 1*
Entering repertoire of skills and abilities

*Stage 2*
Period of instructional manipulations and learning experiences

*Stage 3*
Terminal repertoire of skills and abilities

In the foregoing process, stage 1 leads to stage 2 and stage 2 leads to stage 3. For further discussion of training and education as well as research information on training techniques, books by Glaser (1962) and Holding (1965) are recommended.

Perhaps most of the material in this book refers directly to or has implications for effective training procedures. The purpose of this chapter is to present a guide to the factors usually associated with and involved in training.[1] The following topics will be discussed: knowledge of results (feedback); drill; whole versus part method; mental practice; verbalization; process versus product; application of principles; habit interferences; guidance, demonstration, and instruction; psychological tolerance; cues and aids; and technological aids.

---

[1] For example, the reader may want to refer to the following source: Dael Wolfle. Training. In S. S. Stevens (Ed.), *Handbook of experimental psychology*. New York: Wiley, 1951.

## KNOWLEDGE OF RESULTS (FEEDBACK)

For performance to be improved, a minimal amount of relevant information must be provided to the learner on the outcome of his acts. This information can come from one or both of two sources: from the performer himself on the basis of his response, or from an outsider's later comments. Whatever the source, there can be little doubt that some knowledge of results, or "feedback" as it is popularly called today, is necessary for improvement.

A person can practice a task over and over but show no improvement if information on the outcome of each execution is withheld. For example, in a classic study by Trowbridge & Cason, blindfolded subjects were told to draw a three-inch line. From the data in Table 8-1, it can be seen that four groups of subjects were formed and that each subject had 100 trials at the task. One group received no information after trials, another was given meaningless nonsense syllables, a third was given generalized information, and the last was given exact information on each trial. The data are what we expect: no knowledge of results permits no improvement, and the most precise information yields the most beneficial results.

Actually, the research literature is quite confusing about the interchangeable use of such terms as "knowledge of results," "reinforcement," "reward," and "feedback" (for instance, see Bilodeau, 1966). These terms have many overlapping connotations, as well as specific and important differentiating aspects. Such problems are not important in this book, however; what is important is to apply the theory of feedback to a realistic setting, the gymnasium.

TABLE 8-1   Effect of learning on providing subjects with different amounts of information about results on each trial

| Information given subjects after each trial | Average errors in inches | | |
|---|---|---|---|
| | First 30 trials | Middle 40 trials | Last 30 trials |
| None (control group) | 0.75 | 0.86 | 0.80 |
| Nonsense syllables | 1.11 | 1.07 | 1.05 |
| "Right" or "wrong" | 0.92 | 0.67 | 0.49 |
| Exact information | 0.24 | 0.14 | 0.12 |

*Source:* M. H. Trowbridge & H. Cason. An experimental study of Thorndike's theory of learning. *Journal of General Psychology*, 1932, **7**, 245–258. Reprinted in Dael Wolfle. Training. In S. S. Stevens (Ed.), *Handbook of Experimental psychology.* New York: Wiley, 1951. P. 1268.

As mentioned earlier, feedback can occur from a few sources. Indeed, in the case of athletic skills, there are probably few if any instances in which the performer has no information at all. In the line-drawing task, the investigators made a deliberate attempt to withhold feedback, but in most motor skills, information feedback is intrinsic. That is, by merely completing an act under normal circumstances, a person receives continuous visual and proprioceptive information. The difference between "input" (what the athlete sees and wants to do) and "output" (his actual response) constitutes his error "feedback."

The pitcher sees where he threw the ball, observes what "stuff" was on it, and experiences the feel of the act. He makes appropriate adjustments on the next pitch in order to make the actual response more like the desired response or goal. And this is the function of information feedback—to allow the person to realize the discrepancy between his output and his desired output.

In athletic situations, some sort of signal, or information, occurs during or after the response, informing the performer of the accuracy or acceptability of his movements. The necessity of this condition in learning or maintaining a skill is apparent. Such information allows the archer whose shot is off to one side of the target to compensate to the opposite side in the next shot. The basketball player who shoots short on his first few attempts can adjust by shooting higher or aiming past the front rim.

Not only visual information but also kinesthetic information is present during and after performance of many motor skills. The quarterback not only sees that his passes are off target but may also feel that his throwing pattern is not as smooth as usual. The tennis player can see the results of his response and also sense the coordination and smoothness of his stroking patterns. If a movement in any sport does not feel right and the outcome is not desirable, obviously an adjustment is needed. Response-produced kinesthetic cues are available to all athletes, and the athletes should be conscious of them and should compensate when necessary. Visual control is more prominent in the early stages of learning, kinesthetic control in the later stages. The athlete's vision is thus freed to detect other cues as he performs.

In many cases, the information provided to the performer by his own efforts is incomplete or inadequate, and he needs another source of knowledge about his results. Such supplementary information has been termed "augmented information feedback," and an example occurs when the coach or instructor tells the student how he is doing. Another example is specific training in which extra information is present, with the intent of transferring developed skills to the standard task, as in basketball, when rims are luminated or marks placed on the backboard in practice.

The athlete is often not aware of the faults in his movement patterns that lead to undesired outcomes, but the experienced coach can point out the faults and offer suggestions to rectify them. In addition, the coach's general comments and the manner in which they are stated provide the athlete with knowledge that may affect his next actions. In some sports, such as gymnastics and diving, form is one of the requisites of successful performance. Frequently, an outsider's description of the performer's appearance in the activity can call the athlete's attention to certain aspects of the routine he was not aware needed polishing up.

Research indicates that in many cases augmented information feedback can be beneficial in the learning process, especially when the learning situation is inadequate in itself to advance learning levels quickly. Naturally, the more knowledge is present, the less the need for additional information. If the basketball player scores a basket (and sees it), obviously there is no practical need for the coach to tell him that it was a good shot. This supplementary knowledge of results is not necessary to enhance learning, although it may serve as a motivator.

In the study illustrated in Figure 8-1 it was shown that more knowledge of performance enhanced the learning of a motor skill. One group of subjects received normal feedback, verbal reports of how long they maintained the stylus on target on a pursuit rotor. The other group received verbal reports and were also allowed to see their scores on a counter. The augmented knowledge of results group performed consistently better throughout the study, although both groups improved.

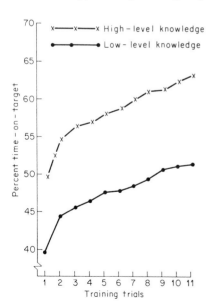

FIGURE 8-1 *Comparison of high-level knowledge of performance with low level of performance. (Source: A. Smode. Learning and performance in a tracking task under two levels of achievement information feedback.* Journal of Experimental Psychology, *1958,* **56,** *297–304. P. 300. Copyright 1958 by the American Psychological Association and reproduced by permission.)*

In practice sessions, added information may be provided that is not a usual consequence of the responses. Extra kinesthetic feedback, verbal feedback, or visual feedback has been afforded to subjects in psychological laboratory tasks, and performances have been compared on standard tasks. Naturally when additional feedback is provided in one sense modality, the nature of the task changes, and the practice is no longer a standard practice. The results of such studies are not conclusive, but in general it seems that standard practice is best in promoting skill acquisition, practice with supplementary visual guidance is second, kinesthetic third, and verbal last.

It may be that in most athletic skills enough feedback occurs that there is no need for additional information. This was the conclusion Bell (1968) arrived at after she tested the effect of augmented knowledge of results on the learning of a badminton skill. Furthermore, this study lends additional support to the theory that practice conditions should simulate game conditions as nearly as possible. In activities where feedback is deficient, or for athletes who show poor performances that might possibly be improved upon with extra guidance in a specific sense modality, however, all potential avenues should be exhausted.

It can be generally stated that (1) there is no improvement in motor activity without some knowledge of results; (2) there is improvement with it; and (3) performance suffers when it is taken away. A practical problem which has been rather well researched is the effect of a delay in feedback. What difference in performance, if any, may be expected when feedback is delayed until the end of performance or is given in summary form rather than immediately? A coach can comment at the end of each act, each fencing lunge, for example, or can wait until the athlete has made a number of practice tries and then comment on the performance as a whole. Immediate feedback appears to be best, and specific comments are more effective than general reactions.

Finally, information feedback may actually serve three functions: (1) to reinforce acts, (2) to motivate the performers, and (3) to provide information and guidance. Some researchers believe that the first two are of secondary importance, and thus the coach's main concern should perhaps be with the role of feedback in directing the athlete toward ideal skill levels and eventually establishing and strengthening associations.

## DRILL

Unfortunately, the word "drill" often becomes synonymous with "training." "Military training program" has always suggested routines requiring drill, and to many people, "athletic training program" implies constant drilling in skills. Actually, a training program includes many aspects of the learning process, only one of which is the potential of drill as an effective learning technique.

Although psychologists rarely use the term "drill," the techniques of drilling have been the subject of much research and theoretical construction. Association theory, bond theory, stimulus-response (S-R) theory, and behaviorism all are concerned with repetition of an act to produce a consistent response. No matter what theory name is used, repeated presentation of the same stimulus will, all things being equal, eventually cause development of a consistent response. There is no substitute for practice in development of skill.

Drill is therefore basic to S-R theory, as it calls for many repetitions of a response to the same stimulus and usually lends to conditioning. The highest levels of skill are achieved only after intensive practice, so that responses occur as if automatically because they are so well learned. The article below by Wickstrom describes the uses of drills and the techniques that should be employed to promote more effective results from drill. Although intended for physical education classes, the material is certainly applicable to the coaching situation.

_____

## IN DEFENSE OF DRILLS[2]

R. L. Wickstrom

Nearly every physical education teacher who does any serious teaching uses drills in connection with his teaching. In terms of effective teaching it is not so much a matter of *whether* drills are used, but more precisely it is a question of *how* they are used. Therefore, an effort will be made to scrutinize the common use of drills and then suggest and defend an extraordinary approach.

### Common practice

Even in what might be termed the "better" physical education programs the usual practice is to employ a few drills at the beginning of a new unit to introduce the students to the skills involved in the game. As soon as the drills are finished the class is plunged irretrievably into the game. There is

[2] Reprinted from *The Physical Educator,* 1967, **24**, 38–39.

another slightly different but equally common version of this approach. After the first few class sessions the drills are largely forgotten or used unintentionally as a barrier to playing the game. That is, the class must get the drills out of the way at the beginning of the period before being permitted to play the game. These seem to be very common and accepted practices. They are also indefensible practices when compared to high standards based upon a knowledge of the nature of motor learning.

The problem with this type of approach is its relationship to the process of motor learning. A learned skill is one which is performed correctly, habitually, automatically without conscious attention to the details of the movements involved. In a drill there is ample opportunity to concentrate on form and technique without the complication of competition or other distractions. When the child is thrust into the game he reverts to the automatic level for his skills and directs his attention to strategy and the other aspects of the game. If he is moved into the game situation too early, his weak or incorrectly developed movements are repeated and become habitual. Faulty form is reinforced and consequently is learned. Considering this complication it would seem that the purposeful and forceful concentration on appropriate drills would be a significant part of any early learning situation. It is perhaps this extraordinary use of drills that needs to be explained and defended.

## Extraordinary use of drills

At the outset it should be made clear that the extraordinary use of drills does not mean an exclusive, restrictive or oppressive use. More accurately it refers to the proper balance of drills with play in accordance with the nature of motor learning. There is a critical point in the learning process at which playing the game can be of more harm than benefit. Similarly there is a point at which continued use of drills without relating them to the game can be detrimental to the learning process. Obviously the identification of this crucial point is the key to the successful use of drills. The point is a highly variable one and is related to the skills being practiced, the group doing the practicing and the nature of the game.

The instructor must be aware of the progress of the class and be sensitive to the manifestation of a consistency in performance. Consistency in performance in a drill is first evidence of a significant level of motor learning. Once this point has been reached the danger of changing the balance from the drill to play is lessened. Furthermore, the balance does not then swing from one extreme to the other but is a gradual change of emphasis. The general approach is to emphasize controlled practice of skills until they are developed in a consistent pattern of correct movements and then move into the modified game to retain the control of play. As the skills develop the use of drills and modified games is reduced in favor of the full scale game. This approach is extraordinary primarily because it is so seldom used. The instructor can become so concerned about interest and fun that his judgment is often impaired. To abandon drills too early as a concession to fun is a grave error and is deadly in terms of motor learning.

Interest is important to motor learning but there are many ways of developing and maintaining it other than playing the game. The instructor must be skillful in manipulating his teaching techniques to provide activity that is interesting and fun *and* still leads to motor learning. To be successful the teacher must believe, unequivocally, that skillful play is more fun and more interesting than mediocre play. He must communicate this belief to his students by his attitude and his presentation. Once the stage has been set, the play can continue. And the primary character is the teacher who must be convincing and realistic to be effective in his role.

*Suggestions for successful use of drills*

1. Concentrate on drills until basically correct form starts to become automatic and thereby habitual. Drills need not be the only form of skill practice employed but they should be emphasized.

2. Encourage students to concentrate on the correct execution of the skill or skills used in the drills. Drills which are performed sloppily are useless and probably far more harmful than beneficial. If students do not improve in performance the situation must be analyzed to determine the cause.

3. Constantly make corrections during drills to keep attention on the proper techniques of performance. Early corrections of a general nature made with enthusiasm and to the entire group are stimulating and effective. Along with the corrections, general comments on the correct fundamentals are positive in nature and of particular value. The students should be kept aware of the purpose and objectives of the drill while they are doing it. It should be remembered that the drill is an opportunity to concentrate on certain aspects of correct performance and develop a consistency in the performance.

4. Make drills game-like as often as possible. Drills of this sort are more interesting and challenging because they are a movement in the direction of regular play.

5. Advance to the use of multiple-skill drills to emphasize the proper use of combined skills. The transition from drills to the game is easier if drills have been devised to reflect the choices and problems possible in the actual game.

6. Make extensive use of modified games to create the much desired com-

petitive atmosphere. Most games can be modified to emphasize one or two skills and still offer controlled practice. The modified game is one of the easiest ways to maintain a high level of interest and still retain the essential spirit of the drill.

7. Keep drills moving at a brisk pace and involve as many participants as possible. This procedure will increase the amount of individual participation and practice. Since motor learning involves the factor of trial-and-error, the student needs many opportunities to participate, evaluate and change. One or two chances per individual in a drill would not have much impact on learning.

### Student interest

Student interest is as significantly related to *how* things are done as to *what* things are done. Again, it is not the question of whether drills are used in connection with the teaching of motor skills, but it is definitely a matter of *how* they are used. Students want to be successful, to make progress and when they see how drills are a means to success they will accept them on those terms.

It has been suggested that the effective use of drills is extraordinary in terms of common practice and therefore in need of explanation and defense. At the root of that statement is the assumption that skill learning requires a spirited and enthusiastic use of drills and modified games until skills are developed, so that there can be a safe but gradual change in the emphasis from drills to the regular game. Then movement into the game situation will be effective and probably not detrimental to ultimate skill development. A concomitant will be a high level of enjoyments for further skill development.

———————

There is, of course, the danger of overdrilling the athlete. Responses that are too well conditioned and not flexible enough in a given situation may act to the detriment of the performance. The diver who can perform perfectly on one type of board, in one pool, under specific conditions, may not be able to adjust to changed situations. The basketball player who is conditioned to shoot every time he gets his hands on the ball may ignore open teammates and not pass to them.

It would appear that drill is effective to a point. It can also be reasoned that the effectiveness of extensive drill may be greatly determined by the nature of the activity. Activities apparently fall primarily into one of two classifications, although a considerable amount of overlap in characteristics is associated with the classifications. Consider inner-directed activities and outer-directed activities, for example.

*Inner-directed activities* are self-pacing. The environment is relatively stable and predictable, the performer acts within his own time allocation, and he has, in a sense, only himself to compete with. Sports that could be included in this category are diving, gymnastics, golf, and archery.

By contrast, *outer-directed activities* take place in more dynamic situations, in which the timing and spatial location of stimuli are unpredictable. The appropriate response must be adapted to the given situation, and the situation is ever-changing. Football, tennis, and basketball are examples of activities in which responses must be well executed but adapted to the appropriate signals, which requires a wide repertoire of skills and flexibility in their usage.

The athlete performing an inner-directed activity also needs a large store of skills, but for the most part, he performs them under more controlled circumstances. He is more concerned with the response; the bowling pins do not move, the ball does not roll, until the bowler initiates the action. He must repeatedly practice bowling until his skill levels are advanced for every possible pin leave. The athlete performing an outer-directed activity, on the other hand, is more concerned with the stimulus; the basketball player, except when he is making foul shots, must call forth an array of well-learned acts which he can adapt to defensive and offensive situations that change from moment to moment. He must take his shot when there is an opening, not when he feels like it. Figure 8-2 illustrates a possible arrangement of sports along a continuum from inner-directed to outer-directed.

Obviously, inner-directed activities are individual activities, and sports in which responses are dependent on the activities of other performers are

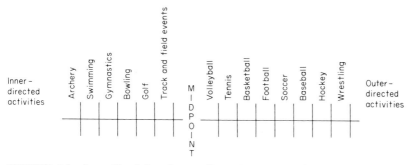

FIGURE 8-2 *Inner-directed and outer-directed activities arranged along a continuum.*

outer-directed. Self-pacing tasks, performed in a relatively permanent and stable environment, can probably benefit most from constant drill. The focus in such tasks is on the act, and drill allows the act to become habitual.

In outer-directed activities, however, drill can help to build up skilled responses, but practice in a wide variety of situations is also necessary. The act is important, but so is being able to perform correctly under all sorts of circumstances, many of which cannot be predicted from moment to moment. Strategy is relevant to success, and there may be a need for more and better strategies in the outer-directed activity. Meaningful practice experiences in general therefore become important to the athlete. He is, in a sense, a problem solver. The problem-solving approach allows for expression of individuality and a thoughtful approach, whereas drill often, though not always, implies group standards and a loss of individuality as well as being told what to do instead of figuring it out for oneself.

Skill per se may be more important in inner-directed activities. Self-pacing tests require tremendous amounts of drill to develop the precision necessary for a high level of performance. In an outer-directed activity, such as basketball, skill is important, but so are other factors. The golfer must develop extremely skillful maneuvers in order to be recognized as superior, but a basketball player can become a starter primarily because of size, aggressiveness, and hustle.

It is evident that both drill and expressive freedom are necessary in all sports. Drill develops the basic skills to a high level, maintains the level, and helps to keep the skills resistant to fluctuation. Problem solving requires the learner to think more and to emphasize the process more than the goal. Emphasis on either technique might very well be determined by the degree to which a sport and the skills associated with it fall into the inner-directed or the outer-directed category.

## WHOLE METHOD VERSUS PART METHOD

Almost any skill can be broken down into its component parts. Each coach is faced with a decision about whether his athletes should practice skills in their entirety or in parts. Because the athlete needs to master so many types of skills in a given sport and because people react differently to different training techniques, the decision is by no means easy.

Let us define our terms before examining the research and making some practical applications to sport. The "whole method" of practice refers to the practicing of a skill in its totality, whereas the "part method" refers to the practicing of the component parts in equal time allotments. There is often disagreement about what constitutes the whole of a skill, and even about what its parts are, but this point is not as important as the general issue.

The tennis serve is a good example of a skill that could be learned by either method. Under the whole method, the entire movement involved in the execution of this act would be completed in continuous fashion. Part practice of this skill would entail first placing the feet and practicing a rocking motion; then tossing the ball until ideal height and placement were achieved; then bringing the racket to the proper point behind the head (without tossing the ball); then practicing the remainder of the swing, from behind the head to extension of the arm, imaginary contact, and follow-through.

Combinations of these practice methods include (1) "whole-part" practice, in which the whole skill is practiced for a limited number of times, followed by practice on its components, and (2) "progressive-part" or "continuous-part" practice, in which each additional component learned is practiced along with the preceding learned matter. Still other combinations are possible.

Research has been done on a number of psychomotor and athletic skills, using a wide variety of such combinations, with different results in different sports: (1) the whole and progressive-part methods were almost equally effective in gymnastics and tumbling stunts; (2) the whole method was most effective in golf; (3) the part method was better in volleyball skills; (4) the whole method was advantageous in swimming; and (5) the whole and part methods were equally effective in badminton. Research in laboratory situations indicates similar conflicting findings.

Perhaps the most consideration should be given to the nature of the skill to be learned. If the skill is relatively simple, there is no need to break it down further; and hence, the whole method is advocated. More complex skills probably need to be practiced by the part method until their components have been mastered and can be performed in sequence. The more unrelated, independent components there are in a given task, the more complex it is.

For example, we may view the crawl in swimming as a complex activity involving elements that are somewhat unrelated and need to be unified. The arm and leg strokes require different movement patterns, and correct breathing is an additional problem. Perhaps it might be best to practice these components separately and then to put them all together. In archery, since the components are small in number and closely related, the whole method might be expected to be most beneficial, though the part method may be useful with individual problems.

The learner's view of the complexity of a skill will be greatly affected by his past experiences in similar activities, and his view must of course be taken into consideration in determining the best method to use in his particular case. In conclusion, the whole method is preferable to the part method whenever possible. Skills that are difficult to the learner should be practiced under the part method until they can be adequately completed in sequence, and task components that are independent should be practiced separately and then integrated.

## MENTAL PRACTICE

Everyone involved in physical education or athletics realizes the importance of the saying, "Learn by doing." In order to acquire skill in throwing a baseball, you have to throw it a great number of times; to become proficient in archery requires countless attempts at the target; and to execute a complex gymnastic task with a high degree of skill demands innumerable experiences.

There is no doubt that skill is acquired by physical or overt practice. At the same time, there is little doubt that every athlete "intellectualizes" his experience, which is to say that he does not go through a physical routine without thinking. He thinks about it beforehand, makes appropriate adjustments and movements according to circumstances, and often mentally reviews preceding activity. In other words, as far as the athlete is concerned, most skilled activity is the result of the interaction of both cognitive and motor processes.

Recently there has been much interest in official designation of time for mental practice of skills—conceptualizing, imagining, mentally rehearsing—as an aid to improving motor performance. There has been a formidable amount of research in this area on a wide assortment of tasks and subjects (although typically not on varsity athletes). Experimentally speaking, the general design of studies investigating the effects of mental practice includes the formation of a control group (which does not practice the skill at all), and three experimental groups (one which practices the skill mentally only, during a set time; one which practices the skill physically only, or in typical fashion; and one which performs some combination of physical and mental practice). All four groups are then tested for skill achievement. Invariably, it is found that physical practice results in the best performance, the combination of mental and physical practice results in performance almost as good, and mental practice results in poorer performance than that of the first two groups but still significantly better than that of the control group which had no practice. In other words, mental practice is better than no practice at all.[3]

---

[3] For an excellent up-to-date summary of the research in this area, the reader might examine Alan Richardson. Mental practice: a review and discussion, *Research Quarterly*, Part I, 1967, **38**, 95–107; Part II, 1967, **38**, 263–273.

In one of the few studies on this topic in which athletes served as subjects, Clark (1960) asked groups of varsity athletes, junior varsity athletes, and novices to practice the Pacific Coast one-hand foul shot. The shooting of the physical practice groups combined and of the mental practice groups combined improved significantly. The following is a breakdown of the relative effects of mental and physical practice within each group:

| | Percentage of improvement | |
| Group | Physical practice | Mental practice |
| --- | --- | --- |
| Varsity............... | 16 | 15 |
| Junior varsity.......... | 24 | 23 |
| Novice............... | 44 | 26 |

The varsity and junior groups improved approximately the same amount from mental and physical practice whereas physical practice was apparently more beneficial to the novices.

Typically, subjects mentally practice tasks by reading prepared material or by listening to the experimenter's directions and then mentally rehearsing the act a certain number of times during a specified time period. The effectiveness of this procedure for the highly skilled is open to speculation, as most studies have been concerned with the learning process and the learning of newly introduced skills. The research does indicate that mental practice is more appropriate after the learner has had physical experience with the skill, but the degree to which the skill should be learned before mental practice has yet to be agreed on.

Overt verbalization of an experience, before or during that experience, has been found to assist learning in certain cases, especially at the beginning stages. Thinking, which consists of internal verbalization of an act (unspoken words), has its role in the acquisition and performnce of a skill. Most outstanding athletes admit to some form of verbalization before, during, or after competition. Bill Sharman, an extremely accurate basketball shooter with the Boston Celtics for a number of years, believes strongly in creating an image of the basket area (1967). He favors staring at the basket from different areas of the floor until the images are strongly memorized. Ideally, all these mental images would be brought by the player to the game itself.

Coaches might do well to stay abreast of the latest findings in this area and perhaps to make some informal experiments of their own. Mental practice sessions could be used in place of practice on rainy days. Injured athletes who are unable to practice physically could be instructed to rehearse tasks mentally in an attempt to maintain their levels of skill. There are many possible uses for mental practice, but what everyone in athletics needs to be more aware of is that the thought processes are active before, during, and after the performance of athletic skills. Determining how formal mental rehearsal of skills can best help the athlete is the challenge that lies ahead.

## VERBALIZATION

As mentioned in the preceding section, the athlete does not typically perform mechanically but usually intellectualizes his experience. Although he may not set specific mental practice routines for himself, his cognitive processes certainly participate directly or indirectly in his motor accomplishments. Psychologists use the term "verbalization" to refer to talking or thinking oneself through an activity.

In his book *The Natural Way to Better Golf* (1954), Jack Burke has included a brief chapter entitled "Making Use of Your Imagination," in which he advocates thinking through each shot before actually making it. During the address, however, he suggests concentration on hitting the ball only.

Naturally, the preceding comments are all validated only unscientifically. We have no way of knowing whether athletes would be as good as they are if they did not use some form of verbalization. Nevertheless, it is interesting to observe the training procedures of outstanding athletes and to note the similarity in their mental approaches to their respective sports.

There is also a danger in thinking too much at the wrong time. Many times it is better to "do it" rather than "think about it" during the actual execution of an act. The skilled athlete's movements appear to be almost habitual. Worrying over the backswing or the wrist action in the midst of the movement may cause a complete breakdown of the stroke. The highly proficient performer apparently knows when to go through his response routinely and when to activate cerebral centers so as to adjust to or compensate for unexpected events.

## PROCESS VERSUS PRODUCT

Another decision that the coach must make is whether to emphasize the process toward a goal or the end product itself. On the one hand, the coach could attempt to intellectualize the learning process by encouraging the athlete to reason, evaluate, and make judgments, in the hope that he might learn to respond in the appropriate manner to reaching the final objectives.

Concentrating only on the end product usually implies having little concern for the learner or his method as long as he gets results. The coach who drills all athletes the same way is usually concerned more with the product than with the learning process. A coach who wants all his athletes to have similar forms or styles is also concerned mainly with the end product.

Whether it is wiser to emphasize process or product may be determined primarily by the nature of the task. For the motor tasks whose ultimate proficiency depends on intellectual components, or on the operation of the cognitive process at a high level, it would seem that emphasis should be on the process rather than on the end product. Many if not most athletic skills fall into this category. The learner should be led to understand why he is doing what he does and what is eventually expected of him. Various methods that might lead to successful execution of the skills may be offered and explained to the athlete.

Emphasis on the process may not always be desirable, however. In self-initiated (self-paced) sports, the end product may be more important than the process. In such sports, an act is practiced repeatedly in order to make it habitual or even, as in diving and gymnastics, to make it conform to a set standard. Achievement in such sports, once skill has been acquired, is not very dependent on symbolic or intellectual components.

Obviously, all coaches are ultimately concerned with the final product, but the means of attaining goals differ, as in some cases emphasis on the process will have more desirable outcomes and in others emphasis on the product will be of most benefit. One means of emphasizing the process is to use the principles of mechanics, psychology, and other disciplines, in the hope that better understanding will lead to better performance.

## APPLICATION OF PRINCIPLES

If the coach is interested in furthering the intellectualization process in the acquisition of motor skill, one means he has available to him is to attempt to explain the principles underlying the activity. The principles would supposedly hold true in a variety of similar situations and assist the athlete in learning new skills. In other words, transfer would occur from principle to practice.

Numerous principles are associated with the mechanics and physics of movement, and physiological and psychological learning principles have been found to hold true in many circumstances. Thus, we know of their existence and range of application, but what needs to be determined is whether teaching them to athletes has a beneficial effect on the learning of athletic skills. Variables in the learning situation that must be considered are whether principles should be taught during physical practice or in separate sessions substituted for some practice time, and the possibility that principles may be taught but not comprehended. Without understanding, application is almost impossible.

These variables may help to explain why research results have been conflicting. A number of investigators have reported beneficial results, whereas other researchers have noted no advantage. The explanation in the latter case may be that learners did not care much about the process but cared only for the product, or by the same token, that they did not understand the principles they were taught and were thus unable to make the appropriate application. Burack & Moos's results (1956) contradict one commonly accepted belief that a person need only be aware of basic principles in the solution of a task in order to apply them.

A typical experimental study on the effects of learning a principle and applying it to motor performance is reported by Hendrickson & Schroeder (1941). The subjects were 90 eighth-grade boys divided into three groups. The control group received no special instruction; the second group learned a theory of refraction; and the third group received more information on refraction than group II. The boys shot air guns into water six inches deep and then into water two inches deep. Performances at the two depths were almost the same within each group; group II did better than the control, and group III did better than group II.

However, experimental results (e.g., Colville, 1957) do not totally support the teaching of principles as a training aid. Nevertheless, with the evidence presently available and with an awareness of the possible reasons why some studies did not show favorable results from the introduction of principles, there is no reason for coaches not to include pertinent information on principles in the practice sessions or in supplementary time periods. Assuming that the coaches have a good understanding of the principles and are able to teach them to the athletes, there is reason to believe, in theory at least, that the learning process might be facilitated.

## HABIT INTERFERENCE

Many sports require actions that are produced readily, or habitually. These acts required much practice, but the practice eventually pays off in that it frees the performer to anticipate new developments and changing stimuli. In the training process, the acquisition of skill is enhanced when little habit interference exists.

"Habit interference," or "negative transfer," occurs when the learning or performance of one task is inhibited by the earlier or later learning of another task. When a skill is not well learned, it is easily interfered with. Since competing responses to similar stimuli confuse the learner, it would seem that training situations should be such as to minimize the possibility of such occurrences until the acts have been well learned. Negative and positive transfer have been discussed in detail in the preceding chapter and need not be elaborated upon here; it will suffice to say that the learning of each new act should be impeded as little as possible.

The baseball player who is still in the stage of learning to be a good hitter does not practice a few bunts, a few hits to the opposite field, and a regular swing in the same batting session, though this procedure would be acceptable for the skilled batter who has had much previous experience in each type of batting. When the batter is learning to swing, it is most important to develop a consistent, smooth stroke of the bat, and the best way of attaining this objective is through constant practice. After reaching this goal, he may attempt to swing late and hit to the opposite field; this maneuver, too, should be constantly practiced until the proper timing has been developed. While each batting skill is being learned, it is practiced with a minimum amount of interference from other batting techniques, but after the individual batting skills have reached a high level, they can be practiced interchangeably without any deleterious effects.

The same principle holds true of the simultaneous learning of different sport activities. If movements and elements are similar in two situations, but the appropriate acts have not been well learned, habit interference occurs. If the two acts are well learned, however, there is little reason to expect an inhibiting effect. Also if two sports are apparently unrelated, there is probably little need for concern. In Nelson's study (1957), for instance, one group of athletes swam and learned gross motor skills on alternate days, and a second group learned the gross motor skills but did not swim. Contrary to general expectations, swimming did not negatively affect the learning of the skills, as no difference in performance was noted between the two groups.

## GUIDANCE, DEMONSTRATION, AND INSTRUCTION

There is no substitute for physical activity and practice in the attainment of high skill levels. However, there are a number of methods available to the coach for facilitating the learning process by enhancing the practice routines. Among the many possibilities are guidance, demonstration, and instruction.

In early stages of learning and even at more advanced levels, the athlete, for one reason or another, may have difficulty in executing movement patterns to the satisfaction of the coach. The performer may know what he is supposed to do but not be able to make the transition to actually doing it. In such cases, a method sometimes employed by coaches is to ask the athlete to relax and then to guide him through the skill physically; manual or external manipulation permits the athlete to experience the desired responses, to "get the feel" of the movement. The hope is that the kinesthetic receptors which usually provide the necessary feedback in the skill will be activated by this process, that the athlete, in a state of passivity, will become consciously aware of the coordination of body parts as the coach manipulates his body through the act. As there has been only a sparse amount of research on the relative effectiveness of this technique, we must rely on a subjective evaluation: that there is logic behind the practice and it may be an effective approach for some athletes who have problems in acquiring a skill.

More common forms of guidance have to do with verbal instruction and direction. Typically, skills or strategies to be learned by the athlete are explained before actual practice begins. How detailed these instructions are will depend on the complexity of the skill, the athlete's level of skill, and his ability to comprehend and apply the instructions. Further comments are offered by the coach while the athlete is actually in practice. These are usually specific to the situation at hand and tend to correct, modify, and advance the activity of the performer. Still other comments may be made after the completion of the skill, play, or event, and sometimes after the entire practice period is over. Verbal instructions in motor performance can be effective if the advice is correct, precise, and clear, and if the learner understands and is able to make the association between the words and the appropriate responses. The messages conveyed by the coach provide direction for the athlete.

An interesting experiment demonstrating the importance of oral guidance during training on a motor task is illustrated in Figure 8-3. Group I received no formal training, group II received "common-sense" or traditional training, and group III received the same guidance as the second group plus special guidance at certain points of training. Because it has been found that certain abilities are more important and more relevant to success at different stages of practice (see Chapter 6), these abilities were emphasized at the crucial times. The visual (spatial) aspects of the task were concentrated on early in training, kinesthetic (coordination) aspects were inserted later in training, and knowledge of various task components was emphasized primarily in the terminal stages. Group III performed best throughout the study and, in fact, improved 39 percent over group II. It would seem, therefore, that when coaches introduce new skills, they might consider emphasizing in the different stages of instruction the abilities that are most important in those stages.

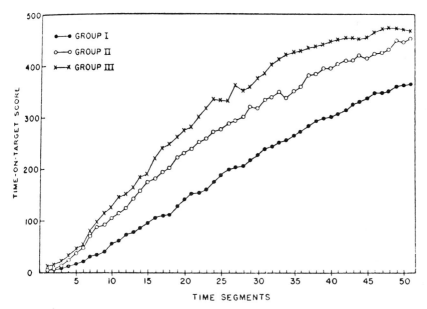

FIGURE 8-3    *The effects of instruction in the training process. (*Source: *James F. Parker, Jr., & Edwin A. Fleishman. Use of analytical information concerning task requirements to increase the effectiveness of skill training.* Journal of Applied Psychology, 1961, **45**, 295–302. P. 299. Copyright 1961 by the American Psychological Association and reproduced by permission.)*

Verbal guidance facilitates the initial mastery of a skill or tactic, although it can be effective throughout the various stages of skill acquisition. It is important that responses be well formed from the beginning for it is easier to verbally or manually guide appropriate responses than to undo incorrect or undesirable ones.

The research literature does indicate the importance of the speed and frequency with which advice and comments are given. Ideally speaking, the sooner after the actual act the comments are made, the more effective they will be. Immediacy is a key word here. It would also be ideal if comments could be made as often as needed, which would almost require a one-to-one relationship. Unfortunately, in the typical situation one or a few coaches must guide and shape the behavior of many athletes. Practical necessity must therefore override the ideal, and the coach must make decisions accordingly.

Words also often serve as a motivator. Paying direct attention to each athlete and his performance usually results in a heightening of his motivation. If he knows that the coach is interested, his performance may improve.

In addition to oral instruction and manual manipulation, demonstration of the skills or maneuvers to be learned appears to help the learner to gain quicker insight into their mastery. The demonstration may be by the coach, an athlete, or an outsider, and may appear on film or be made in person. Seeing what a performance looks like is only beneficial if it is executed expertly. Again, there has been little research in this area, and the use of such a procedure is based more on common sense than on experimental verification. Most people apparently learn, at least in the beginning, through observation and imitation. The demonstration of an act permits delayed imitation, which in turn provides direction and gives meaning to the activity. It is extremely difficult to undertake a task unless there is a model to refer to, and once some form of demonstration has been offered to the learner, he can proceed with a set goal in mind.

## PSYCHOLOGICAL TOLERANCE

The extent to which man can achieve is virtually untapped. Hereditary factors do place limits on potential accomplishments, but there is a wide gap between what a person typically achieves and what he could achieve. In the world of sports, the greatest athletes are often acknowledged as such not only because of their skill but also for their physiological and psychological makeups.

In sports requiring great daring, speed, strength, and endurance, physiological factors play an important role in determining successful performance. In endurance events, for example, the trained athlete must have a remarkable cardiorespiratory system that allows a high oxygen intake, a maximal stroke volume, and the like. Physiological variables distinguish the great from the average in many grueling activities. The bodily changes that occur during intensive training need not be discussed here as they are aptly described in a number of books on the physiology of exercise.[4]

Physiological properties and their contributions to outstanding athletic performance have been researched, explained, and acknowledged for many years. Psychological factors affecting successful performance have had less attention and are less well understood. Whether a person is able to endure

---

[4] E.g.: de Vries, Herbert. *Physiology of exercise for physical education and athletics*. Dubuque, Iowa: Wm. C. Brown, 1966.

     Karpovich, Peter. *Physiology of muscular activity*. Philadelphia: Saunders, 1966.

     Morehouse, Laurence E., & Miller, Augustus T. *Physiology of exercise*. St. Louis: C. V. Mosby, 1967.

     Ricci, Benjamin. *Physiological basis of human performance*. Philadelphia: Lea & Febiger, 1967.

the punishment of a contest is determined by his physiological training. What is not yet understood is the role of psychological components in driving the athlete to goals never before reached. Many athletes possess the necessary physical and physiological characteristics but, because of fear, lack of utmost drive, and the like, do not push themselves to attain unusual goals.

From a psychological point of view, it has been shown that well-trained athletes can tolerate a diminution of blood oxygen and an increase in carbon dioxide concentration better under certain conditions than others. More specifically, when the athlete thinks of something positive that is emotionally satisfying to him, his output is increased. Puni (1965) reports a breath-holding experiment in which athletes were requested to hold their breath as long as possible under four different conditions. The subjects all received the same direction, to choose among (1) thinking of anything they chose, (2) working out arithmetical problems, (3) concentrating on a frightening situation such as drowning, or (4) imagining a pleasant experience. The results of the study are given in Table 8-2. As can be seen, when one's consciousness is filled with positive emotional content, breath-holding time is increased. Coaches might consider the voluntary regulation of physiological states caused by prolonged endurance events. Perhaps thinking positively about something other than the immediate activity is the answer.

In fact, conceptually speaking, we may borrow the "hurt-pain-agony" framework expressed by Dr. James Counsilman (Counsilman, 1968), the acclaimed swimming coach at the University of Indiana. Perhaps athletes, in terms of their success, go through these zones of tolerance—hurt, pain, and agony—in that order. According to Counsilman, the boys who exert themselves to the highest levels of agony typically become his greatest

TABLE 8-2    The effect of the contents of consciousness on duration of breath holding

| Series of experiments | Contents of consciousness | Duration of breath holding |
|---|---|---|
| I............................ | Voluntary | 1 min 25 sec |
| II............................ | Picturing of crucial situations | 1 min 20.3 sec |
| III............................ | Solution of arithmetical sums | 1 min 31.3 sec |
| IV............................ | Picturing of pleasant situations | 1 min 37.8 sec |

*Source:* A. T. Puni. Problem of voluntary regulation of motor activity in sports. In Antonelli, Ferruccio (Ed.), *Proceedings of the 1st International Congress of Sports Psychology,* 1965, pp. 103–113. P. 113.

swimmers. Every person has a psychological tolerance for every activity he participates in. The goals at stake, the meaningfulness of the outcome, and the temperament of the person all help to determine the possible levels of attainment.

A study recently reported by Ryan and Kovacic provides some interesting data on the relationship between participation in athletics and tolerance of pain. Since athletes, especially those in contact sports, undergo tremendous amounts of training to achieve peak operating levels, it would appear that they might have an exceptionally high tolerance to pain. They practice beyond the point at which the "average" person would quit. Ryan and Kovacic (1966) tested this and other hypotheses on three groups: contact-sport athletes, noncontact-sport athletes, and nonathletes. The contact-sport athletes were football players and wrestlers, and the noncontact-sport athletes were golf and tennis players. All subjects were given tests of pain tolerance and pain threshold; although the groups did not differ in threshold, they demonstrated dissimilarities in tolerance. As might be expected, the contact-sport athletes showed the greatest tolerance levels, the noncontact-sport athletes showed less, and the nonathletes showed least of all. Evidently, the ability to tolerate pain is associated with participation in athletics and the nature of the sport participated in. The data do not answer, of course, the question whether a person accepts pain more easily because of participation in sports or whether he participates in certain sports because of his ability to tolerate pain.

Furthermore, Roudik (1965), a Russian researcher, states:

> The achievement of worse results in competition than in previous training is in many cases due to the fact that the athletic condition attained by the athlete includes excellent indices only of physical, technical, and tactical training, but does not contain the necessary elements of volitional training for competition.
>
> Our experience of studying various forms of athletic activity psychologically shows that the most important objective of volitional training of an athlete is the education of this ability to overcome difficulties he experiences during training and in completion [pp. 79–80].

We may speculate that on many occasions athletic endeavors are hindered more by psychological than by physiological factors. Recent attempts at determining psychological traits as associated with outstanding athletes in various sports provide interesting data. It is possible to distinguish the champion from the average athlete or the nonathlete on the basis of traits and personality profile as described in Chapter 3.

There is every reason to believe that the training that results in today's superior performances has physiological and psychological overtones. Better training techniques and methodologies are associated with higher achievement, as are the abilities to tolerate, to drive, to want something badly enough that pain and suffering become bearable.

## CUES AND AIDS

Training in situations similar to those found in the actual contest has unchallenged merit. According to laws of transfer, the more closely the practice setting and the skills practiced resemble the "real thing," the more favorable the results should be. For several reasons, there may arise a need to manipulate training techniques somewhat. First, the traditional setting may prove to be boring to some athletes and to cause a drop in motivational levels. Second, athletes may encounter difficulty in learning skills or aspects of them under conventional instruction methods, and may require some specific supplementary programs. In motor learning and performance, the visual and kinesthetic sense channels typically operate, and the auditory channel to a lesser degree. If the learner is not advancing to higher levels of skill as might be expected, presenting information in a manner that emphasizes a sense of involvement in the particular activity may prove beneficial.

### Auditory Cues

The use of verbal directions and cues as well as the implementation of principles of various sorts in the learning of motor skills have been discussed above. This information is usually received through the auditory mechanism, perceived, and acted upon immediately or in due course in time. For the coach to present cues to the athlete in the practice situation and even in the contest is a commonly accepted characteristic of the relationship between coach and athlete. Comments made before a response is initiated serve as warnings and place the athlete in a state of preparation and alertness; during the movement, they guide the athlete; and after the response, they provide knowledge of results and reinforce the actions taken.

### Auditory Aids

One possible influence on motor learning and performance that is transmitted through auditory receptors is music. Music varies in tempo and volume, and as an addition to the environment it may produce some interesting results. Some people use it as a relaxer, some as a stimulator and motivator. Others use music to improve motor coordination, specifically

through the sense of rhythm; this practice occurs in some physical education classes and some athletic team workouts. Music, with appropriate
rhythm and tempo, is either played along with or before the execution of
certain skills. If it is played before the activity, the music may be accompanied by special movements or even by dancing in the attempt to develop
rhythmic ability. It is hoped that the transfer effects will be such that experience in the situation will lead to faster and better athletic performance.
Research on the topic, which is almost nonexistent, does not support the
hypothesis. One investigator has observed no meaningful relationship between rhythmic ability and achievement on tests of motor skill (Bond,
1959). Further research is needed to determine the effectiveness of such
training routines, for more and better-designed studies may help to advance
the stage of knowledge on the use of rhythmic melodies to enhance motor
coordination and agility.

As to the idea that performance output is increased by music, playing
music of varying types does not seem to make a difference when the tasks
at hand are relatively simple and monotonous, at least in industrial situations. There has been little research on such complex skills as those involved
in athletics, and hence no conclusions can be drawn. In practice, music may
serve as a motivator for some or a relaxer for others. In the athletic game,
a band playing may have a positive effect on performance, as at least one
researcher has reported (Ayres, 1911).

### Visual Cues

Success in most sports is dependent upon the selection of and reaction
to appropriate stimuli. Athletes learning new skills can be directed by the
coach to the cues that are most important in the situation in order to hasten
the learning process. Not only can emphasis be placed on already existing
cues, but artificial ones may be added to benefit the learner.

Highly skilled performance is associated with selective attention, the discrimination of present stimuli and concentration on the most relevant ones.
The learner must display what psychologists term "set"; that is, a state of
readiness for certain stimuli. The focusing process comes with experience
but certainly can be facilitated by appropriate guidance.

Visual cues not inherent in the target areas themselves are often added
in practice or in the actual event. Artificial cues are found in such sports as
bowling, archery, and basketball. In archery, at nearer distances to the
target, the archer may aim at an object in the ground located nearer to him
than the target itself, but at very great distances, he will aim at some
specific point over the target. Figure 8-4 illustrates points of aim at various
distances from the target. In bowling, the bowler has the option of aiming

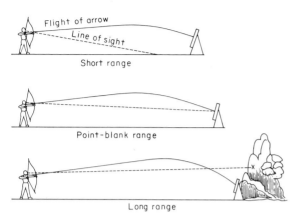

FIGURE 8-4    *Point of aim at various distances. (*Source:
*John H. Shaw, Carl A. Troester, & Milton A. Gabrielsen.*
Individual sports for men. *Philadelphia: Saunders, 1955.*
*P. 46.)*

directly at the pins or at spots placed on the alley near where he releases
the ball. In basketball, marks may be placed on the backboard in order for
the player to aim at these when shooting at an angle to the basket instead
of at the backboard in general, or he may be instructed to concentrate on a
specific area of the rim instead of the entire rim.

The value of such cues lies more on a theoretical foundation than on
substantial supportive research evidence, although there has been some
favorable indication for the use of artificial visual cues. It seems logical
that nearer cues are easier to attend to than those farther away, hence the
use of spots in bowling. Specific and precise cues are more effective than
general and vague ones, which explains the use of marks on the backboard
or concentration on a specific area of the rim in basketball.

### Visual Aids

We usually think of visual aids as consisting of movies, loop films, slides,
pictured representation of skills, or any accessories to an object or target
that aid concentration on it. Many forms of visual aids have been employed
in coaching and teaching situations, with varying degrees of success.

Holding (1965) offers the following advice on the use and benefits of
visual aids:

> There is no magic about visual aids. They are effective when they are ap-
> propriate. It would be idle to deny that well-designed visual data properly
> integrated into the training scheme may assist learning, but any advantages

they have derive from the same principles of learning already described. Unfortunately, visual gadgets, like illuminated charts and brightly colored models, possess what psychologists call "face validity;" that is to say they have an immediate, superficial appeal which is not necessarily justified, but which tends to generate enthusiasm among their sponsors [p. 62].[5]

Research has generally demonstrated that the use of various visual aids, whether static (pictures or charts) or dynamic (films), has not lived up to expectations. The explanation may be overoptimism about the effectiveness of such aids. A number of studies indicate increased learning when such visual aids are added to traditional teaching situations; a smaller number do not indicate increased learning. If two groups are provided with the same amount of training time, and if one group views the film not on extra time but within the provided amount of training time while the second group never sees the film, the two groups will probably learn the skill about the same. A major problem with most films is that they run continuously at a set speed, providing no opportunity for review. Showing films in a situation in which they can be slowed down, reversed, and examined closely may yield more productive results than the usual method.

Pertinent films that display the desired responses accurately are probably most beneficial. Many college and professional athletic teams take films of the athletes in action, and the athletes later view and analyze the films. Although there has been little research on the benefits of such practices, there is a common-sense reason for them. A recent study by Watkins (1963) does in fact indicate the effectiveness of analyzing one's own performance on film. It was found that baseball players on a college baseball team who viewed films of themselves batting decreased their batting faults more than did players to whom this opportunity was not extended. Experiments concerned with color and black-and-white films have not found an advantage in use of one type of film instead of the other, and hence, the lower cost of the black-and-white films may be at least one advantage. Research does not indicate whether it is better to watch oneself or to watch an expert in action. There are probably favorable aspects to both methods, and perhaps both might be used together with good results.

In various sports, targets have been manipulated during practice in hopes of improving performance on regulation targets in actual competition. A good example of this procedure may be found in basketball: oversized and undersized rims are employed in the practice sessions of some teams. The benefits of such practice have been experimentally investigated in Selk's study (1967); each of 11 participating high school basketball teams was

---

[5] Reprinted with permission from D. H. Holding, *Principles of Training*, 1965, Pergamon Press Ltd.

divided into a small-rim group and a regulation-rim group for practice purposes. Half the members of each of the 11 squads practiced free throws on a 15-inch rim while the other half practiced on the regulation 18-inch rim. No significant difference between the groups in foul-shooting accuracy was observed in game competition, as the small-rim group scored on 61.1 percent of free-throw attempts as compared with 60.8 percent scored by the regulation-rim group.

Changes in the stimulus situation, as exemplified in Selk's study, actually constitute, in psychological terms, changes in display. A "display" is the specific learning situation or task with which someone is faced. In a laboratory experiment, it is the task, equipment, and cues. In piloting a plane, it is the flight conditions and response panel. In almost every task some sort of display is present, and these displays may be manipulated so as to provide varying degrees of information to the learner. Presumably changes in the display during practice cause positive transfer effects to the display found in the actual contest. When requiring basketball players to shoot at a smaller rim, greater accuracy in shooting is required. It is hoped that the transfer effects from the difficult to the easier task will be favorable, although such effects were not evident in Selk's investigation.

Elements may be added to or subtracted from displays. In basketball, special paint may be applied to rims, backboards may be removed, or baskets may be raised or lowered. These changes in display create either more difficult or easier shooting conditions than usual. Although there can be justification for such practices utilizing principles of transfer and knowledge of the theoretical advantage in the emphasis of certain visual cues, the paucity of research in physical education and athletics on such factors is a serious problem.

### Kinesthetic Cues

Although many types of visual and verbal cues are appropriate in learning situations, it seems impossible to talk in terms of kinesthetic cues. It is probably more accurate to describe assistance in this sense modality as coming from kinesthetic aids.

### Kinesthetic Aids

Intrinsic feedback, or kinesthetic awareness of movements, is a part of most motor acts. An underlying contributor to success in sport, the kinesthetic sense apparently is of great importance, especially in the latter stages of the acquisition of skill. How to sharpen the activity of this sense is the problem.

One technique available to the coach is external manipulation, discussed earlier in this chapter. The subject remains passive while the trainer moves his body parts through the range of movements demanded in the performance of the particular skill. The purpose is to allow the learner to get the feel of the movement, and to activate the appropriate proprioceptors.

A second technique is the blindfolded or eyes-closed method. Diminishing the feedback and competition of vision may increase the effectiveness of kinesthesis. In an early study (Griffith, 1932), it was reported that blindfolded subjects learning how to play golf improved more than subjects with no impaired vision. The blindfolded golfers were not visually distracted and were able to concentrate on the swing itself.

Durentini's results (1967) did not confirm those found in the preceding study. In her investigation, a group of blindfolded subjects practiced foul shots while another group practiced in the usual manner. An analysis of the data revealed no differences in improvement between the groups; the lack of visual cues did not improve the kinesthetic sense. Evidently, more research is needed in this area.

A third possible technique in proprioceptive facilitation is to employ objects heavier or lighter than the regulation ones and note the transfer effects when athletes perform with regulation objects. It is possible that sharpened kinesthetic sensitivity may occur as a result of practicing with lighter or heavier equipment before using regulation equipment. Egstrom, Logan, & Wallis (1960), testing a throwing skill with projectiles of different weights, found that more positive effects transferred from the lighter projectiles than from the heavier ones. Use of lighter balls, it was speculated, sharpened the functioning of the proprioceptors more than did use of heavier ones.

### Laboratory Aids

Because coaches are aware that certain attributes appear to be related to success in a number of sports, the natural inclination is to attempt to develop these factors as much as possible. It is not unusual for a coach to go to a researcher for advice on how to use laboratory equipment to raise the levels of certain abilities in athletes. Let us assume, for example, that in a particular sport, coordination, reaction time, balance, speed, spatial orientation, and kinesthesis are considered extremely important variables, highly related to ultimate achievement. Can laboratory equipment increase the sense of kinesthesis in the sport? Will practice on a stabilometer improve general balancing ability? Is the experience acquired with a reaction-time apparatus beneficial to the reactions needed in athletics?

There is no reason to believe that laboratory equipment can work magic. The general adage should hold true: the more similar the practice is to the real contest situation, the higher the likelihood of positive transfer. Unfortunately, in almost all cases, the tasks performed in the laboratory are quite different from those executed in the swimming pool, on the athletic field, and in the gymnasium. There are many abilities, and in each ability, there are many ways of showing skill.

Why should practice on the stabilometer improve the football player's balance? How much relationship is there between the reaction-time experiment—which tests the speed with which the subject can lift his finger from a button at the onset of a stimulus—and the reactions displayed in typical sports skills? Can practice on positioning tests, which supposedly measure kinesthetic awareness, assist the proprioceptive activity involved in the golf swing, the jump shot, or the bowler's approach and release of the ball.

With the present state of knowledge, all indications are that skills may be developed only to the extent that the practice situations resemble the actual situations. If laboratory situations can approximate real conditions, the possibility of favorable transfer is enhanced. Many types of acts can represent a single ability such as balance: the wrestler maintains balance on the mat, the tennis player in a wide variety of strokes, the basketball player in assorted shots at the basket, and the trampolinist in a series of complicated movements. So many variables influence the successful completion of each of the tasks that a balance factor can hardly be isolated. Therefore, there is no reason to expect that learning to balance on a movable platform would enhance the balancing ability of wrestlers, tennis players, basketball players, or trampolinists.

*Technological Aids*

Coaching aids assume many forms. We have discussed numerous methods of rearranging displays and modifying responses as well as pertinent research findings, but we have not examined the use of mechanical devices as possible additions to the practice sessions. Many devices are currently on the market that can be employed in an array of sports.

In education today, as a result of the initial work of Pressey in the 1920s and the later efforts of Skinner, teaching machines and programmed texts have become quite popular. In driver and safety education, equipment has been built to simulate the actual driving of a car. Similarly, the military forces have at their command equipment to simulate various weapons, situations, and means of transportation; in a simulated cockpit, the pilot goes through activities as if he were in a real plane, and rifle targets are in the shape of a man. Likewise, industry trains equipment operators in situations that resemble the actual situation. Today, teachers of physical education classes and coaches of athletic teams are also utilizing special equipment for the learning and maintenance of motor skills more than ever before.

In all these fields, simulators, or devices which reproduce a large portion of the actual situation to be faced by the learner, evoke operations and movement patterns that will be called forth in the real situation. They are typically used at advanced levels of skill, to permit consolidation and maintenance of skill in the final stages of learning.

Other forms of technological aids include trainers for the early stages of learning, programmed learning machines for beginners, and special films. The concern in this book is primarily with equipment that can be used by athletes who are already operating at fairly high skill levels. There are three prime advantages in the use of simulators:

1  They can be controlled. For instance, a ball-throwing machine may be instructed to toss the ball at set speeds and from set distances. The athlete can gain practice under the condition he wishes to experience.
2  As mentioned earlier, they are very like the "real thing," and possibilities of transfer to real situations are of course increased under such conditions.
3  Certain aspects of the real situation can be omitted to allow the athlete to concentrate on his responses, which necessitates decreased variability and increased predictability of stimulus events. Again, a ball-throwing machine can be instructed to throw the ball to a given point.

Thus it can be seen that training with special equipment may play an important role in improving performance. Changes in the equipment used in the contest may also cause improvement, as in pole valuting, where new records may be at least in part attributed to the use of fiber glass poles.

Training devices permit the practice of isolated skills. Coaches of each sport are aware of much of the commercial equipment available, but they are less aware of some of the research evidence which suggests the desirable outcomes that may result from use of special equipment in certain situations. There is also concern about the scientific validation of the commercial products. Only a few investigations have been conducted on the benefits that special training devices may have over traditional practice regimens, and these few have primarily used subjects who were enrolled in physical education classes, not varsity performers.

The type of apparatus that is most often used in practice is some sort of ball-throwing machine in baseball and tennis, which can be preset to toss balls at designated speeds and allow the player to concentrate on the correct swing. Since the person can reasonably predict the speed with which and certainly the direction from which the ball is tossed, his task is simplified.

One experiment on college beginning tennis classes compared various combinations of practice on the Ball-Boy tennis machine and practice by traditional methods (Solley & Borders, 1965). The most beneficial schedule was found to be starting with conventional practice and switching to the Ball-Boy machine after a number of class periods. Another study (Chui, 1965) used the Golf-O-Tron, which simulates a golf course and on which the player hits the golf ball with regulation clubs. Little final difference in performance was noted between the group practicing with the Golf-O-Tron and the conventional practice group. Mathews & McDaniel (1962), working with college students, used the Golf-Lite, a light powered by a battery and attached to the shaft of the club. Benefits greater than those obtained with the traditional method were noted.

Aside from these studies and perhaps a few others, the use of such special equipment in practice to promote better performance is based more on theoretical grounds than on research. It is to be hoped that more research will be done, especially with varsity performers as subjects.

In almost every sport, practice equipment is currently being developed to improve aspects of practice. In swimming, the Pull-Buoy (Figure 8-5) can be placed between the thighs and adjusted to various leg sizes, to allow the swimmer to concentrate on his arm stroke while in a normal swimming position. The swimmer's attention can be focused on correct execution of the arm stroke, since there are fewer responses that need to be attended to.

The Electronic Golf Range (Figure 8-6) provides realistic, accurate playing conditions indoors or outdoors. Regulation woods, irons, and balls are used with this computerized apparatus, which simulates a golf course and true playing conditions. Golfers can improve their strokes, have the opportunity to play all year round, and enjoy the competitiveness and reality of the golfing situation.

Special rebounding devices are used in basketball practice sessions to help players develop their rebounding ability. They can be used in tipping, timing, and coordination drills. A replica of a player can be used in basketball practice sessions to simulate a defensive player in game situations (illustrated in Figure 8-7). Cut and drill cones for basketball (Figure 8-8) and

FIGURE 8-5   *The Pull-Buoy.* (Pull-Buoy, Inc., 1623 Kingsmere, Rochester, Mich.)

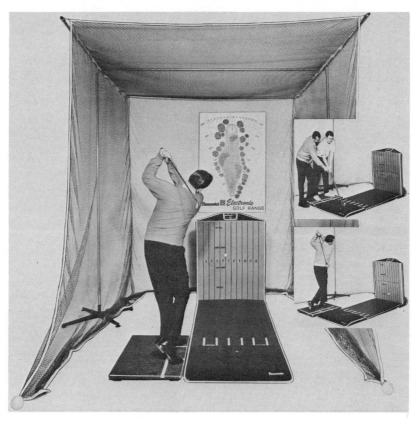

FIGURE 8-6    *The Electronic Golf Range. This apparatus includes a computer, distance meter, tee area, Astro-Turf, and other accessories.* (Brunswick Corporation, Bowling Division, 69 W. Washington, Chicago, Ill.*)*

football (Figure 8-9) allow practice of particular formations and plays. The Blaster (Figure 8-10) gives the football player the experience of being hit hard while carrying the ball. The Knee-High Trainer (Figure 8-11) is for training football players to step and run with their knees high, a desirable characteristic of good running backs. The Powerator is also geared for football players, with the purpose of improving hitting force and reaction time (Figure 8-12).

In tennis, ball-throwing machines are commonly used to allow players to concentrate on their strokes. The recently developed Server, illustrated in Figure 8-13, holds a tennis ball at preset height, and releases it when hit; the ball travels in the direction it was stroked without interference. It eliminates many of the variables of the serve and allows complete attention on

FIGURE 8-7   *Sacker Sam. This life-size replica of a player has movable rotating arms with a reach of 10 feet. It encourages shooting concentration and creates a shooting situation similar to that found in a game.* (Sacker Sam, 812 Patterson Drive, South Daytona, Fla.)

FIGURE 8-8   *Basketball drill and cut cones.* (Wolverine Sports Supply, 745 State Circle, Ann Arbor, Mich.)

FIGURE 8-9  *Football drill and cut cones.* (Wolverine
Sports Supply, 745 State Circle, Ann Arbor, Mich.)

the stroke itself, as do so many of the devices that are being developed for
practice in various sports.

A similar apparatus used in baseball practice is the Batting Tee (Figure
8-14), which enables the batter to concentrate on his swing and practice hitting balls at different levels and to different areas of the field. The Baseball
Pitching Machine (Figure 8-15) delivers pitches at preset speeds and accuracy. This automatic machine allows the athlete to perfect his response
to predictable stimuli. Since the speed and accuracy of the ball are predetermined, development of the appropriate movement patterns becomes
easier. Another advantage in use of such equipment is that skill can be
maintained throughout the year.

A popular piece of equipment today in all sports is the videotape machine. Ease of operation and reasonable costs have encouraged the purchas-

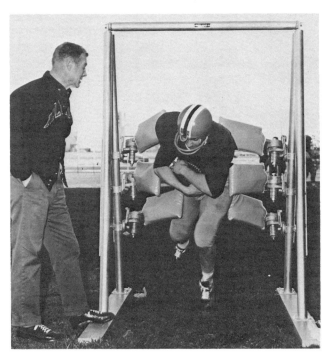

FIGURE 8-10  *The Blaster. University of Illinois fullback Jim Grabowski explodes through the Smitty's Blaster trainer as head coach Pete Elliot watches.* (Universal Bleacher Company, P. O. Box 640, Champaign, Ill.)

ing of these machines on a broad scale. With this apparatus, the athlete may view his performance immediately after actual execution. Videotaping allows immediate terminal feedback, a process which should encourage a quicker recognition and correction of faults and faster learning. Videotape equipment is illustrated in Figures 8-16 to 8-19.

SUMMARY

As the trainer of a select group of people, the coach must constantly be aware of situations which he can alter to produce more favorable performance results. Training factors that he might want to consider are as follows:

*Knowledge of results*  Immediate and specific information after the execution of an act is best. Augmented information (feedback) may be bene-

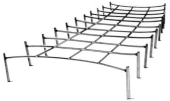

FIGURE 8-11   *The Knee-High Trainer.* (Wolverine Sports Supply, 745 State Circle, Ann Arbor, Mich.)

ficial in certain cases. Knowledge of results serves to reinforce acts, provide guidance, and motivate the performers.

*Drill*   Drill and spontaneity of activity are essential for the mastery of skills and for success in sport. The relative emphasis on each may depend on the nature of the activity, whether it is inner-directed (self-pacing) or outer-directed (in which occurrences are unpredictable, as they are controlled by the environment).

*Whole method versus part method*   Whether a skill should be taught in parts or as a whole will depend on how difficult it is for the learner and on the nature of the task components. Whole methods are favored where possible, but part methods are encouraged in difficult skills, especially those whose components are fairly independent.

*Mental practice*   Formal mental rehearsal of an act has been shown to be a beneficial approach to the learning of motor skills. Although actual overt or physical practice is most effective, some form of mental practice is better than no practice at all.

*Verbalization*   Thinking, or "unspoken words," as verbalization is called, is apparently a frequent practice with outstanding athletes. This informal method varies in nature from athlete to athlete, but usually precedes the actual execution of a skill or participation in a contest.

*Application of principles*   The learning of concepts or principles underlying the execution of movements may transfer to future similar situations

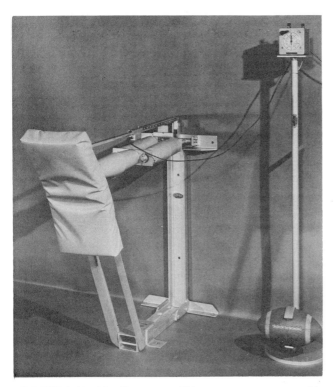

FIGURE 8-12    *The Powerator. This apparatus measures hitting force and reaction time.* (Leflar, 6840 S. W. Macadam Avenue, Portland, Oreg.)

FIGURE 8-13    *The Server.* (The Ball-Boy Company, Inc., 26 Milburn Street, Bronxville, N.Y.)

FIGURE 8-14    *The Batting Tee.* (Dudley Sports Co., Inc., 12-12 37th Avenue, Long Island City, N.Y.)

FIGURE 8-15    *The Baseball Pitching Machine.* (Dudley Sports Co., Inc., 12-12 37th Avenue, Long Island City, N.Y.)

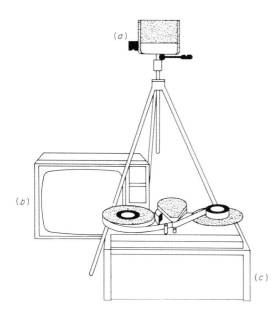

FIGURE 8-16 *Basic videotape equipment: camera (a), monitor-receiver (b), and videotape recorder (records and reproducers) (c).* (Ampex, 5422 W. Touhy Avenue, Skokie, Ill.)

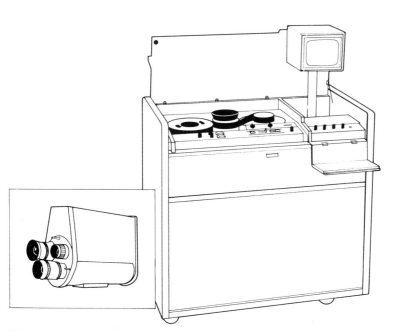

FIGURE 8-17 *A complete videotape system for recording and playing back which incorporates many of the latest advances in technology.* (Ampex, 5422 W. Touhy Avenue, Skokie, Ill.)

FIGURE 8-18 *Action videotaped and recorded in a football game can be played back to the group at the end of practice or the game, or sooner.* (Sony, VTR Division, 47-47 Van Dam Street, Long Island City, N.Y.)

and promote quicker insight into the solution of problems. This may or may not prove to be true, depending on how the principles are taught and how well the learner understands them, among other things.

*Habit interference*   When a skill is not well learned, there is a tendency for other closely related skills to interfere and be interfered with. Competing responses result in poorly demonstrated acts.

*Guidance, demonstration, and instruction*   Manual or external manipula-

FIGURE 8-19  *Videotaping a female athlete stroking a tennis ball.* (Ampex, 5422 W. Touhy Avenue, Skokie, Ill.)

tion allows the athlete to experience the desired movement, demonstration permits observation and imitation, and instruction serves to guide and motivate.

*Psychological tolerance*  There are physical limitations to a person's potential achievement, but because of psychological factors, most people do not push themselves to their limits. Psychological endurance and ability to tolerate pain and punishment often determine which athlete will be the best trained and will exert himself most in a contest.

*Cues and aids*  Cues and aids associated with specific sense modalities may help to improve motivation and supplement traditional training programs.

*Auditory cues,* in the form of coaches' comments, prepare the athlete, guide him through an act, and provide a knowledge of results.

*Auditory aids,* as exemplified by music in the background, may or may not improve the learning and performing of athletic skills.

*Visual cues* which are closer to the athlete and more precise are easier to attend to than those which are more general and farther away. The athlete should attend to the relevant cues and disregard others.

*Visual aids,* such as movies, may prove to be helpful when supplements to regular practice sessions, but as a substitute for actual practice, their value is questionable. Modifications in visual displays, such as smaller or larger basketball rims, for practice sessions can often be justified on theoretical grounds, but research on reported outcomes is conflicting.

*Kinesthetic cues* are not thought of as functional in athletic contexts, as there are many cues inherent in motor activities.

*Kinesthetic aids* may be obtained from manual manipulation of body parts or from practicing while blindfolded. The limited research on this topic provides little substantiation or refutation of such practices.

*Laboratory aids* contain no magic. As far as developing an ability is concerned, the closer laboratory practice comes to the actual situation in which the practiced task will be used, the more beneficial it will be.

*Technological aids* have proved to be of value in education, the military, driver education, and industry. They typically simulate portions of tasks and may promote learning. The real value of the aids that are being used in athletics, such as ball-throwing machines, has not yet been determined.

## REFERENCES

Ayres, L. P. The influence of music on speed in the six day bicycle race. *American Physical Education Association Review,* 1911, **16**, 321–346.

Bell, Virginia L. Augmented knowledge of results and its effect upon acquisition and retention of a gross motor skill. *Research Quarterly,* 1968, **39**, 25–30.

Bilodeau, Ina M. Information feedback. In Bilodeau, E. A. (Ed.), *Acquisition of skill.* New York: Academic Press, 1966.

Bond, Marjorie H. Rhythmic performance and gross motor performance. *Research Quarterly,* 1959, **30**, 259–265.

Burack, Benjamin, & Moos, Donald. Effect of knowing the principle basic to solution of a problem, *Journal of Educational Research,* 1956, **50**, 203–208.

Burke, Jack. *The natural way to better golf.* New York: Hanover House, 1954.

Chui, Edward F. A study of Golf-O-Tron utilization as a teaching aid in relation to improvement and transfer. *Research Quarterly,* 1965, **36**, 147–152.

Clark, L. Verdelle. Effect of mental practice on the development of a certain motor skill. *Research Quarterly,* 1960, **31**, 560–569.

Colville, F. H. The learning of motor skills as influenced by knowledge of mechanical principles. *Journal of Educational Psychology,* 1957, **48**, 321–327.

Counsilman, James E. *The science of swimming.* Englewood Cliffs, N.J.: Prentice-Hall, 1968.

Dembowski, Michael. A comparison of the peripheral vision of high school varsity basketball players and nonathletes. *Your Challenge,* Toledo University, 1968, **3**, 3–7.

Durentini, Carol L. The relationship of a purported measure of kinesthesis to the learning of a simple motor skill, the basketball free throw, projected with and without vision. Unpublished master's thesis, University of Massachusetts, 1967.

Egstrom, Glen H., Logan, Gene A., & Wallis, Earl L. Acquisition of throwing skill involving projectiles of varying weights. *Research Quarterly,* 1960, **31**, 420–425.

Glaser, Robert (Ed.) *Training research and education.* New York: Wiley, 1962.

Griffith, Coleman R. *Psychology of coaching.* New York: Scribner, 1932.

Hendrickson, Gordon, & Schroeder, William W. Transfer of training in learning to hit a submerged target. *Journal of Educational Psychology,* 1941, **32**, 205–213.

Holding, D. H. *Principles of training.* New York: Pergamon Press, 1965.

Mathews, Donald K., & McDaniel, Joe. Effectiveness of using Golf-Lite in learning the golf swing. *Research Quarterly,* 1962, **33**, 488–491.

Nelson, Dale O. Effect of swimming on the learning of selected gross motor skills. *Research Quarterly,* 1957, **28**, 364–373.

Puni, A. T. Problem of voluntary regulation of motor activity in sports. In Antonelli, Ferruccio (Ed.), *Proceedings of the 1st International Congress of Sports Psychology,* 1965, pp. 103–113.

Roudik, Petre A. Psychophysiological mechanisms of surmounting difficulties in sports. In Antonelli, Ferruccio (Ed.), *Proceedings of the 1st International Congress of Sports Psychology,* 1965, pp. 79–83.

Ryan, E., & Kovacic, C. R. Pain tolerance and athletic participation. *Perceptual and Motor Skills,* 1966, **22**, 383–390.

Selk, Larry B. A comparison of different methods of free throwing practice among selected high school basketball players in North Dakota and Minnesota with respect to accuracy in games. Unpublished master's thesis, University of North Dakota, 1966.

Sharman, Bill. *Sharman on shooting.* Englewood Cliffs, N.J.: Prentice-Hall, 1967.

Solley, William H., & Borders, Susan. Relative effects of two methods of teaching the forehand drive in tennis. *Research Quarterly,* 1964, **36**, 120–122.

Watkins, David L. Motion pictures as an aid in correcting baseball batting faults. *Research Quarterly,* 1963, **34**, 228–233.

# CHAPTER NINE

# Research and Sports

The material in the preceding chapters has held general implications for the coach and the athlete. Psychological research has been presented in such a manner as to be applied across situations that might be found in any sport. Naturally, there is a limit to the extent to which this approach contains value. The person associated with a given sport wants to know about the psychological research on that particular sport. This chapter has been designed with that thought in mind.

Although much research on athletic skills and performance is published in the *Research Quarterly,* the research publication of the American Association of Health, Physical Education, and Recreation, the subjects of the studies are usually members of physical education classes or students referred to as nonathletes, and the same trend is apparent in thesis and dissertation work. The results of such research may be generalizable to athletes, but then again, they may not. Surprisingly, of all the research done by physical educators, only a small portion has dealt with the athletically gifted performer. However, only studies in which varsity or professional athletes served as subjects and which are psychologically oriented, concerned with learning or training methods or personality variables, are included in this chapter.

One limitation of much of the research presented in this chapter is that select groups of athletes were used in the studies. The numbers of subjects are usually small, and the caliber of the athletes is difficult to determine. Furthermore, much of the evidence comes from projects submitted to meet graduate school requirements, in the form of theses or dissertations. Therefore, although athletes, as defined by the individual experimenters, were employed in the reported investigations, the results must still be interpreted with caution.

A serious search of athletic journals, research publications, and theses and dissertations reveals that some sports have been more intently investigated than others. Greater interest in some sports and more favorable conditions for research in them are two of the reasons. The sports on which the most psychological research has been done are basketball, football, baseball, and wrestling, and gymnastics, tennis, swimming, track and field, volleyball, and golf have been studied to a lesser degree.

The research in this chapter is categorized by sport[1] and has been chosen because it has dealt primarily with psychology of learning and training, not with physiological or kinesiological material, which has been handled adequately in other sources. Investigations of personality factors relevant to athletic groups are also included.

## BASEBALL

### Batting

Many researchers have attempted to investigate the relationship between batting success and certain abilities and characteristics, and also to find ways of improving batting productivity. Since reaction time is thought to be an important determiner of hitting success, Ness (1967) attempted to determine the extent of the relationship. The subjects were a combined group of 30 high school and college baseball players and another group of 30 college students. The baseball players' reaction times were recorded and correlated against a criterion of coaches' ratings and batting averages. Variations of the reaction time test were administered, and most of the correlations of the test scores with each other and the criterion were low to moderate, the highest being .41.

The batter must react mentally and physically within a very short period of time after the release of a pitched ball. This point has been statistically documented by Slater-Hammel & Stumpner (1951). Their subjects moved a baseball bat upon the presentation of a visual stimulus, and the average reaction time was observed to be 0.21 second. Hubbard & Seng (1954) concluded that professional batters react between 0.24 to 0.28 second to the flight of a baseball. In the Slater-Hammel study, to change the direction of a moving baseball bat took approximately 0.27 second. The major implication of this study is that the batter's decision to swing or not to swing must be made when the ball has traveled about half the distance from the pitcher's mound. Therefore, the ball must be watched carefully when it is pitched, and the decision-making process must be begun immediately in order to get satisfactory results.

The ability to judge a pitched ball quickly could be related to the stance of the batter. Lande (1968) observed that most of the best batters use a closed stance. Individual differences in various characteristics certainly must be evaluated before a particular stance is recommended, however.

[1] Acknowledgment is given to Dennis Riccio, who at the time of this writing is teaching physical education at Wheeling High School in Illinois, for his assistance in collecting and organizing a portion of the material that is contained in this chapter.

Weiskopf (1960), studying the outstanding professional batters of all time, reported that four of the best batters used a parallel stance with a short stride. In a study of the relationship between stance and batting reaction and movement times, Herman (1968) used 29 Illinois State University baseball players. The subjects took five swings in each stance (parallel, open, and closed) upon the activation of a light stimulus. Reaction time was measured upon the initiation of bat movement in response to the stimulus, while movement time was represented by the time it took to complete the swing. Special apparatus was constructed for testing purposes. No differences were obtained when performances for reaction time and movement time were compared in the three stances. Generally speaking, a person who demonstrated a fast batting reaction time or movement time in one stance did the same in another stance.

An early study (Bates, 1948) in which films were used indicated that the batters who visually followed the ball longest got the best hitting results. Maintaining eye contact with the ball was found to be extremely important. Furthermore, Burpee & Stroll (1936) report that Babe Ruth's reaction time was twice as fast as average when it was measured at the psychological laboratories at Columbia University.

Little wonder that various researchers have attempted to devise ways of improving reaction time, since it is so important in the batting swing. For instance, Trenbeath (1966) used 18 freshman baseball candidates at the University of North Dakota in an attempt to find some answers. One group used the variable-speed rotating pitching machine, and a second acted as a control. The experimental group practiced with the machine three days a week for six weeks, and the control group had regular daily practice without use of the pitching machine. Reaction time was measured before the six-week period, and when it was measured again after the period, the experimental group was significantly faster in reaction time.

There are a number of possible approaches to the improvement of batting. If we assume that the ability to swing the bat quickly is associated with a better chance of hitting the ball, then a thesis by Deese (1962) provides some interesting information. He found that weight training increased batting movement time. Supplementary information is offered by Harold Wertich's (1967) investigation. Two groups of South Dakota State freshman baseball candidates were formed, one of which received traditional weight training while the other received resistance training with the Exer-Genie. The velocity of the batting swing was measured before and after training. It was found that: (1) both programs increased the velocity of the batting swing; (2) the two methods were equally effective; and (3) swinging a weighted bat immediately before batting did not affect the velocity of the swing.

Ewart Bagg (1966) investigated the possibility of improvement in batting performance as a result of mental rehearsals of the act. Working with 20 varsity players at the University of California at Los Angeles, he administered a criterion batting test which was based on distance and accuracy of a batted ball. A pitching machine was used to serve up the pitches. Two groups of players were formed; one received nine 15-minute sessions of mental practice in addition to physical practice, and the other acted as a control and received only physical practice. Both groups had prebatting and postbatting tests. On the basis of a statistical analysis of the data, Bagg reported that the experimental group performed significantly better than the control group.

Visual aids such as slides, motion pictures, and loop films may assist in improving performance. The subject in such aids may be the player himself so that he can observe and analyze his strengths and weaknesses, or an outstanding athlete who serves as an example. In David Watkins' (1963) study, 20 members of the varsity team at the State University of Iowa were used to study the effectiveness of motion pictures as an aid in correcting batting faults. A control and an experimental group were formed. The individual members of the latter group were filmed at the beginning of the test period, at the end of the third week, and at the end of the fifth week, which was also the end of the experimental period. Once a week during the five weeks this group reviewed the most recent films of their batting; the film was shown, and each subject received three minutes of instruction. During regular batting practice, the two groups received equal amounts of instruction. The experimental group performed significantly better than the control group when the gain between the first and the fifth weeks was compared. In other words, motion picture instruction coupled with batting practice can decrease batting errors.

The relationship between batting success and eye dominance and unilaterality has been investigated by Adams (1964). The players on two college baseball teams were analyzed for crossed laterals (those who had one eye dominant but batted from the opposite side of the plate) and unilaterals (same-sidedness). Unilaterals were superior to crossed laterals in most batting categories. Unilaterals who had an open stance generally outperformed those with a closed stance.

*Pitching*

Robert Blank (1966) had three groups of freshman and varsity pitchers throw at different targets during a four-week training period. The targets were (1) the catcher's preliminary signal with his ungloved hand as to where the pitcher should throw the ball, (2) the catcher's glove alone, and (3) targets 1 and 2 combined. The three methods produced similar results and were therefore considered equally effective. The pitching accuracy of all players significantly improved.

Gellinger (1965) was also concerned with pitching control. He experimented with presence and absence of cues, or more specifically, with the effect of blindfolds on pitchers' control. Three groups of subjects, comprising 18 freshman and varsity pitchers, practiced in the following way: the members of group I were blindfolded and their scores were reported after each pitch, but no suggestions given; group II could see each pitch and in addition were advised and instructed; and group III acted as a control. During each of six practice sessions held in a three-week period, the subjects first warmed up and then threw 20 fast balls at a target. When pretest and post-test scores were compared, no statistically significant gains were made among the groups, although the blindfolded group showed the highest mean gain in performance.

A study of the effects of warmup and special practice on the throwing performance of varsity-caliber baseball players was done by Van Huss, Albrecht, Nelson, & Hagerman (1962). They tested 50 members of the Michigan State University freshman baseball team for throwing velocity and accuracy with a regulation 5-ounce baseball before and after throwing an 11-ounce baseball. Overload warmup was found to improve throwing velocity, but the effects on accuracy were unclear. Data from this study are illustrated in Chapter 6 in the section on warmup.

In Donald Brose's thesis (1964), 21 candidates for a college freshman team were divided into three groups and were trained three days a week for six weeks. One group threw leaded baseballs (10 ounces); the second trained on a wall pulley that provided 10 pounds of resistance; and the third group, the control, threw regulation baseballs. The post-test performance scores of the three groups when using regulation baseballs showed no differences in velocity and accuracy. However, the two overload-trained groups did improve significantly from pretest to post-test scores.

In the same area of investigation, Logan, McKinney, Rowe, & Lumpe (1966), studied college baseball players in an attempt to determine means of increasing throwing velocity. Group I received six weeks of Exer-Genie range-of-throwing motion exercises; group II threw 30 pitches a day, five days a week, and did some exercises; and group III acted as a control. On tests administered before and after the six weeks of the study, the only group to make a significant gain in performance was group I.

## Predicting Baseball Ability

Very little work has been done on predicting baseball ability. Everett (1952) reported a study in which 30 University of Iowa baseball players were rated by their coach. They were measured on a number of performance tests: throwing for distance, speed and agility in running, eye-hand co-ordination, reaction time, ability to judge distance, ability to visualize spatial relationships (Thurstone's $S$ test), Sargent jump, ability to make decisions quickly (blocks test), ability to relax, and ability to throw accurately. The Sargent jump was the best single predictor of baseball ability ($r = .52$). The best combination of predictors was the Sarget jump, the $S$ test, and the blocks test.

Another battery of tests was administered by Kelson (1953) to boys between the ages of 8 and 12 participating in Little League. Playing ability was determined by batting ability, ability to throw for distance and with accuracy, ability to catch fly balls, and ability to field ground balls. When all these measures were compiled and one representative score was determined, ability to throw for distance was most closely related to the score (a very high correlation of .85). Evidently, with boys this age, a distance throw is fairly indicative of baseball ability.

Robert Imlay (1966) evaluated the physiques of 151 college baseball players and found that they differed in somatotype from the general population. Furthermore, certain positions in the batting order and certain defense positions could be distinguished by somatotype.

## Personality

Interesting data have been collected on the behavioral characteristics of Little Leaguers. Skubic (1956) compared two baseball groups—Little Leaguers and Middle Leaguers—with nonplayers. Questionnaires were sent to parents and players, and an analysis of the ratings showed that the players were better adjusted emotionally and socially than the nonplayers. Seymour (1956) compared Little Leaguers with nonparticipants by studying 114 subjects in each group before and after a season. The results indicated that the needs and problems of the groups were similar, but Little Leaguers scored higher than nonplayers on personality traits and social acceptance both before and after the baseball season.

The personalities of college baseball players at Ohio State University were investigated by Singer (1969) by comparing data collected on the Edwards Personal Preference Schedule with normative data. The baseball group scored lower in autonomy (independence of others) and intraception (self-analysis and analysis of others), and higher in abasement (easy acceptance of blame; giving in readily). Fifty-nine baseball players, taken from the freshman and varsity teams, were rated by their respective coaches. The 10 highest-ranked varsity and the 10 highest-ranked freshman players were placed in one group, for statistical analysis, to be compared with the 10 lowest-ranked varsity and the 10 lowest-ranked freshman players. Personality profiles were found to be similar between the groups when treated with multiple discriminant analysis, and individual personality traits were also observed to be the same for both groups.

John La Place (1954) attempted to determine what personality traits might be associated with success in professional baseball. He designated major leaguers as a successful group and minor league players as an unsuccessful group. On the Minnesota Multiphasic Personality Inventory, major league players were found to be better able

1    To apply their strong "drive" toward a definite objective by exercising self-discipline
2    To adjust to occupations, such as professional baseball, requiring social contact or the ability to get along well with other people
3    To exercise initiative

The two groups are compared with each other and with norms on each personality measure in Figure 9-1.

## BASKETBALL

### Training Techniques and the Basket

The majority of basketball studies have dealt with the effects of practice in which the target or the ball is varied in some way, and the most attention has been given to the effect on shooting ability of practicing with a rim that is smaller than the regulation size.

Maaske (1960) matched two groups of freshman basketball players according to a test of accuracy in shooting at official baskets. After the groups practiced with smaller and with regulation baskets, they attempted 50 field goals with regulation baskets at each of nine stations marked on the floor. In the shooting test, the small-basket group scored significantly higher than the standard-basket group. In 15 practice and intercollegiate games, the small-basket group made 43.4 percent of field-goal attempts and 68.5 percent of free-throw attempts, whereas the official-basket group scored 31.3 percent of field-goal attempts and 60.3 percent of free-throw attempts.

Sell (1963), in a similar experimental design, randomly divided 22 high school basketball players into two groups. A shooting test of 450 shots from nine stations on the floor was administered to both groups at the beginning and again at the end of the season. Throughout the season one group practiced with baskets 15 inches in diameter while the other group practiced

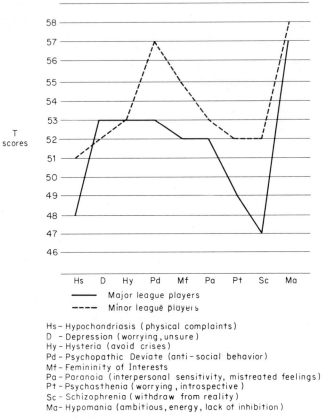

T scores

Hs  D  Hy  Pd  Mf  Pa  Pt  Sc  Ma

——————  Major league players

– – – –  Minor league players

Hs – Hypochondriasis ( physical complaints )
D  – Depression ( worrying, unsure )
Hy – Hysteria ( avoid crises )
Pd – Psychopathic Deviate ( anti-social behavior )
Mf – Femininity of Interests
Pa – Paranoia ( interpersonal sensitivity, mistreated feelings )
Pt – Psychasthenia ( worrying, introspective )
Sc – Schizophrenia ( withdraw from reality )
Ma – Hypomania ( ambitious, energy, lack of inhibition )

FIGURE 9-1  *MMPI profiles of major league and minor league players. A T score of more than T54 indicates a significant profile score over the general population. The major leaguers scored higher in hypomania (strong aggressive drive), and the minor leaguers had significant scores on the psychopathic deviate, interest, and hypomania scales (associated with people who have behavior problems).* (Source: *John P. La Place. Personality and its relationship to success in professional baseball.* Research Quarterly, *1954,* **25,** *313–319. P. 314.*)

with official 18-inch baskets. On the final test the scores from three of the nine stations were significantly higher for the group that practiced with the smaller baskets. In addition, in 16 interscholastic games, the small-basket group made 36.4 percent of the field goals attempted, and the official basket group made 32.3 percent. The differences in performance are less markedly in favor of the small-basket group than those reported by Maaske.

Minahan (1963) tested a group of 50 ninth-grade boys on a regulation basket and another similar group on a basket that had a restrictive device inserted in it. There was no significant difference in the performances of the two groups. Joseph Kite (1964) also found no significant differences when high school groups practiced with an official basket, a 15-inch basket, an 18-inch basket with a target, and a 21-inch basket. Similar results were obtained in studies by Fisk (1967), Selk (1966), and Takacs (1965). These studies indicate that no benefits are derived from practicing with a smaller basket, and consequently that the popular restrictive devices that are placed in the official baskets may be useless.

Visual areas are extremely important in basketball, and the basketball player relies on many of them during a game. Both specific vision (directly concentrating on the rim) and peripheral vision (absorbing the visual "field" surrounding the action) are important. Ten college basketball players were tested by Sills & Troutman (1966) for visual acuity, depth perception, and peripheral vision to determine the relationship of these factors to shooting ability. The subjects took 100 shots at the basket under each of five conditions: (1) sighting directly on the rim, (2) sighting on an object 10° from the center of the basket, (3) sighting on an object 20° from the center of the basket, (4) sighting on an object 30° from the center of the basket, and (5) blindfolded. Differences in performance output were noted in all possible mean-score comparisons except (1) normal sighting and sighting 10° from the basket, (2) sighting 20° and 30° from the basket, and (3) sighting 30° from the basket and shooting blindfolded. Evidently a player shooting from a stationary position can shoot as effectively when sighting directly on the rim as when sighting on an object 10° from the center of the basket. At high levels of skill, therefore, concentrating on the rim may be less important than believed.

### Basket Height

The increasing trend toward taller basketball players has necessitated the adoption of certain rules in order to make the game more difficult and lower the score per game, and a recent suggestion along this line is to raise the height of the basket. The relative shooting advantages and disadvantages for the "little" man and the "big" man must, of course, be analyzed before any such change is made. Bob Chaloupecky (1967) attempted to determine differences in performance in 22 freshman and varsity Illinois State University basketball players when shooting at 10-foot and 11-foot baskets. The players took 100 shots (25 on each of four days), a mixture of free throws, jump shots, and set shots, at each basketball rim height. Some of the more important conclusions are as follows:

1. Shooting ability at the 10-foot basket was significantly better than at the 11-foot basket.
2. Accuracy, when compared between the three shots (set shot, jump shot, and free throw) and at the two baskets, was significantly different for all means tested. The two highest means were obtained on the free throws at both basket heights. Jump shots revealed the second highest means at the baskets. The two lowest mean shooting accuracy were obtained on set shots at both basket heights.
3. Shorter players were significantly better shooters at both basket heights.
4. Taller players adjusted easier than the shorter players when transferring from the 10-foot to the 11-foot basket while shooting the set shot and jump shot.
5. Shorter players adjusted easier than the taller players when transferring from the 10-foot to the 11-foot basket while shooting the free throw.
6. The accuracy of the free throw attempts at both basket heights were highly correlated; set shots at both basket heights were moderately correlated and jump shots resulted in the lowest correlation between performances at the different basket heights.
7. From a questionnaire form submitted to leading professional and college basketball coaches, it was found that 83% of them favored keeping the basket at the traditional height [pp. 46–47].

### Training Cues

There is much discussion among coaches about the effect of extraneous cues on shooting accuracy. Some coaches feel that players shoot most accurately when they concentrate solely on the basketball rim, whereas others believe that cues are needed to allow the player to have a better association with the basket. William Guerin (1966) tested this theory at Eastern Illinois University. He recorded data on 20 varsity players taking a number of shots from varying positions under light and dark conditions. Under the dark conditions only the rim of the basket was visible. The shooting of the players was more accurate under the light conditions.

Scanlon (1968) tested 15 college varsity players under dark conditions. The players shot from three different positions on the floor, and only the designated target area was visible. Analysis of the data revealed that focusing on the entire target—the basket rim covered with luminous paint—led to better performance than focusing on either the front or the back of the rim. Furthermore, focusing on the back of the rim was more effective than focusing on the front of the rim.

Looking at the problem from a different point of view, Gene Gephart (1954) tested three groups on foul shooting. A blindfolded and a sighted group practiced for six weeks under these conditions, and the control group did not practice. It was found that the blindfolded subjects improved significantly more than either the sighted practice subjects or the control group in free-throw performance.

### Training Techniques and the Ball

The effects of altering the size of the ball have also been studied. In the first study reported below, an attempt was made to determine whether altering the size of the ball would help to lower scoring. In the second study below, the transfer effects of training with balls of various sizes were investigated.

Lindeburg & Hewitt (1965) observed 26 experienced male basketball players on a short shot test, a foul shooting test, a passing test, and a dribble test. One group used a regulation ball, $29\frac{3}{4}$ inches in circumference and just over 20 ounces in weight, and another group used an experimental ball that was 31 inches in circumference and over 22 ounces in weight. In general, there was no difference between performances with the two balls except that passing was less effective with the larger ball.

Jay Kinser (1966) tested subjects with three balls of different weights: a one-pound ball, a regulation ball, and a ball slightly under three pounds. The subjects practiced free throwing with the nonpreferred hand for four weeks. The group that practiced with the lightest ball developed significantly greater accuracy, but no mention was made of testing this group with a regulation ball.

### Training Techniques for Jumping

Other special training techniques used by coaches have been investigated by researchers. Anderson (1961) attempted to determine the relative effects of weighted ankle spats on various measures of physical performance. One group of high school basketball players trained with the spats; the other trained in the usual manner. The subjects were tested before and after a six-week training period. The difference between test scores showed that the spat group improved more than the control group in vertical jumping agility and a 360-yard run. The effects of weighted training shoes on vertical jumping, agility, and endurance were also investigated by Wayne Lukas (1960), who placed 18 basketball players in three groups: a control, a group that trained wearing regular shoes, and a group that trained wearing weighted shoes. Analysis of the data revealed that the weighted-shoe group showed the greatest gains on all three tests. Contrarily, Howell (1967), also using high school players, found no differences in jumping performance between such groups during a four-week program. Also, Dave

Genzmer (1960) noted no significant differences in Sargent jump performance as a result of special weight training programs designed to increase achievement. Basketball players were placed in one of four groups: a squat-jump group, a knee-bend group, a board-rhythm group, and a control group. The three groups were trained under similar and increased weights for each week of the experiment.

Brees (1961) studied the effectiveness of trampoline training in improving performance as measured on tests similar to those used in Anderson's thesis. Junior varsity high school basketball players were assigned to one of three groups: (1) trampoline work, (2) jumping exercises, or (3) control. Performance tests in the vertical jump, agility, standing broad jump, 30-yard dash, and 300-yard shuttle run were administered at various intervals during a five-week period. The three groups did not differ in the standing broad jump or the 30-yard dash. The trampoline group showed a significant increase over the control group in the 300-yard shuttle run, the vertical jump, and the agility run.

### Practice Techniques

Practice methodology is a very important factor in the coaching of any sport. Should practice be massed or distributed? Should it be mental, physical, or a combination of mental and physical? Practice methods have been researched extensively but there have been few concerned exclusively with basketball. Brassie (1965) had one group of college basketball players practice free throws consecutively and another practice them intermittently. On the initial and final tests both groups shot both consecutively and intermittently. No difference between the mean scores was found on the final test, but in games, the intermittent-practice group scored on 4.8 percent more free throws than the consecutive-practice group. This study would seem to indicate that in a game situation a team that had practiced free throws on an intermittent schedule would perform better than one that had practiced on a consecutive schedule.

Lowell Swartzendruber (1965), in an investigation of the effects of physical and a combination of mental and physical practice on basketball shooting, found no significant difference in performance.

Hugh Thompson (1958) did a study to determine whether warmup is beneficial to shooting. The subjects were 20 Pennsylvania State University freshman basketball players. Foul-shooting tests were administered to the same players (20 shots each) three times with warmup and three times without warmup on different days. Warmup consisted of general floor shooting for 10 minutes, foul shooting, and a passing drill. When test scores were compared, it was observed that the average number of baskets made out of 60 attempts was as follows: after no warmup, 37.55; after warmup, 44.35. The indications were significantly in favor of warmup.

Ever since men began to coach they have been looking for a successful and objective way of selecting team members and starters. A successful method would be very beneficial to the coach in this important aspect of coaching. The problems are that successful players have a larger number of qualities which must be accurately identified, and that constructing a test that can somehow be used to evaluate performance and predict achievement is quite difficult.

Boyd, McCachren, & Waglow (1955) used the Knox Basketball Test[2] to try to predict squad members of the University of Florida junior varsity team. They concluded that the Knox test has merit as a squad predictor, as it can readily distinguish between varsity and nonvarsity performers, but that it is not subtle enough to distinguish between levels of ability within a squad.

Mack (1964) worked with other measures in an attempt to determine the association of certain test scores with basketball achievement. A total of 70 subjects (25 college basketball players, 25 nonathletes, and 21 high school basketball players) were tested. Basketball playing ability was rated by the coach, and the measurements included the Knox penny cup test, Sargent jump, running speed, grip strength, and peripheral vision. With all the basketball players combined, the following significant correlations were obtained:

| r | Basketball ability and test |
|---|---|
| .60 | Peripheral vision |
| .60 | Speed |
| .58 | Penny cup test |
| .47 | Sargent jump |
| .45 | Right-hand grip strength |
| .36 | Left-hand grip strength |

Judging by the correlations, the qualities that are most associated with higher basketball ratings are vision, running speed, and change of direction with speed ability (penny cup test). When the three groups of subjects were compared, the college basketball players were found to be significantly better than the high school players in everything except height. They were

[2] The test (Knox, 1947) contains a speed dribble test, dribble-shoot test, wall-bounce test, and penny cup test. Knox found his test to be an excellent predictor of high school teams that made a tournament as well as first-team players.

also significantly better than the nonathletes in all tests except right-hand grip strength and peripheral vision.

Similar and other tests have been employed by other investigators and coaches interested in predicting achievement. George McGinnis (1955), working with eighth-grade boys, used one-on-one (man-to-man) basketball games—with point systems derived—as a criterion of basketball aptitude. He found a fairly high multiple correlation of .80 when the following tests and resultant performance scores were correlated with the criterion: wall bounce, jumping height, free throws (number scored out of 25), 35-yard dash, and vertical jump. Whether these same tests correlate well with basketball accomplishments in a regular game is open to conjecture.

Stroup (1957) suggested field of motion perception as a criterion for selecting players. He tested physical education majors and men who had played high school and college basketball. His results showed that the basketball players scored higher on the field-of-motion perception test. However, since all groups improved with training, there was an indication that basketball develops this ability.

### Body Constitution

Anthropometrical measures may distinguish better from less good players. Patty (1953) reported that a group of 101 successful basketball players exceeded a group of 170 unsuccessful basketball players in agility, vertical jump, right- and left-hand grip strength, weight, finger dexterity, arm pull, speed, arm span, hand width, leg lift, leg length, height, arm push, total strength, endurance, foot length, hand length, and foot width. The only measurement in which the unsuccessful athletes did better was trunk extension. No difference was found in back lift strength, trunk flexion, shoulder flexion, and ankle flexion.

### Aspects of the Game

Kay (1966) has developed a profile technique, which has proved to be highly objective, for the evaluation of basketball players. Managers could make valid ratings after one practice with familiar high school players and two practices with unfamiliar players. The profile technique, Kay states, can be used as a test, as a measure of basketball ability over four or five games, and as a basis for inferences about basketball ability in a single game.

A summary and comparison of coaching techniques in the teaching of various basketball skills has been made by Garretson (1962). Of 25 college basketball coaches in the Pacific Northwest who were contacted, 18 replied and completed questionnaires. Little agreement was noted among the coaches about the teaching of many of the skills.

Coaches are very much concerned to acquire information and statistics on various aspects of the game in order to determine the relative importance of various factors that might contribute to success. A master's thesis by Fred Brendice (1965) offers some interesting facts. Field goals attempted and made, foul shots attempted and made, rebounds, passes, personal fouls, and total scores for the 1965 Springfield College freshman team were compared with their opponents' scores. The most important game-outcome factor was found to be skill in shooting, and passing was the second most important. The researcher concludes that a short team can compensate for lack of height by expertise in other aspects of the game. Further data are offered by Arietta (1967). After making observations in basketball games, he concluded that most missed free throws rebound into the foul lane in front of the basket. This supports the contention that the foul shooter should be blocked by the opposite team so that he cannot get the ball on the rebound from his own missed shot. As expected, Arietta states that the two most effective positions for rebounding are the two positions nearest the basket.

Lutes' thesis (1961) is recommended to readers interested in areas of concentration of rebounds of shots taken from specified zones of the court. High school and college games played at Springfield College provided the necessary data. An attempt has been made by Fisher (1961) to equalize game scoring by changing the conventional method of scoring basketball games. A zone scoring plan was used; for example, shots made in the zone from 15 to 27 feet in front of the basket and from 20 to 32 feet on either side were worth three points. A particular high school team was studied, and after the season, all game scores were retallied according to the zone method. Score differences were changed in every game, and the outcome of one game was actually reversed.

Studying free throws, Thomas Vizard (1967) determined whether there were differences in the number of successful first shots in one-and-one and two-shot situations. Tournament high school and college contests provided the data. No difference in success was found between the first shots under each circumstance for either group of athletes. Furthermore, it made little difference whether the shots were attempted in the first or second half of the game, or whether they were made with a point difference in score from 0 to 5, from 6 to 9, or 10 and higher. Vizard concludes, "The lack of significant differences in performances between the first shots of the one-and-one and two-shot fouls, and between levels of experience, and the lack of significant combination between these variables seem to be the most conclusive and valuable findings of this study" (p. 35). Vizard also passed on some information given to him by Dr. E. S. Steitz, former chairman of the NCAA

Basketball Research Committee. Steitz stated that the national free-throw percentage for over 4,000 games was 69, and that for tournament shooting it was lower. These data provide guidelines for coaches about expectancies in foul-shooting performance, in regular season and tournament games.

Findings by Stotts (1967) suggest that although Brendice's statement that height limitations can be compensated for may be true to a certain extent, the taller team usually wins the contest. He collected data from players and games in Big Eight and NAIA tournaments. From the mean heights taken, it was determined that taller teams won 59 percent of the games against shorter teams. Also, the taller team out-rebounded the shorter team 59 percent of the time in games played. In 66 percent of the games played, the team with the most rebounds won. In general, increased scoring and rebounding were associated with greater height. Taller men are usually involved in center jumps, and Warnock's thesis (1960) was concerned with a comparison of two methods of executing the jump and the relative effectiveness of each.

In Stroup's study (1955), the scores of competing teams in actual basketball games were compared with the "skill score" averages of the teams (the skill score rating was computed from scores on tests of passing, dribbling, and shooting). The results showed that 83.87 percent of the 38 games played were won by the teams that had the higher skill score rating.

## Personality

Very little research has been done on the personalities of basketball players, and in much of what has been done (reviewed in Chapter 3) basketball players were usually compared with other athletic groups in personality. In one of the few studies that have dealt specifically with basketball players, Frank (1968) administered the Washburne Social-Adjustment Inventory to 10 Central Missouri State College basketball players before and after the season. The preseason level of adjustment was interpreted as being low normal for the group. A season of basketball did not change scores on the subtests of happiness, alienation, purpose, sympathy, and impulse-judgment.

Richard Havel (1959) analyzed and compared the personality needs of college varsity basketball players, junior varsity players, nonathletes, and norms, using the Edwards Personal Preference Schedule. Among the findings were that varsity athletes scored higher than other groups in need to achieve, deference, order, abasement, and aggression. When the coach's rankings of the team members were associated with each personality trait, low correlations were obtained. No particular trait was related to achievement in basketball.

In another experiment, Edgar Larson (1966) tested the galvanic skin responses (GSRs), which are an index of emotions, of college varsity players. Three responses were taken at various times during the season and before and after games. One interesting finding was the GSRs were higher, showing greater emotionality, during the regular season than before the practice season started. The highest GSRs were recorded after conference games, the next highest after games that were lost, and the third highest before games that were won. No relationship was found between GSRs and scoring in games.

Because of the nature of the game, basketball teams need "leaders." The question often arises whether leaders and nonleaders can be distinguished in certain personality traits and physical characteristics. In an attempt to find some answers, Dale Nelson (1966) tested subjects from 31 Class A high school basketball teams in Utah and southeast Idaho. Leaders and nonleaders were designated by the "guess who" technique (by which coaches and team members respond to a questionnaire, filling in the name of the player who best fits as the answer to each question) and by coaches' ratings. Two personality tests were administered. It was found that both groups scored above the normal range in intelligence and that the two groups differed on 5 of 16 personality factors measured,[3] although they were in the normal range when compared with standardized scores.

## FOOTBALL

### Training Aids

Audio-visual aids are probably used to a greater extent in football than in any other sport. Almost all football coaches use some sort of films or pictures as teaching devices. Damron (1955) investigated the use of slides for instructing high school football players in recognition of defenses. He divided 52 squad members of the Indiana University high school team randomly into two groups; one group was trained on two-dimensional slides and one on three-dimensional slides. Both groups were shown slides of eight defenses viewed from six offensive positions in the line (excluding center) and from the quarterback position. There was no difference in the recognition of the groups, but recognition increased for both groups. This study indicates that there is benefit to be derived from the use of slides as an instructional device.

Londeree (1967) investigated the comparative training effects of motion

---

[3] The five traits on which they differed were sociability versus aloofness, maturity versus immaturity, enthusiasm versus glumness, adventurousness versus shyness, and sophistication versus unpretentiousness.

pictures and flash cards upon recognition of plays. He divided 28 high
school players into two equal groups based on football experience and intelligence. One group was trained for play recognition from the the defensive end position by using motion pictures, the other by using flash cards.
Both groups were then tested for recognition of plays in a live situation. The
group trained with motion pictures had significantly shorter response times.
It was also discovered that differences in intelligence, over the limited range
used in the study, did not result in differences in response time. This study reinforces the feeling that the more similar the training is to the actual situation, the better the transfer results, as motion pictures are of course much
more similar to actual football play than flash cards are.

Football coaches have experimented with all types of starting signals, and
there are many differing opinions about what type is best. Almost all signals
involve names, colors, or numbers, and they may be either rhythmic or nonrhythmic. Thompson, Nagle, & Dobias (1958) tested different starting signals and the movement times that each elicited. Their subjects were high
school and college football lettermen. The three types of signals tested were
the rhythmic digit, the nonrhythmic word digit, and the nonrhythmic color
digit. The results showed that the rhythmic digit produced the fastest movement time.

These results have been confirmed by Schroeder (1966), who tested 38
football players, using an apparatus which tape-recorded starting signals
to activate a timer. The timer was deactivated when the player released a
hand switch as he charged forward to make a block. Each subject received
15 rhythmic signals and 15 nonrhythmic signals. Rhythmic signals resulted
in significantly faster reaction times than nonrhythmic signals, but approximately 4.5 times more off sides were produced by the rhythmic signals than
by the nonrhythmic signals. Furthermore, a football player who reacted
quickly under one condition did not necessarily do so under the other. The
correlation between the reaction-time scores for the football players under
both conditions was a low to moderate .23. If a coach is primarily concerned
with having his team get off the line fast, it is evident that a rhythmic signal
is the best type of starting signal, but there are many other considerations
that some coaches feel are more important. It would seem that this type of
signal would also give an advantage to the defense because they could be
more ready (that is, could anticipate more quickly) when they were
charging.

The effects of audible play signals at the line of scrimmage on reaction
time and response time were investigated by Finn (1968). South Dakota
State freshman and varsity players were tested with audible and nonaudible play signals. When the data were analyzed, it was found that nonaudible and audible play signals resulted in no significant differences in

performance. Nevertheless, nonaudible play signals produced generally faster performances and less errors.

Roll-out passing was investigated by John Mikszewski (1968). From distances of 6, 12, and 25 yards, six quarterbacks rolled out, right or left, and passed the football when in motion. Right-handed quarterbacks were significantly more accurate at the 6-yard distance while rolling to the right than while rolling to the left. At the other distances, performances were similar when rolling either way.

Practice early in the season is very important for a successful football team. This is the time when most of the teaching must take place, and the more material learned before practice begins, the further ahead the team will be. The traditional method of teaching is to distribute playbooks from which the players learn assignments and other material.

Jim Dupont (1966) experimented with a new method at New Haven Indiana High School. He used programmed instruction to teach play formation and other material before the start of practice. In programmed instruction each player can work along at his own pace, and it is a competitive way of learning. Dupont has found that the material is better learned by this method.

Whether practice with a heavier than standard projectile helps to improve speed and accuracy in the contest is difficult to ascertain. Various researchers, using different types of equipment from various sports, have published conflicting results, but only rarely have varsity athletes been the subjects of these investigations. Richard Hopek (1967) had 12 backfield players throw at a moving target. One group of six threw with a regulation ball, the other with a weighted ball. No significant differences were noted between the groups on a test of passing accuracy, although the weighted-ball group improved more. More research is needed before any definite conclusions can be reached.

Mudra did a dissertation (1965) on the coaching practices of a number of football coaches with regard to learning principles. He contrasted Gestalt and S-R learning principles advocated by 71 college coaches and 56 college administrators, and also made comparisons between coaches of winning and losing teams and coaches of small and major college teams. He interpreted statements made by his subjects "Gestalt-field-oriented" or "S-R-oriented." More authoritarianism and a formal drill atmosphere is associated with the S-R approach than with the Gestalt approach. Administrators averaged about five Gestalt-field responses higher than the coaches. Winning and losing coaches' responses paralleled each other. Nevertheless, most of the coaches who had high "Gestalt-field scores" came from small colleges and most of the coaches who scored high on S-R came from major colleges.

Most coaches use some type of psychological method in order to get a team "up" for a game. Vic Rowan (1967), the football coach at San Francisco State, discusses the different methods he favors, which are representative of the methods most coaches use. He awards helmet insignias for outstanding achievement, which can range from intercepting a pass to scoring a touchdown. He also uses different colors of practice jerseys for the offense, defense, and other smaller groups to promote group pride and unity. Offensive and defensive statistics charts are posted to allow team members to see their performance and progress. Rowan has pictures of all his school's successful teams on the dressing room walls, as well as slogans to produce a motivational effect. He also has music played in the locker room, which is varied for different effects on the players. Many other methods are used, but these are representative.

### Body Constitution

As in every other sport, there have been attempts to establish what "makes" a football player, anatomically, physiologically, and psychologically. These attempts have met with limited success. Sigerseth & Haleski (1950) compared the flexibility of football players and nonfootball players. The subjects were 100 football players at the University of Oregon who had played at least two years of high school and one year of college football, and 56 University of Oregon students in elective physical education courses. Twenty-four measures of flexibility were recorded including all the major joints of the body. The nonfootball players were more flexible on 15 measures, the football players were more flexible on only one measure, and there was no difference on eight measures. In general this study indicates that football players are less flexible than nonfootball players. It would be very helpful if norms were established showing the degrees of flexibility that football players possess.

### Predicting Football Ability

Doyle Seely (1964) has taken an inventory of motivational factors associated with All-American football players, and they appear in his unpublished master's thesis. Wilhelm (1951) undertook an extensive study to determine measurable traits related to success in football. At Indiana University, he tested 65 freshman football players and 65 freshman nonfootball players. The measures that were taken were anthropometrical, strength, physiological, and mental. The football players recorded superior scores in all strength and muscle-girth measurements, in power, speed, agility, kinesthetic sense, depth perception, and visual acuity. The nonplayers were better in only one mental test. No differences were found in height, finger dexterity, cardiovascular endurance, balance, reaction time, near and far fusion (an aspect of depth perception), and three other mental tests.

## Personality

In Don Littlefield's (1967) study, the California Psychological Inventory was administered to three groups of college students: (1) outstanding football players; (2) ordinary football athletes; and (3) nonathletes. Nonathletes scored significantly higher than athletes on the composite CPI score, and outstanding athletes scored significantly lower than the other two groups. Participation in football, in this case, was not associated with more favorable characteristics of social interaction and social living. No difference was found between athletes and nonathletes on the Scholastic Aptitude Test.

Carder (1965) investigated the relationship between manifest anxiety and performance in college football. The subjects, 40 freshman football players, were ranked by the coaches according to total performance and according to skill in blocking, tackling, movement agility, and running speed. They were also tested on the Manifest Anxiety Scale and three tests of motor ability. No significant relationship was found between scores on the MAS and any of the performance rankings.

Cowell & Ismail (1961) tested Purdue University freshman players to study the validity of a football rating scale and its relationship to social integration and academic ability. Each player was rated on a scale for condition, aggressiveness, perseverance, team play, attitude toward coaching, ability to play his position, blocking, tackling, and football knowledge. On the basis of their results, the researchers suggested that attitude toward coaching and ability to play the position be used in selecting varsity football players from freshman squads. It was established that the social integration of the team increases as the players play together over a period of time. The social integration of the team appears to be affected also by intense competition for places on the team. Finally, football and academic abilities were found to be independent of each other, but football ability and social acceptance were found to be interrelated.

For some reason, athletes, especially football players, are popularly considered to be different from the normal population. Although the football player's athletic talents are admitted to be superior to those of the average person, the public stereotypes him as possessing lower intelligence and undesirable personality traits. The findings of an investigation by Cassel & Childers (1963) are most enlightening on this matter. The subjects, 45 high school football players, were compared with the norms of the school as well as with national norms on such tests as the California Test of Mental Maturity, the Group Personality Projective Test, the Test of Social Insight, and the Leadership Ability Evaluation Test. The conclusions were as follows:

1   There were no significant differences between football players and school norms in intelligence, and the football players were found to be significantly brighter than the national norms.
2   Football players scored higher than most norms on academic tests, except English.
3   No differences among the three groups were noted in leadership patterns, social insight, and personality tension needs.

In Rinne's study (1968) of high school students, 50 interscholastic players were compared with 50 football nonparticipants in aggressive attitudes. The EPPS was administered to all subjects. Rinne was particularly interested in the scores on the need to achieve and dominance variables, and he found that football players tended to be no more aggressive than their nonparticipating peers. Bend (1968) says that Ogilvie and Tutko have tested college football players at Santa Clara, Stanford, San Jose State, and the Air Force Academy. Football players and nonplayers did not differ on emotional factors. The athletes were characterized by

. . . more ambition and need of success, more respect for authorities, fewer exhibitionistic tendencies, more leadership potential, greater potential for expressing aggressions outwardly, greater endurance (seeing things through to a conclusion), and a greater sense of order and organization [p. 6].

Rushall (1968) has undertaken extensive personality testing of University of Indiana athletes. His data on football players, collected on the Cattell Sixteen Personality Factor Questionnaire did not show differences among three groups of players—first, second, and third string. When the football players were tested over three years, no changes in personality were found. Rushall concludes that personality is not a significant factor in athletic performance.

Clarence Johnson (1966) attempted to determine the influence of a season of football on the personalities of high school football players. He selected subjects from three public secondary schools which were comparable in size and classification. Before the football season, the Guilford-Zimmerman Temperament Survey was administered to 160 football players and 180 nonfootball players, and the same procedure was followed at the end of the season. Various analyses were made between and within the schools. When the samples were compared, it was found that football players gained significantly over nonfootball players in two traits, ascendance and objectivity.

However, when the data from the three schools were compared, inconsistent patterns of changes were noted as a result of a season of football.

Personality testing on football players has taken interesting directions. For example, the possibility exists that winning and losing teams may demonstrate dissimilar personality profiles. Kroll & Petersen (1965a) selected five collegiate football teams: "The winning teams were represented by undefeated nationally ranked teams either in major or small college classifications from the university, state college, and private church college categories. Losing teams were represented by sister schools who finished at or near the bottom in the same athletic conference from the state college and private church college categories" (p. 434). At the end of the season, personality tests were administered to the teams. The personality profiles of the groups were shown to be different.

The same authors (Kroll & Petersen, 1965b) have done further work in this area. The values of three winning and three losing college football teams were compared. (Essentially, the values test measured six value variables: theoretical, economic, aesthetic, social, political, and religious.) Value structures, it was concluded, were dissimilar when analyzed by type of school and type of season. Winning teams scored lower on social values than losing teams; and universities scored lowest on the social variable, state colleges next, and private schools highest. The association between sport and values is also discussed in Chapter 5.

The National Football Foundation supported a project which resulted in a research-documented publication (Bend, 1968) that is well worth the reader's time.

## GOLF

Aside from the early study by Coleman Griffith (1931) which showed that blindfolded beginning golfers improved more than a group with sighted practice in learning to drive a golf ball, few studies of golf class members or team representatives have been reported. In activity classes, the effectiveness of various techniques has been compared, including (1) various teaching methods, (2) testing of the relationship between physical characteristics and performance in an attempt to relate success with certain characteristics, (3) loop films, (4) training aids such as Golf-Lite and Golf-O-Tron, and (5) various golf grips. The qualities of the excellent golfer have hardly been investigated at all.

Gold (1955) found similar personality traits when he compared college varsity and professional golfers (as he did when making the same comparison with tennis players).

In a study of 51 golfers with handicaps from 0 to 14, Wiren (1969) took 33 anthropometric, flexibility, and strength measurements, and also recorded driving distance scores and made films. The differences between the longest and shortest drivers were determined, and correlations among all variables were also computed. Among the findings was that strength was an important factor in the drive, but only if accompanied by good flexibility of the wrist. Timing variables correlated highest with the criterion of all the variables investigated. A predictive mathematical model was developed to estimate driving distance.


## GYMNASTICS

Various teaching methodologies have been used in gymnastic classes, but there has been no research on training techniques for gymnasts.

Gene Wettstone (1938) attempted to determine the traits of outstanding gymnasts by studying 22 members of the University of Iowa gymnastic team. Numerous measurements were recorded, such as height, physical courage, interest and determination, strength, gross motor coordination, kinesthetic sense, heart condition, flexibility, musical timing, rhythm, motor educability, and limb and body proportions and sizes. Height, strength, and gross motor coordination (as measured by the Burpee test) predicted potential gymnastic ability fairly well, as a multiple correlation of .79 with the criterion was obtained.

Of 10 body measurements taken by Williams (1963), 5 showed a combined significant correlation of .64 with gymnastic ability. However, the investigator believes that this coefficient is not high enough to have confidence that the measurements can be used to select squad members.

James Bosco (1962) administered the Cattell Sixteen Personality Factor Questionnaire to 84 champion gymnasts and 9 college men of comparable age. The gymnasts scored higher in emotional stability and maturity, confidence and security, and conventionality and seriousness. Kjeldsen (1961) had his subjects, members of a gymnastic class and members of the freshman gymnastic team, complete the EPPS. Different variables were found to be associated with success in each group. When the two groups were compared, the team members scored higher on deference, order, abasement, and endurance than the class members.

Using female college subjects, Mary Brennan (1967) attempted to determine differences on various performance measures among four groups: skilled gymnasts, skilled dancers, skilled sport participants, and nonathletes. Data were collected on strength, kinesthesis, balance, flexibility, rhythm, and motor performance. With multivariate discriminant analysis, it was found that the gymnastic and dance groups were similar to each other but not to the other two groups. (The interested reader is also referred to a questionnaire study of college women gymnasts involving emotional reactions [Knapp, 1966].)

## JUDO

The investigation of judo by Min (1967) is the only one found in the literature. Various measures of physical factors, performance, and experience were correlated to determine their interrelationships. Data were collected on 34 participants in the first Southeastern Judo Championship. Measures of foot and hip reaction times, age, weight, height, experience in judo, and belt rank yielded generally low and positive correlations. The correlation between experience and belt rank, as might be expected, was quite high ($r = .85$). The only two factors that had meaningful relationships with contest scores were experience ($r = .61$) and belt rank ($r = .67$).

## KARATE

Only one study of karate participants was found in the literature. Carlson & Kroll (1967) selected 71 subjects participating in a tournament held among five karate clubs from several colleges. The subjects were divided into three groups, advanced, intermediate, and novice, according to years of experience and belt ranks. The Cattell Sixteen Personality Factor Questionnaire was administered to the subjects, and it was concluded that no profile or patterns in personality were found to distinguish among levels of participation and proficiency in karate, or between participants and the nonparticipating population.

## SWIMMING

Although a reasonable amount of anthropometrical and physiological research on swimmers has been undertaken,[4] a surprisingly small number of studies have been done in the psychological domain. The majority of those that have been done deal with the personality makeup of the swimmer.

---

[4] This is evident from reading John A. Faulkner. *What research tells the coach about swimming.* Washington, D.C.: American Association for Health, Physical Education, and Recreation, 1967.

Perhaps in no other sport has the personality of the athlete been analyzed to the extent it has in swimming.

## Training Techniques

The quickness of the racing start is extremely important in determining the winner of short-distance swimming events. Mowerson, McAdam, & O'Brien (1964) investigated and compared two racing-start techniques: the arms-forward and arms-backward starts. Nine college varsity swimmers were tested for time in both dives. Although results were not conclusive, the recommendation was that the arms-forward start should be taught to a beginning competitor, but that an experienced competitor who consistently demonstrated a good arms-backward start should not be changed.

Constantine (1961) has published an interesting discussion on the relationship between swimming speed and water depth. He compared and analyzed principles involved in the movement of ships and swimmers, and reached the conclusion that shallow water is more detrimental to swimming speed than deep water. The shallower the water and the closer the competitors on each side of the swimmer, the slower his pace will be.

The swimming turn is also a major consideration in winning a particular event. In the first of three studies to be reported here, William King (1957) worked with two age groups: 17 and younger, and 18 and older. With both groups, it was determined that of two backstroke turns, the experimental one-arm glide yielded faster performance times than the standard two-arm glide. In another experiment, Scharf & King (1964) studied 47 college and high school swimmers in freestyle swimming turns. The experimental tumble turn with a one-arm glide was faster than the conventional tumble turn with a two-arm glide. Both these glides are illustrated in Figure 9-2. Finally, Michael Schiesel (1966), using cinematographic techniques, examined the freestyle turns of four swimmers with regard to time. The time of the turn cycle was affected by the nature of the turn. The pike underarm turn was found to be faster than the conventional tumble turn.

Many investigations have been done on the physical conditioning of swimmers. Lawrence (1965) has polled a large number of college coaches in order to discover common practices. Larry Hamilton (1967) has done some typical research in the area of the physical training of the swimming athlete. In the Hamilton study, college swimmers were paired for each of five swimming events. No difference between groups was noted when the effects of resistance and nonresistance training techniques were compared.

A competitive swimming group and a nonswimmer group were compared in flexibility by Jacobson (1967). At the start of a three-week stretching program, swimmers were observed to be more flexible than nonswimmers.

Two-arm glide method    One-arm glide method

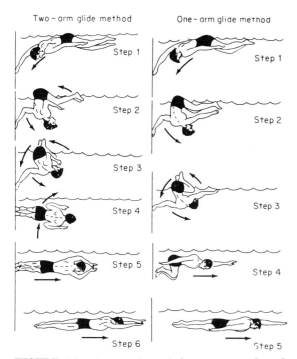

FIGURE 9-2    *A comparison of the two-arm glide and
one-arm glide methods. (*Source: *Raphael J. Scharf, &
William H. King. Time and motion analysis of competitive freestyle swimming turns.* Research Quarterly,
1964, **35**, 37–44. P. 39.)

They also maintained greater flexibility during a four-week nontraining
period after the three-week program.

The purpose of a thesis by Alseth (1968) was to determine the relationship between ability to perceive hand pressure and speed in the 100-yard
crawl. Ten college swimmers were asked to distinguish among various gram
weights placed on their hands. The two abilities studied were found to be
unrelated.

The need for warmup preceding performance in swimming, as in other
sports, has yet to be fully supported by research findings. In two similar
theses undertaken at Springfield College by Filipponi and Middlebrooks,
the value of warmup was not supported. Filipponi (1951) tested 12 varsity
swimmers in the 100-yard freestyle event. Five trials were given to each
subject with warmup, and five without warmup. No difference in performance times was noted. In Middlebrooks' study (1966), the American crawl,

back crawl, and backstroke were tested in 100-yard and 500-yard events. Twelve college varsity swimmers were divided into three groups. Each subject was tested 10 times (5 with warmup, 5 without warmup) for a particular event. Warmup consisted of practice of the stroke used in the test, and the duration of the warmup was based on the time it usually took to swim that stroke. No differences for any group in any stroke at either distance were determined between "warm" and "cold" trials. In a published study, however, Herbert de Vries (1959) found that swimmers as a group made significantly better times with warmup than without warmup.

### Body Constitution

Swimmers have been body-typed by a few researchers. Using the somatotype method, Cureton (1951) concluded that Olympic swimmers have a mesomorphic (muscular) body build. Swimmers associated with different events can usually be distinguished according to body build (e.g., Hirata, 1966). Researchers have usually found that long-distance swimmers are endo-mesomorphic, that is, have larger fat deposits than short-distance swimmers (e.g., Pugh et al., 1960).

### Personality

It was mentioned above that a number of studies have been done on the personality of the swimmer. Where research shows psychological properties, it mainly concerns personality traits of varsity swimmers as compared with norms, less expert swimmers, or nonswimmers. John Kelso (1967) administered the CPI to 29 college varsity and freshman swimmers. When swimmers were compared with the college norm, they scored lower in responsibility and femininity and higher in communality. A Practices and Attitudes Questionnaire was answered by poorer (nonlettermen) swimmers and better (lettermen) swimmers. No difference in responses was observed.

David Parsons (1963) tested two groups of swimmers, "selected" (to represent Canada on a team) and "nonselected." They were compared with each other as well as with the average population on the 16 personality traits measured by the Cattell Sixteen Personality Factor Questionnaire. The results indicated that there were no significant differences in personality between the selected and nonselected champion swimmers, but the subjects, as a group, showed differences from the average population on 15 of the 16 traits.

Faster and slower competitive swimmers have been the subject of study by Earl Newman (1968). The Thurstone Temperament Schedule, derived from several personality tests, was administered to 21 high school swimmers competing in different events. Each swimmer had been timed throughout the season and ranked accordingly. Correlations[5] were recorded between swimming speed in an event and each of seven personality factors. The following three correlations were determined to be significant (although the highest was only .50): (1) a negative correlation between 100-yard breast stroke performance and the sociable trait; (2) a positive correlation between the dominant trait and 100-yard freestyle ranking; and (3) a negative correlation between the reflective trait and 200-yard freestyle performance. Evidently, faster and slower swimmers can be distinguished by certain personality traits. Although Robert Behrman (1967) did not use varsity-caliber swimmers, he found in a study of college freshmen that a group with low swimming ability could be differentiated on six scales of the Guilford-Zimmerman Temperament Survey from a group with high ability.

Four psychological personality tests were administered by Ogilvie, Tutko, & Young (1965) to 27 United States Olympic swimmers. In a comparison with typical college students, the swimmers were reported to score much higher in need to be the best performer, in need for freedom and self-direction, and in need for attention and acclaim. No difference was found in emotional maturity. When medalist and nonmedalist Olympic swimmers were compared, no significant trait differences were determined, but trends were discussed.

Ogilvie (1967) has made some general statements about teen-age swimmers and personality changes, with special attention to female competitors. In a more sophisticated article (1968), he describes longitudinal data collected on swimmers as well as related research findings. He feels there is sufficient evidence to show that emotional stability comes with competition and age. Other personality traits are also related to swimming competition and achievement.

Brent Rushall (1968) has also investigated the relationship between personality factors and physical performance, and his data are in contrast with Ogilvie's findings. His University of Indiana swimmers displayed a wide range of scores on all personality traits, and he also reports that over a three-year period, no changes in personality were exhibited.

Possible trends in personality and social dimension of competitors were analyzed by Hendry & Whiting (1968). Two different groups composed of boys and girls in the age range from 13 to 16 were compared. Data were collected on one group in 1964 and on the other group in 1967. Both groups

[5] A significant positive correlation indicates that a high score on a personality trait was associated with better swimming performance, and vice versa. A significant negative correlation indicates that a low score on a personality trait was associated with poorer swimming performance, and vice versa.

were selected by performance standards, as set by the Amateur Swimming Association in England. The 1967 group had a significantly lower mean age, showed a marked increase in the number of weekly training hours, and demonstrated a severe anxiety symptom, nail biting. The 1964 group contained 37 percent nail-biters, whereas the 1967 group contained 83 persistent nail-biters. Hendry & Whiting conclude:

> The overall picture which emerges of these young swimmers is that of excessive involvement in a sub-culture of competitive sport such that a majority of the time and interest is devoted to physical achievement and personal attainment, leaving little time for other adolescent interests. The young competitive swimmer's life would appear to be one of school, swimming training, competitive sport and sleep! [p. 202]

Anxiety level and swimming performance have been investigated by James Lampman (1967), who administered the IPAT-8 Parallel Form Anxiety Battery test to 15 university varsity swimmers first in a noncompetitive situation and then one hour before each of six meets. Premeet anxiety and percentage of improvement over the season were negatively related. No difference in anxiety level and performance were noted between champion and nonchampion swimmers. There was some indication, though, that less anxious subjects, as determined in noncompetitive situations, do better in performance if their premeet anxiety is also low.

The relationship between coach and swimmer was analyzed by Hendry (1968), by testing 126 swimmers and 56 coaches on the Cattell Sixteen Personality Factor Questionnaire in order to measure their personality traits objectively. The coaches and swimmers then made subjective ratings of each other. The coaches were able to assess the swimmers more effectively and correctly than the swimmers were able to assess the coaches.

## TENNIS

The strokes of champion tennis players have been analyzed kinesiologically and cinematographically, but few psychological studies have been done of high-caliber tennis athletes. McAdams (1964) used women subjects in a study of tennis skill with the use of rebound nets; 56 beginners, 36 intermediates, and 4 varsity players were tested with the rebound net at varied times and distances from the net. Data from round-robin tournaments served as the criterion. The 20-foot distance, 30-second test proved to be the most valid test, correlated against the criterion.

Marvin Gold (1955) found that college varsity and professional players tended to score similarly on personality tests. The athletes ranked fairly high on desirable personality traits as compared with the normal population. Edward Olson (1966) interviewed 12 nationally known tennis players and studied their personalities in various ways. Certain characteristics seemed typical of the outstanding athletes: they were (1) intense and serious; (2) inner-directed; (3) usually deeply depressed after a loss but greatly exhilarated after a win; (4) not very much aware of crowds; and (5) constantly practicing—they never had "to take a break."

Michael Malmisur (1966) undertook a study to find the relationship between certain physical characteristics and success in tennis among Junior Davis Cup players. The test items were reaction time and movement time, dynamic balance, depth perception, height, weight, speed in the 50-yard dash, agility, arm-shoulder coordination and strength as measured by a softball throw for distance, and tennis ability as measured by the Dyer Backboard Test. There was no apparent association between these items and tennis success, which was determined by national rankings, tournament placements, and ability as indicated by judges' ratings. Evidently, the various physical attributes measured in this study cannot be used to differentiate among superb tennis athletes.

## TRACK AND FIELD

The literature on the relationship of psychology to track and field is sparse. As with swimming, much more research has been undertaken on physiology, kinesiology, and anatomy. A good article generally showing the role psychology plays in track performance has been written by Epskamp (1962), and aspects of motivation and competitiveness in track, already discussed in Chapter 7, are presented by Ryan (1958). Further information on motivation in track and field has been compiled by Harold Harris (1962).

With regard to motivation, Timmons (1965) has suggested a technique to be used in distance track or cross-country practice. Timmons advocates having the athlete run a golf course from tee to green, in order to establish his par. In additional runs, the athlete is to try to break par. Possible methods of scoring are offered by Timmons, who states that the plan can be modified in many ways.

### Training Techniques

Erikson (1967) has surveyed track coaches to discover what techniques they use in training shot putters, and Briedwell (1967) has analyzed questionnaire data received from 68 Texas high school coaches about the techniques they use in training track athletes. Bobby Fries (1963) has suggested methods for coaching track and field in high school.

Methods of starting and finishing a race have been studied, for any slight advantage might make the difference between winning and losing. Lloyd Kolker (1968) compared the effects of vertical starting blocks and conventional blocks on performance times in a study of members of the track teams of South Dakota State University. After training programs had been conducted, Kolker found that vertical starting blocks produced a significant improvement in both starting time and performance time. Carl Myllymaki (1966) compared five methods of sprint finishes: lean, dip, lunge, shrug, and run-through. Nine college sprinters were timed after a one-week instruction period for each finish. No differences in times were observed.

The use of handweights to improve sprinting speed has been investigated by McCullough (1966). Three groups of subjects were formed: (1) one group was trained in a sprint program, (2) another group was trained with three-pound weights in the hand-wrist area, and (3) a control group received no training. No differences in improvement were noted between the groups.

In studying the effects of warmup on performance, Myers (1967) had Springfield College team members throw the hammer 108 times after each of these conditions: heavy warmup, light warmup, and no warmup. No performance dissimilarities were found as a result of varying intensities of informal warmup. However, a smaller number of fouls did occur after light warmup.

*Personality*

The personality of the track athlete has been studied by a few researchers. James Crakes (1960), in research for his doctoral dissertation, administered the California Psychological Inventory, the EPPS, and a Rorschach test to 11 distance runners. Two categories of mile runners were formed: one containing athletes with times of 4 minutes 17 seconds or lower; the other with athletes with times of 4 minutes 18 seconds or higher. When the data from the three personality tests were analyzed, differences in various traits were found between the two groups.

Elliot Baker (1966) classified college middle- and long-distance runners according to various criteria and tested their personalities with the EPPS. The classifications formed were related to performance times within ability: high or low aspirations, arrived at on the basis of the differences between the runners' own predictions and their actual times; and performance under

competitive stress. A relationship was found between competitive performance in running and intraception, succorance, dominance, and change. A
higher level of aspiration was related to autonomy, intraception, nurturance,
endurance, and aggression. Baker concludes:

> There is evidence that middle and long distance runners deviate on some
> personality traits from the college student means published in the Edwards
> Personal Preference Schedule Manual.
> Evidence indicates that several personality traits may have an effect on how
> well an individual will compete, how high he will aspire, and how he will react
> to a competitive situation in the middle or long distance event with runners of
> comparable ability [p. 51].

Arthur Miller (1960) has undertaken an interesting research project on
the relationship of competition and emotional stress, using 44 high school
track and field athletes as subjects. Based on performance at six meets, each
athlete was classified as an outstanding, average, or poor competitor.
Measurements taken on the athletes before each meet and compared with
controls included meet score, reported self-confidence, pulse, respiration
rate, and palmar perspiration. Miller concludes that some form of emotional
stress exists in connection with competition. Significant self-confidence ratings and palmar perspiration measurements reflected the existence of stress
on meet days as compared to nonmeet days. It was found that a high level
of confidence leads to good performance. With regard to difficult and less
difficult meets, the only change noted was that average competitors felt
more confident before less difficult meets. Finally, a significant relationship
was observed between degree of confidence and the physiological measures.

## VOLLEYBALL

Although a number of studies have included students in volleyball classes,
the high-caliber volleyball athlete has not been the subject of intense investigation. Bushman (1963) used film analyses to determine the most desirable
speed and height of an excellent overhand flat volleyball serve as judged by
a board of experts and as tested by the ability of an opposing team to return
the serve. The most difficult serve to return was the one that traveled low
to the net and with maximum speed but stayed in bounds.
    Slaymaker (1966) classified 32 volleyball players into three levels of com-
petition, and placed them in corresponding groups. In an attempt to determine group differences, the players were tested on various physical and performance factors: reaction time, movement time, grip strength, leg power,

height, wrist flexibility, and agility. The highest-caliber group of volleyball players were significantly better than the other two groups in vertical jump and right-hand grip strength. The first two groups, which were made up of tournament players, scored higher on most measures than the last group, which was composed of college volleyball class members.

Clarena Bakker. (1968) used college women volleyball players in a study to determine the relationship between degree of success in volleyball and certain physical, motor, and anthropometrical factors. Twenty-eight players were rated on playing ability, and variables were correlated with this criterion score. Significant correlations were obtained between reaction time and the criterion, and between jumping ability and the criterion. Reaction time and jumping ability together correlated .53 with playing ability. All variables combined, including height, weight, jumping ability, reaction time, movement time, grip strength, strength of the extensors of both legs, and skinfold measurements, correlated .73 with the criterion.

## WRESTLING[6]

### *Body Constitution*

There seems to be a popular image of the wrestler's physique: a huge chest and bulging muscles. Walter Kroll (1954) tested 35 varsity wrestlers from four Big Ten universities. He found that they had a mean somatotype of 3-5-4 and a reciprocal ponderal index (RPI) of 12.9. The mean RPI for young American males is 13.0, an indication that the wrestlers in the study were similar to the average young American male. In somatotype the wrestlers had a good balance among the ectomorph, mesomorph, and endomorph classifications. The wrestlers were much more agile than many people imagine, rather than being ponderous.

Meyer (1945) examined freshman wrestlers at the University of Michigan and found a mean RPI of 12.6. Russel Bush (1950) supported the findings of Kroll and Meyer. He evaluated 50 competitors in the 1950 NCAA wrestling tournament and noted a mean RPI of 12.57. These studies indicate that successful wrestlers have no particular or special build.

Quick reactions and movements have always been considered to be an integral part of the success of any wrestler. Rasch, Pierson, O'Connell, & Hunt (1961) investigated the response time of amateur wrestlers. They

---

[6] For a thorough report on all research related to wrestling, the following source is recommended: Phillip J. Rasch & Walter Kroll. *What research tells the coach about wrestling.* Washington, D.C.: American Association for Health, Physical Education, and Recreation, 1964.

tested nonathletes, college wrestlers, outstanding Amateur Athletic Union wrestlers, and the Japanese Amateur Wrestling Association team, and found that the groups did not differ in reaction time or movement time. Ken Reed (1963) administered speed-of-movement tests to high school wrestlers before and after the season. There was no significant difference between the initial and final scores, and there was no significant relationship between the results and wrestling success. These studies seem to indicate that quick reactions are not necessary to the success of a wrestler. However, there is a possibility that the movements tested may not be related to the movements used in wrestling.

## Predicting Wrestling Ability

Sievers (1934), in a very early study, tried to measure potential wrestling ability. He tested 30 high school wrestlers who were also subjectively rated according to wrestling ability. The Sargent jump, a breath-holding test, a test of applied forces, and a "switch" test were of little value in estimating ability, but the Athletic Index, a sustained grip test, and a front and back leaning rest test gave a better estimate of ability when compared with subjective ratings.

In a more recent study, Bremner (1964) also attempted to measure wrestling ability. The subjects were 30 college wrestlers, and their wrestling ability was evaluated by coaches on an 80-point scale. Various tests, including the Sievers Test of Potential Wrestling Ability and measures of balance and reaction time, were administered. The Sievers test correlated a rather low .37 with ratings of wrestling ability. The best multiple correlation (.68) was obtained from the following tests: a dipping test, the Bass Stick Test (balance), and a balanciometer (balance) test. This correlation indicates a fair degree of success in prediction of potential wrestling ability from such performance tests.

Alan Schultz (1960) investigated the balancing ability of college wrestlers. The wrestlers and matched nonathletes were tested on the Bass Stick Test and the Bass Test of Dynamic Balance. The wrestlers did not perform significantly better than the nonathletes. The study seems to indicate that balance is another factor which cannot be used to predict wrestling ability.

Can factors be identified that are associated with wrestling success? William Yensen's (1963) thesis includes some interesting information related to this problem. Questionnaires were sent to NCAA wrestling champions, and the following are some of the highlights of their responses:

1   They began wrestling because they wanted combative activity and recognition.

*2*  The personal qualities which they believed to be important were balance, perseverance, desire, and determination.

*3*  The average college wrestler was a physical education major with a 2.5 grade-point average out of a possible 4.0.

*4*  Most of them felt that wrestling had helped them to gain their present status.

As to laboratory measures of performance in relation to wrestling success, Kroll (1958) noted the following with 90 Illinois high school varsity wrestlers:

*1*  Two response-time measures of actual takedown maneuvers were not related to competitive initial takedown ability as calculated in 1,029 individual matches and 815 initial takedowns.

*2*  The Four-Item Proportional Strength Test/Body Weight was also not significantly related to the criterion.

*3*  When successful wrestlers were compared with unsuccessful wrestlers, the former were significantly better than the latter in the following measures: (a) right-hand grip strength; (b) left-hand grip strength, and (c) back lift strength.

*4*  Successful wrestlers secured the initial takedown 70 percent of the time and lost it 9 percent of the time. Unsuccessful wrestlers gained the first takedown 38 percent of the time and lost it 37 percent of the time. In the remaining percentage of the time, no takedowns took place.

Kroll concludes his study in the following way:

> The results seem to give credence to the feelings of many wrestling coaches who believe that, although strength and speed are naturally desirable in any wrestler, "setting up" an opponent and skillful execution of a continuous series of attempts at take downs are of more importance [p. 405].

Knutzen (1962) devoted his thesis to determining which of two approaches, counter wrestling and aggressive wrestling, was more effective. "Aggressive wrestling" was defined as wrestling in which the first moves were made in the neutral position and the top position. Data from six high school and college wrestling tournaments indicated that the more aggressive wrestlers had the best chance of winning their matches. The wrestlers who made the greater number of aggressive moves from the two positions won 336 and lost 68 matches.

## Personality

Warren Johnson & Daniel Hutton (1955) investigated the effects of wrestling upon personality dynamics. The House-Tree-Person Projective Technique (HTP) was given to eight wrestlers and evaluated by a clinical psychologist. Testing was done three weeks before, four or five hours before, and the morning after an intercollegiate match. The precontest test revealed an increase in aggression directed inward rather than outward toward the environment. The postcontest results indicated a diminished level of undirected aggression, and increased self-assurance replaced feelings of inferiority. Whether the match was won or lost had no effect on personality changes. This study shows that temporary personality changes do take place around the time of the contest.

Along the same lines, Sullivan (1964) conducted a thesis that involved University of Massachusetts varsity and freshman wrestlers. Novice and experienced wrestlers were identified, and the wrestlers' own ratings of how they expected to perform in contest competition were taken three times: the night before the match, at weigh-in time, and 15 minutes before the match. Approach-avoidance data were also collected, at nine intervals of time before the match. These data measured tension, and whether the athlete was looking forward to competition or fearing it. In general, anticipation of wrestling affected novices and experienced wrestlers differently, and differences in feelings were shown at the various testing times.

Rasch & Hunt (1960) tested 14 United States Olympic wrestlers and concluded that they did not differ appreciably from male freshman norms on masculinity-femininity ratings.

Ten Central Missouri State College wrestlers were analyzed for social and emotional adjustment before and at the end of the wrestling season by Omer Frank (1968). The preseason level of adjustment for the group was borderline, as indicated by the Washburne Social-Adjustment Inventory, and no changes in the traits measured were noted as a result of the season of practice. Kroll (1967) studied 94 amateur and collegiate wrestlers in three groups formed according to level of achievement: (1) a superior group composed of Olympic wrestlers, (2) an excellent group composed of varsity collegiate wrestlers who had won at least 60 percent of their seasonal matches, and (3) an average to below-average group of wrestlers. No differences in personality profiles among the groups were observed. When compared with norms, the wrestlers were found to score higher in tough-mindedness, self-reliance, and masculinity. Kroll states that no support was found for the suggestion that wrestlers may possess a neurotic profile. This is in contrast to the findings of Slusher (1964).

In another comparison of groups of wrestlers, Brown (1958) used 79 high school wrestlers. On the basis of coaches' subjective evaluations of competitiveness-aggressiveness, two groups of wrestlers were formed, one considered high and one low in the attribute. All subjects were administered the EPPS. The groups differed on only two of the 15 "needs" or traits measured: the high group scored higher on aggression, as might have been expected, and the low group scored higher on endurance. In this case, "endurance" means persisting at a task, seeing something through to completion. It might have been expected that the high group would demonstrate a greater need to endure than the low group.

Measures of anxiety and match performance were compared by Richard Newman (1967). During one season, 24 high school wrestlers received an anxiety test before each home match, and their wrestling performances were evaluated by a panel of three wrestling judges. No relationship existed between anxiety, as measured by an IPAT (Institute for Personality and Ability Testing) test, and match performance, as determined by the judges' evaluations. The anxiety measures were therefore not useful in predicting wrestling performance.

REFERENCES

*Baseball*

Adams, Gary. The effect of eye dominance on baseball batting. Unpublished master's thesis, University of California, Los Angeles, 1964.

Bagg, Ewart J. Effect of mental and physical practice on baseball batting. Unpublished master's thesis, University of California, Los Angeles, 1966.

Bates, Frank H. Relationship of hand and eye coordination to accuracy in baseball batting. Unpublished master's thesis, University of Iowa, 1948.

Blank, Robert G. A study of the use of three targets for improving control in baseball pitching. Unpublished master's thesis, Washington State University, 1966.

Brose, Donald E. The effect of overload training on the velocity and accuracy of baseball throwing. Unpublished master's thesis, University of Maryland, 1964.

Burpee, R., & Stroll, W. Measuring reaction time of athletes. *Research Quarterly,* 1936, **7**, 110–118.

Deese, D. W. The effect of weight training on batting movement time. Unpublished master's thesis, University of Illinois, 1962.

Everett, Peter W. The prediction of baseball ability. *Research Quarterly,* 1952, **23**, 15–19.

Gellinger, Terrence J. The effect of blindfolded and instructed practice on pitching control. Unpublished master's thesis, University of Illinois, 1965.

Herman, Leslie A. The effect of three baseball batting stances upon reaction and movement times. Unpublished master's thesis, Illinois State University, 1968.

Hubbard, Alfred W., & Seng, C. N. Visual movements of batters, *Research Quarterly,* 1954, **25**, 42–57.

Imlay, Robert D. The physiques of college baseball players in San Diego, California. Unpublished master's thesis, San Diego State College, 1966.

Kelson, Robert E. Baseball classification plan for boys. *Research Quarterly*, 1953, **24**, 304–307.

Lande, Leon. What causes hitting errors? *Athletic Journal*, 1968, **58**, 66, 86.

La Place, John P. Personality and its relationship to success in professional baseball. *Research Quarterly*, 1954, **25**, 313–319.

Logan, Gene A., McKinney, Wayne C., Rowe, William, Jr., & Lumpe, Jerry. Effect of resistance through a throwing range-of-motion on the velocity of a baseball. *Perceptual and Motor Skills*, 1966, **23**, 55–58.

Ness, Richard A. Determination of the relationship between baseball hitting success and the Nelson Reaction Timer. Unpublished master's thesis, University of Illinois, 1967.

Seymour, Emery W. Comparative study of certain behavior characteristics of participant and non-participant boys in Little League baseball. *Research Quarterly*, 1956, **27**, 338–346.

Singer, Robert N. Personality differences between and within baseball and tennis players. *Research Quarterly*, 1969, **40**, 582–588.

Skubic, Elvera. Studies of Little League and Middle League baseball. *Research Quarterly*, 1956, **27**, 97–110.

Slater-Hammel, A. T., & Stumpner, R. L. Batting reaction-time. *Research Quarterly*, 1951, **21**, 353–356.

Trenbeath, William. A comparison of reaction time changes in freshman baseball players elicited by practice with the variable speed rotating pitching machine. Unpublished master's thesis, University of North Dakota, 1966.

Van Huss, W. D., Albrecht, L., Nelson R., & Hagerman, R. Effect of overload warm-up on the velocity and accuracy of throwing. *Research Quarterly*, 1962, **33**, 472–475.

Watkins, David L. Motion pictures as an aid in correcting baseball batting faults. *Research Quarterly*, 1963, **34**, 228–233.

Weiskopf, D. Batting styles of world champions. *Athletic Journal*, 1960, **40**, 8–13.

Wertich, Harold G., Jr. The velocity of the baseball batting swing as affected by the addition of a select resistance exercise to a traditional pre-season weight training program. Unpublished master's thesis, South Dakota State University, 1967.

*Basketball*

Anderson, Kenneth A. The effect of the weighted ankle spat on the jumping performance, agility, and endurance of high school basketball players. Unpublished master's thesis, University of Wisconsin, 1961.

Arietta, Ralph J. Defensive positioning for rebounding free throws. Unpublished master's thesis, Springfield College, 1967.

Boyd, Clifford, McCachren, James, & Waglow, T. F. Predictive ability of a selected basketball test. *Research Quarterly*, 1955, **26**, 364.

Brassie, Paul Stanley. Effectiveness of intermittent and consecutive methods of practicing free throws. Unpublished master's thesis, State University of Iowa, 1965.

Brees, Clifford D. The effects of trampoline training upon the jumping performance, agility, running speed, and endurance of high school basketball players. Unpublished master's thesis, University of Wisconsin, 1961.

Brendice, Frederick A. Effect of skill performance on game outcome in basketball. Unpublished master's thesis, Springfield College, 1965.

Chaloupecky, Robert. A comparison of basketball shooting skill at a ten-foot and eleven-foot basket. Unpublished master's thesis, Illinois State University, 1967.

Fisher, Edward S. A comparison of the conventional and zone systems of basketball scoring. Unpublished master's thesis, University of Washington, 1961.

Fisk, Timothy. Development of basketball shooting accuracy as affected by varying goal sizes. Unpublished master's thesis, South Dakota State University, 1967.

Frank, Omer V. A comparison of the social and emotional adjustment of basketball players and wrestlers. Unpublished master's thesis, Central Missouri State College, 1968.

Garretson, Rodney R. An analysis of selected basketball skills by coaches of the institutions of higher learning of the Pacific Northwest. Unpublished master's thesis, University of Washington, 1962.

Genzmer, Dave E. The effect of three systematic weight training methods on the jumping ability of high school basketball players. Unpublished master's thesis, University of Wisconsin, 1960.

Gephart, Gene C. The relative effect of blindfold, sighted and no practice on free throw accuracy. Unpublished master's thesis, University of Illinois, 1954.

Guerin, William T. A study to determine the effects of extraneous visual cues on the accuracy of shooting a basketball. Unpublished master's thesis, Eastern Illinois University, 1966.

Havel, Richard C. Personality variables of college basketball players, *Proceedings of the National College Physical Education Association for Men*, 1959, **62**, 10–14.

Howell, William T. The influence of ankle weights on jumping height of high school basketball players. Unpublished master's thesis, Drake University, 1967.

Kay, H. Kenner. A statistical analysis of the profile technique for the evaluation of competitive basketball performance. Unpublished master's thesis, University of Alberta, 1966.

Kinser, Jay. The effect of practicing with varied weights of basketballs on free throw skills. Unpublished master's thesis, Southwest Missouri State College, 1966.

Kite, Joseph. The effects of variations in target size and two methods of practice on the development of accuracy in a motor skill. Unpublished doctoral dissertation, Louisiana State University, 1964.

Knox, Robert D. Basketball ability tests. *Scholastic Coach*, 1947, **17**, 45.

Larson, Edgar D. Emotional responses of basketball players. Unpublished doctoral dissertation, University of Oregon, 1966.

Lindeburg, Franklin A., & Hewitt, Jack E. Effect of an oversized basketball on shooting ability and ball handling. *Research Quarterly*, 1965, **36**, 164–167.

Lukas, Wayne. The effect of a weighted training shoe on the jumping performance, agility, running speed, and endurance of college basketball players. Unpublished master's thesis, University of Wisconsin, 1960.

Lutes, Warren C. A study to determine the best locations for obtaining rebounds. Unpublished master's thesis, Springfield College, 1961.

Maaske, Paul W. The effect of the practice of shooting at small baskets on the accuracy of shooting in basketball. Unpublished master's thesis, State University of Iowa, 1960.

McGinnis, George. Screening for basketball aptitude. *Scholastic Coach*, 1955, **25**, 44–47.

Mack, Arthur E. The relationship of selected traits to basketball success. Unpublished master's thesis, University of Massachusetts, 1964.

Minahan, Fred B. An experiment with a restrictive goal device designated to improve basketball free throw shooting accuracy of ninth grade boys. Unpublished master's thesis, University of Washington, 1963.

Nelson, Dale O. Leadership in sports. *Research Quarterly*, 1966, **37**, 268–275.

Patty, Elbert K. The relationship of selected measurable traits to success in basketball. Unpublished doctoral dissertation, Indiana University, 1953.

Scanlon, William M. A study to determine the results of focusing attention on a point of reference in basketball field goal shooting. Unpublished master's thesis, Springfield College, 1968.

Selk, Larry. A comparison of different methods of free-throwing practice among selected high school basketball players in North Dakota and Minnesota with respect to accuracy in games. Unpublished master's thesis, University of North Dakota, 1966.

Sell, Veryl L. Use of fifteen-inch goal in development of shooting accuracy in basketball (high school). Unpublished master's thesis, State University of Iowa, 1963.

Sills, Frank, & Troutman, Donald. Peripheral vision and accuracy in shooting a basketball. *Proceedings of the National College Physical Education Association for Men*, 1966, **69**, 112–114.

Stotts, James. Height as related to the success of basketball players. Unpublished master's thesis, University of Kansas, 1967.

Stroup, Francis. Game results as a criterion for validating basketball skill test. *Research Quarterly*, 1955, **26**, 353–357.

Stroup, Francis. Relationship between measurements of field of motion perception and basketball ability in college men. *Research Quarterly*, 1957, **28**, 72–76.

Swartzendruber, Lowell. A comparison of physical and mental-physical practice on the performance of basketball shooting. Unpublished master's thesis, Pennsylvania State University, 1965.

Takacs, Robert. A comparison of the effect of two methods of practice on basketball free throw shooting. Unpublished master's thesis, Arkansas State College, 1965.

Thompson, Hugh. Effect of warm-up upon physical performance in selected activities. *Research Quarterly*, 1958, **29**, 231–246.

Vizard, Thomas C. The effects of increased emotional pressure on foul-shooting performance in college and high school basketball tournaments. Unpublished master's thesis, University of Massachusetts, 1967.

Warnock, Ronald H. A comparative analysis between two methods of executing a center jump in basketball. Unpublished master's thesis, Washington State University, 1960.

*Football*

Bend, Elmer. *The impact of athletic participation on academic and career aspiration and achievement.* New Brunswick, N.J.: National Football Foundation, 1968.

Carder, Brent. The relationship between manifest anxiety and performance in college football. Unpublished master's thesis, University of California, 1965.

Cassel, Russel, & Childers, Richard. A study of certain attributes of 45 high-school varsity football team members by use of psychological test scores. *Journal of Educational Research,* 1963, **57**, 64–67.

Cowell, C. C., & Ismail, A. H. Validity of a football rating scale and its relationship to social integration and academic ability. *Research Quarterly,* 1961, **32**, 461–467.

Damron, D. Frazier. Second and third dimensional slide images used with tachistoscopic training techniques in instructing high school football players in defenses. *Research Quarterly,* 1955, **26**, 36–43.

Dupont, Jim. Programmed learning in the athletic program. *Athletic Journal,* 1966, **46**, 62, 91.

Finn, Edward P. Reaction and response time of football players as affected by an audible change of play. Unpublished master's thesis. South Dakota State University, 1968.

Hopek, Richard. Effect of overload on the accuracy of throwing a football. Unpublished master's thesis, Eastern Illinois University, 1967.

Johnson, Clarence. Personality traits affected by high school football as measured by the Guilford-Zimmerman Temperament Survey. Unpublished doctoral dissertation, University of Arkansas, 1966.

Kroll, Walter, & Petersen, Kay H. Personality factor profiles of collegiate football teams. *Research Quarterly,* 1965, **36**, 433–440. (a)

Kroll, Walter, & Petersen, Kay H. Study of values test and collegiate football teams. *Research Quarterly,* 1965, **36**, 441–447. (b)

Littlefield, Donald H. Comparison between college football players and non-participants on selected psychological characteristics. Unpublished master's thesis, Texas Technological College, 1967.

Londeree, Ben R. Effect of training with motion pictures versus flash cards upon football play recognition. *Research Quarterly,* 1967, **38**, 202–207.

Mikszewski, John C. A comparison of direction and distance on the accuracy of roll-out passing. Unpublished master's thesis, Springfield College, 1968.

Mudra, Darrell E. The critical analysis of football coaching practices in the light of a selected group of learning principles. Unpublished doctoral dissertation, Colorado State College, 1965.

Rinne, James L. A descriptive study of the aggressive attitudes of high school football players as compared to the aggressive attitudes of non-participating students. Unpublished master's thesis, Sacramento State College, 1968.

Rowan, Vic. Psychological gimmicks in coaching football. *Scholastic Coach,* 1967, **37**, 62.

Rushall, Brent S. The demonstration and evaluation of a research model for the investigation of the relationship between personality and physical performance categories. Unpublished doctoral dissertation, Indiana University, 1968.

Schroeder, John R. A comparison of reaction times of football players to two types of audible starting signals. Unpublished master's thesis, University of Massachusetts, 1966.

Seely, Doyle G. An inventory of motivational factors among selected All-American football players. Unpublished master's thesis, Brigham Young University, 1964.

Sigerseth, Peter, & Haleski, Chester C. The flexibility of football players. *Research Quarterly*, 1950, **21**, 394–398.

Thompson, Clem W., Nagle, Francis J., & Dobias, Robert. Football starting signals and movement times of high school and college football players. *Research Quarterly*, 1958, **29**, 222–230.

Wilhelm, Arnold W. The relationship of certain measurable traits to success in football. Unpublished doctoral dissertation, Indiana University, 1951.

*Golf*

Gold, Marvin. A comparison of personality characteristics of professional and college varsity tennis and golf players as measured by the Guilford-Martin Personality Inventory. Unpublished master's thesis, University of Maryland, 1955.

Griffith, Coleman. An experiment of learning to drive a golf ball. *Athletic Journal*, 1931, **10**, 11.

Wiren, Gary. Human factors influencing the golf drive for distance. Paper presented at the annual convention of the American Association for Health, Physical Education and Recreation, Boston, Mass., 1969.

*Gymnastics*

Bosco, James. The physical and personality characteristics of champion male gymnasts. *Proceedings of the National College Physical Education Association for Men*, 1962, **66**, 66–72.

Brennan, Mary Alice. A comparative study of skilled gymnasts and dancers on 13 selected characteristics. Unpublished master's thesis, University of Wisconsin, 1967.

Kjeldsen, Eric. A study to determine the relationship between the Edwards Personal Preference Schedule and participation in gymnastics. Unpublished master's thesis, Springfield College, 1961.

Knapp, Joann. Emotional reactions of college women gymnasts as a function of time to competition. Unpublished master's thesis, University of Massachusetts, 1966.

Wettstone, Eugene. Tests for predicting potential ability in gymnastics and tumbling. *Research Quarterly*, 1938, **9**, 115–125.

Williams, Edward C. Relationship of certain body proportions to success in the sport of gymnastics. Unpublished master's thesis, Pennsylvania State University, 1963.

*Judo*

Min, Kyung-Ho. Correlations among factors in judo contest performance. *Perceptual and Motor Skills*, 1967, **24**, 1243–1248.

*Karate*

Kroll, Walter, & Carlson, B. Robert. Discriminant function and hierarchal analysis of karate participants' personality profiles. *Research Quarterly*, 1967, **38**, 405–411.

*Swimming*

Alseth, Alfred R. Pressure perception ability as related to athletic performance in swimming the crawl stroke. Unpublished master's thesis, Washington State University, 1968.

Behrman, Robert M. Personality differences between nonswimmers and swimmers. *Research Quarterly*, 1967, **38**, 163–171.

Constantine, T. The effect of lane width and depth on the speed of swimming. *Swimming Pool Age*, 1961, **35**, 40.

Cureton, Thomas K. *Physical fitness of champion athletes*. Urbana, Ill.: University of Illinois Press, 1951.

de Vries, Herbert. Effects of various warm-up procedures on 100-yard time of competitive swimmers. *Research Quarterly*, 1959, **30**, 11–20.

Filipponi, Mervyn L. The effect of warming-up upon speed of swimming 100 yards. Unpublished master's thesis, Springfield College, 1951.

Hamilton, Larry M. A comparison between the effects of resistance and nonresistance training on varsity competitive swimmers. Unpublished master's thesis, Central Missouri State College, 1967.

Hendry, L. B. Assessment of personality traits in the coach-swimmer relationship and a preliminary examination of the father-figure stereotype. *Research Quarterly*, 1968, **39**, 543–551.

Hendry, L. B., & Whiting, H. T. A. Social and psychological trends in national championship calibre Junior Swimmers: a three-year replication study. *Journal of Sports Medicine and Physical Fitness*, 1968, **8**, 198–203.

Hirata, Kin-Itsu. Physique and age of Tokyo Olympic champions. *Journal of Sports Medicine and Physical Fitness*, 1966, **6**, 207–222.

Jacobson, Richard Lee. An experimental study of flexibility and its retention in competitive swimmers. Unpublished master's thesis, University of California, Los Angeles, 1967.

Kelso, John G. A study of the personality characteristics and the practices and attitudes of college varsity and freshman swimming team members. Unpublished master's thesis, University of Oregon, 1967.

King, William H. A time and motion study of competitive backstroke swimming turns. *Research Quarterly*, 1957, **28**, 257–268.

Lampman, James J. Anxiety and its effects on the performance of competitive swimmers. Unpublished master's thesis, University of Florida, 1967.

Lawrence, Lee W. Practices in conditioning of competitive swimmers. Unpublished master's thesis, Springfield College, 1965.

Middlebrooks, Gwendolyn H. The effect of warming-up upon swimming performance. Unpublished master's thesis, Springfield College, 1966.

Mowerson, G. R., McAdam, Robert E., & O'Brien, Ronald. Comparison of two
methods of performing the racing start in competitive swimming. *Swimming
World,* 1964, **5**, 4.

Newman, Earl N. Personality traits of faster and slower competitive swimmers.
*Research Quarterly,* 1968, **39**, 1049–1053.

Ogilvie, Bruce C. What is an athlete? *Journal of Health, Physical Education, and
Recreation,* 1967, **38**, 48.

Ogilvie, Bruce C. Psychological consistencies within the personality of high-level
competitors. *Journal of the American Medical Association,* 1968, **205**, 156–162.

Ogilvie, Bruce C., Tutko, T. A., & Young, Irving. The psychological profile of
Olympic champions. In Antonelli, F. (Ed.), *Proceedings of the 1st International
Congress of Sports Psychology,* 1965, pp. 201–203.

Parsons, David R. Personality traits of national representative swimmers—Canada,
1962. Unpublished master's thesis, University of British Columbia, 1963.

Pugh, L. G. C., et al. A physiological study of channel swimming. *Clinical Science,*
1960, **19**, 257–273.

Rushall, Brent S. An evaluation of the relationship between personality and
physical performance categories. Paper presented at the 2d International Congress of Sports Psychology, Washington, D.C., 1968.

Scharf, Raphael J., & King, William H. Time and motion analysis of competitive
freestyle swimming turns. *Research Quarterly,* 1964, **35**, 37–44.

Schiesel, Michael L. An analysis of competitive free-style swimming turns. Unpublished master's thesis, University of California, 1966.

*Tennis*

Gold, Marvin. A comparison of personality characteristics of professional and college varsity tennis and golf players as measured by the Guilford-Martin Personality Inventory. Unpublished master's thesis, University of Maryland, 1955.

McAdams, Linda Butler. The use of rebound nets as a means of determining
tennis skill. Unpublished master's thesis, Washington State University, 1964.

Malmisur, Michael. Selected physical characteristics of Junior Davis Cup players
and their relation to success in tennis. Unpublished doctoral dissertation, Ohio
State University, 1966.

Olson, Edward. Identification of personality differences among male tennis champions. Unpublished doctoral dissertation, Ohio State University, 1966.

*Track and Field*

Baker, Elliot. Psychological factors affecting competitive performance in middle
and long distance running. Unpublished master's thesis, Temple University, 1966.

Briedwell, William. A study of present methods used in training participants in the
University of Texas State high school cross country meet. Unpublished master's
thesis, North Texas State University, 1967.

Crakes, James G. The anatomical, physiological, and psychological differences between distance runners of varying abilities. Unpublished doctoral dissertation, University of Oregon, 1960.

Epskamp, Robert. Psychology and the track coach. *Scholastic Coach,* 1962, **31,** 50–51, 56–57.

Erikson, Roger D. An analytical survey of shot putting techniques and training methods utilized by selected collegiate track coaches. Unpublished master's thesis, University of Washington, 1967.

Fries, Bobby Conrad. Methods of organization for coaching high school track and field. Unpublished master's thesis, Fresno State College, 1963.

Harris, Harold E. An analysis of motivation components in track and field. Unpublished master's thesis, University of Illinois, 1962.

Kolker, Lloyd L. The new vertical starting block and its effect on sprint starting time. Unpublished master's thesis, South Dakota State University, 1968.

McCullough, James. The effect of handweights in starting practice on speed of sprinters. Unpublished master's thesis, University of North Dakota, 1966.

Miller, Leonard Arthur. The effect of emotional stress on high school track and field performance. Unpublished master's thesis, University of California, 1960.

Myers, Douglas G. The effects of varied intensities of informal warm-up upon performance in throwing the hammer. Unpublished master's thesis, Springfield College, 1967.

Myllymaki, Carl W. A study to compare five methods of sprint finishes. Unpublished master's thesis, Springfield College, 1966.

Ryan, Francis J. An investigation of personality differences associated with competitive ability in athletics. In Wedge, B. M. (Ed.), *Psychosocial problems of college men.* New Haven: Yale University Press, 1958.

Timmons, Bob. Running golf. *Athletic Journal,* 1965, **46,** 38.

*Volleyball*

Bakker, Clarena K. Factors associated with success in volleyball. Unpublished master's thesis, Illinois State University, 1968.

Bushman, Ben Robert. Analysis of the speed and height of the overhand flat volleyball serve. Unpublished master's thesis, University of Utah, 1963.

Slaymaker, Thomas E. A comparison of selected physical characteristics of volleyball players at three levels of competition, including national championship participants, regional tournament participants, and college activity class participants. Unpublished doctoral dissertation, Colorado State College, 1966.

*Wrestling*

Bremner, J. Barron. Measurement of potential wrestling ability. Unpublished master's thesis, University of Iowa, 1964.

Brown, Edward A. Personality characteristics of wrestlers. Unpublished master's thesis, University of Minnesota, 1958.

Bush, Russel L. A study of the relationships between anthropometric measurements and wrestling maneuvers. Unpublished master's thesis, Purdue University, 1950.

Frank, Omer V. A comparison of the social and emotional adjustment of basketball players and wrestlers. Unpublished master's thesis, Central Missouri State College, 1968.

Johnson, Warren R., & Hutton, Daniel C. Effects of combative sports upon personality dynamics as measured by a projective test. *Research Quarterly*, 1955, **26**, 49–53.

Knutzen, Gary H. The role of aggressiveness in wrestling. Unpublished master's thesis, University of Illinois, 1962.

Kroll, Walter. An anthropometrical study of some Big Ten varsity wrestlers. *Research Quarterly*, 1954, **25**, 307–312.

Kroll, Walter. Selected factors associated with wrestling success. *Research Quarterly*, 1958, **29**, 396–406.

Kroll, Walter. Sixteen personality factor profiles of collegiate wrestlers. *Research Quarterly*, 1967, **38**, 49–57.

Meyer, Herbert H. Anthropometry of athletes. Unpublished master's thesis, University of Michigan, 1945.

Newman, Richard E. A comparison of the anxiety measures and match performance evaluations of high school wrestlers. Unpublished master's thesis, South Dakota State University, 1967.

Rasch, Philip J., & Hunt, M. Briggs. Some personality attributes of champion amateur wrestlers. *Journal of the Association for Physical and Mental Rehabilitation*, 1960, **14**, 163–164.

Rasch, Philip J., Pierson, William R., O'Connell, Eugene R., & Hunt, M. Briggs. Response time of amateur wrestlers. *Research Quarterly*, 1961, **32**, 416–418.

Reed, Kenneth L. Speed-of-movement tests as measures of wrestling ability (high-school wrestlers). Unpublished master's thesis, State University of Iowa, 1963.

Schultz, Alan E. The effect of a wrestling program on balance in college physical education classes and amongst members of a college wrestling squad. Unpublished master's thesis, South Dakota State College, 1960.

Sievers, Harry L. The measurement of potential wrestling ability. Unpublished master's thesis, State University of Iowa, 1934.

Slusher, Howard S. Personality and intelligence characteristics of selected high school athletes and nonathletes. *Research Quarterly*, 1964, **35**, 539–545.

Sperling, Abraham P. The relationship between personality adjustment and achievement in physical education activities. *Research Quarterly*, 1942, **13**, 351–363.

Sullivan, Edward. Emotional reactions and grip strength in college wrestlers as a function of time to competition. Unpublished master's thesis, University of Massachusetts, 1964.

Yensen, William Arthur. An investigation of factors that contributed to the success of NCAA wrestling champions. Unpublished master's thesis, San Diego State College, 1963.

CHAPTER TEN

# The Coach

In this brief final chapter, a few additional roles of the coach will be identified. The many and varied responsibilities of the coach in the application of aspects of psychology to sport and athletes have been pointed out on previous pages. Many of these functions could, of course, be executed by the athlete without the guidance of the coach. The well-educated, mature athlete is sometimes able to apply principles of psychology to his own training regimen. But the coach must still tie it all together, mold the team into a cohesive, optimally functioning unit. His personal professional commitment to specified objectives demands that he continue to acquire knowledge of the scientific underpinnings of sport.

The reader is well aware by now that "psychology of sport," as used in its fullest sense, encompasses many interrelationships among the coach, the athlete, and the sport. Although psychology may be applied in common-sense ways, it is also useful for its research support. Ideally, the coach should make decisions on the basis of scientific logic and good judgment. If he does so, he becomes the core of the functioning unit. If he is to shape winning teams, outstanding skilled athletes, and decent, well-adjusted human beings, his talents must be diverse, relevant, and well received. His effect on his charges, in many ways, is potentially unlimited.

## IMPRESSION ON ATHLETES (FRAME OF REFERENCE)

The many hours which the coach spends with the athlete suggest the potential influence which he may have on the athlete's development. The athlete's development may very well be affected by his feelings toward the coach—e.g., respect, admiration, fear, dissociation. A person's frame of reference, or how something or somebody appears to him, is affected by his perceptions, and in turn affects what he learns.

A frame of reference is a perceptual judgment or attitude about persons, objects, or events, based on comparative information. It is therefore a relative matter. One's view of materials or skills to be learned determines the extent to which they will be acquired and retained. Research shows that people tend to remember best that which supports their social attitudes rather than that which conflicts with them. In sport, if the athlete agrees with the coach's strategy or technique for executing a task, he has a tendency to learn it well. If the athlete likes and respects the coach, he will probably also agree with the coach's suggestions and will consequently learn sports skills at a level that will suit the objectives of the coach. Singer (1968) has elaborated further on the consequences of the athlete's frame of reference:

> If the athlete . . . does not respect the coach . . . or agree with what is being taught, these negative attitudes will suppress learning effectiveness. Many times a person thinks he knows how a skill should be performed, and if he is set in his attitude, his unwillingness to accept a new learning approach will be evidenced in his lack of progress. Perhaps even more serious is the situation whereby the coach . . . is not respected either as a person or for his seeming lack of knowledge and poor teaching ability. The barrier formed between learner and teacher will be difficult to overcome and certainly will not represent a favorable learning situation [p. 316].

It is obvious, then, that when two people perceive each other in the same way, e.g., as having similar ideas, mutual respect occurs and the follower's reactions to the leader are favorable. Judgments are partially affected by background, and a person's attitudes determine how he evaluates others. Unfortunately, previous experiences may distort present situations. For example, if an athlete liked his former coach very much and dislikes his present coach, his reactions to the latter may be exaggerated, and his interpretations of the coach's actions and words may be warped. The present relationship between coach and athlete in such a case suffers by comparison with the earlier one. In turn, morale may be lowered and output may be diminished.

Ideally, the athlete's frame of reference toward his coach is one of high esteem. Favorable player attitudes toward the coach should be encouraged and the competitive philosophies of the coach and players should be similar if team objectives are to be met. Attitudes toward learning must be considered in the process of skill acquisition. The wise and sensitive coach attempts to determine what kind of rapport he has established with his athletes and tries to improve his relationships with them whenever possible.

## PREDICTING SUCCESS IN ATHLETICS
## WITH THE AID OF PSYCHOLOGICAL RESEARCH[1]

One crucial problem of the coach is selection. How should he choose his team members? What are the criteria? What relationship is there between initial performance (the basis for selection) and performance in the contests? For the same sport, are there different criteria for initial selection, depending on the age and maturation of the group? What primarily determines athletic achievement—genetics or environmental experiences?

These and many other questions are related to the same issue. Considering the athlete's stage of growth and development, can the coach predict his potential levels of achievement from initial observations and past data? Many aspects of the problem have been discussed in other sections of this book. However, the seriousness of the coach's function in this area demands a synthesis of pertinent research.

### Heredity and Experience

A moderate correlation of about .50 is obtained from averaging research findings on succeeding generations of a family in such physical qualities as height, weight, and body build. To the extent that physical characteristics are associated with athletic achievement, there is an indication that heredity plays a role. Further, research has demonstrated that the Olympic athlete and his family tend to engage in similar physical activities, and that specific physical and psychological qualities of the Olympians can be attributed to heredity.

Heredity usually has more influence on intelligence and anthropometric characteristics than do environmental experiences. It would seem that for a person to become expert in a particular sport or event, a hereditary stereotype in favor of the motor skills involved can be of some advantage. However, desire and motivation can drive those who are less well endowed physically to succeed in athletics.

### Body Type

Hard training can overcome many personal limitations. Although a certain body type or build may lead to achievement in a specific activity, it is

[1] This section is based on a paper presented at Research Section Meetings, Michigan Association of Health, Physical Education, and Recreation (Boyne Mountain, Michigan), October 31, 1969.

by no means necessary. Nevertheless, the presence of certain bodily, emotional, and intellectual characteristics will probably contribute to a greater probability of success in a particular endeavor.

### Early Experiences

Another consideration in predicting success in athletics is the types of early experiences which the athlete has had. A childhood filled with enriched movement experiences serves as a foundation for learning the more complex athletic skills later in life. Proficiency in related skills and sports increases the probability of success in a given sport. Therefore, knowledge about the athlete's background and his other athletic accomplishments helps the coach to know what to expect.

Research on mammals and birds has disclosed optimal periods for learning certain behaviors. An "optimal" or "critical" learning period is that time in the organism's life span when the maximum sensory, motor, psychological, and maturational capacities are present for the learning of a particular thing. Unfortunately, information is not available on the optimal point in life for learning athletic skills such as golf, tennis, and bowling. There is no doubt, however, that sports skills can be taught earlier, though perhaps in a modified form, than is usually attempted. For the sake of developing skill in adulthood, however, what is important is not how early a skill is taught but how timely its teaching is. A history of the individual person's athletic experiences at each stage of development (maturational age) might suggest behavioral expectations to the coach.

### Personality

Some personality traits that appear to be related to athletic success are persistence, aggressiveness, and drive. Insight and sensitivity to the personality characteristics of hopeful athletes may help the coach to detect behavioral patterns. When traits can be ascribed with a reasonable degree of confidence to typical athletes in a sport, or to certain events or positions in a sport, statistical analysis will be able to predict the probability that a person will perform successfully on a team, in an event, or in a position.

### General Abilities

In predicting proficiency in athletics, it is likely that very young athletes will have more "generalizable" abilities than high school or older athletes; that is, they will be more apt to show all-round athletic qualities. With age, however, a process of maturation and differentiation occurs. As the athlete develops toward maturity, he must continuously and conscientiously practice complex and specialized tasks in order to attain relatively high degrees of skill, which obviously means devoting less time to other pursuits. The athletic endeavors of youngsters demand gross movements and are fairly similar from activity to activity, but in the adolescent years, the maturing person becomes capable of undertaking and completing more highly refined tasks. His interests also change and may become more specialized.

Evidently, then, a test designed to measure general motor ability is almost meaningless in differentiating among the highly skilled. A sport requires intricate and refined movements. It is inconceivable that one test or even a battery of tests could make discriminating judgments among athletes and among sports. Specialized tests of skills needed in a given sport will do a more acceptable job. Even so, successful participation in athletics is related to so many variables that the practices of isolating particular skills and testing potential team members for purposes of classification and prediction are of questionable value. It is true, for example, that Knox found his test of basketball skills to be an excellent predictor of high school teams that made a tournament as well as designating first-team players. However, other researchers, although they conceded that the Knox test has merit as a squad predictor and readily distinguishes among varsity and nonvarsity performers, found that it was not sensitive enough to differentiate between levels of ability within a squad.

### Prediction from Initial Status

Another point to consider is that present levels of proficiency are not necessarily a valid basis for predicting future levels of proficiency. Although there are fast learners and slow learners, a person is not typically an overall fast learner or a generally slow learner. Rather, each person's achievement in different tasks is obtained by varying speeds and at different levels. For example, there is no indication of a general learning ability or a general improvement factor. A coach would do well to bear this concept in mind in forming expectations of achievement for his many athletes.

When athletes have practiced a skill for some time, prediction of relative achievement within a group becomes easier and more accurate. Relative improvement in performance of simple skills is more predictable than performance of complex tasks. The number and nature of abilities necessary in complex tasks apparently change as performance improves during practice. In other words, the coach may expect different abilities to be important in different phases of the learning of a skill. Once the abilities that are relevant to a particular skill are ascertained, they should be emphasized at the pertinent stages of development.

*Practice and Game Situations*

Finally, suitable prediction from performance is most likely to occur when test conditions are most closely related to actual contest conditions. Performance in three-man, half-court basketball is little indication of playing ability on a full court, and shooting in practice by oneself is not the same as performing in a game.

*Concluding Thought*

Forecasting athletic status, selecting team members, and making game substitution decisions are only a few of the major problems that coaches face. In the future, coaches will be better educated, and research material will be better prepared and more appropriate—a combination which must result in greater success in the handling and training of promising young athletes.

## TREATMENT OF INDIVIDUAL PLAYERS

The very nature of athletics requires the coach to consider the team as a whole and to consider individual problems as well. Throughout this book an attempt has been made to emphasize the general behavioral principles that lead to the effective training of groups of athletes, but frequently, special attention has also been given to individual differences. A final discussion on the treatment of individual athletes is in order here.

One of the qualities of the coach is his ability to be very perceptive of and responsive to individual needs. A study reported by Wotruba & Golden (1968) indicates ". . . that the coach who is functioning at a high level on the empathic, positive regard, concreteness, and genuineness scales, is the one who is developing the 'true' champion provided the athlete is willing to listen and learn" (p. 23). Furthermore, they claim that the ". . . athlete is not willing to learn unless the coach provides him with the right atmosphere and feeling that he really cares about him as a person" (p. 23).

"Empathic understanding" by the coach is sensitivity to each athlete's needs. "Positive regard" refers to the coach's ability to communicate respect and concern for each athlete, regardless of their present status. Openness, or just being oneself, in personal relationships describes the quality of "genuineness." Finally, "concreteness" indicates the degree to which the athlete can talk with the coach about his own ideas on the athletic program.

Individual relationships between coach and athlete have an important effect on the personal achievements of the athlete and on the overall functioning level of the team. Robert Epskamp (1962), track coach at Miami University of Ohio, has made the following conclusions (p. 57):

1. An individualistic approach should be used in coaching due to the variety of moods, temperaments, goals, emotions, and other behavioral characteristics exhibited by individual athletes.

2. The coach has responsibility to recognize different behavioral characteristics and make accurate assessments of each individual athlete.

There is no doubt that it is easier to deal with groups and to train people collectively than to address oneself to individual problems, but the psychological literature on the nature of individual differences strongly suggests individual considerations in individual or group efforts. Apparently, coaches too are recognizing the importance of such considerations today, as evidenced by their practices and writings.

Going a step further, coaches may want to heed the advice of the noted philosopher Paul Weiss. In *Sport: A Philosophic Inquiry* (1969), Weiss analyzes sport in an attempt to make meaning of its various aspects. He stresses the inadequacies of the traditional, rigid, old-fashioned coaching style, and emphasizes the need for creativity in athletics. Coaches should approach their endeavors with creative minds, for this, according to Weiss, is the age of the creative, individualistic athlete. Exhortations on behalf of team, community, or country, he writes, please those in positions of authority but they usually leave the rest unmoved. It is to be hoped that, with the coach's creative guidance, the athlete will be driven to excellence through self-motivation.

## TREATMENT OF WINNING AND LOSING TEAMS

Research evidence does not suggest different techniques for guiding successful and unsuccessful teams. However, common sense indicates that the approach that seems to be working with the winning team may be continued, but that various techniques will have to be attempted with the losing team until it gets on the right track. A "winning formula," once established, is usually perpetuated until a need for change is demonstrated. The coach in the midst of a series of losses must continually try new approaches, which implies making training, tactical, mechanical, and psychological modifications in dealing with the team members.

Some successful coaches are noted for their aggressiveness and ability to drive their athletes. Enthusiasm, pep talks, and general fiery oratory are characteristics associated with such coaches. Other winning coaches demonstrate a good deal of reservation and calmness. They appear to be cool, calculating, and determined under a variety of conditions. Both these extreme personality profiles are associated with satisfactory coaching results. The winning coach can afford the luxury of continuing his usual tactics and general psychological approach to each contest, although he may make variations on appropriate occasions. The losing coach, on the other hand, is forced to experiment until the performances of the individual athletes and the team as a whole become successful.

In any event, successful coaches usually sense when to maintain the status quo and when to modify their strategies. The winning coach has to sustain the winning effort by continuing to instill confidence and enthusiasm in his athletes. The unsuccessful coach must elevate the sights of the team members, and use whatever other tactics might result in a winning effort. Obviously, athletes with inferior skills will probably not win no matter what psychological tactics are employed. However, when there is a reasonable degree of similarity between individual or team competitors in levels of skill and training, the psychological techniques employed by coaches may very well make a difference in the final outcome of a contest. General factors that may contribute to successful results in competition are illustrated in Figure 10-1. The ultimate determining factor in achievement is the relationships among the coach, the team, and the individual players.

## MENTAL ATTITUDE AND PREPARATION FOR THE CONTEST

Many tales have been spun and many popular articles written on the mental disposition of the athlete before the contest. Presumably, being in an ideal frame of mind puts the athlete in a good position to perform his skills well and attain ultimate victory. The mental attitude of an individual athlete or a team can help to overcome many obstacles or can lead to unexpected defeat. Coaches agree that the physical characteristics, skills, and training of the athletes are extremely important, but they also indicate that good mental preparation for competition is a necessary component of the winner.

Coaches do not agree about how to help athletes to develop such an attitude. Each coach seems to have his own techniques, which work for him. Much probably depends on the personality of the coach and his ability to influence the attitudes of the team members. Nevertheless, the development of an appropriate mental attitude, set, or preparation is an integral part of the athletic scene. One has to want to win. He has to believe in himself and the team, and to believe that winning is not only possible but indeed probable. The presence of such an attitude is necessary not only on the day

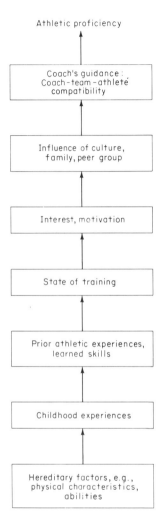

Athletic proficiency

Coach's guidance :
Coach-team-athlete
compatibility

Influence of culture,
family, peer group

Interest, motivation

State of training

Prior athletic experiences,
learned skills

Childhood experiences

Hereditary factors, e.g.,
physical characteristics,
abilities

FIGURE 10-1  *Foundation blocks in building athletic excellence.*

of the contest, but during the previous week and even during the entire year.

The amounts of enthusiasm and energy expended during practice provide an indication of what is in store the day of the contest. Keeping morale high among the team members is a key function of the coach. The coach, through his attitudes and actions, shapes the feeling of the group. This was very evident when Duffy Daugherty, the prominent Michigan State football coach, described to the author the events leading to a certain game between Michigan State and Notre Dame a number of years ago. Michigan State was heavily favored to win. Notre Dame's team, although Paul Horning was on the team at the time, was having an average season; but the Notre Dame spirit and school morale were undeniable. When Michigan State arrived at Notre Dame to practice the day before the game, someone asked Daugherty if it would be all right for some of the old-time Notre Dame greats to watch the practice session. Duffy agreed. The psychology worked for Notre Dame, for the Michigan State boys were awed and overwhelmed by the presence of the Four Horsemen and other men who helped to create football history, and they could not concentrate on their practice routines. A deathly silence reigned. It was as if the ghosts from the past had spellbound the would-be victors.

On the day of the game the situation was the same: the MSU athletes were serious, tight, and not mentally prepared to win. The Notre Dame players, however, were as high as they could be. At the end of the first half, the score was 14 to 7 in favor of Notre Dame, and if Michigan had not had a few breaks, Notre Dame's score could easily have been much higher. When the MSU players came in for half-time, they expected to hear the typical review of the first-half play: what went wrong or right, why, and how. Duffy, however, threw the expected routine out the window. He asked one of the leading wits on the team to tell a joke. After a moment of disbelief, he did, and there were a few chuckles. Next, a few players who had developed a hilarious pantomime of slow-motion football films, forward and in reverse, were asked to put on their act. They did, and as usual were received with much laughter. This procedure continued until the players were in hysterics.

When the players were notified to report to the field for the second half, they were slow to respond, for they were weak from laughing so hard. They finally ran onto the field laughing, to the surprise of the fans, who probably thought the MSU players had cracked. However, the second-half statistics indicated quite the opposite, for MSU ended up with over 40 points to the original 14 points scored by Notre Dame.

What Duffy did was to throw the book away and employ an unusual technique to loosen up the boys. It evidently worked; he created a feeling among the athletes that precipitated victory. This is an example of the coach's role as an amateur psychologist. The importance of mental preparation for competition cannot be denied and should never be underestimated.

Further testimony on the importance of psychological factors in sport is provided by Bob Pettit (1967), professional basketball star for many years. He writes, "Being mentally up for a game insures a top effort" (p. 147). One must take pride in his performance. Pettit writes further, "The mental aspect of basketball is 50 percent of the battle" (p. 27). If you think you are the best, you have a better chance of realizing hoped-for goals.

Preparation for a contest may take still another form. In a news release in the *Washington Post* on October 30, 1968, it was reported that the Soviet newspapers had expressed dissatisfaction with the poor showing of the Russians as compared with the Americans in the Olympics; criticisms had been leveled and analyses of causative factors offered. There was a call for "better training and better psychological preparation to foster feelings of responsibility for the honor of the banner of our national team." Patriotic feelings (loyalty to one's country, state, community, or school) are one other aspect of the mental preparation of athletes.

## THE COACH AS AN INDIVIDUAL

It has been stressed before that each athlete or each coach is an individual with his own unique characteristics and ways of behaving, and no further emphasis on this fact is necessary. Coaches in general, however, are looked upon as possessing certain qualities that distinguish them from the average population.

For example, Beisser (1967) recognizes that the term "old man" was once reserved for the male head of the household. In our society today the coach receives a similar connotation. Beisser writes:

> The model of the good coach is the same as the model of the good father. He is strong, tough, and virile, deserves and expects respect, is not punitive, but neither is he easy. Though firm discipline has almost disappeared in many homes it is still expected in athletics. The coach demands and receives obedience. He is the expert and the teacher. . . . The successful coach is one who gains the respect of his team, and whom the young athlete generally obeys [p. 200].

According to Beisser, even the alumni, parents, and spectators look upon the coach as a father. If there is little age difference between the coach and his charges, however, his image may be that of an older brother. In all levels of competition, from elementary school to professional athletics, the coach is responsible for the players and for the team's output. Beisser suggests further:

> The athletes that make up the team are not ordinarily held responsible for a loss—they are to be excused for they are only the "boys." It is the coach who carries the burden of responsibility. On a losing team, the team members are rarely replaced; rather, the coach or manager is "fired." This is a magical symbolic gesture, for often a team is simply inadequate and the coach may be doing the best possible job, nevertheless he is the one who is replaced [p. 200].

Not only does the coach's image as a father figure usually place him in a favorable and acceptable leadership role, but also it can be hoped that he will be able to use it to inspire a winning attitude. No matter what the coach's image, whether that of a father or that of an older brother, he is expected to win. Our culture has come to expect and demand the best in team output, and the coach is expected to fulfill these wishes.

Some data on the personality profile of a "typical" coach have been reported by Ogilvie & Tutko (1966). Data on a group of selected coaches were compared with normative data on college males in order to see whether personality traits were distinguishable between the two groups. Ogilvie & Tutko state that the coaches' profile was similar to that of outstanding athletes from numerous sports, and different in a number of respects from the college norm. Here is a summary of the characteristics of their sample:

*a*. Highly success-driven men with an outstanding need to be on top. Only U.S. Air Force Cadets had a greater need as a group than they.

*b*. They were highly orderly, organized men who preferred to plan ahead and be concerned with looking ahead into the future.

*c*. They tended to be outgoing and warm people who enjoyed being with others.

*d*. They had finely developed consciences and were very much in tune with the appropriate values in our culture.

*e*. They seemed unusually well equipped by personality and temperament for handling their emotions when under considerable stress.

*f*. They were, as a group, open, trusting people who were not excessively defensive in their relationships with others.

*g*. They scored very high in leadership qualities when compared with norms based upon men who were selected or elected leaders.

*h*. They were, as a sample, more dominant, take-charge types of persons who would actively seek roles of leadership.

*i*. They were more prone to blame themselves and accept blame when things go wrong than to pass the responsibility over to someone else.

*j*. They exhibited the highest average of psychological endurance of any sample of men we have ever studied. It appears that "stick-to-it-ness" is the most prominent feature of the personality of successful coaches.

*k*. They were unusually mature emotionally and would be described on the basis of their tests as persons who would face reality in a direct manner.

*l*. They were free to express their natural aggressive tendencies in a manner appropriate to their role as a coach [pp. 22–23].[2]

On the negative side, the coaches revealed a tendency not to be interested

[2] Reproduced from *Problem athletes and how to handle them,* by Dr. Bruce C. Ogilvie & Dr. Thomas A. Tutko, published by Pelham Books, London, and distributed in the U.S.A. by Track and Field News, Los Altos, California.

in the dependency needs of others. They were not concerned with the problems of their athletes. Offering support or counseling in emotional or social disturbances was not of interest to these coaches. Whether the traits listed by Ogilvie & Tutko are typical of all coaches is difficult to ascertain at the present time. Coaches are individuals and therefore may be expected to respond to situations accordingly—in an individualistic manner. Nevertheless, the personality data reported do provide some interesting speculations on the nature of a coach. They should be viewed as preliminary data, awaiting confirmation or refutation by more rigorously controlled research.

## THE SUCCESSFUL COACH

If we could accurately or even adequately describe the characteristics of the champion athlete and the successful coach, many problems in athletics would be resolved. Although attempts have been made, much remains to be done. Indications of general behavioral characteristics have been gathered by empirical observations and by personality assessment. Let us take a brief look at both sources of information.

On the basis of personal experience and observation, Stampfl (1955) suggests, "The coach's job is twenty percent technical and eighty percent inspirational" (p. 146). He says further that the successful coach is one who gains the confidence and comradeship of his athletes. Although most coaches agree on the fundamentals of execution of skill, the method of application and the degree of responsiveness of the athletes may be what separate the successful from the unsuccessful coach. Stampfl says, "Confidence is the most important quality in all athlete-coach relationships" (p. 150). The athlete must at all times trust the coach. "Guide, philosopher and friend, counsellor and confessor, a prop at times of mental tension, a coach's job is big enough for any man" (p. 141).

It is interesting to note that whereas Stampfl emphasized the importance of guidance and counseling on the part of the coach, Ogilvie & Tutko did not notice that such practices were common among the coaches they analyzed. Other attributes of the successful coach are discussed by Counsilman (1965). He suggests that each coach adopt a coaching style that is designed to fit his unique personality, but that, whatever his style, the coach should have the affection and respect of the athlete.

> One of the greatest motivators to keep an athlete working hard in practice is the affection and respect he has for the coach. This affection and respect is not the coach's due; it must be earned. In order to earn it, he must present the athletes with a good training program and with well-planned and organized practice sessions [p. 729].

Counsilman writes further:

> The old belief that a coach is a stern disciplinarian who drives the athletes through their hard training routines much as a mule driver drives an unquestioning mule team across Death Valley must be replaced with the belief that the coach is an educated director of young people who are striving for a common goal. He must not drive them relentlessly, but should guide them intelligently toward this goal [p. 728].

The successful coach's attitude toward all his charges is positive. He is able to build and maintain morale throughout daily routine practice sessions and during the course of the competitive season. Counsilman thinks that the good coach is democratic, not authoritarian. He reasons that the mature, intelligent, emotionally stable athlete cannot identify with the autocrat. The coach should be fair but firm about rules and practice schedules.

Research has enabled the designation and comparison of the traits of so-called "good teachers" and "poor teachers." Differences have been established, but they are not necessarily consistent from study to study. Differences in samples, trait-measuring devices, and statistical evaluation procedures also confuse the picture. However, if there are indeed identifiable differences between good and poor teachers, successful and unsuccessful coaches can certainly also be distinguished.

Hendry (1969) has attempted to examine coaches' and swimmers' views of the ideal coach and the degree to which these views are comparable to the actual personality traits of highly successful swimming coaches. On the basis of certain criteria,[3] 30 outstanding coaches were selected from a group of 56, and their personality profiles were assessed. Data that had been previously acquired were used to construct a picture of the personality of the ideal coach. On the basis of the Cattell Sixteen Personality Factor Questionnaire, comparisons between less successful and more successful coaches led to the conclusion that no clear-cut personality differences existed. Hendry suggests that since differences in the achievements of coaches were not due to personality factors, they might possibly be attributed to other considerations, "such as better training techniques, better human relationships, better motivational techniques, and so forth" (p. 302).

Further analysis of Hendry's data revealed that the personality traits of successful coaches and of the constructed ideal coach were not at all alike. This surprising finding leads to interesting speculations. Differences

---

[3] The criteria were (1) competitively successful swimmers, (2) the coach's own background and technical knowledge, and (3) the coach's being held in high esteem by other coaches.

# Name Index

Adams, Gary, 306, 340
Adams, Jack A., 250, 255
Albrecht, L., 207
Allport, Gordon W., 67, 90
Alseth, Alfred R., 329, 346
Anastasi, Anne, 26, 63
Anderson, Kenneth A., 313, 341
Annarino, A. A., 164, 187
Annett, John, 13, 21
Arietta, Ralph J., 317, 341
Armer, J. Michael, 124, 133
Arond, H., 163, 189
Atkinson, John W., 221, 225
Ayres, L. P., 282, 300

Back, John, 200, 216
Bagg, Ewart J., 305, 340
Baker, Blaine L., 58
Baker, Elliot, 334, 347
Bakker, Clarena K., 336, 348
Bannister, Roger, 221, 255
Bartlett, F. C., 213, 216
Bartley, S. Howard, 213
Bastian, J. R., 225, 255
Bates, Frank H., 47, 63, 305, 340
Bee, Claire, 196, 216
Behrman, Robert, 331, 346
Beisser, Arnold R., 97, 141, 144, 163, 187, 361, 366
Bell, Virginia L., 262, 300
Bend, Elmer, 324, 344
Benington, John, 199, 216
Berelson, Bernard, 167, 187
Bilodeau, Ina McD., 259, 300
Binet, A., 7
Birren, James H., 58, 63
Blank, Robert G., 306, 340
Blum, Milton L., 146
Bond, M. H., 282, 300
Booth, E., 71, 90
Borders, S., 289, 301
Bosco, James S., 326, 345
Boyd, Clifford, 315, 341
Boyle, Robert H., 159, 162, 169, 187
Bradley, Bill W., 140
Brassie, Paul Stanley, 314, 341
Brees, Clifford D., 314, 341
Bremner, J. Barron, 337, 348
Brenci, G., 73, 91
Brendice, Frederick A., 317, 342

Brennan, Mary, 326, 345
Briedwell, William, 333, 347
Brose, Donald E., 206–207, 216, 307, 340
Brown, Edward A., 339, 348
Burack, Benjamin, 274, 300
Burdeshan, Dorothy, 109, 133
Burke, Jack, 272, 300
Burpee, R., 305, 340
Bush, Russel L., 336, 348
Bushman, Ben Robert, 335, 348
Buxton, C. E., 209, 216

Carder, Brent, 323, 344
Carlson, B. Robert, 80, 90, 327, 346
Carron, Albert V., 126, 133
Carter, J. E. Lindsay, 95, 96, 133
Carter, L., 156, 187
Cassel, Russel, 323, 344
Cattell, R. B., 67, 90
Chaloupecky, Robert, 311, 342
Childers, Richard, 323, 344
Chui, E. F., 289, 300
Clark, L. Verdelle, 47, 63, 271, 300
Clarke, H. Harrison, 37
Cofer, C. N., 137, 189
Coleman, James S., 41, 63
Colville, F. H., 274, 300
Constantine, T., 328, 346
Cooper, Lowell, 71, 90
Cortés, J. B., 69, 90
Counsilman, James, 279, 300, 363, 364, 366
Cowell, C. C., 32, 63, 323, 344
Crakes, James G., 344, 347
Cratty, Bryant J., 136, 145, 158, 187
Crawford, Meredith P., 196, 216
Cureton, Thomas K., 114, 133, 330, 346

Damron, C. Frazier, 319, 344
Daniels, Diane, 242, 255
Darley, J., 136, 187
Deese, D. W., 305, 340
Dembowski, Michael, 116
Denny, M. R., 194
DeVries, Herbert, 203, 205, 216, 330, 346
Dickson, W. J., 230, 256
Digman, J. M., 195
Dixon, N. F., 213, 216
Dobias, Robert, 320, 345
Dolan, Joseph P., 160, 188
Dupont, Jim, 48, 63, 321, 344

Durentini, Carol L., 286, 301

Earl, R. W., 225, 255
Egstrom, Glen H., 286, 301
Ellis, Henry C., 240
Entwisle, D. G., 241, 255
Epskamp, Robert, 333, 348, 357, 366
Erikson, Roger D., 333, 348
Espenschade, Anna, 35, 63
Everett, Peter W., 307–308, 340

Faulkner, John A., 327
Ferguson, Don P., 109, 133
Fiedler, F. E., 136, 156, 157, 188
Filipponi, Mervyn L., 329, 346
Finn, Edward P., 320, 344
Fisher, Edward S., 317, 342
Fisk, Timothy, 311, 342
Flanagan, Lance, 78, 91
Fleishman, Edwin A., 17, 21, 43, 45, 110–
    113, 133, 194, 209, 216, 249, 255, 277
Foster, Harriett, 245, 255
Fowler, William H., 83, 91
Francis, Roy G., 175, 188
Frank, Omer V., 318, 339, 342, 349
Freud, Sigmund, 7, 26, 32
Fries, Bobby Conrad, 334, 348
Frisbey, N., 194
Fulton, Ruth E., 247, 255

Gabrielsen, Milton A., 283
Gagné, Robert M., 17, 21, 194, 216, 245,
    255
Garretson, Rodney R., 316, 342
Gatti, F. M., 69, 90
Gedda, Luigi, 73, 91
Gellinger, Terrence J., 307, 340
Genzmer, Dave E., 314, 342
Gephert, Gene C., 312, 342
Geurin, William T., 312, 342
Glaser, Robert, 258, 301
Gold, Marvin, 80, 91, 325, 333, 345, 347
Goldenberg, Joseph, 197, 216
Gorsuch, H. R., 72, 91
Gottheil, Edward, 73, 92
Graybiel, A., 117, 133
Griffith, Coleman, 192, 193, 216, 286, 301,
    325, 345
Gross, N., 136, 187

Hagerman, R., 207
Haider, M., 213, 216
Hale, Creighton J., 32, 63
Haleski, Chester C., 322, 345
Hamilton, Larry M., 328, 346
Harlow, H. F., 246, 255
Harris, Dorothy V., 79, 91
Harris, Harold E., 333, 348
Havel, Richard C., 318, 342

Haythorn, W., 156, 187
Heise, Bryan, 30, 63
Hempel, Walter E., 209, 216
Hemphill, John K., 156, 188
Hendrickson, Gordon, 274, 301
Hendry, L. B., 85, 91, 332, 346, 364, 366
Henry, Franklin M., 18, 19, 21, 115, 133
Herman, Leslie A., 305, 340
Hewitt, Jack E., 313, 342
Hirata, Kin-Itsu, 51, 63, 97, 103, 133
Holding, D. H., 258, 283, 301
Hollingworth, N. C., 184, 230, 255
Hopek, Richard, 321, 344
Howell, Fred E., 200, 216
Howell, M., 156, 187
Howell, William T., 48, 63, 313, 342
Hubbard, Alfred W., 304, 340
Humphreys, L. G., 209, 216
Hunt, M. Briggs, 339, 349
Hurlock, E. B., 237, 256
Hutton, Daniel C., 83, 91, 399, 349

Ibrahim, Hilmi, 78, 91, 170, 188
Imlay, Robert C., 308, 340
Irion, A. L., 250, 256
Ismail, A. H., 32, 63, 323, 344

Jacobson, Richard Lee, 328, 346
Jersild, Arthur T., 46, 63
Johnson, Clarence, 324, 344
Johnson, Granville B., 83, 91
Johnson, Harry W., 13–16
Johnson, Warren R., 83, 91, 206, 217, 339,
    349
Jokl, Ernst, 51, 63, 117, 133
Jones, M. B., 211
Jones, Thomas A., 58
Joseph, Newton, 172–173, 188

Kane, John E., 83, 91
Karpovich, Peter V., 204, 205, 216
Kay, H. Kenner, 316, 342
Kay, Harry, 13, 21
Keating, James W., 155, 188
Kelso, John G., 330, 346
Kelson, Robert E., 308, 341
King, William H., 328, 346
Kingsmore, John M., 180, 188
Kinser, Jay, 313, 342
Kistler, Joy W., 74, 91, 149, 188
Kite, Joseph, 311, 342
Kjeldsen, Eric, 326, 345
Kleiner, R. J., 137, 188
Klingbeil, Jerrold L., 123, 133
Knapp, Joann, 327, 345
Knapp, Robert H., 2, 21
Knox, Robert D., 46, 63, 315, 342
Knutzen, Gary H., 338, 349
Kolker, Lloyd L., 334, 348

Kovacic, Charles R., 280, 301
Kramer, G. F., 206, 217
Kroll, Walter, 76, 80, 86, 91, 97, 101, 133, 325, 327, 336, 338, 339, 344, 349
Krueger, W. C. F., 202

Lakie, William L., 75, 91, 149, 188
LaLone, Patricia Anne, 196, 217
Lambert, Ward, 207, 217
Lampman, James Joseph, 127, 133, 332, 346
Lande, Leon, 304, 341
LaPlace, John E., 83, 91, 309, 341
Larson, Edgar D., 318, 342
Lashley, K. S., 196, 217
Lawrence, Lee W., 328, 346
Leavitt, B., 200, 217
Lehman, Harvey C., 51–57, 63, 64
Levitt, Stuart, 224, 256
Lindeburg, Franklin A., 313, 342
Littlefield, Donald H., 323, 344
Litwin, G. H., 225, 255
Locke, Edwin A., 224, 256
Logan, Gene A., 286, 301, 307, 341
Londeree, Ben R., 319, 344
Loy, John, 162, 188
Lukas, Wayne, 313, 342
Lumpe, Jerry, 307, 341
Lutes, Warren C., 317, 343

Maaske, Paul W., 309, 343
McAdam, Robert E., 328, 347
McAdams, Linda Butler, 332, 347
McCachren, James, 315, 341
Mack, Arthur E., 315, 343
McCullough, James, 334, 348
McDaniel, Joe, 289, 301
McGeoch, J. A., 250, 256
McGinnis, George, 316, 343
McGraw, Myrtle, 27, 64
McIntyre, Thomas D., 162, 188
McKinney, Wayne C., 307, 341
McPhee, John, 117, 133, 140, 188
Malmisur, Michael, 333, 347
Martin, W., 136, 187
Massey, B. H., 206, 217
Mathews, Donald K., 289, 301
Mead, Margaret, 139, 188
Meyer, Herbert H., 336, 349
Meyers, Carlton R., 72, 91
Meyers, Judith L., 251, 256
Middlebrooks, Gwendolyn H., 329, 347
Mikszewski, John C., 321, 344
Milani-Comparetta, M., 73, 91
Miller, Leonard Arthur, 335, 348
Min, Kyung-Ho, 327, 346
Minahan, Fred B., 311, 343
Mohr, Dorothy R., 193, 217
Moore, Robert A., 88, 92

Moos, Donald, 274, 300
Mowerson, G. R., 328, 347
Mudra, Darrell E., 321, 344
Müller, E. A., 205, 217
Murphy, Herbert H., 197, 217
Myers, Douglas G., 334, 348
Myllymaki, Carl W., 334, 348

Nagle, Francis J., 320, 345
Naylor, James C., 146
Nelson, Dale O., 275, 301, 319, 343
Nelson, R., 207, 217
Ness, Richard A., 304, 341
Newell, Pete, 199, 216
Newman, Earl H., 47, 64, 330, 347
Newman, Richard E., 340, 349
Nisbett, Richard E., 160, 161, 188
Noble, Clyde E., 58
Norton, Ken, 196, 216
Nunney, Derek N., 214, 217

O'Brien, Ronald, 328, 347
Ogilvie, Bruce C., 2, 3, 21, 40, 64, 71–73, 82, 88, 89, 92, 229, 324, 331, 347, 362, 363, 366
Ohnmacht, Fred W., 72, 91
Olsen, Jack, 170–171, 188
Olson, Edward C., 83, 92, 33, 347
Olson, Willard C., 122, 133

Parker, James F., 249, 277
Parsons, David R., 330, 347
Partch, Andrew F., 164, 188
Patty, Elbert K., 316, 343
Pavlov, I., 7
Petersen, Kay H., 86, 91, 325, 344
Peterson, Sheri L., 76, 92
Pettit, Bob, 140, 188, 360, 366
Phillips, William H., 213, 217
Postman, Leo, 128, 133
Puni, A. T., 279, 301

Rarick, G. Lawrence, 29, 30, 64
Rasch, Phillip J., 336, 339, 349
Reed, Kenneth L., 337, 349
Rehberg, Richard, 164, 189
Reitman, Walter R., 225, 255
Rhine, R. J., 147, 189
Riccio, Dennis, 304
Rich, Simon, 112, 113, 133
Richardson, Alan, 270
Richardson, Deane, 74, 92, 149, 189
Riddle, Lynne, 78, 92
Rinne, James L., 47, 64, 324, 344
Roethlisberger, F. J., 230, 256
Rosen, Bernard C., 163, 189
Rosenthal, D., 137, 189
Roudik, Petre A., 280, 301
Rowan, Vic, 322, 344

Rowe, William, 307, 341
Ruhling, Robert O., 80, 92
Rushall, Brent S., 84, 92, 324, 331, 345, 347
Ryan, E. Dean, 280, 301
Ryan, Francis J., 141–144, 189, 229, 256, 333, 348

Sauter, Waldo, 196, 217
Savage, Howard J., 148, 189
Scanlon, William M., 312, 343
Schafer, Walter E., 124, 133, 164, 189
Scharf, Raphael J., 328, 347
Schendel, Jack, 36, 38, 39, 64
Schiesel, Michael L., 328, 347
Schiltz, Jack H., 224, 256
Schreckengaust, V. J., 76, 92
Schroeder, John R., 320, 345
Schroeder, William W., 274, 301
Schrupp, M. H., 164, 189
Schultz, Alan E., 337, 349
Scott, J. P., 28, 64
Seely, Doyle G., 322, 345
Selk, Larry B., 284, 301, 311, 343
Sell, Veryl L., 309, 343
Seng, C. N., 304, 340
Seymour, Emery W., 31, 64, 308, 341
Sharman, Bill, 271, 301
Shaw, John H., 283
Sievers, Harry L., 337, 349
Sigerseth, Peter, 322, 345
Sills, Frank, 311, 343
Sims, Verner M., 228, 256
Singer, R. N., 12, 19–21, 76, 77, 80–82, 92, 118, 150–154, 182–184, 189, 244, 308, 341, 352, 366
Singleton, W. T., 241, 256
Skubic, Elvera, 31, 51, 64, 308, 341
Slater-Hammel, A. T., 118, 134, 246, 256, 304, 341
Slaymaker, Thomas E., 335, 348
Slusher, Howard S., 75, 92, 339, 349
Smith, Karl U., 8
Smith, William M., 8
Smode, A., 261
Solley, W. H., 289, 301
Sperling, Abraham P., 71, 92
Stampfl, Franz, 87, 92, 363, 366
Steiner, Gary A., 167, 187
Stevens, S. S., 258
Stotts, James, 318, 343
Stotz, Carl, 28
Stroll, W., 305, 340
Stroup, Francis, 116, 134, 316, 318, 343
Stumpner, R. L., 304, 341
Sullivan, Edward, 339, 349
Swartzendruber, Lowell, 314, 343

Takacs, Robert, 40, 64, 311, 343
Tanner, J. M., 41, 64, 96, 109, 134

Thisted, M. N., 164, 189
Thompson, Clem W., 320, 345
Thompson, Hugh, 314, 343
Thorndike, E. L., 243, 256
Thune, John B., 75, 92
Tillman, Kenneth, 79, 92
Timmons, Bob, 333, 348
Trapp, C., 117, 133
Trapp, William J., 165, 166, 189
Travis, L. E., 182, 189
Trenbeath, William, 305, 341
Triplett, Norman, 181, 189
Troester, Carl A., 283
Trousdale, William W., 76, 92
Troutman, Donald, 311, 343
Turner, Edward T., 180, 189
Tutki, Thomas A., 2, 21, 82, 88, 89, 92, 229, 324, 331, 347, 362, 363, 366

Vanderburgh, Bill, 158, 189
Van Huss, W. D., 207, 307, 341
Vizard, Thomas C., 128, 134, 317, 343

Waglow, T. F., 315, 341
Wallis, Earl L., 286, 301
Ward, L. B., 246, 256
Warnock, Ronald H., 318, 343
Watkins, David C., 284, 301, 306, 341
Weaver, J., 194
Weber, Jerome C., 76, 92
Wedge, Bryant M., 143
Weinberg, K. S., 163, 189
Weiskopf, D., 305, 341
Weiss, Paul, 357, 366
Welford, A. T., 58–61, 64
Werner, Alfred, 73, 92
Wertich, Harold G., 305, 341
Wettstone, Eugene, 326, 345
Weyner, Norma, 137, 189
Whiting, H. T. A., 332, 346
Wickstrom, R. L., 263–265
Wilhelm, Arnold W., 322, 345
Wilkinson James J., 115, 134
Williams, Edward C., 326, 345
Winter, Robert B., 123, 134
Wiren, Gary, 110, 134, 232–240, 326, 345
Wolfle, Dael, 200, 217, 259
Wolman, Benjamin B., 7, 21
Woodrow, Herbert, 208, 217
Woods, John B., 248, 256
Woodworth, R. S., 243, 256
Wotruba, Richard T., 356, 366
Wundt, Wilhelm, 7

Yensen, William Arthur, 337, 349
Young, Irving, 331, 347

Zeaman, David, 137, 189

# Subject Index

Ability, 17
  general motor, 18, 354, 355
  permanent, 17
  relation to physical characteristics, 121–123
  types of, 17
Academic achievement and athletes, 123–125
Aging process, 56–60
  effects on speed and accuracy, 58–60
Anxiety level, 126
Athlete:
  differing emotional tendencies, 127–128
  personality trait characteristics, 362
Athletic versus sociocultural activity on campus, 179
Athletic achievement, 50–63, 56
  optimal age for, 50–53, 56
Attitudes and values, 147–150
Auditory aids (see Cues and aids)

Baseball, 304–309
  batting, 304–306
  personality, 308–309
  pitching, 306–307
  predicting baseball ability, 307–308
Basketball, 309–319
  aspects of the game, 316–318
  basket height, 311–312
  body constitution, 316
  personality, 318–319
  practice techniques, 314–316
  training cues, 312–313
  training techniques: and the ball, 313
    and the basket, 309–311
    for jumping, 313–314
Behaviorism, 8–9
Body build, 94
  predicting athletic success, 95–96
  racial differences, 108–109
  sport differences, 95–108

Case histories, 28
Coach, 351–366
  impression on athletes, 351–352
  as an individual, 361–363
  psychological research and predicting athletic success, 353–356
    body type, 353–354
    early experiences, 354

Coach:
  psychological research and predicting athletic success: general abilities, 354–355
    heredity and experience, 353
    personality, 354
    practice and game situations, 356
    prediction from initial status, 355
  successful, 363–365
Coaching success determiners:
  coach's roles, 1
  continuing education, 4–5
  human relations, 3
  personal experience, 3–4
  personal qualities, 2–3
College athletes, 49
Competing responses theory, 252–253
Competition and cooperation, 138–141
Competitive ability, 141–144
  good and bad competitors, 143–144
Critical learning periods, 354
Cues and aids, 281–293
  auditory aids, 281–282
  auditory cues, 281
  kinesthetic aids, 285–286
    external manipulation method, 285–286
    eyes closed method, 286
    kinesthetic cues, 285
    laboratory aids, 286–287
    visual aids, 283–285
    visual cues, 282–283

Dating, 166
Demonstration (see Training)
Diathermy, as warmup, 205
Discrimination, 167–171
Dismissals, 174
Display in stimulus situation, 285
Drill, 262–268
  inner-directed activities, 267
  outer-directed activities, 267

Early experiences, 354
Early movement considerations, 27–28
Elementary school athletes, 28–32
  benefit versus harm, 28–30
  coaching of, 30
  competition and cooperation, 30–31

Elementary school athletes:
    maturational influences, 31–32
Emotions, 125–128
    competition considerations, 127–128
    expression of, 129
    general considerations, 126–127
Enriched movement experiences, 354
Equilibrium, 117–118
Extinction, 252

Family and the athlete, 159–162
    first-born children, 160–161
    "Plimsoll Point," 160
Fatigue, 212–215
Feedback, 258–262
Football, 319–325
    body constitution, 322
    personality, 323–325
    predicting football ability, 322–323
    training aids, 319–322
Form, 130
    imitation of, 130
    physiological and anatomical limitations,
        130
Formal discipline theory, 243
Frustration, 129

Game situations, 356
    research and predicting success, 356
Goals, 146
    common, 146
Golf, 325–326
Group acceptance, 165
Group interaction, 135–138
    cohesiveness, 136
    effects of group size, 137
    fraternization versus specified tasks and
        goals, 136
    individual's attractiveness to the group,
        138
    personal identity within the group, 138
    primary group, 136
    secondary group, 136
Growth and developmental factors:
    early movement considerations, 27–28
    general considerations, 24
    influence of environment and heredity,
        25–26
    optimal learning periods, 26–27
Guidance (see Training)
Gymnastics, 326–327

Hair, 172–174
Handling individuals, 165–176
    dating, 166
    discrimination, 167–171
    dismissals, 174
    group acceptance and social integration,
        165

Handling individuals:
    hair, 172–174
    married athlete, 166–167
    newsmen and communications personnel,
        174–175
    psychological approach of sports recruit-
        ers, 176
    school and community people, 175–176
    training rules and absence from practice,
        171–172
Heredity:
    predicting athletic success, 353
    role in personality, 362
High school athlete, 40–49
    instructional method research, 48
    learning and training research, 48
    personality testing, 47
    predicting ability, 46–47
    psychology in sports, 48–49
    socially influenced participation, 41, 46
Hot showers, as warmup, 205

Identical elements theory, 242–243
Improvement in practice, 207–212
    ability patterns in performance, 209–210
    predicted achievement from early suc-
        cess, 207–209
    variability in performance, 211–212
Incentives, 147
Individual and team performance relation-
    ships, 145
Instruction (see Training)
Intellectual attributes, 121–125
    athletes and academic achievement, 123–
        125
    intelligence, motor performance, and
        physical characteristics, 121–123
Interaction among team members, 135–138
Interscholastic athletics, 33–35
    pro and con, 34–35

Judo, 327
Junior high school athletes, 32–40
    cross-sectional data, 35–36
    interscholastic athletics, pro and con,
        34–35
    maturational influences, 32–33
    personality data, 36, 40
    safeguards, 33

Karate, 327
Kinesthesis, 117
Kinesthetic aftereffects, 120–121
Kinesthetic aids, 285–286
Kinesthetic illusions in warmup, 207
Knowledge of results (feedback), 258–262

Laboratory aids, 286–287
Leadership, 146, 155–159

Learning, 219–221
Learning sets, 246
Level of aspiration, 223

Married athlete, 166–167
Massage, as warmup, 205
Massed (continuous) practice, 192–195
Maturational readiness, 24–25
Mental attitude and preparation for the
    contest, 358–361
Mental practice (*see* Training)
Morale and spirit, 145–147
  common goals, 146
  incentives, 147
  interaction, 146
  leadership, 146
Motivation, 221–231
  competition, 228 229
  external comments, 227–228
  goal setting, 223–225
  Hawthorne effect, 229–230
  ideal level of, 221
  material versus ideal rewards, 222
  need to achieve, 225–226
  optimal level, 226–227
  social presence, 230–231
Motor specificity, 18–19

Natural athlete, 18–21
Negative transfer, 241–242
Newsmen and communications personnel,
    174–175

Optimal age for achievement, 50–56
Optimal learning periods, 26–27

Pain tolerance, 280–281
Perceptual distortions in warmup tasks,
    120
Perceptual mechanism, 118–121
  kinesthetic aftereffects, 120–121
  selective attention, 119–120
Personal factors and the athlete, 93–94
Personality:
  of athlete, coach's effect on, 69–70
  athlete's versus nonathlete's, 70–73
  of baseball players, 308–309
  of basketball players, 318–319
  changes as a result of athletic experi-
    ence, 73–74
  of coach and team, 85
  comparisons between sport groups, 74–
    78
  data and the coach, 84
  defined, 67
  explained, 65–67
  of football players, 323–325
  predicting athletic success, 353
  related to physical fitness, 79

Personality:
  relationship to recreational and activity
    interests, 78–79
  research on sports and, 67–69
  role of heredity, 73
  of superior athlete, 79–80
  of track and field athletes, 334–335
  type of school, 85–86
  of typical athletes, 71–72
  of wrestlers, 339–340
Physical and motor measures, 110–111
Physiological and anatomical differences,
    130
Physiology, 203
Post college athletics, 50
Practice:
  changes in ability, 209–210
  mental, 270–272
  research and predicting success, 7
Practice sessions:
  administration of practice periods, 192–
    197
  practice periods, 192–195
Practicing for perfection, 197–202
  attention, 199
  conditions, 199–201
  importance of, 201
  intent to learn, 197–198
  meaningfulness, 198
  overpractice, 201–202
  readiness, 198–199
Professional athletics, effect of, 177–178
Psychological injuries, 87–89
  situations leading to, 88–89
Psychological tolerance, 278–281
Psychologists:
  clinical, 11
  developmental, 10–11
  learning, 11
  physiological, 11
  social, 11
Psychology:
  animal experimentation, 7
  applied to coaching, 10–12
  applied to society, 9–10
  behaviorism, 8–9
  historical aspects, 5–9
  human behavior, 6
  mental tests, 7
  psychiatry, 7–8
  public relations, 174–176
  in tactical advantages, 86–87

Reinforcement, 231–240
  negative and positive, 231–234
  praise and criticism, 237–238
  reinforcement considerations, 238–240
  shaping behavior, 237